This Realm of England
1399 to 1688

A HISTORY OF ENGLAND
General Editor: Lacey Baldwin Smith

THE MAKING OF ENGLAND: 55 B.C. to 1399
C. Warren Hollister
University of California, Santa Barbara

THIS REALM OF ENGLAND: 1399 to 1688
Lacey Baldwin Smith
Northwestern University

THE AGE OF ARISTOCRACY: 1688 to 1830
William B. Willcox

Walter L. Arnstein
University of Illinois, Urbana-Champaign

BRITAIN YESTERDAY & TODAY:
1830 to the Present
Walter L. Arnstein
University of Illinois, Urbana-Champaign

This Realm of England
1399 to 1688

SEVENTH EDITION

Lacey Baldwin Smith
Northwestern University

D. C. HEATH AND COMPANY
Lexington, Massachusetts   Toronto

Address editorial correspondence to:
D. C. Heath and Company
125 Spring Street
Lexington, MA 02173

Acquisitions Editor: James Miller
Developmental Editor: Lauren Johnson
Production Editor: Carolyn Ingalls
Designer: Alwyn R. Velásquez
Photo Researcher: Sue McDermott
Production Coordinator: Charles Dutton

Published simultaneously in Canada.

Printed in the United States of America.

International Standard Book Number: 0-669-39717-2

Library of Congress Catalog Card Number: 94-74305

10 9 8 7 6 5 4 3 2 1

To J. R. S.,
who has endured and improved
seven editions. Bless her!

Foreword

Carl Becker once complained that everybody knows the job of the historian is "to discover and set forth the 'facts' of history." The facts, it is often said, speak for themselves. The businessperson talks about hard facts; the statistician refers to cold facts; the lawyer is eloquent about the facts of the case; and the historian, who deals with the incontrovertible facts of life and death, is called a very lucky fellow. Those who speak so confidently about the historian's craft are generally not historians themselves; they are readers of textbooks that more often than not are mere recordings of vital information and listings of dull generalizations. It is not surprising, then, that historians' reputations have suffered; they have become known as peddlers of facts and chroniclers who say, "This is what happened." The shorter the historical survey, the more textbook writers are likely to assume godlike detachment, spurning the minor tragedies and daily comedies of humanity and immortalizing the rise and fall of civilizations, the clash of economic and social forces, and the deeds of titans. Anglo-Saxon warriors were sick with fear when Viking "swift sea-kings" swept down on England to plunder, rape, and kill, but historians dispassionately note that the Norse invasions were a good thing; they allowed the kingdom of Wessex to unite and "liberate" the island in the name of Saxon and Christian defense against heathen marauders. The chronicler moves nimbly from the indisputable fact that Henry VIII annulled his marriage with Catherine of Aragon and wedded Anne Boleyn to the confident assertion that this helped produce the Reformation in England. The result is sublime but emasculated history. Her subjects wept when Good Queen Bess died, but historians merely comment that she had lived her allotted three score years and ten. British soldiers rotted by the thousands in the trenches of the First World War, but the terror and agony of that holocaust are lost in the dehumanized statistic that 765,399 British troops died in the four years of war.

In a brief history of even one "tight little island," the chronology of events must of necessity predominate, but if these four volumes are in any way fresh and new, it is because their authors have tried by artistry to step beyond the usual confines of a textbook and to conjure up something of the drama of politics, of the wealth of personalities, and even the pettiness, as well as the greatness, of human motivation. The price paid will be obvious to anyone seeking total coverage. There is relatively little in these pages on literature, the fine arts, or philosophy, except as they throw light on the uniqueness of English history. On the other hand, the complexities, uncertainties, endless variations, and above all the accidents that bedevil the design of human events — these are the very stuff of which history is made and the "truths" that this series seeks to narrate and preserve. Moreover, the flavor of each volume varies according to the tastes of its author. Sometimes the emphasis is political, sometimes economic or social, but the presentation is always impressionistic — shading, underscoring, or highlighting to achieve an image that will be more than a bare outline and will recapture something of the smell and temper of the past.

Even though each book was conceived and executed as an entity capable of standing by itself, the four volumes were designed as a unit. They tell the story of how a small and insignificant outpost of the Roman Empire hesitantly, and not always heroically, evolved into the nation that has probably produced and disseminated more ideas and institutions, both good and bad, than any state since Athens. Our hope is that these volumes will appeal both individually, to those interested in a balanced portrait of particular segments of English history, and collectively, to those who seek the majestic sweep of the story of a people whose activities have been wonderfully rich, exciting, and varied. In this spirit this series was originally written and has now been revised for a sixth time, not only to keep pace with new scholarship but, equally important, to keep it fresh and thought-provoking to a world becoming both more nostalgic and more impatient of its past.

Lacey Baldwin Smith

Preface

History is not lived as it is told. It is experienced as a series of largely unexpected disastrous or advantageous personal encounters, the outcomes of which depend on luck, circumstance, and personality. But history is recorded collectively and given direction and focus through the advantage of hindsight, and all sorts of messages about the meaning and purpose of the historical process are imposed upon this collective experience.

The fundamental question is whether history belongs to the living or to the dead. Should historians, using their knowledge of how events actually turned out, direct their research and artistry at reconstructing history as it affects and interests the present? Or should they write about the past as if they were contemporary to it, blind to what will happen? Today, the neo-Whig interpretation — history written with the benefit of hindsight and evaluated through the eyes of the living — is branded by the so-called revisionist historians as false. Such scholars argue on the grounds that it is wrong to presume the existence in history of men and women possessed of providential knowledge who strove to achieve, or conversely to block, those ideals and institutions that would become important to the twentieth century. Far better, so the revisionists maintain, is to present history as it really was: the product not of heroes and villains obsessed with a sense of manifest destiny but of accident, misunderstanding, and the perversity of events. The gospel according to the revisionists insists that great events in history — wars, revolutions, and heresies — do not require great causes. In recent years the story of the English Civil War has been rewritten in that belief. Today, revisionism has seeped back into the fifteenth and sixteenth centuries. The Wars of the Roses are no longer seen as the result of some malfunction in society but as the product of the peevish personality and mistakes of Henry VI. The Protestant Reformation is now said to be more the work of political factions in the court of Henry VIII than a response to changing religious aspirations operating within a society transformed by economic forces and a mounting secular perspective.

In the fifth edition of *This Realm of England,* the chapters dealing with the early Stuarts and the coming of civil war were heavily modified to soften their Whiggish tone and to incorporate the revisionist school of history. In the sixth edition, the sections on the Lancastrian, Yorkist, and early Tudor reigns were similarly revised. This seventh edition has sought to resolve one of the basic dilemmas of textbook writing: how to incorporate social, intellectual, economic, family, and cultural history into the story of the past without losing the chronological thread. Many texts prefer to cluster together in a separate chapter those themes that do not fit neatly into a political time frame. This volume used to be no exception. Chapter 13, "Paternalism, Profiteers, and Pioneers," was Fibber Magee's closet that kept the rest of the story tidy. Its contents have now been woven into the text to give the story a stronger social and cultural flavor. Not even a volume that makes no apology for its political emphasis can afford to ignore the essential role played by the family, local government, education, and women in the building of English history between 1399 and 1689.

Two notes of caution are in order when reading a text that has been thirty years in the making and that tries to do justice to the past as well as the present. First, there are fashions in history as in other human activities. Ideology and determinism — both economic and sociopsychological — as driving forces in the affairs of men and women are out of style. Some evidence suggests, however, that the pendulum is beginning to swing. Second, the story of the past, especially when it is encapsulated into a survey that seeks to lead the anxious reader through a maze of events, must have direction and must highlight those developments that contributed to the making of today. Although it may be essential to remind ourselves of the importance of the irrational — pride, prejudice, and paranoia — and of the inescapable shapelessness of the past, it is equally important to realize that history is a continuum and by definition a prelude to the present. It had its winners and losers, and the historian's job is to explain how and why certain people, institutions, and ideas triumphed or failed, and in doing so how they produced the world as we perceive it. The trick in writing a textbook is always to be faithful both to men and women long dead, who had little or no sense of the future, and to readers, who want to understand the present in terms of the past. In a sense, then, history belongs to neither the past nor the present but to the magician-historian who handles the lighting and stage-manages the effect. The novelist Samuel Butler sensed this paradox when he wrote:

> It has been said that although God cannot alter the past, historians can; it is perhaps because they can be useful to Him in this respect that He tolerates their existence. — *Erewhon*

L. B. S.

Contents

Illustrations

Maps

Genealogical Charts

This Realm of England
1399 to 1688

Medieval Twilight

1399 to 1485

On preceding page: TROOPS SCALING THE WALLS OF A TOWN
From a fourteenth-century illuminated manuscript. *(E.T. Archive)*

CHAPTER 1

The Curse of Disputed Succession

There is nothing quite as satisfying as a good, clean, substantial fact. It can be cherished and recorded, memorized and scrutinized, dropped casually in the middle of a conversation, or used with impressive effect to begin or destroy an argument. It is indeed a fact that Richard Plantagenet, King of England, died during the first weeks of the year 1400 A.D. On closer inspection, however, this event may not be one of those tidy and unadulterated facts, devoid of controversy and free of confusion and mystification. The manner of the royal passing remains in doubt; whether Richard II was strangled, starved, or "perished heartbroken" of sheer melancholy still inspires intense debate. Moreover, the fact of the king's death, although a matter to be recorded, attains historical significance only in terms of what came before and after. In death Richard proved infinitely more important than in life because of another not-so-simple fact: he was the last Plantagenet king of England to inherit through the eldest son.[1]

The Fall of Richard II (1377–1399)

The historical Richard — his failure, abdication, and death — has been confounded by a literary image. The fertile genius of William Shakespeare has conjured up the specter of an introspective sovereign whose boastful words and eloquent appeals to God's law and the divinity of kings concealed both political timidity and moral obtuseness. Only in recent years has Richard Plantagenet been divorced from Richard the fumbling, incompetent neurotic, whose inept urge to tyranny was translated into grand tragedy by the magic of the poet's verse. Richard, the historical reality, fell victim to the political mores of his time and to the fair

---

[1]The standard survey of the fifteenth century is J. R. Lander, *Government and Community: England, 1450–1509* (1980). Indispensable are K. B. McFarlane's essays in *England in the Fifteenth Century* (1951). See also A. L. Brown, *The Governance of Late Medieval England, 1272–1461* (1989). By far the best work on constitutional history is S. B. Chrimes, *English Constitutional Ideas in the Fifteenth Century* (1936).

words and broken promises of the man who replaced him on the throne and who engineered his "abdication."[2]

Richard's failure reflects the basic confusion and instability inherent in medieval political theory and governmental organization. The legal position of the feudal monarch was summarized in the oft-quoted words of Henry de Bracton: "The king himself ought not to be subject to any man, but he ought to be subject to God and the law." The unsolved riddle of politics was how the sovereign could be both limited and unrestrained, above man but under law. The dilemma was further complicated by the presence of a body of powerful barons who regarded themselves as the rightful watchdogs of government, but whose definition of good government was sometimes synonymous with no government, and who were at pains to emphasize the dependence of the sovereign on law as interpreted by themselves. Conversely, the aim of every great feudal monarch had been to be master in his own house, and to free himself of the factional and irresponsible interference of men, especially noblemen. As the fountain of justice, the medieval king sought to administer law and justice impartially and to root out the private law of strong and violent subjects who championed a mixture of the divine right of aristocracy and the doctrine that might makes right. That Richard had a surfeit of uncles — the dukes of Gloucester, Lancaster, and York — was discomforting but not necessarily fatal. More fundamental was the question of the king's council: was it to serve as an instrument of aristocratic rule through which the magnates could control both king and realm, or was it to be a weapon of royal authority, filled with men of the monarch's choosing, and exercising and enforcing the king's law throughout the realm?

An era of growing baronial control of crown policy had set in when Edward II had been forced to abdicate in 1327 and was then murdered in the name of good government. The prolonged conflict with France, in which Edward III had had to rely on his knights and henchmen to fight even a losing war, swung the balance even further in favor of baronial influence. Finally, a decade of minority rule under Richard II, who had ascended the throne in 1377 as a boy of ten, upset the equilibrium completely. In 1397, however, Richard II struck out both against his uncles and against the weight of aristocratic influence in his council and government. In a rapid coup d'état, he destroyed the authority of his baronial masters, the so-called Lords Appellant of the king's council. His uncle, the duke of Gloucester, was imprisoned and quietly smothered; the earl of Arundel was publicly tried and executed for high treason; and the earl of Warwick was exiled to the Isle of Wight. Then, in order to build an

---

[2]Most of this story and the interpretation of Richard II have been taken from H. F. Hutchison, *The Hollow Crown: A Life of Richard II* (1961). For two other quite different views, see A. Steel, *Richard II* (1941), and Shakespeare's *Richard II*. See also A. Tuck, *Richard II and the English Nobility* (1973), and C. Given-Wilson, ed. and trans., *Chronicles of the Revolution, 1397–1400: The Reign of Richard II* (n.d.), for a useful compilation of sources.

aristocratic faction loyal to himself, Richard created five new dukedoms from the lands and estates of Gloucester and Warwick. Whether this was tyranny or merely the efforts of a monarch determined to be master in his own council is not a question of fact but of opinion. Richard failed, and the dynasty that followed him on the throne branded his actions as tyrannical and despotic. Yet it may be well to recall the words of the proverb: "Treason never prospers, what's the reason? Why if it prospers, none dare call it treason."

Rightfully or wrongfully, Richard placed a dangerous interpretation on the formula that the sovereign should be subject to no man. His enemies claimed that he voiced the extreme doctrine that "laws were in his own mouth and frequently in his own breast and that only he himself could change and make the laws of his realm." More dangerous yet, in February of 1399, he translated theory into practice when, on the death of his uncle John of Gaunt, duke of Lancaster, he confiscated the estates and dignities of the duchy of Lancaster. From one perspective, Richard's actions fitted the pattern of strong medieval kingship — the extension of royal authority and the destruction of provincialism, privilege, and private law. The duchy of Lancaster was in effect a state within a state. The old duke had maintained his own council and exercised his own justice, and royal writs held no authority. Stated differently, Richard committed an act of unmitigated tyranny. He ignored the ancient constitution, which stipulated that "to the king belongs authority over all men, but to subjects belongs property," and he denied to his cousin Henry Bolingbroke, earl of Derby and son of Gaunt, his rightful inheritance.

When Richard seized power in 1397 from the Lords Appellant, he did not touch, but had not forgotten, two other important noblemen: his cousin, the earl of Derby, and the duke of Norfolk, both of whom had been associated with the Lords Appellant in their rule of England. In 1398 Norfolk and Derby fell out, and the earl accused Norfolk of suggesting that the two men attack the king before Richard had a chance to move against them. The truth of the accusation has never been settled. Nor was the voice of the deity allowed to decide the issue, for, although a trial by combat was ordered, Richard called off the ordeal and exiled both noblemen — Norfolk for life, Derby for ten years. The king, however, promised the exiles that their right of inheritance would be recognized. When Richard sequestered the lands of old Gaunt, he broke his bounden word, and in denying the right of his cousin to inherit from his father, Richard touched the most sensitive chord in all men of property. The duty that a subject owed his sovereign was placed in doubt when the monarch himself violated the rights of his people. Shakespeare does not overstate the case when he has the duke of York warn his royal nephew that if he wrongfully seized Derby's inheritance, "you pluck a thousand dangers on your head, you lose a thousand well-disposed hearts." So when Henry Bolingbroke defied the king's will and returned to England to claim his inheritance — the dukedom of Lancaster — in his eyes he landed not as a traitor but as a liberator. As the victim of royal injustice, he could call on the support of all who sought to safeguard their rights from the encroachment of arbitrary government.

Returning from exile, Henry landed at Ravenspur on July 4, 1399, and immediately trumpeted to the four corners of the realm his rightful claim to the duchy of Lancaster. The response was overwhelming, dangerously so because many great baronial clans — the Percys of Northumberland and the Nevilles of the northern shires — lent their support. They did not so much seek to win Bolingbroke his ducal title as to seize for themselves the control and direction of government and to secure their independence from royal interference in the conduct of their own affairs.

Fortune's wheel was turning against Richard. Part of his reason for confiscating Bolingbroke's inheritance was to pay the cost of putting down rebellion in Ireland. When he returned to England, he suddenly found himself alone and trapped at Conway Castle in northern Wales, facing the overwhelming forces of an embittered and ambitious enemy. Although Shakespearean legend has it that Richard meekly bowed to the inevitable and allowed himself to be led captive into the presence of his cousin Derby, Richard's surrender involved Bolingbroke's deceit, not the king's spinelessness. Conway Castle was a military stronghold with escape by sea to Ireland and France, and it was not easy to induce the king to leave the safety of his fortified port. As yet Bolingbroke had made no claim to the throne, and he sent Henry Percy, earl of Northumberland, to offer terms and lure Richard from his sanctuary. Derby, who now styled himself duke of Lancaster, demanded recognition of his rightful inheritance and the surrender of five of the king's council to be tried before Parliament. Growling darkly that he would "flay some people alive," Richard agreed to his rival's terms and accepted Northumberland's promise of safe conduct to London. Once enticed from Conway, the king was ambushed and taken to the Tower, where he was "guarded as strictly as a thief or a murderer."

The seizure of a king is one thing; to remove his crown legally is another. By what authority could the anointed king be dethroned and divested of powers conferred on him by God? The question facing Henry was how to legalize a revolution. With Richard securely in the Tower of London, Bolingbroke first reorganized the royal court and council, removing his enemies and rewarding his friends. Actually he made surprisingly few changes in administrative personnel, a fact that casts doubt on the Lancastrian claim that the crown was usurped in the name of justice and honest government for the realm. More significant, he appointed two colleagues in arms to high office — Henry Percy, earl of Northumberland, as lord constable, and Ralph Neville, earl of Westmorland, as lord marshal.

Control of the machinery of government still did not give title to the throne. Henry now had to come out into the open and publicly claim the crown. Three roads lay open to him — he could demand title by family descent, by parliamentary decree, or by right of conquest. The duke's hereditary rights were dubious from the start, for if there were a legal heir to the throne, it was the eight-year-old Edmund Mortimer, eighth earl of March, who was Edward III's great-great-grandson by this third son, Lionel, duke of Clarence. Henry of Lancaster was closer to Edward III in generations but more distant in legal descent, for his father was John of Gaunt, Edward's fourth son (see genealogy, page 12). The best that the new government could do was to accuse Richard of "perjuries, sacrileges, unnatural crimes, exactions from his subjects, reduction of his people to slavery, cowardice, and weakness of rule," and to demand that he be deposed by "the authority of the clergy and people." Dimly, hesitantly, a new and pregnant concept was being voiced — that a king could be tried and deposed by a Parliament, which presumably embodied the "authority of the clergy and people." There were, however, serious drawbacks to claiming the throne on the basis of a parliamentary mandate. Historically, Parliament could be summoned only by the king and could act only if it had been convened by legal writs of summons. In deposing the monarch, Parliament was in effect destroying itself, and, once the sovereign had been set aside, it was highly questionable whether Parliament retained sufficient authority to bestow the crown on anyone, let alone on Henry Bolingbroke.

The constitutional issue was obscure, but the danger to Henry in claiming his throne by grace of Parliament was manifest. The duke was already obligated to the great lords for their military assistance against Richard, and he was determined to suppress any notion that he had received his crown as a gift, given him on the basis of baronial authority in Parliament. As a consequence, Henry insisted that he was king by right of inheritance and conquest. The former claim was the sheerest fabrication, and the latter was darkly suspect in the eyes of constitutionalists who wondered how Bolingbroke could justify his actions against Richard on the grounds of law yet deny to his royal cousin his legal right to be king.

England in the summer of 1399 had to have a king who could rule. Right, in the person of the reigning monarch, was powerless; but might, in the guise of the duke of Lancaster, lacked the mantle of legality. Under the circumstances, the best compromise lay in engineering an abdication in which Richard II would step down of his own free will; Richard's own Parliament, legally summoned, would declare his throne vacant; and Henry would claim the crown by right of lawful descent. On these foundations the Lancastrian legend was concocted. Richard cheerfully (*hilari vultu*) abdicated his sovereignty, absolved his vassals of their feudal oath of obedience, and surrendered his signet seal to Henry. Indeed, the records show no evidence of cheerfulness, only of an angry and embittered man who had been denied fair trial and ordered to sign on the dotted line.

On September 30, Parliament was assembled to acknowledge the abdication and declare Richard "utterly unworthy and useless to rule and govern the realm." In fact, the Parliament convened was no legal body,

The Funeral of Richard II "The only remaining impediment was the physical existence of Sir Richard, who was helped to a 'natural' death within five months of his cousin's coronation." *(Reproduced by permission of the British Library)*

for it lacked a legitimate king and its members were heavily outnumbered by a disorderly host of London citizens, most of whom were favorably disposed to the Lancastrian cause. At best the assemblage that met at Westminster might be called a convention or ad hoc Parliament; at worst it was a gathering collected to lend the appearance of legality to a political coup d'état. Finally, Henry rose and "challenged the throne," stating that "God of His grace" had sent him with the aid of his friends and kin "to recover" the crown of England and to claim it as his due right. On October 13, Bolingbroke was crowned king and anointed with the "true" and sacred oil used at the coronation of Edward the Confessor. The fact that the oil had been conveniently rediscovered just in time for the ceremony casts doubt, if not upon the effectiveness, at least upon the authenticity, of the fluid. Henry now stood as king by God's grace, and Richard became "Sir Richard of Bordeaux, a simple knight." The only remaining impediment was the physical existence of Sir Richard, who was helped to a "natural" death within five months of his cousin's coronation.

NIl laui de noftre
feigniur mil.
quatrecene vn
monie adunit

torre la plui quant paitie. et
en aprce p furent tous lefpir
contre et nobles dudit vtni
me et auffi du commun &c

Coronation of Henry IV "A precedent . . . had been established: a legitimate king had been forced to abdicate and had been replaced, not by a legal heir but by an overmighty subject." *(British Library, London/Bridgeman Art Library, London)*

Henry IV (1399–1413)

As Henry IV's dying words — "Only God knows by what right I took the throne" — revealed, the new king's right to rule was fragile in the extreme. Force of arms had won him a crown, and he would have to fight again and again to keep it upon his head. The first Lancastrian claimed all the divinity and prerogatives of his predecessor, but a precedent, nevertheless, had been established: a legitimate king had been compelled to abdicate and had been replaced, not by a legal heir but by an overmighty subject.[3] Once the house of Lancaster faltered in its power, the curse of disputed succession would haunt the English throne. Henry's victory was not so much what Lancastrian propaganda maintained, the triumph of law and justice over tyranny, as it was a giant stride in the already

---

[3]Although Edward II had been forced to "abdicate," an important difference existed: he was replaced by an undisputed heir, his eldest son, Edward III.

century-old transformation of a feudal monarchy into a feudal oligarchy. A Neville and a Percy had been instrumental in elevating a baronial colleague to the throne; within three years Percy would endeavor to help him down again, and within two generations another Neville would bear the name of kingmaker.

The man who assumed the burdens of monarchy in October of 1399 was a veteran of forty-two, skilled in war and government.[4] As the first step in Henry's newfound royalty, he freed himself from his many allies who expected rich rewards for their services. The king's original council was aristocratic in composition, reflecting the influence of those "natural councillors" of the crown whose claims to political recognition rested on birth, on services rendered, and on political and economic power in the shires. During the first year of the reign, an average of fifteen barons were invited to attend the council, but the number rapidly fell to seven, while the proportion of professionally trained administrators steadily rose. The new monarch drew heavily from those who had run the duchy of Lancaster, and the three most important governmental posts — the chancellor, the treasurer, and the keeper of the seal — were all filled with relatively humble but loyal servants of the king. Yet no matter how hard he tried, Henry IV was never able to free himself entirely of baronial influence and interference.

The same was true of church and Parliament. Immediately after his coronation, Henry called a new convocation of the clergy and a new Parliament. In the former, he tried to win ecclesiastical support for his dynasty by promising to exterminate the heresy of Lollardy; in the latter, he proved more demanding, and insisted on a tax on the export of wool for a period of three years. The king's relations with his Parliaments throughout the reign were rarely harmonious. Even with the addition of the revenues from the duchy of Lancaster, Henry became financially more dependent on Parliament than his predecessors had been. A multitude of baronial "friends" had to be rewarded with fat annuities and grants taken from crown lands, while those who demanded too much had to be destroyed, an even more expensive procedure. Richard's income had averaged over £100,000 annually; Henry rarely equaled this figure, yet his expenses during the first eight years of the reign rose to £140,000 a year. The deficit was made up by loans, by an export tax on wool, by subsidies (parliamentary taxes imposed on land), and by import and export duties known as tunnage and poundage. The dilemma of all feudal governments was that financial reality did not correspond to political theory, and even a strong monarch could not finance his government from his normal or private sources of revenue. In other words, he could not live on his own. Unfortunately, this was exactly what political theory required: Parlia-

---

[4] J. L. Kirby's *Henry IV of England* (1970) is the standard biography of the king.

ment argued there was historic justification[5] that during normal times the king should support himself with rents from crown lands, fees from the administration of justice, and profits from feudal law. Parliamentary sources of money, it claimed, should be reserved only for extraordinary occasions of great emergency.

Both Lords and Commons tended to view the financial plight of the crown not on the basis of economic reality but in terms of governmental extravagance, corruption, and inefficiency. The theories and demands voiced by the Stuart Parliaments two centuries later had a long and distinguished heritage under the Lancastrian Parliaments. Their definition of good government tended to be cheap government, and in the name of efficiency and economy they began to encroach on royal authority. Commons demanded that the king refrain from giving away the profits of crown lands to reward his friends with lucrative annuities; it insisted that income from parliamentary subsidies and excise taxes be audited, and that the expenses of the household be curbed and inspected by a parliamentary committee. Henry IV endeavored to resist these pressures, but his financial situation was such that he dared not antagonize this essential source of money. In 1406 he told the Commons that kings were not wont to render account to Parliament, but he allowed the auditing of moneys granted him two years before. There were, however, limits to how far he was willing to go; and Henry curtly dismissed the claim that members of his council should take personal responsibility for any part of the grant that Parliament felt had been misspent.

Henry's rebellion had been made possible by the united opposition of all men of property to the violation of ancient law. Public sentiment had supported Bolingbroke's claim to the duchy of Lancaster, but his seizure of the throne shocked important elements of the landed elite. Moreover, the baronial leaders soon discerned that in elevating Henry to the throne they had a tiger by the tail, and they began to question the wisdom of having replaced the unstable and emotional Richard with a veteran campaigner such as Lancaster. The first of the king's allies to fall out was Harry Hotspur, the son of Henry Percy, earl of Northumberland. Hotspur had won fame by defeating the Scots in 1401, and as a consequence of his victory, he held the earl of Douglas prisoner. The Percys were growing increasingly restless under Lancastrian rule, and Harry refused to yield the earl of Douglas to the king. Instead he claimed the ransom money for himself on the grounds that victory had exacted a heavy toll and that to the victor belonged the spoils. At issue was the historic right of the crown to hold all important prisoners of war, and Hotspur's action clearly constituted open defiance of royal authority. Henry had no choice but to

---

[5]This is a matter of considerable debate, but by the fifteenth century Parliament was certainly voicing such a theory.

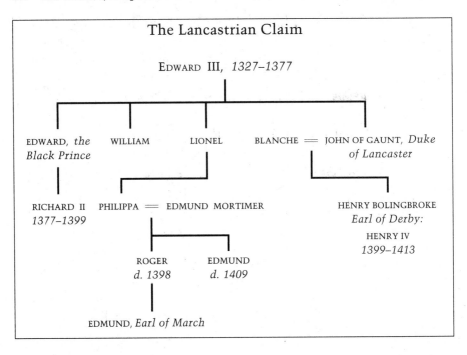

The Lancastrian Claim

EDWARD III, *1327–1377*

EDWARD, *the*   WILLIAM   LIONEL   BLANCHE = JOHN OF GAUNT, *Duke*
Black Prince   *of Lancaster*

RICHARD II   PHILIPPA = EDMUND MORTIMER   HENRY BOLINGBROKE
1377–1399   *Earl of Derby:*

                                                         HENRY IV
                                                         1399–1413

ROGER   EDMUND
d. 1398   *d. 1409*

EDMUND, *Earl of March*

crush his erstwhile friend; Hotspur was defeated and killed at the Battle of Shrewsbury in 1403.

Equally serious was the uprising of Hotspur's father, the earl of Northumberland, in league with Owen Glendower and Sir Edmund Mortimer, uncle to the young earl of March and himself a possible contender for the throne. Glendower was the leader of a Welsh insurrection against English rule and influence, and his daughter was Sir Edmund's wife. He had allied himself with Hotspur in 1402, and three years later he entered into the treasonous agreement to divide England into three parts — Glendower to take Wales and the adjacent English shires; Northumberland, the northern counties; and Mortimer, what remained, which wasn't much. Henry now faced not one but three potential usurpers, and it took two years of continual fighting to defend his kingdom and secure his crown. In the end Glendower was driven back into his inaccessible Welsh hills, Northumberland was caught and executed, and Mortimer was trapped in 1409 at Harlech Castle, where he chose starvation rather than surrender.

Henry spent fourteen weary years scolding his Parliaments but never daring to dispense with them, plucking down the baronial caterpillars of his commonwealth but never having the strength to wipe them out, and struggling with a dread of disease and infection. The strain of constant campaigning and the weight of regal responsibility slowly destroyed the king's health. He degenerated into a neurotic hypochondriac plagued by eczema, which contemporaries took for leprosy visited upon him by God in retribution for his usurpation of the throne. The concluding years of his life were troubled by the dilemma of all monarchies — the relationship between a father who is a ruling sovereign and a son and heir who is a potential king. The story that young Prince Hal tried on the crown while his father still lived is legend, but it symbolizes the strain that existed between the two men. As the years slipped by, it became painfully apparent that the elder stood for senility, sickness, and death; the younger, for youth, energy, and life. All who looked to the future, who hoped to profit from change, turned away from the dying sovereign to his dynamic son. The end came on March 20, 1413, and Prince Hal succeeded his father upon a usurped throne, breathing new vigor into the Lancastrian dynasty.

Henry V (1413–1422) and the War Against France

Every society creates its own particular brand of horror, and every civilization has its own methods and reasons for fighting wars. Often the ideals that lend distinctive vitality to a society breed the wars that in the end destroy those same ideals. The revival of conflict between France and England in the fifteenth century provides a case in point. Feudal society, for all its Gothic spires and exquisite stained glass windows, rested on a military ideal — the code of the armed and mounted knight, which appealed to violence. Lawlessness did not spring entirely from the lack of law enforcement; instead it was built into the creed itself. When the major pastime of the leaders of society was the mock warfare of the joust, and when feats of arms were the mark of social success, the human instinct to settle personal and international disputes by recourse to arms was unrestrained and elevated to a position of virtue. That the cannon, the musket, and the longbow were rapidly replacing the armored knight in battle mattered not at all; the medieval military code remained intact and esteemed by society. Knights were by tradition, if not in reality, full-time soldiers; the language of military chivalry still held in bondage the minds of men; and the kingly ideal continued to be Richard Coeur de Lion, not Henry II or Edward I, the builders of strong royal government. The fact that the first Richard had drained his realm of coin and lived in England less than six months in a reign of ten years was of no importance. Richard I had united chivalry with piety, military prowess with the spread of God's word. His was the ideal to be followed, especially by the youthful Henry V, who eagerly sought to prove his manhood and his kingship. Given the nature of the feudal code, as embodied in the expenses of Prince Hal's education ("eight pence for harpstrings, twelve pence for a new scabbard, four pence for seven books of grammar in one volume"), the young king inevitably turned his eyes toward France, remembered the glorious victories of Crécy and Poitiers, and renewed the ancient conflict between the two kingdoms.

The renewal of the Hundred Years' War was certainly an outgrowth of the structure and code of feudal society, but evidence indicates that war in the fifteenth century was also closely related to a particular

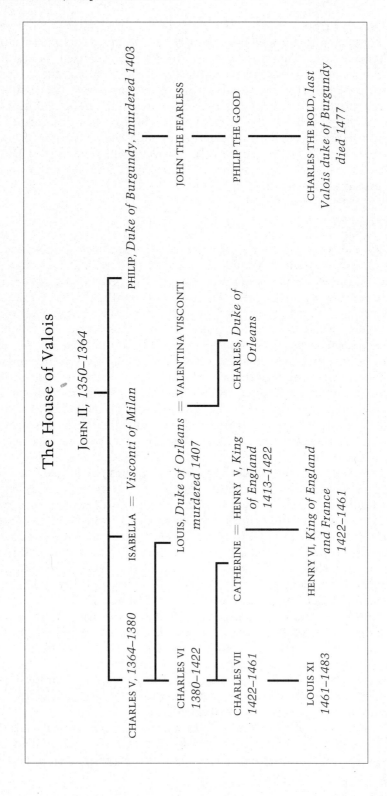

The House of Valois

JOHN II, *1350–1364*

CHARLES V, 1364–1380

PHILIP, *Duke of Burgundy, murdered 1403*

JOHN THE FEARLESS

PHILIP THE GOOD

CHARLES THE BOLD, *last Valois duke of Burgundy died 1477*

ISABELLA = *Visconti of Milan*

CHARLES VI
1380–1422

LOUIS, *Duke of Orleans murdered 1407* = VALENTINA VISCONTI

CHARLES, *Duke of Orleans*

CATHERINE = HENRY V, *King of England 1413–1422*

CHARLES VII
1422–1461

HENRY VI, *King of England and France 1422–1461*

LOUIS XI
1461–1483

problem of medieval government — the difficulty of maintaining law and order at home. Behind the tenuous claims of the English crown to the throne of France lay the reality of domestic politics. A combination of lawlessness and heresy confronted the new reign in 1413, and the simplest solution to the internal turmoil was to send the troublemakers to fight in France. Heresy and sedition marched hand in hand in 1414 when Henry's old comrade-in-arms, Sir John Oldcastle, turned against his sovereign. Oldcastle, had he lived two hundred years later, would have been labeled a militant Puritan who sought to apply the standards of heaven to human affairs. He was aghast at the perfidy and corruption that marred church and state, and he demanded the liquidation of what was generally regarded as the source of all ecclesiastical evil: the church's landed wealth and temporal powers. Behind him stood the restless knights of the shires, who cast covetous eyes on ecclesiastical lands, and an array of men, some desperate, some ambitious, some idealistic, who had one thing in common — the desire to change the existing order of things. The old warrior seems to have organized an ill-conceived and subterranean plot to kidnap the king and lead the city of London in a revolt against the godless leaders of society. The plan came to nothing, and although Oldcastle escaped capture until 1417, his followers were systematically hunted down and hanged as traitors or burned as heretics. In the end the old knight was caught in Wales and executed. He died a martyr to ideals that would not be realized for two centuries, an example of the restlessness and violence of his age. Under such circumstances, it was not surprising that men argued that the prestige of a doubtful monarchy and the peace of the realm would be enhanced if such domestic strife were directed into foreign parts and if England were to gain victory abroad.

The international scene proved particularly propitious for such a policy. France, like England, was moving into a century of overmighty subjects, irresponsible magnates, insane monarchs, minority rule, and wicked princely uncles. Unlike England, however, France had no Henry V to catch the imagination and to curb the forces of anarchy and misrule. In 1380 the death of the able Charles V and the succession of the eleven-year-old Charles VI exposed France to a combination of minority government and monarchy crippled by a sovereign who passed from adolescence into imbecility. The situation was made worse by the consequences of French dynastic policy. The kings of France had introduced a policy of endowing members of their family with the ducal titles of the various semi-independent provinces of the kingdom in the hope that bonds of blood would secure those territories more closely to the crown. King John in 1361 had presented the duchy of Burgundy to his son Philip, while Charles VI gave his brother Louis the duchy of Orleans. The results were the opposite of those expected. When Charles went mad in 1392, his ducal relatives began to fight over the control of the royal government. Factional rivalry deteriorated into armed conflict in 1407 when Philip's successor, John of Burgundy, conspired in the murder of the duke of Orleans. Racked by civil discord and paralyzed by an insane monarch,

Henry V   "A professional soldier who combined boundless energy with the mystique of leadership and an absolute conviction that God stood at his elbow." *(National Portrait Gallery, London)*

France in 1414 was ripe for the picking when Henry V of England revived the Plantagenet claim to the French crown. His assertion rang hollow, for the house of Lancaster had only a doubtful right to its own crown, let alone the throne of France. But legality is by necessity a question of interpretation, and Henry V had no doubt as to the just and righteous nature of his title. The king's attitude was more a reflection of his character than a matter of legal niceties.

Henry V, the legendary hero, the paragon of kingly and soldierly virtues — loyal, just, upright, honorable, able, chivalric, and pious — turns out on closer inspection to have had feet not of clay but of iron. The wonderful image of an irresponsible prince taking part in escapades of juvenile bravado with that engaging and boisterous bag of wind Sir John Falstaff is Shakespearean fiction, not history. At sixteen Prince Hal was an adult, experienced in war and the trials of campaigning in the Welsh mountains. When he mounted the throne at twenty-five, he was a veteran, the most effective of military men: a professional soldier who combined boundless energy with the mystique of leadership and an absolute conviction that God stood at his elbow. Conventionally orthodox in his religious creed but almost a fanatic in the intensity with which he adhered to his faith, Henry believed implicitly that victory in war was a question not of numbers but of "the power of God." The justice of his historic right to the duchy of Normandy and to the crown of Valois France verged on a religious obsession for which no price was too great to pay, either by him or by his kingdom. More than a conqueror, Henry was a visionary who included most of the traditional values of his century in his view of proper kingship. More important, he came close to realizing those ideals because, when he sailed for France in August 1415, he left behind a country remarkably united both in the justice of the venture and in its praise of the king.[6]

For almost fifty years, England had lacked the single political ingredient that could make premodern government work properly — aggressive and inspirational royal leadership. In scarcely two years, Henry displayed the charismatic energy that could remake a feudal kingdom. A medieval sovereign was expected to be a model for his subjects and the fountain of justice for all. By the judicious use of intimidation, arbitration, and encouragement, he was meant to maintain law and order, which depended heavily on the honesty of such royal officials as the sheriff, the justice of the peace, and the coroner, and on the cooperation of the local landed elite. Unless the king's servants were selected without favor or "brokerage," and the chronic land disputes and personal animosities between rival baronial families were adjudicated, there could be justice for neither rich nor poor. Henry proved himself to be adept in settling disputes, in his choice of honest councillors and officials, in the administration of his laws, and in his conciliatory handling of Parliament. In fact, he applied the same attention to fiscal and military details and governmental accounts that his more "modern" and notorious namesake, the seventh Henry, would later do, but with markedly different results. Instead of being branded a miser and hated for his actions, he was able to channel crown and parliamentary funds into his war effort and still retain the respect and devotion of his subjects. Shakespeare's Henry V may have spoken the truth when he said that he knew he left "not one behind that doth not wish success and conquest to attend on us."

The army raised by the king and the war fought in France reflected most of the new forces operating in late medieval society. The ancient and always somewhat theoretical method of raising troops on the basis of military service rendered in return for land tenure had long since disappeared. Instead, an indenture system had emerged by which captains contracted to raise specific numbers of archers and men-at-arms. The contract or indenture set the size of the company, its rate of pay, the length of service, the place of assembly, and the composition of the unit, which

---

[6]Henry's reputation has improved markedly in recent years. See especially G. L. Harriss (ed.), *Henry V, the Practice of Kingship* (1985) and E. Powell, *Kingship, Law and Society: Criminal Justice in the Reign of Henry V* (1989). Standard biographies include C. T. Allmand, *Henry V* (1993), and H. F. Hutchison, *Henry V: A Biography* (1967). For a decidedly unfriendly approach, see D. Seward, *Henry V: the Scourge of God* (1988). The best general accounts of the Hundred Years' War are C. T. Allmand, *The Hundred Years' War: England and France at War c. 1300–1450* (1988), and A. Curry, *The Hundred Years' War* (1993).

generally consisted of mounted knights with their esquires and pages, mounted and foot archers, and pikemen. By the fifteenth century, such armies had developed extensive headquarters — staffs of armorers, surgeons, clerks of the stable, carpenters, trumpeters, and the like. The more important members of the headquarters unit supplied their own archers — the sergeant of the king's tent brought 28; the master smith and master carpenter had 41 and 124, respectively; and the yeomen of the king's bedchamber financed 86.

Henry landed in France with a force of 2,000 mounted men-at-arms, 6,000 archers (half of whom were also on horseback), and possibly another 1,000 in his headquarters company. The channel port of Harfleur was the first objective, and in late September it surrendered in the face of English cannons. The king was so convinced of the moral and military weakness of the French that he determined to march his tiny army overland through Normandy to winter quarters at Calais. On October 25, a wet, tired, and isolated English force found itself confronted by a French host that may have numbered as many as 50,000. At Agincourt, Henry's belief that God, not man, gave victory, was confirmed by the crushing defeat of the French army. English archers; the cramped nature of the battlefront, which prevented the French from capitalizing on their numerical superiority; and the sodden state of the battlefield contributed to victory; but to contemporaries the hand of God was manifest in a battle that butchered the flower of French chivalry. The French dead included 3 dukes, a grand constable, 8 counts, 1,500 knights, and 4,000 to 5,000 men-at-arms. The English lost fewer than 300 men, including the duke of York, the earl of Suffolk, and 6 or 7 knights.

Agincourt was a staggering moral victory, but further conquests and the English bid for the French crown were made possible by two other factors: first, hard, unheroic and extremely expensive fighting in which "the King's Daughter, the Messenger, the London" (all names of siege cannons used to breach the walls of French towns) played a more important role than armored knights; and second, the Burgundian alliance caused by another eruption of the Burgundy-Orleans feud. On August 28, 1417, the leaders of the Orleans faction, in league with Charles VI's son, the dauphin of France, arranged a meeting with John of Burgundy to discuss the plight of France and the possibility of concerted action against the English. The hope of unity was dashed by the murder of John of Burgundy, who was attacked and killed by the Orleans party. Instantly, his son Philip joined the English, and together in 1420 they dictated the Treaty of Troyes to a torn and prostrate France. Charles VI was allowed to keep his crown, but Henry V was to marry the king's daughter, the princess Catherine, and was pronounced Charles's true and rightful heir. In return, Henry undertook to defend all of France that acknowledged the treaty and to reduce those sections that still held out for the disinherited dauphin. In May 1420, the English Parliament ratified the treaty and bound its members and "their heirs and successors to observe and fulfill

The Battle of Agincourt "At Agincourt, Henry's belief that God, not man, gave victory was confirmed by the crushing defeat of the French army." *(Bibliothèque Nationale, Paris)*

its terms." The dual monarchy had been created. In part Henry V's vision had been realized; it now remained to be seen whether a defeated France would accept such a dream or a victorious England could enforce it.

The first and most disastrous blow to the success of the dual kingdom came with the death of Henry V on August 31, 1422. He died of dysentery and exhaustion, victim of an obsession and martyr to a defunct ideal: a medieval Europe devoid of national consciousness and tolerant of an international ruling elite that placed chivalry, piety, and nobility above Englishness or Frenchness. Had he lived two months longer, he would have become king of both realms, for Charles VI of France followed him to the grave on October 11. The heir to the two kingdoms was now a nine-month-old baby — Henry, the sixth of his name.

The momentum of English victories was not stopped by the king's death; under Henry's brother, the duke of Bedford, the tide of conquest spread deep into France. By 1429 the reality of a dual kingdom seemed almost within grasp. The dauphin of France, the future Charles VII, remained uncrowned, unloved, and ineffective; and an English army stood at the gates of Orleans, the last major bastion holding out for Charles. Bedford's successes, however, were more a symptom of French moral and military paralysis than a sign of English strength or an indication of real enthusiasm for the infant Henry VI. In 1429 the tide of war began to ebb as rapidly as it had risen, and the conquerors were driven, battle after

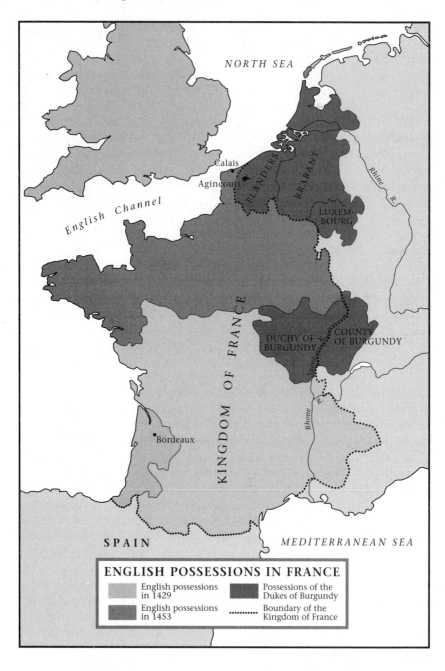

NORTH SEA

English Channel

Calais

Agincourt

FLANDERS

BRABANT

Rhine R.

LUXEM-
BOURG

KINGDOM OF FRANCE

DUCHY OF
BURGUNDY

COUNTY
OF BURGUNDY

Saône R.

Rhone R.

Bordeaux

SPAIN

MEDITERRANEAN SEA

ENGLISH POSSESSIONS IN FRANCE

English possessions in 1429	Possessions of the Dukes of Burgundy
English possessions in 1453	·········· Boundary of the Kingdom of France

battle, back toward the English Channel. The story of Joan of Arc and the resurgence of French arms is an oft-told tale. Joan poured new spirit into France; she even goaded the feckless dauphin into activity and finally persuaded him into forcing his way to Rheims to be crowned. Urged on by her "voices," who told her, "Fille de Dieu, va, va, va! Je serai à ton aide,"[7] she accomplished a miracle. Today we question that miracle, preferring to explain her success in terms of nationalism, politics, and the power of finance. But the fifteenth century thought otherwise, and it seemed to the English of the utmost importance to prove that she was a "disciple and limb of the fiend." When she was captured by the Burgundians and bought by the English for 10,000 gold crowns, Bedford considered the prize cheap at twice the price. The moral influence of the Maid of Orleans had, at all costs, to be destroyed, and Joan was sacrificed upon the altar of a child-king and the dual crown that he wore. She was tried, found guilty of heresy and witchcraft, and burned at the stake at the age of nineteen on May 30, 1431. Although Bedford acknowledged the deed to be an act of political necessity, an English soldier at the scene cried out: "God forgive us; we have burned a saint."

When Bedford died in 1435, exhausted by his impossible labors defending the regal title of his young nephew, and when in the same year Burgundy deserted its English ally, the tide of defeat turned into a flood. At home in England, a bankrupt crown, a child-king, a weary and uncooperative Parliament, and an increasingly irresponsible aristocracy paralyzed the English will to fight, and it became simply a matter of time before the invaders were driven into the channel.

Henry VI (1422–1461, 1471): Part I, the Years of Minority

The story of Henry VI's reign is difficult to categorize, consisting as it did of nearly fifteen years of minority rule; another sixteen years of chronic administrative mismanagement; eight more years of varying degrees of mental and physical collapse, culminating in dethronement in 1461; and a final, year-long restoration in 1471 before the last Lancastrian was put away once and for all at the age of fifty.

The king's childhood years in a sense properly belong to the conclusion of his father's reign because the new government was dominated by the dead king's brothers — the dukes of Bedford and Gloucester — and by his half-uncle, Henry Cardinal Beaufort. Moreover, the momentum of strong, efficient administration still lingered on, and the council, established to rule in the name of a child-king, was absolutely committed to extending English conquests in France and defending the dual monarchy that the conqueror had established.

Unfortunately, the financial condition of the realm made the task well-nigh impossible. In 1433 the normal expenses of the government

---

[7]Daughter of God, go go, go! I will be your support.

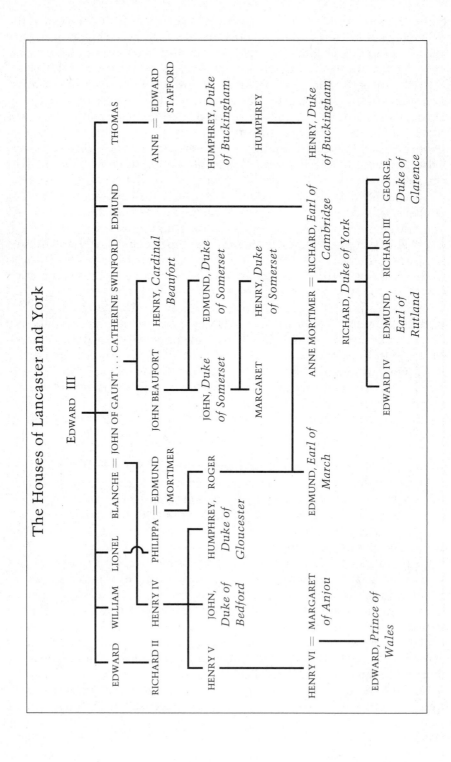

The Houses of Lancaster and York

were estimated at £57,000, while the cost of the war in France added another £44,800. The traditional peacetime revenues of the crown, derived mainly from the duchy of Lancaster and other crown lands, amounted to £38,000 but, after a multitude of fixed fees and annuities had been deducted, it fell to only £8,400. The customs on wool yielded £27,000, and parliamentary and ecclesiastical taxes supplied approximately £45,000, for a total of £80,400. Consequently, the government was operating at a deficit of over £21,000 a year and faced an accumulated indebtedness of £164,815. The constant burden of war made the English insist that the conquered territories in France pay for their own defense and contribute to the financial support of the dual kingdom, but such a policy merely alienated whatever affections Henry's French subjects may have felt, and earned for the English the nickname "God-damns."

The burdens of government were compounded by the presence of an infant king. From the start, the council was split between the Gloucester and Beaufort factions, and partly as a consequence the government maintained the fiction of personal rule by a child monarch, even requiring the infant sovereign to order his own educational disciplining. At the age of two, he informed his "very dear and well beloved" councillors that, because it was necessary for a king to learn good manners, he gave them permission "to reasonably chastise us from time to time as the case shall require," and he further assured his teachers that they would "not be molested, hurt or injured for this cause in future time." The lords of the council had little to fear because, as one observer remarked, Henry was "very young and inexperienced and watched over as a Carthusian [monk]." This observation was alarming because it was made as late as 1450 when the king, who had technically come of age in 1437, was a man of twenty-nine. Henry became a monarch who looked the part but was temperamentally unsuited to the role, almost the opposite of his father. Henry V had been the charismatic warrior, workaholic administrator, and dispassionate judge and arbiter. The son, in contrast, avoided personal involvement in battle, was careless of administrative details, easily bored by the duties of his office, and politically partisan to the point of folly. The strongest word he was ever heard to utter in anger was *forsooth*, and his associates correctly guessed the truth when they noted that he had not the "manliness to be a king," caring more for "his soul's health" than the labors of kingship.

It is unfair to say that, almost alone, Henry succeeded in turning a realm, which at his succession had reached its military and political zenith, into a morally, financially, and politically bankrupt and paralyzed kingdom. He was officially a minor for the first fifteen years of his reign, and probably nothing could have prevented the military disasters in France that by 1453 had reduced his father's conquests to the single channel port of Calais. Nevertheless, Henry bears heavy responsibility for the destruction of his crown. His vacillating and capricious personality — which fluctuated wildly between bouts of uncontrollable generosity, petty vindictiveness, and almost total disregard for the political and financial consequences of his actions — inflamed the already festering factionalism at court and fostered the growing violence and collapse of "good governance" throughout the kingdom. Instead of standing above factions, he allowed himself to become caught up in the mire of baronial rivalries that beset the country; far from curbing the "caterpillars of the commonwealth," he allowed their expansion to the point that the crown itself became associated with partisanship in the public eye. The story of the deterioration of the Lancastrian monarchy during the 1440s and 1450s cannot, however, be told simply in terms of the character defects of the king. Throughout the realm, economic, spiritual, and political forces operated independently of the personality of Henry and his favorites. These factors, as much as the sovereign's lavish generosity and blindness to political and financial reality, led to a decade of civil war during the 1450s and early 1460s.

CHAPTER 2

Economic Collapse and Social Dislocation

The twilight years of medieval England — the second half of the fourteenth and much of the fifteenth centuries — endured social, economic, and demographic disasters common to all of Europe. Different segments of the population responded in varying ways to these catastrophes, but no one could assign to them comprehensible causes except to speak in terms of God's wrath at the multiple sins of humanity.

Changes in the Structure and Spirit of Feudalism

By the early years of the fifteenth century, the cornerstones of the ancient feudal edifice were rapidly disintegrating. Three hundred and fifty years before, the overwhelming need had been for immediate and massive local defense. The armed knight, who did military service in return for land tenure, had then been a necessity and a reality. The fief and the manor had worked reasonably well as an economic and legal means of uniting land and labor into a productive union sufficient to support the knight and his retainers; and the economy of England and Europe had remained so marginal as to make any other form of military or political organization unrealistic. By 1400 all this had changed radically.[1]

The increasing use of money was reshaping the contractual relationship between the vassal and his overlord, whereby land in return for service had been the essential part of the agreement. Money also profoundly affected the structure of the manor, changing the nature of landholding and the legal status of the peasantry. At the same time, the king's law and the king's peace had long since secured a sufficient, if not complete, defense of the realm. The knight, although he still clung tenaciously to his

---

[1]Trevor Rowley, *The High Middle Ages 1200–1550* (1986), is a splendid social and economic survey. See also Kate Mertes, *The English Noble Household, 1250–1600* (1988); J. M. W. Bean, *The Decline of English Feudalism 1215–1540* (1968) and his *From Lord to Patron: Lordship in Late Medieval England* (1989); J. Hatcher, *Plague, Population, and the English Economy, 1348–1530* (1977); L. R. Poos, *A Rural Society After the Black Death: Essex 1350–1525* (1991); and K. B. McFarlane, *Lancastrian Kings and Lollard Knights* (1972), as well as the works cited in the beginning of Chapter 1. For the pre-Reformation church, see R. M. Haines, *Ecclesia Anglicana: Studies in the English Church of the Later Middle Ages* (1989), and R. N. Swanson, *Church and Society in Later Medieval England* (1989).

warrior ideal, had lost most of his military reason for being, and the military obligations connected with his land tenure had dwindled away. Although the term *knight* lingered on, either as a personal dignity or as a generic term to describe those worthy of a seat in the House of Commons, the status of knighthood was evaded by most landed proprietors anxious to avoid the financial and military duties associated with the position. As the fifteenth century advanced, the feudal knight tended more and more to become the sixteenth-century gentleman. Typical of the class were such boisterous and aggressive country gentlemen as Thomas Paston and John Howard. They fought a noisy duel for local preeminence in Norfolk, not with the venerable weapons of war but with lawsuits, disputed elections to Parliament, rival mercantile ventures, marriage alliances, and occasional jail sentences, depending on which one had exercised greater influence at court or intimidated the larger number of judges and juries in the shires by their association with rival baronial factions (see pages 40–43).

The ideal of knighthood was the theme of Sir Thomas Malory's *Morte d'Arthur* (1472), in which the knights of the Round Table were all sworn to observe the chivalric code. They were bound "never to do outrageousity, nor murder, and always to be free from treason." They were expected "by no means to be cruel, but to give mercy unto him that deserveth mercy." On pain of death, they were sworn "always to do ladies, damsels, and gentlewomen succour," and no knight was to "do battle in a wrongful quarrel for no law, nay for no world's goods." Yet reality was quite otherwise; the knightly order was branded as "mere disorder," and the knight who took to the field of battle was described as laden "not with steel but with wine, not with spears but with cheese, not with swords but with wineskins, not with javelin but with spits."

As the joust in the fifteenth century had deteriorated into a spectacle hedged in by regulations, wooden barriers, and rigid pageantry, and had lost all relationship to the realities of war, so the chivalric ideal had become a social myth totally out of line with the actions of living men. Even Froissart, the chronicler of the Hundred Years' War, had a singularly commercial view of chivalry. In one breath he claimed to be recording the "honorable and noble adventures of feats of arms" as encouragement to the "brave and hearty" of future generations. In the next breath he decried the English slaughter of their prisoners, not because it was an act of unchivalric brutality but because it was unprofitable; "one with another" the captives would have been worth "400,000 francs."

As for the fief and manor, those economic keystones of the medieval past were eroding with each passing generation. Originally, the fief was a political division of the land, held by the vassal of a lord in return for feudal services. The manor was a unit of agrarian exploitation, consisting of the union of land, labor, and legal rights. A fief often included many manors or might include only part of a manor, depending on the productivity of the soil. Private property in the modern sense did not exist; instead the lord of the manor, who was usually, but not always, a baron or a

The Chivalric Ideal: A Knight Receiving a Helmet from a Lady
The knight was sworn " 'always to do ladies, damsels, and gentlewomen succour' " and never " 'to do battle in a wrongful quarrel for no law, nay for no world's goods.' " *(Mary Evans Picture Library)*

member of the knightly class, possessed rights only to the fruits of the soil. He did not own the land itself. Only the king could be said to own land, and all medieval land tenure rested on this concept of proprietorship whereby property rights were limited to the profits of the land, and landholding was carefully prescribed by the custom of the manor or by the terms of the tenure. In the same way that the vassal held his fief from someone above him in the feudal structure in return for rather hypothetical military services, so within the manor itself freemen and bondsmen held land on the basis of various types of tenurial relationships.

The property of the manor was generally of three kinds: (1) demesne land over which the lord of the manor possessed full proprietorship and which he exploited directly through his serfs or hired laborers, or which he leased to tenants for life or for a set number of years; (2) freehold land held of the lord for a fixed rent and passed from generation to generation unchanged in the family of the freeholder; and (3) copyhold land held on the basis of the custom of the manor, which might involve financial or personal services whereby the holder was required to give to the lord of the manor a percentage of his labor or his produce or both. The nature of these obligations might be recorded in the manor court and, if so, the tenure was known as a copyhold; or the tenant's rights and services might be unwritten, resting on the historic custom of the manor. In both cases it was possible for the lord of the manor to modify and increase the nature of the services attached to the property; or, in the case of tenure protected only by custom, he could claim it as demesne land, evict the peasant, and rent the fields to whomsoever he pleased at the highest price he could command. The landholding that eventually proved most resistant to the encroachment of the lord of the manor was freehold property, which tended to become a fixed and permanent tenure approaching that of private property.

At the root of the land problem in the fifteenth century lay the rationalization of feudal property agreements. The confusion of conflicting and overlapping rights to the profits of land protected by custom gave way to the ownership of land legally recorded and protected by law. The various types of tenure dictated by historic custom evolved into the modern twofold division of private land and rented land, and these changes in turn led to bitterness and violence because the common law lacked the necessary terminology and machinery to handle such disputes. Scarcely a baronial or wealthy knightly family was not embroiled in land disputes. Scarcely a manor escaped the economic pressure to rationalize land use and ownership. Indeed, much of the political unrest under the Lancastrian monarchy stemmed from the litigious nature of the century and the slowness with which the common law responded to the needs of a changing society.

Equally serious strains were being placed on the labor supply of the manor, which tended to fall into two types — free and bond. By 1500 most laborers were free, but in 1399 perhaps a third to a half of the peasant population remained in a state of bondage — owing personal service to the lord of the manor, obliged to pay death and inheritance taxes and other financial extractions, and still legally bound to the land. It was quite possible for a serf or unfree laborer to hold free land. Conversely, it was not uncommon for freemen to farm unfree property and for both, bond and free, to lease demesne land from the lord of the manor. By 1399 two things tended to happen. First, freemen with freeholds evolved into substantial landed proprietors, and this provided the agricultural element out of which the yeoman class of the fifteenth century developed. Starting as freeholders or wealthy peasants, some of them even rose to be lords of the manor in their own right, and as a group they soon began to merge with the lower fringes of the knightly class. Second, the bondsmen and copyholders tended to fall to the level of wage laborers, usually free, occasionally renting land, but generally working the soil for wages paid them by the lord or yeomen of the manor. The result of this twofold process was the weakening and eventual destruction of the bonds that had once welded land and labor into an economic unit in which both lord and peasant had legal rights and shared in the produce of the soil.

Finally, the simple agrarian economy of the medieval past disappeared along with the professional knight and the fief. The merchant, the

A Manor Court "The confusion of conflicting and overlapping rights to the profits of the land protected by custom gave way to the ownership of land legally recorded and protected by law." *(The Granger Collection)*

moneylender, the financial speculator, and the cloth manufacturer had become, by the fifteenth century, just as important to society as the knight and the cleric. The laws regulating the just price in trade and commerce continued on the statute books; the doctrine that "riches exist for man, not man for riches" remained the official creed; and the military-chivalric ideal held captive the minds of men. Nevertheless, commerce and a money economy predominated. Long before 1399, the crown had become dependent on the wool trade as a source of revenue, and the customs on wool equaled in importance land subsidies granted by Parliament.

The Black Death (1348, 1361, 1369)

The origins of most of the economic, social, and legal tensions within late medieval society can be found long before the second half of the fourteenth century. There is excellent reason to believe, however, that the plague contributed heavily to the economic dislocation, emotional instability, and political weakness of the fifteenth century. In the summer of 1348, two strains of the plague descended upon England like bolts of

The Dance of Death, by Hans Holbein the Younger   "The death toll offered
by contemporaries indicates the magnitude and horror of the affliction and its
impact on the imagination. . . ." *(Mary Evans Picture Library)*

divine retribution — the bubonic infection spread by rats and other animals and transmitted by the bite of an infected flea, and the more lethal
and unpredictable pneumonic variety spread by coughing and sneezing.
Three times — in 1348, 1361, and 1369 — the plague reached devastating, epidemic proportions.

The total number dead is beyond count, especially since historians
disagree over the precise population of England before 1348. The death
toll offered by contemporaries indicates the magnitude and horror of the
affliction and its impact on the imagination, but it is otherwise unbeliev-
able because the medieval world was never given to statistical accuracy.
A sense of reliability is not conveyed when we read that Norwich, a city
that did not exceed 17,000, lost 57,000 souls. The customary estimate is
that between 30 percent and 50 percent of England's population may
have died, or in round and unreliable figures, possibly 2 million in a population of between 4 and 5 million.[2] More important demographically
speaking, after 1369 the plague became endemic, preventing the population from recovering: during the first half of the fifteenth century, 50
percent of the population had no surviving sons after the first generation,
and 75 percent failed to produce a male heir in the third generation.

---

[2]If the total is computed at 6 million, the mortality could have been as high as 3 million.

The spiritual, economic, and social consequences of the plague are incalculable. Whether a causal relationship exists between the communal graves of the plague victims and what followed chronologically — social revolt, civil anarchy, and heresy — is impossible to say, but the Black Death certainly set the stage on which these events took place. The intellectual and spiritual vigor of the high middle ages had been declining long before the plague struck down both rich and poor, in seeming disregard for reason, cosmic order, or prayer. Under such circumstances, the ultimate plague victims may have been the medieval doctrine of moderation — "all enthusiasm is the foe of salvation and all excess is a fault"[3] — and the belief in a rational and merciful deity. Religious expression turned away from reason and intellect to unreason and imagination. The intelligible God of the great medieval scholastics seemed quite incomprehensible: what good and sufficient reason could there be for a supposedly rational deity to bring upon mankind the catastrophe of the Black Death? Confronted with such unreason, the medieval world looked instead toward a God who need not be understood intellectually but who could be experienced emotionally and imaginatively. Humanity, however, is extraordinarily resilient, and both church and state, although profoundly shaken, emerged in the fifteenth century remarkably unaffected by the demographic disasters of the previous century.

The economic consequences of the plague are just as difficult to evaluate as the spiritual but somewhat easier to record. At first the lords of the manor had little difficulty in finding laborers, because the rural population in the previous century had been so abundant that not even the catastrophic crop failures and famines of the early decades of the century plus the disaster of the plague could seriously reduce their numbers. By 1400, however, the cumulative impact of the Black Death, along with the Gray Death of 1361, began to take effect, and England moved into a century of contracting economy: the prevailing economic theme was one of land surplus with seriously curtailed rentals, and labor shortage with consequent high wages. A shrinking population did not necessarily mean hard times for all. Peasants and yeomen prospered in an era of abundant land. But for the large landed proprietors, who were dependent on rents and farm labor, a major agricultural recession commenced in 1400 and lasted for the better part of the century.

A demographic mystery shrouds the fifteenth century for which there is no ready answer. By 1400, even though the mortality rate remained desperately high, all the conditions for a population recovery had emerged — food and land surplus, high wages, depressed rents, and considerable, if spotty, economic prosperity; yet the fertility rate failed to respond. Although the population of the continent began to recover, not until 1470, three generations later, did clear evidence exist in England of "more families with more children and fewer families with no children."

---

[3]*The Statesman's Book of John of Salisbury,* trans. John Dickinson (1963), ch. IX, pp. 43–44.

The trauma of the Black Death clearly included psychological factors that limited the birthrate and that the economic, political, and spiritual troubles of the century did nothing to mitigate.[4]

Economic Crisis (1400–1475)

The economic crisis that reached its height during the 1440s was not caused solely by the plague; other factors were involved, both domestic and international. Certainly the Hundred Years' War, with its ugly step-sisters plunder, piracy, and violence, lay heavy upon Europe, driving up the risk of commerce and reducing the buying power of some of the most prosperous areas of northern France. War can act as an economic stimulus, but prolonged guerrilla warfare, as was fought between France and England in the fifteenth century, may end by destroying the very basis of trade — a reasonable chance for making a profit and customers who are able and willing to buy. For centuries England's major export had been sacks of raw wool sent to Flanders and Florence for manufacture into cloth, but in the fifteenth century, war began to curtail this trade. In 1448 French pirates looted the Kentish coast, burning towns located many miles inland and destroying warehouses filled with wool. In the same year, England's traditional ally, the duchy of Burgundy, actively joined France in the Hundred Years' War and closed its Flemish ports to English wool. The results are recorded in the trade statistics of the town of Sandwich in Kent: between 1448 and 1449, exports of sacks of wool dropped from 182 to 25, and imports of wine fell from 1,042 to 271 tuns.

Throughout the fifteenth century, English merchants faced increased competition from abroad and at the same time were less able to defend themselves. This proved particularly true in relation to the Hanseatic League, a union of German towns that exported corn, timber, pitch, and fur and controlled the sale of Flemish cloth. As the century progressed, the Hanseatic merchants were able to extend their extraterritorial rights in England, securing the virtual independence of their place of business in London. The Steelyard, as the area was called, became a state within a state, and the Hansa merchants claimed immunity from English law. At the same time, they gained the right to export wool at special rates, which were in some cases more advantageous than those regulating English merchants. The crowning blow came in 1450 when Hanseatic merchants drove the English out of the Baltic and closed the lucrative Icelandic waters to English traders and fishermen.

If care is taken in the selection of the data, the economic picture of the first half of the century can be made to appear black and oppressive. Towns experienced a long decline in population, and between 1350 and

---

[4]See R. S. Gottfried, *Epidemic Disease in Fifteenth-Century England* (1978), p. 221; but for one possible answer, see P. J. P. Goldberg, *Women, Work, and Life Cycle in a Medieval Economy: Women in York and Yorkshire c. 1300–1520* (1992).

1500 more than 1,300 villages disappeared, their inhabitants having died or migrated to more prosperous farming areas. Wool exports between 1448 and 1450 alone dropped by 35 percent, miscellaneous trade was down 23 percent, and wine imports were cut by 50 percent. The earls of Northumberland may have faced a 35 percent cut in land revenues during the first fifty years of the century, and throughout the kingdom the decline of rents may have exceeded the drop in prices by as much as 11 percent. The poverty of the realm is reflected in the reduction of the crown's income; the parliamentary subsidy for the county of Surrey was set at £587 in 1334, but by 1440 the estimate had been reduced to £506. A tax that generated £37,000 before the Black Death yielded only £29,000 a century later.

Like most economic matters, the total design is difficult to distinguish. Economic recession and agricultural depression hurt some individuals and groups, but they also helped others. Certainly, the overall economic profile is not one of unrelenting gloom. Before the plague, England was approaching the point of "critical population density," a social-science euphemism for starvation in a society where the population outstrips its food supply. Agriculturally, the kingdom was desperately underdeveloped, and farm production was probably no better than in twentieth-century Ghana, where in 1970 one worker could feed only one and a half persons. (In the United States a single farmer could feed forty-two.) Although the total economic pie shrank after 1349, those who survived the Black Death had more of almost everything; food prices declined sharply, inferior farmland now lay uncultivated, and real wages may have doubled. As inferior farmland was left uncultivated, the relative agricultural productivity of the kingdom increased, and seed yield for wheat, which had stood at 4.2 to 1 in 1300, rose to 5 to 1 by 1400. Obviously, more could be grown for less cost and labor.

Landlords responded to falling rents, shortage of labor, and the search for higher profits in varying ways and with different economic and social results that further befuddle the total economic picture. Some proprietors sought to reestablish their "seignorial" rights over the labor of their serfs. Others turned to sheep farming, seeing the shepherd and his dog as a practical answer to falling wheat prices, the high cost of labor, and the tendency of peasants to flee their manors and renegotiate their freedom elsewhere. Still others began to introduce new farming methods, which by the late sixteenth and early seventeenth centuries had reached revolutionary proportions (see page 83).

The wool trade reveals an equally mixed picture. The decline in the export of wool, if taken alone, would indeed be an alarming index of commercial disaster, for the average number of sacks exported during the 1390s had stood at 19,357 and by 1446 it had fallen to 7,654. These figures, however, must be presented against the equally dramatic rise in the export of woolen broadcloth, for during the century following the plague, England evolved from a wool-exporting kingdom into a cloth-manufacturing country. In 1354 the export of wool broadcloth totaled

4,774 pieces; by 1440 the average had risen to 56,317; and by 1509 it had reached 84,789 pieces. Export figures can be translated into mercantile success or failure, depending on the interests involved. The Staplers, an association of three to four hundred merchants with their headquarters (or staple) located at Calais, were on the decline during the century, but their commercial welfare was geared to the export of raw wool. Conversely, the Merchant Adventurers, a newer organization concentrating in and eventually monopolizing the export of wool broadcloth, grew increasingly prosperous throughout the same period. The truth of the matter is that economic boom or depression varied from individual to individual and group to group, and had very little to do with the total picture of expansion or contraction.

The Peasantry

Of all the elements of medieval society, the peasantry remained the largest in numbers, the weakest in influence, the most important to the economy, and the skimpiest in terms of historical documentation. Medieval recorded history has been the story of a small, dominant, and literate minority who took the trouble to record and preserve its opinions and activities. Consequently, the historian's image of the voiceless and inarticulate majority is haphazard at best and heavily distorted by feudal upper-class prejudice against manual labor and by the medieval conviction that social groups were ordained by God to play a prescribed function within the social organism — the aristocracy to lead, the clergy to pray, the merchant to pay taxes, and the peasants to labor "with their hands from dawn to vespers." In the highly exaggerated words of those who could document their sentiments, the toiler of the soil was "marvellously ugly and hideous. His head was big and blacker than smoked meat; the palm of your hand could easily have gone between his two eyes; he had very large cheeks and a monstrous flat nose with great nostrils; lips redder than uncooked flesh; teeth yellow and foul. . . . Upon his back was a rough cloak; and he stood leaning on a huge club."

Richard II summoned up the aristocratic attitude toward the peasantry when he exclaimed, "Villains you have been and are; in bondage you shall remain," but economic reality determined otherwise. Time, if not politics, was on the side of the serf, and his economic position was improving. The plague and the consequent shortage of labor accelerated a process that had for decades been working in favor of the serf, transforming him into something other than a bondsman, tied to the land, "owning nothing but his belly," and subject to his lord's legal and economic domination. Faced with a depleted labor supply, the lord of the manor was forced to grant far better terms to his serfs. Bondsmen became freemen either by formal agreement or by the informal lapse of ancient obligations. Occasionally the serf simply ran away to a distant manor where the local landed proprietor asked no questions and hired him for wages.

Iulius, Augustus, nec non et Iunius Aestas · AESTAS Adolet · · *Frugiferas aruis fert Aestas torrida meßeis ·*

Working on the Manor   "The peasant's most valuable asset, his labor, was suddenly placed at a premium, and he could use it to win his legal freedom." *(The Metropolitan Museum of Art, Harris Brisbane Dick Fund, 1926; 26.72.23)*

The peasant's most valuable asset, his labor, was suddenly placed at a premium, and he could use it to win his legal freedom. As the years passed, the lords of the manor found it easier to pay wages than to enforce personal service or labor statutes. By 1500 the serf was almost extinct. His place had been taken by three groups: the wage-earning rural proletarian who was free but landless; the free customary tenant or copyholder who paid rent but had a right to bequeath and inherit his land "according to the custom of the manor"; and the freeholder who had become in fact, if not yet in theory, the owner of land that owed no service (see also Enclosures, pages 80–83).

The Yeomanry

Above the rural laborer in the social hierarchy stood another group, less definable and even more elusive than the peasantry. This was the element sometimes referred to as freeholders, sometimes as yeomanry, and sometimes simply as prosperous peasants. Whatever the name, they constituted an agricultural laboring elite, which by dint of hard work and efficient farming had prospered as a consequence of the agricultural depression and labor shortage. Rents were low and leases were easily negotiated on long-term bases, and many a humble man who may have started life as a serf ended up a substantial farmer, controlling a freehold, leasing a sheep run, and employing a handful of laborers. Agricultural statistics give impressive evidence of the prosperity of this group; on Redgrave Manor the average size of a peasant's landholding rose from 12 acres in 1300 to 30 acres in 1400. There were possibly five thousand such farmers throughout the kingdom, earning anywhere from £5 to £25 a year. They constituted the lowest level within the ruling elite that represented scarcely 2 percent of the total male population. Bishop Hugh Latimer's father belonged to this group. His assessed income was £4 a year. Owning no land but leasing 200 acres, raising a hundred sheep and thirty cows, hiring six laborers, and himself working from dawn till dusk, he sent a son to college, financed good marriages for his daughters, and paid for the hospitality that more than anything else was the mark of social status and success.

The Gentry

The higher one mounted the social pyramid, the more unpredictable the economic, demographic, and financial picture became. Above the yeomanry stood the gentry, divided according to their incomes into gentlemen, esquires, and knights. These men represented only about 1 percent of the adult male population — possibly two thousand to three thousand individuals — but collectively they were the largest landowners in the kingdom, possessing over 50 percent of all property not in ecclesiastical hands. In contrast, the nobility controlled less than 4 percent. Gentry incomes varied: the privileged minority at the top had assembled wealth of £300 a year; and those at the bottom managed on considerably less than Bishop Latimer's father. What distinguished the gentry, especially the upper echelons, from those below was their political connection with the royal court and the great barons, which assured them the profitable lease of royal and episcopal lands, gave them control of politically important local offices, and awarded them favorable treatment at law. The ranks of the gentry were in constant flux as well-to-do yeomen moved up the social and political ladder, and as wealthy lawyers, merchants, and war profiteers sought to set themselves up as landed gentlemen. Once these newcomers had earned, married, or acquired gentility, they insisted on recording and protecting their newly acquired status. To this demand the crown acquiesced in 1510 by establishing the College of Heralds to legalize and prove their real or fabricated family pedigrees. The gentry were the heart of the political nation. They supplied the lion's share of its governance, linking the king and his household to the shires and, as the clients of the great magnates, they wove the kingdom into a web of interacting political alliances or "affinities."

Building Houses in a Fifteenth-Century Town Even though the mortality rate remained desperately high, all the conditions for a population boom existed — food and land surplus and considerable economic prosperity. *(The Granger Collection)*

How cohesive or economically solvent the gentry were is difficult to judge. Some were closer economically and socially to the yeomanry below them. Others were in effect untitled members of the nobility, but most seemed to have been confronted with a major economic crisis during much of the fifteenth century. The dislocation of the wool trade; the incessant cry for higher wages; the collapse of rental income from land; and, after 1470, the increasing size of their families, which were growing faster than the rest of the realm, hit them hard. Plagued by curtailed means, rising expectations, and the cost of maintaining their social position, the gentry not surprisingly sought relief through war, litigation, and increasing political irresponsibility. The case of Thomas Hargrave during the civil wars of the Roses, although scarcely typical of the gentry as a whole, is nevertheless symptomatic of the growing use of violence. Hargrave returned in haste from the Yorkist victory over the Lancastrians at Tewkesbury in 1471, ready and willing to capitalize on the military success of his party. Hargrave intended to evict Peter Marion from lands that Marion had held for years but that Hargrave coveted. The unfortunate Marion was suspected of Lancastrian sympathies and lacked friends or influence in high places. Hargrave seized his rival, tied him up with a dog collar around his neck, and chained him in the great hall of the manor house that had once been his. Then Hargrave sent for the recorder of Winchester, who arrived to discover the new "owner" mounted on a raised chair with Marion cowering at his feet. Under the circumstances, it is not surprising that Marion was persuaded to deed the manor to

Hargrave, or that the transaction was duly recorded at law, or that Marion, the instant he achieved his freedom, repudiated his act and sought the aid of important men who could help him regain his property. No one can say what percentage of the responsible elements of society acted like Hargrave, but when the social element that represented the natural rulers of society, and from which sheriffs and justices of the peace were drawn, used force, fraud, and favoritism to gain its ends, the collapse of good government and the advent of civil war were simply a matter of time.

The Baronage

On a legal and restricted pinnacle far above the ranks of lesser folk stood the baronage of England, exclusive in numbers but not always financially distinguishable from the wealthier knights of the shires. In 1436 the realm had only fifty-one barons, and although their number varied from decade to decade, there were rarely more than a few dozen who were of sufficient age, ability, and wealth to exercise real power. Their average income was in the neighborhood of £865 a year, but the lower economic echelons of the group managed with as little as £300, while the favored few rose as high as £5,000.

The lesser barons faced many of the economic problems confronting the gentry and renter classes, and they took similar steps to alleviate their woes. Like their cousins, the knights of the shires, they also turned to violence, law, and political factionalism. The great barons, however, were in a far more favorable position than most of the lesser landowners. Their historic position as the natural advisers of the king gave them entry to court and the potential to influence directly the sovereign's policies and manipulate his bounty. Social and economic forces conspired to concentrate in their hands unparalleled wealth and potential political power. The closer they stood to the crown in birth and association, the greater their revenues. Richard, duke of York, commanded an income of £3,231, and possibly twice this sum if his Welsh manors are included. Richard, earl of Warwick, jogged along on £3,116 and could count on another £2,422 from his Welsh estates. The duke of Buckingham managed with £4,400, and the Percys of Northumberland trailed with £2,825.

The principle "to him who hath shall be given" prevailed. Not only the incomes but also the estates of the great magnates tended to grow larger as the vagaries of marriage, mortality, and violence began to operate at an accelerated pace. As families died out, estates escheated back to their overlords or were passed through the female line into the great baronial clans whose daughters were legion. The greatest, the most prolific, the most predatory, and therefore the most successful and dangerous of these noble dynasties were the Nevilles. Younger than the Percys in noble rank, but their rivals for control of the northern shires, the Nevilles began their spectacular rise with John, third Baron Neville. By the judicious marriages of his many sisters and daughters, he converted a distinguished northern baronial family into a dynasty equal in wealth and power to the royal houses of York and Lancaster. His eldest son, Ralph (1364–1425), became first earl of Westmorland and carried on the family policy of marital aggrandizement. Ralph married twice, and his second wife was Joan Beaufort, daughter of John of Gaunt by his mistress Catherine Swinford, and thus a half-sister of Henry IV. In all, Ralph had eleven sons and twelve daughters, and hardly an important family in England escaped a Neville son- or daughter-in-law. Neville daughters became duchesses of Norfolk, Buckingham, and York; Neville sons inherited through their wives such important titles as Latimer, Furnival, Fauconberg, Salisbury, and Abergavenny. Through the marriage of his daughter Cecily, Ralph became father-in-law to the Yorkist heir to the throne and grandfather of two Yorkist kings of England — Edward IV and Richard III. By his son Richard, he became the grandfather of the mightiest baron of them all — Richard, earl of Warwick, known in history as the kingmaker. The earl entered London in February 1454 marching at the head of six hundred men dressed in brilliant livery and decorated with the Neville heraldic emblem of the ragged staff. When he sat down to breakfast, his household consumed six oxen. It was said that six thousand friends and acquaintances came to celebrate the installation of his brother George as archbishop of York in 1467. If the number cited is correct, the entire ruling elite of England, including much of the yeomanry, must have been gathered together at a single function.

The story that six thousand guests came to partake of Warwick's hospitality is probably another example of medieval exaggeration, but it dramatizes two important aspects of the baronial style of living: its costliness and its political implications. No matter the immense revenues of the great magnates, their incomes were never enough, and during much of the fifteenth century they were on the decline. The duke of York confronted a 22 percent reduction in rents during the 1440s, the rents for the dukes of Norfolk fell by 40 percent, and the earl of Northumberland experienced a rental decrease of 35 percent. To add to their financial plight, the loss of their lands in France further curtailed their incomes, while their expenses, especially those associated with what is called bastard feudalism, were rising. The great barons, like Warwick, had to prove their political power by their largesse and the number of followers who displayed their colors, wore their livery, and partook of their hospitality. The system demanded that the magnates attract into their political circles a wide assortment of retainers, who had to be bought with annuities, gifts, favors, and offices. Given their retainer bills, baronial poverty "may, after all, have been the spur to political gangsterism."[5]

---

[5]C. D. Ross, "The Estates and Finances of Richard, Duke of York," *Welsh Historical Review,* 3 (1967), p. 302.

Bastard Feudalism

Historians generally refer to the political system that prevailed in fifteenth-century England as bastard feudalism, a phrase that confuses and distorts more than it clarifies, but that nevertheless conveys the essential psychological and emotional ties that held late medieval society together. The expression conveys three half-truths: (1) that once there was something called pure feudalism capable of later becoming bastardized; (2) that some sort of feudalism actually existed in the fifteenth century; and (3) that this malformed system was a cancerous affliction of the body politic, which produced weak government, endemic violence, judicial corruption, and eventually civil war.

Only in the most theoretical and idealized sense is it correct to depict feudalism as a political structure shaped like a pyramid and based on proprietorship over land that had been given to a vassal by an overlord in return for military, judicial, and financial services and obligations. Historically speaking, feudal reality was neither particularly systematic nor rational, and as it matured, any claim to tidiness disintegrated into a welter of legal confusion and lapsed obligations. It is difficult to say that by the fifteenth century feudalism survived in any formal political, contractual, or hierarchical sense. What remained, however, was much of the emotional underpinning that sustained feudalism, which from the start was more a state of mind than a formal political structure. Used in its broadest and least institutional sense, feudalism embodied most of humanity's innate fears and virtues: instinctive dislike of change, rigid adherence to custom, deep suspicion of public authority, and a preference for private over public law.

It is difficult for the twentieth century to sniff the feudal atmosphere that reeked of strong emotions, especially myopic loyalty to friend, kin, village, and overlord. Membership in and loyalty to the group — the guild, town, monastery, college, family, or the entourage of a great nobleman, each of which gave to the individual a sense of importance and status — was a more potent attraction and inspired far deeper emotional attachment than any concept of nation or nationality. The individual yeoman or gentleman might regard himself as the king's man, but he did so primarily because the monarch could personally inspire his loyalty. He had only a vague and ill-formed idea of the theory of service owed by a subject to the state.

What distinguishes fifteenth-century feudalism is the increased use of money and written contractual agreements (called indentures) to shore up and strengthen the personal and political ties between lord and vassal, master and retainer. In the distant past, these agreements had of necessity involved the exchange of land for services rendered and had rested on verbal promises — oaths of fealty and homage — and the force of custom to sustain them. In a more litigious, educated, and money-oriented society, the overlord rarely offered land for service. Instead he promised political favors, annuities, or cash payments. The terms of the contract were

The Tree of Battles A fifteenth-century satirical depiction of the violence that existed in both church and state. *(E. T. Archive)*

written and explicit, and this was regarded by both parties as a vast improvement over the older system.

The ancient relationship whereby a vassal looked to his lord for military protection, and the lord in turn depended on his vassal to fulfill his own military obligations to the king or to fight his personal wars against rival barons, waned in the fifteenth century, but the economic, political, and social dependence of the gentry and yeomanry on the local baron and their willingness to serve their betters remained. Nothing is more important to the operation of early modern society than the concept of personal service, and it will remain the dominant human response throughout the centuries encompassed in this volume. To be in service today has acquired the stigma of servility. In the fifteenth century, almost everyone was in service because to serve was both profitable and honorable. To the lord, service guaranteed power. Not only did service supply him with legal, managerial, military, and political expertise in his constant struggle to expand or defend his estates, but it also gave him reputation. The number of people who were in his service, belonged to his affinity, and wore his livery formed the hallmark of his political clout. To the retainer, service gave economic advantage, political office, legal protection, and above all status in a society that judged a man by his patron.

The relationship between service and patronage was interlocking. Good lordship, in other words the favor and influence of a nobleman, might be offered to a retainer in anticipation of future services, but it could also be given as the reward for services already performed. The great as well as the lesser magnates were constantly pestered with offers of service because it was "the law and the profit" to find a "good lord." Exactly how important the favor of a lord was can be sensed from the popularity of charms sold as a guarantee that the bearer "shall have love of great masters and they shall not refuse his asking but grant him with good will" all that he desired.[6] The principle of lordship encompassed all levels of the political elite. Lord Hasting's ninety retainers included twenty individuals described as gentlemen, fifty-nine as esquires, nine as knights, and two as peers of the realm. Even more significant, twenty served as sheriffs and thirty-three as justices of the peace. They received royal and episcopal patronage in the form of leases and offices as a consequence of Lord Hasting's influence at court. In return they did political and judicial favors for Hasting's friends by selecting friendly juries or bribing judges. If judicial extortion failed, they could try outright intimidation of the judge and jury, as when Lord Fanhope sat outside the town hall of Bedford with fifty armed retainers to secure a "proper" judgment (see also pages 50–51).

Service expressed itself only occasionally in armed retainers committing what was called, then and now, the crime of maintenance, the corrupting and intimidation of the legal process. Most service took the form of household positions — the lord's bailiff, steward, forester, or stable master — offices almost invariably offered only to family relations or neighboring gentry. Indeed, service could be as tenuous as simply being the lord's tenant and thus owing him rent. Together, household staff, indentured retainers, tenants, family, political well wishers, and neighborhood friends constituted the lord's affinity or structure of good lordship. When such associations were headed by a great magnate who possessed entry to the king's court and could influence his policies, they could grow into kingdomwide alliances of individuals obligated "to take their overlord's full part and quarrel and be with him against all persons save the king."

Understandably, modern observers tend to focus on the quarreling and disruptive aspects of bastard feudalism. The military flavor of the indenture system cannot be minimized when Sir John Trafford contracted with the earl of Warwick in 1461 to "be ready at the desire or commandment of the earl to come unto him . . . horsed, harnessed, arrayed and accompanied as the case shall require, and according to what the earl shall

---

[6]Quoted in R. Horrox, *Richard III, A Study of Service* (1989).

call him to do." But bastard feudalism was as useful and necessary to the effective governance of the kingdom as it was politically dangerous, and the exception written into all indentures that service did not mean warring against the sovereign was crucial to a society that possessed deep respect for kingship.

In medieval England, two systems of government existed, in one sense side by side, in another sense one on top of the other. One was the king's law, common to all subjects. The other was baronial law, which originated in a few cases directly from the historic rights of the local magnate to hold his own court, council, chancellory, and exchequer but more often simply reflected the prestige and wealth of the nobleman to whom the county gentry owed loyalty and service. The king's government was helpless without baronial support, and if a Percy or a Neville did not sit on the Commission of the Peace, there could be no peace in the shire. It did little good for the sovereign to send strangers from London into the shires because the local justices of the peace would accept only the authority of the man who was known and respected and whose affinity ran throughout the locale. Ultimately, it was not the king's courts of law or his administration standing in isolation that preserved order throughout the realm. Instead, as Thomas Starkey observed in the sixteenth century, "the office and duty of the nobility and gentry of every shire is to see justice among their servants and subjects and to keep them in unity and concord."[7] What made the situation in the fifteenth century so politically explosive was not bastard feudalism as such but the existence of an authority vacuum at the apex of the political hierarchy: the crown itself. It took strong royal government to arbitrate between rival political factions and to bend them to the royal will and convert them into instruments of effective government. The cancer that beset the kingdom after the death of Henry V was not the presence of overmighty magnates but the failure of kingship as a child-king grew into a pious but unstable and incompetent adult.

The Church

Economic and political tensions plagued Henry VI's reign, but far more important to the young monarch himself was the deeply religious atmosphere into which he had been born and the paramount position that the church continued to hold despite the ravages of the Black Death. Nothing symbolizes the pivotal role of the church in society as much as Henry's own intense concern for spiritual and ecclesiastical matters and the presence in his government of the wealthiest churchman of his day — his great-uncle, Henry Beaufort, Cardinal Bishop of Winchester. The cardinal served as the king's chief adviser for most of his early life

---

[7]Quoted in G. L. Harriss, *Henry V, the Practice of Kingship* (1985).

and the crown's most important creditor, having lent the Lancastrian dynasty £212,330 between 1404 and 1446.

The traditional approach to the fifteenth-century church is to view it as the prelude to the Reformation: because the old church was destroyed in the sixteenth century, logic leads the historian to find the causes in the fifteenth century and to emphasize the worst about the old church — its corruption, worldliness, institutional rigidity, and inability to respond to society's changing spiritual aspirations. Such an approach is tempting because it is tidy and sets up an easily understood cause-and-effect relationship; however, it hopelessly distorts reality. In reaction modern historians have been attracted by a more sympathetic view that presents the fifteenth-century church as a healthy, soul-satisfying, and holistic body of beliefs that tied the living to the dead through a set of time-honored rituals. These ceremonies gave meaning to the mystery of human existence, offered solace in the midst of earthly suffering, and presented a satisfactory explanation to an otherwise incomprehensible and frightening cosmos. These scholars argue that pluralism — the holding of more than one ecclesiastical benefice or living — and absenteeism from office were not regarded by contemporaries as particularly grievous abuses, but instead were seen as a perfectly rational response to economic and political reality. Many church livings were too poor to support a clergyman, and many priests, especially bishops like Henry Beaufort, were involved in government. The educational level of the clergy, far from declining, was better than that attained in the thirteenth century. The church may not have built many monasteries in the fifteenth century, but revisionists point out that it expressed its vitality by constructing chantries and chapels. By 1529, 2,374 priests sang masses for the dead in perpetual chantry foundations. In York Cathedral, the faithful endowed fifty-six chantry chapels, and in the city itself forty-one parish churches possessed an additional eighty chantries. The late fifteenth and early sixteenth centuries were also the great age of parish church construction and renovation, and during the 150 years before the Reformation possibly 60 percent of the kingdom's churches were built anew or remodeled in the magnificent perpendicular style of late Gothic architecture.

Revisionists maintain that for the vast majority of the faithful, the church remained a beloved and treasured haven in the midst of suffering, insecurity, and mortality, and it is comforting to believe that Geoffrey Chaucer's picture of the country parson — upright, generous, and devoted to his calling — matched reality:

> There was a Parson, too, that had his cure
> In a small town, a good man and a poor;
> But rich he was in holy thought and work.
> Also he was a learned man, a clerk,
> Seeking Christ's gospel faithfully to preach;
> Most piously his people would he teach.
> . . . .

> To tempt folk unto heaven by high endeavor
> And good example was his purpose ever.

Unfortunately such a romantic view of the old church is as distorted as the one that speaks only of Chaucer's pardoner:

> There was no pardoner could go his pace,
> For in his bag he kept a pillow-case
> That was, he said, our Blessed Lady's veil;
> He claimed to own the fragment of the sail
> That Peter had the time he walked the sea
> And Jesus saved him in his clemency.
> . . . .
>
> In one day he could get more revenue
> Than would the parson in a month or two.
> And thus with tricks and artful flattery
> He fooled both flock and parson thoroughly.
> But let us say, to make the truth less drastic,
> In church he was a fine ecclesiastic.

Without the pardoner, the Reformation becomes inexplicable and is relegated to the level of a rather sordid political trick foisted upon an unsuspecting and spiritually satisfied flock for reasons of greed and dynasty (see pages 132–140).

The late medieval church was neither parson nor pardoner, but both. Structurally, it was an international leviathan with its heart in Rome and its ecclesiastical arteries spread over the length and breadth of Christendom. Like any vast institution — composed as it was of 2 archdioceses, 21 bishoprics, 8,600 parishes, 825 monasteries, with some 13,000 attending monks and nuns, and possibly 30,000 secular priests — the English medieval church was afflicted with most of the failings that beset the human species and most of the flaws that often come with age, privilege, and wealth. Originally, the estates belonging to the church had been bestowed out of respect for an organization that not only held the keys to the kingdom of heaven but also practiced a higher and better way of life on earth. By the fifteenth century, God's church still possessed the keys but it tended to equate entrance into paradise with paying church tithes and state taxes. As an institution, it had significantly more wealth than the crown, holding between one-fourth and one-third of all arable land, a fact that became increasingly important as church and state clashed during the Reformation crisis. Rich, autonomous, and well connected, and eyeing with the deepest misgivings all new ideas — especially those that might endanger its financial and material well-being — the late medieval Catholic church became a universal great-aunt with more of the madame about her than the martyr. It chose the path of safety, whereby church and crown joined in an alliance to maintain the status quo. Pope, priest, and friar preached a single truth: payment of taxes and obedience to authority were necessary to the soul's salvation. In return, the Lancastrian

Illumination from a Dutch Book of Hours c. 1440 Depicting Hell's Mouth "Pope, priest, and friar preached a single truth: payment of taxes and obedience to authority were necessary to the soul's salvation." *(The Granger Collection)*

crown assumed the responsibility for enforcing religious orthodoxy and exterminating heresy.

Anticlericalism and the wish to purify and elevate the church were as old as the medieval world, and in the past the ecclesiastical structure had always been able to absorb and profit from the demand for reform. Fifteenth-century criticism of clerics and their comfortable and worldly way of life was different; much of it lay outside of a church that had grown so rigid and unyielding that it could do nothing but brand all reform as heresy and turn to the Lancastrian kings and parliamentary statutes to exterminate the ideas of Oxford scholar John Wycliffe (1320?–1384) and his Lollard followers.

From the established church's point of view, Wycliffe expounded three darkly pernicious doctrines. First, he put alarming emphasis on the Bible and on individual interpretations of the Scriptures as the source of spiritual inspiration and the guide for a moral life. Clerics could never sanction such a notion because it implicitly denied the authority of the church to interpret God's will and administer His grace. Even more explosive, he insisted that the man was more important than the ecclesiastical office. The wicked priest, in Wycliffe's view, destroyed the benefits derived from the sacraments despite the authority vested in him by his sacred office. Conversely, the good man, filled with a sense of divine grace, could administer the sacraments just as effectively as the ordained priest. Wycliffe challenged the central pillar of the church's spiritual authority, the privileged status of the clergy as an ordained and separate caste within society. Finally, the Oxford scholar attacked the temporal and monetary endowments of the church, arguing that Christ and his apostles had lived in poverty without benefit of gold plate and exorbitant rents. Pomp and circumstance, he complained, were corrupting the spiritual health of the priestly order, and monks with their "red and fat cheeks and great bellies" were more interested in the cure of hams than of souls. In denying the right of the church to possess wealth and land, Wycliffe was only a step away from questioning its position as the custodian of the conscience of Christendom.

Wycliffe's essentially academic and theoretical approach to the spiritual and ecclesiastical issues of his day were often translated by his Lollard followers into commonsense literalism: if a belief or ceremony were not expressly mentioned in the Bible, it was unacceptable; if it were included, it had to be followed to the letter. Consequently, Lollards branded much of the church's spiritual apparatus — creeping to the cross, venerating saints, collecting holy relics, and embarking on pilgrimages — as violations of the biblical commandment: "Thou shalt not make unto thee any graven image" or "bow thyself to them."

For a time in the fourteenth century, Wycliffe and his Lollard followers were immensely popular, and they "multiplied exceedingly like budding plants and filled the whole realm everywhere." Barons who resented ecclesiastical control of high royal offices found comfort in the Lollard belief that a good churchman "dwelleth at home and keepeth well his fold." Likewise, knights of the shire in Parliament must have listened with sympathy in 1410 to the Lollard suggestion that if church lands were nationalized and redistributed to deserving lords and gentlemen, there would be sufficient estates to create 15 earldoms, 1,500 knights, 6,200 esquires, 100 almshouses, and 15 universities, and leave £20,000 for the royal treasury. Such a suggestion found wide support among landlords, both orthodox and heretic, who envied the church's wealth, power, and independence.

But it was with the lesser sort that Lollardy proved most popular. A few of the converts were eccentric and impious fellows, such as the man who split the statue of St. Catherine into kindling to boil his cabbage, or the singular gentleman who took a consecrated wafer used in the mass and consumed one-third of it with oysters, one-third with onions, and one-third with wine, as rather extraordinary proof that it was only common bread and possessed no miraculous qualities. But most Lollards were devout and ordinary folk, drawn from the lesser gentry and yeomanry, or from the urban and artisan population. They represented a numerous, if not powerful, element that was in desperate need of spiritual comfort, which the established church either would not or could not give.

By the fifteenth century, Lollardy was considered to be far more dangerous than it had been in the fourteenth, for the ruling elements of society began to suspect that novelty in religion walked hand in hand with social revolution. The Peasants' Revolt (1381) and the Lollard heresy coincided in time; rightly or wrongly, anxious priests and frightened landlords were quick to assume that heresy in faith produced revolution in society, and that church and state must stand shoulder to shoulder if Christendom were to exterminate the heretical and seditious doctrine that "all goods should be held in common and no one ought to be allowed to have property." Persecution commenced with the triumph of a Lancastrian dynasty anxious to win ecclesiastical support for its shaky throne. Parliament passed laws in 1401 making unrepentant heresy punishable by burning, but such legislation did little save harass and irritate the Lollards. On the death of Henry IV, however, a stern and orthodox monarch, hoping to earn the favor of God, mounted the throne. For Henry V, the link between Lollardy and treason seemed absolutely clear in the Oldcastle rebellion of 1414 (see page 15), and by 1422 the prisons overflowed with heretics awaiting trial or execution. By 1431 Lollardy as a political or religious force was purged.

Church and state were allied in the fifteenth century, giving late medieval society an appearance of psychological stability that helped offset the unsettling presence of royal incompetence, governmental corruption, and baronial feuding and aggrandizement. Not even the events portrayed in the next chapter could undermine the confidence that most people had in the rightness of the existing socio-religious structure.

CHAPTER **3**

The Lion and the Unicorn

In the last chapter, Richard Neville, earl of Warwick was left entertaining six thousand guests, a display of conspicuous consumption which might not have been politically dangerous had the sixteen-year-old Henry VI, his childhood over, not remained politically inept and emotionally unstable, an easy prey for those who sought to use him in the factional struggles that beset the kingdom. It is now time to "sit upon the ground and tell sad stories of the death of kings."[1]

Henry VI (1440–1461, 1471): Part 2, the Years of Incompetence

Political success is notoriously difficult to explain; it so often results from the delicate interaction of accident, personality, and good luck. With the wisdom of hindsight, political failure, however, is easy to diagnose. The fifteenth century preferred to place the blame for what happened between 1440 and 1461 on the king's evil and unscrupulous councillors, the "catchpoles and mushrooms" that fed upon the king's bounty. The twentieth century, less dazzled by the magic of kingship, is more willing to point the finger at the young monarch himself.

Political power bears direct relationship to economic wealth, and Sir John Fortescue correctly analyzed the dilemma confronted by Henry VI when he pleaded that kings should be worth twice the gold of their greatest subjects. When a Warwick, a Percy, or a duke of York could command cash revenues that almost equaled those of the sovereign, subjects possessed the potential to be mightier than kings. Such a situation, of course, could happen only under the most extraordinary conditions:

---

[1]The general bibliography for Chapter 3 is essentially the same as for Chapters 1 and 2, but see also J. R. Lander, *Crown and Nobility, 1450–1509* (1976); R. A. Griffiths's lengthy, *The Reign of King Henry VI: The Exercise of Royal Authority, 1422–1461* (1981); and B. Wolffle's shorter *Henry VI* (1981). Besides K. B. McFarlane's critical *England in the Fifteenth Century* (1981), which is a collection of his key essays, see his *The Nobility of Later Medieval England* (1973). See also R. A. Griffiths and J. Sherborne (eds.), *Kings and Nobles in the Later Middle Ages* (1986) and C. Ross (ed.), *Patronage, Pedigree and Power in Later Medieval England* (1979), both of which are collected papers by diverse writers.

when the crown was confronted by unprecedented war expenses; was burdened with past debts; and, most important of all, was worn by a monarch generous to the point of idiocy, possessing no sense of what constituted "good kingship," and easily influenced by favorites to whom he was blindly devoted. From the year that Henry officially came of age in 1437 to his enforced removal from the throne in 1461, contemporaries had increasing difficulty denying that "the kingdom was out of all governance."

Nature may not abhor a vacuum, but politics does. Without the presence of a strong, charismatic sovereign who knew his own mind and who could command both personal and military respect, the great magnates began to use their positions and influence at court to line their pockets with fat salaries and annuities drawn from crown lands and to provide their friends, servants, and retainers with lucrative government offices. The king's chancery, his exchequer, even his law were invaded, used, and warped, and the royal service degenerated into a vast system of jobbery. "Men," wrote John Paston, "do not lure hawks with empty hands." The aristocratic leaders, if they wanted lesser men to look to them for aid and comfort and come to their support, had to produce the plums of political patronage. Sir John Fortescue perceived the essence of the political process when he noted that the king's council was controlled by the great lords who so occupied themselves with the welfare of "their kin, servants and tenants that they attended but little to the king's matter." He added that no question treated in the council "could be kept privy, for the lords told their servants how their causes had fared and who was against them."

The barons had always claimed the right to counsel the sovereign and had looked to him for wealth and office to reinforce their own authority in the shires, and in all likelihood, politics at court would not have reached crisis proportions had most of the barons been able to profit equally from the king's bounty. Unfortunately, the royal ear and, therefore, his largesse and his government were monopolized by a small faction of Lancastrian relatives and baronial favorites. Possibly even then, the situation would not have exploded into a clash of arms had the crown been able to remain above political factionalism. Instead, kingship became so besmirched by political infighting that Henry was increasingly viewed as the head of a Lancastrian faction and not as the leader of the kingdom. Once this perception had spread, the only way that those barons who had been denied the monarch's patronage could protect their own interests in the shires was to eliminate by force of arms the "caterpillars" and "catchpoles" about the king. The link between shire politics and court politics and the clash of factions that had the potential to spark baronial conflict and to destroy the Lancastrian dynasty is best analyzed in reference to a single political explosion in Bedfordshire, which took place just as Henry VI came of age.

The cause of the trouble was Sir John Cornwall's entrance into local shire politics. Sir John was highly esteemed at court. He had served as a comrade-in-arms with Henry V and had profited hugely from the early English successes in France. He had also married Elizabeth of Lancaster, the widowed sister of Henry IV, and had been created Lord Fanhope in 1432. He wisely decided to invest the profits of war not in France but in England, and he purchased Ampthill Castle in Bedfordshire, seeking to become the prevailing local magnate. In doing so, however, he clashed with the interests of Reginald, Lord Grey of Reuthen, whose family had controlled Bedfordshire politics for generations. Worse, Ampthill Castle lay only five miles from Grey's country residence outside Silsoe. Conflict between the two men erupted in 1437 when the Lancastrian government sent a Commission of the Peace to investigate reports of riots and violence in the county. Because the commission was heavily stacked with Lord Fanhope's appointees and friends, Lord Grey understandably accused it of deliberately trying to place the blame for the shire's disturbances on Lord Grey's tenants and retainers. The allegation was brought before the king's council, and Grey demanded that, when the commission reconvened, his men and political interests be represented in its membership so that he could answer the charges brought against his friends. Both sides marshalled their armed retainers, and the new Commission of the Peace broke up in a brawl.

The government patched up a peace between the two lords, and issued a general pardon for all murders and treasons committed by the rival factions. Fanhope was determined, however, not only to impose his "lordship" on Bedfordshire but also to superimpose it on Grey's "lordship." This feat entailed winning over the justices of the peace, especially when they met collectively for judicial purposes at the town of Bedford. In January 1439, the two rival factions came to blows. Fanhope arrived in town with 140 armed retainers, interrupted the court proceedings, and insulted the justices allied with Grey. Grey in his turn appeared, allegedly with 800 men, and intimidated those justices favorable to Fanhope. In the ensuing scuffle, some eighteen men were thrown down the stairs of the courthouse and several jurors were accidentally killed. Each side accused the other, and when the king's council heard the case, it became clear who had real political clout. The young king personally granted a pardon to his great-uncle by marriage; pardons to Grey's friends, however, were delayed for months, and the new Commission of the Peace for Bedfordshire was purged of its pro-Grey elements. Political success in the counties clearly depended on whom you knew at court and whether you could influence the king. With noblemen like Lord Grey, deprived as they were of a voice at court and confronted with "strangers" moving into their traditional preserves, the kingdom possessed the potential for an anti-Lancastrian party. All it required for Lord Grey's resentment to take political form was, first, a sense of desperation and, second, the presence of a rival claimant to the throne. During the 1450s, both of these conditions were met.

By 1447 the two dominant figures of the early reign, the duke of Gloucester and Cardinal Bishop Beaufort, were dead. Gloucester had

Henry VI and His Queen Receiving a Book from the Earl of Shrewsbury   "In 1445 a new political force put in an appearance: Henry VI's young French queen, Margaret of Anjou." *(The Mansell Collection)*

fallen victim to factional infighting in which his blood ties as the king's uncle proved as much a debit as an asset, and he died accused of high treason. Beaufort was, by the standards of his age, an extremely old man when he died in his mid-seventies. His death left his protégé, John de la Pole, duke of Suffolk, in control of the king's government, and Pole successfully built up a political affinity that extended throughout the kingdom. His influence remained paramount until his murder in 1450, but in 1445 a new political force put in an appearance: Henry VI's young French queen, Margaret of Anjou. The wedding had been arranged in the desperate hope that it would bring peace between England and France before the island lost its last footholds on the continent. But the wedding only increased the king's debts and introduced into court a young princess who grew into "a great and strong laboured woman" and who had even more lavish spending habits than her husband. Her total expenditures for

1452–1453 came to £7,540. Margaret, however, spent money more wisely than did her spouse, amassing her own network of political affinities. As a consequence, the great nobles found it increasingly difficult to dislodge either the queen or the duke of Suffolk from the king's chambers. To make matters worse, the magnates were feeling the economic pinch of a losing war. As the Lancastrian government ran out of funds, those barons at political odds with Suffolk and his allies had trouble persuading the government to reimburse them for their mounting military expenses in France.

By 1450 the crown faced total bankruptcy. The kingdom, as one contemporary put it, found itself in desperate straits because "the king was simple, and led by covetous council and owed more than he was worth." The causes of the financial plight of the monarchy were threefold: (1) the royal inability to collect revenues in a century afflicted with economic dislocation; (2) the channeling of royal resources into private and factional hands; and (3) most serious of all, the narrowing of the gap between the public revenues of the crown and the private incomes of certain overmighty subjects whose economic means had grown almost as sizable as those of the monarch. Rents from crown lands should have been supplying nearly £40,000 annually, but by the time fixed obligations and annuities promised to favorites had been paid off and royal officials had dipped their fingers into the till, the amount came to only slightly over £8,000. By the fifth decade of the century, the king's cash income had shriveled to £5,000, while the normal operating expenses of the household, carrying the added cost of the queen's retinue, ranged between £17,000 and £24,000. As a consequence, the royal debt rose to the staggering sum of £372,000. Understandably, reformers and critics demanded that crown property be returned to the king, that salaries and annuities to court favorites and factional henchmen be cut, that the monarch be assured a fixed and nonparliamentary personal income at least equal to that of his wealthiest subject, and that his debts be paid off. This last point was particularly galling; the king's credit was so bad that favored members of his council could buy up his debts at reduced terms and then turn around and have his exchequer pay them back at full value.

The Failure of Parliament

In years past, the realm had solved the crown's fiscal problems by direct taxation through parliamentary grants; but as the royal coffers were plundered, both houses of Parliament became increasingly reluctant to grant new taxes. The knights and esquires of the shires, burdened by high wages, low rents, contracting markets for wool and wheat and a costly and unprofitable war, demanded economy and retrenchment in government. Unfortunately, Parliament was better at complaining than acting; it had not yet developed a sense of responsibility for the governance of the kingdom. Government remained in the hands of the king and his officials.

The parliamentary body that had met in 1399 to acknowledge Henry IV as king of England, and to which the first Lancastrian monarch promised "not to be guided by his own will nor his own desire or individual opinion but by common advice, counsel and assent," had long since outgrown its early medieval origins. By 1400 the organization of Parliament had evolved into something resembling its present-day structure. What yet remained to develop was the modern legislative mind and the privileges, traditions, and responsibilities of a national body representing all interests and estates within the realm. That process was not completed until the end of the seventeenth century.

The fifteenth century saw the evolution of a body of lords and a group of commoners who were becoming increasingly aware of their own separate and corporate existence. By 1450 the Lords had transformed what had originally been a group of the king's advisers, appointed by the monarch and composed of those individuals whom the king wished to call to his court, into an instrument of oligarchical and aristocratic rule. Royal judges and nonnoble elements were in the process of being removed by aristocratic pressure, and the barons had succeeded in claiming a seat in the House of Lords based solely on inheritance and noble title and not on royal favor. Magna Carta and later royal charters had established the baronial right to advise the sovereign; by 1400 that right of advice had become an excuse to control the royal government. In effect, the king was allowed to rule only upon the sufferance of his nobles.

The temporal lords attended Parliament fairly constantly; possibly half their number sat during any given session. In Henry IV's first Parliament, ninety-seven noblemen of varying ranks were summoned and sixty-three sat. Thereafter, the number of those who could claim noble dignity either by royal writ or by inheritance fell to around fifty and once dropped as low as twenty-three. As for the spiritual lords, the two archbishops and nineteen bishops of the realm were fairly regular, but their brothers, the abbots of the monasteries, were erratic in the extreme; of the twenty-seven who had a historic right to sit, only a handful ever attended. Until the Reformation in the third decade of the sixteenth century, the spiritual lords outnumbered the temporal, but power resided with the lay barons who were the natural leaders of the realm, the possessors of economic and social strength outside of Parliament, and the advisers and controllers of royal government. At one time, five Neville brothers sat in the House of Lords — four barons and one bishop. Family associations such as these, unstable as they often were, guaranteed political control of the legislative and executive process.

The Commons lagged far behind the Lords in corporate self-identity. The term itself simply meant *general* or *public,* and only slowly did it acquire institutional significance. Over three hundred individuals sat in the House of Commons in 1422: 2 knights from each of the 37 shires, 188 representatives from the chartered towns or boroughs, and possibly 30 to

40 others appointed by the crown, such as the king's justices and councillors. By 1450 competition for a seat in Commons could on occasion produce rowdy campaigning and disputed elections. The lower house had become so much an upper-class preserve for landlords, merchants, and lawyers that in 1430 legislation was passed to prevent men "of small substance and no worth" from voting, and the right to vote in the shires was restricted to men of property who held sixty acres of free land producing an annual income of forty shillings. At the same time, borough elections tended to become limited to a small oligarchy of municipal officers and substantial citizens. If the House of Lords was evolving into the closed corporation of the magnates, the House of Commons was developing into a preserve of men of lesser, but still great, wealth. There was nothing common about the incomes or social positions of Commons.

Originally, Commons had played the role of the humble petitioner: the old formula for law enactment in the fourteenth century stated that statutes be made "with the assent of the earls, prelates and barons at the request of the knights of the shires and commons in Parliament." By the mid-fifteenth century, a significant change in phraseology had evolved, one that embodied a revolution in legislative function. Now the formula read: "Be it enacted by the King's Majesty with the advice and consent of the Lords spiritual and temporal and the Commons in the present Parliament assembled and by the authority of the same." Commons had achieved partnership with the Lords, and was no longer simply a petitioner but now a co-creator of law.

Equally important, was the new dignity embodied in the phrase "by the authority of the same." The insolvency of the Lancastrian crown and its financial dependence on parliamentary sources of income added weight to the voice of Commons. Moreover, the new dynasty's doubtful legitimacy and its abdication of political leadership under Henry VI transformed Parliament from a high court of justice into a legislative organ of government capable not only of translating the king's will into law but also of enacting its own opinions. The authority of that indivisible trinity — King, Lords, and Commons — was "so high and so mighty in its nature that it could make law and unmake that which was law."

On the statute books and in the annals of constitutional history, Parliament looks impressive. Six times between 1341 and 1407 it successfully claimed the right to audit royal accounts. In 1367 it impeached a royal minister for dishonesty, and it selected the council of regency during Henry VI's minority. In the fifteenth century, it demanded the privileges of freedom of speech and immunity from arrest, and the right to hold annual sessions. Such pretensions, however, were more illusory than real. Behind the glitter of parliamentary activity stood serious constitutional and psychological limitations, which in the end ensured that the Lancastrian Parliaments would prove as ephemeral as the Lancastrian dynasty. As early as 1399 it was being said of members that "some stammered and mumbled and did not know what they meant to say. Some were afraid to take any step without their master's orders.

Some were so pompous and dull witted that they were hopelessly involved before they reached the end of their speeches, and no one could make out what they wanted to say. . . . Some went with the majority whichever way they went, while some would not commit themselves; and some were so afraid of great men that they forsook righteousness." Embedded in these words are the reasons for Parliament's failure to cast off its feudal origins and develop into a modern representative institution. Constitutionally, Parliament was as yet incapable of exercising powers that would ensure legislative independence because psychologically it was unable to picture itself in the alien role of a sovereign authority rivaling the king. The basic paradox of the medieval constitution remained: only a strong monarch could enforce parliamentary law and win widespread respect for it.

Parliament was still the creature of the king. The monarch issued the writs that summoned Parliament into being. He prorogued and dismissed it, controlled its agenda, and maintained his right of veto and amendment. In fact, it was not absolutely clear whether royal ordinance might not be equal to parliamentary statute, and no one took seriously the suggestion that Parliament should meet annually regardless of need or emergency.

A more serious failing was that Parliament never developed any idea of itself as the watchdog of government or assumed responsibility for good government; the former duty belonged to the barons on the council, the latter to the crown. At best, Parliament's image of its proper role was simply that of a rectifier of bad administration. As long as no financial emergency, corruption of law, or royal mismanagement loomed, it did not expect or desire to be summoned. Lords and Commons may have had most of the forms and structures of their modern counterparts, but they still thought of themselves as feudal institutions, meeting occasionally to exercise their extraordinary powers of taxation and legislation. If affairs of state ran according to form and custom, Parliament was not expected to interfere. The political and economic crises of the fifteenth century, however, produced the extraordinary and largely misunderstood situation in which Parliament had to meet in frequent emergency session. Royal bankruptcy and ineptitude ensured parliamentary existence, but Lords and Commons regarded both as undesirable. They approved of strong, solvent, and competent monarchs who had no need to summon them. As late as 1560, Sir Thomas Smith was still voicing this traditional if unrealistic view when he wrote: "What can a Commonwealth desire more than peace, liberty, quietness, little taking of their money, few parliaments?"

Although Parliament was legislatively active, its failure was most obvious in the realm of law enforcement. As one contemporary put it, "Many acts of Parliament/Few kept with true intent." The power to legislate is worthless without the means to compel obedience, and Parliament depended on a strong national monarch to enforce its will and to ensure its prestige and position as a body representing the voice of the entire land. With monarchy moribund and the machinery of justice and law enforcement in the hands of the great magnates, Parliament was dominated by noblemen who possessed the economic and military means to implement or to ignore statutory law as they saw fit. Law, regardless of whether it was royal or parliamentary, fell victim to the greed and brutality that recognized no authority other than the drawn sword. The evils of livery (the hiring of private armies) and maintenance (the corruption and intimidation of juries and law courts) were legislated against with vigor, but they continued to flourish. In 1404 the earls of Northumberland and Westmorland waged private war; the loser was ultimately brought to trial, accused not of high treason but merely of trespassing. Again in 1411, Parliament thundered against lawlessness and rioting. But such pious, if statutory, good intentions rang hollow when in the following year Sir Robert Tirwhit, justice of the Court of Common Pleas, ambushed Lord Roos with five hundred armed men and pleaded ignorance of the law as his defense.

Even the traditional signs of parliamentary strength and independence provided little more than further evidence of baronial predominance and royal timidity. The case of Mr. Thomas Yonge is often cited as a milestone in the development of parliamentary freedom of speech and immunity from arrest. In 1451 in the House of Commons Yonge proposed that the duke of York be named heir apparent to the throne. The Lancastrian barons surrounding the king were anything but pleased with the idea and promptly clapped Mr. Yonge into the Tower of London for his presumptuous suggestion. After twelve months in jail, he was released, and four years later Mr. Yonge successfully brought suit against the government for damages. On the surface, his success represented a victory for the principle that members of Parliament "ought to have their freedom to speak without any manner of challenge, charge, or punition." In reality, his freedom was made possible by an uneasy reconciliation between the two parties in April of 1451, and the damages he was able to collect were the result of the duke of York's appointment as protector of the realm in 1455. Mr. Thomas Yonge won his liberty and his parliamentary privilege more because he was the duke of York's man than because he was a member of Commons.

Good government, as well as healthy Parliaments, was based on a proper and harmonious balance among crown, Parliament, and barons. In the fifteenth century, the elements of this trinity consisted of an inept king, an ineffectual legislative body, and an irresponsible baronage. Add the presence of a magnate who claimed a right to the throne equal to Henry VI's, and it was only a matter of time before the kingdom was rent in twain, and any semblance of good government lapsed into civil war.

The Dynastic Issue

Fifteenth-century English politics may have been embittered by something called bastard feudalism (see Chapter 2), but it was also confused by the dynastic debate that erupted the moment Henry IV usurped the throne from Richard II in 1399 and established the descendants of John of Gaunt, duke of Lancaster, as the kingdom's legitimate rulers. The Lancastrian line, as Shakespeare's bishop of Carlisle predicted, did indeed seem to be cursed. In 1399 Henry was rich with sons and daughters; forty-eight years later, only a single grandson, Henry VI, was left. The crown might have gone to the Lancastrian descendants of Henry IV's half-brother, John Beaufort; but that line, stemming from Gaunt's mistress, Catherine Swinford, although legitimized by act of Parliament, had been barred from the succession. The ineligibility of the Beaufort dukes of Somerset meant that Henry VI's heir became Richard, duke of York, who was descended from both Edward III's third and fifth sons. In short, York's double Plantagenet blood gave him a better claim to the throne than Henry VI's, whose right to the kingdom was based essentially on the fact that his father and grandfather had worn the crown (see genealogical chart, page 62).

The link between York's dynastic claims and what might be called "bad lordship," which tied shire politics to corruption at court, became dramatically clear in May 1450 when the men of Kent rose up under the leadership of a shadowy figure called John Cade. Cade associated peasant grievances with Yorkist ambitions by styling himself John Mortimer, Mortimer being a Yorkist family name. The rebels were peasants and artisans, but their complaints echoed the mounting cries from Parliament for political and fiscal reform and the search for a scapegoat for English humiliation in France. The duke of Suffolk, as the king's favorite and the head of a particularly unscrupulous and self-serving faction at court, was the perfect evil councillor to blame, and Parliament in the spring of 1450 accused him of treason. To save his friend from Parliament, Henry exiled the duke, who was so detested kingdomwide that he was murdered while leaving the country.

The Kentish rebels under Cade demanded more than Suffolk's blood. They carried their demands directly to London, and the list of their grievances testified to the scope and degree of Lancastrian misgovernment. Six points were singled out for reform: the king was giving away too much of the crown land and consequently could not live on his own; there was extensive corruption in the collection of royal revenues; members of the House of Commons were not elected freely and had fallen to the status of agents of the rich and mighty who controlled their elections; court parasites were using royal justice to seize for themselves the lands of their opponents and of poor folk who had no influence at court; England was losing the war in France, which was a disgrace to the memory of the heroes of Agincourt; and high offices of state were given to favorites and men of mean and humble station while the duke of York was excluded from his rightful place as the king's chief adviser. Eventually, Cade was killed and his brothers-in-arms hanged, but the criticism of the government did not die with them.

More and more, Richard of York was able to pose as the spokesman for reform and good government. Cade and his peasant rabble were more an embarrassment than a political asset to Richard, and no evidence exists that the duke was connected with the uprising except for Cade's seizure of his family name. Nevertheless, the demand for reform mounted. Gentlemen like John Paston began to speak out against corruption. In 1450 he wrote that Lord Moleyns with a thousand men had ejected Mrs. Paston from her manor house of Gresham and had then secured a letter from Henry VI himself instructing the sheriff of Norfolk to "make such a jury as to acquit the Lord Moleyns." It was not long before important segments of the ruling elite began to wonder whether Richard of York would not make a better king than Henry of Lancaster.

Three years later, three events profoundly altered York's relationship to the throne: in July 1453, England endured its final military humiliation with the loss of Gascony; in August the king drifted from simple-mindedness into intermittent insanity; and in October his queen bore him a son. The end of the Hundred Years' War completed the moral bankruptcy of the Lancastrian dynasty. Possibly foreign defeat, more than the corruption and factionalism that besmirched Henry VI's throne, deprived the government of popular support and prepared the way for York's takeover. The king's insanity made it impossible for the Lancastrian faction to keep York out of the government, but the birth of a royal son meant that if Richard of York ever expected to wear the crown, he would have to fight for it.

After almost a year of stalling tactics and efforts to conceal the king's mental state, Queen Margaret and her political ally, the Beaufort duke of Somerset, yielded to reality, and Parliament named York temporary protector. His control, of course, lasted only as long as the king's madness. When Henry VI regained his senses, his queen and her Lancastrian associates recovered their influence over royal administration. Faced with a Lancastrian heir to the throne and with the queen and the Beaufort family firmly in control of the king's person, York turned to force of arms to rid the realm of "evil councillors" and to restore his henchmen to a place in the political sunshine about the king. This was the situation when the duke of York and his first cousin, the earl of Warwick, presented Henry VI with an ultimatum that struck at the heart of the feudal monarchy and made a mockery of the divine right of kings. "Please it, your Majesty Royal, to deliver up such as we will accuse [of our enemies]. This done you to be worshiped as a most rightful king." The Battle of St. Albans, which followed in July 1455, sowed the dragon seeds of hatred and family revenge: one baron fell with his "brains dashed out, another with a broken arm, a third with a cut throat, and a fourth with a pierced chest, and the whole street was full of dead corpses." The battle was a dress rehearsal and preview of coming attractions. It won the Yorkists preeminence within the royal council and rid them of their rival the Beaufort duke of Somerset, killed upon the field of war. It did not change, however, the basic script for civil war. Queen Margaret of Anjou waited in the wings to turn the tables; a young Lancastrian Prince of Wales lived to carry on his royal line; Somerset's son plotted to avenge his father's death; and, most important of all, blood once shed could not be stanched.

The Wars of the Roses[2]

The Wars of the Roses, symbolically represented by the white rose of York and the red of Lancaster, are generally dated from the first Battle of St. Albans in July 1455. That engagement, however, was only a skirmish. It took another five years for the virus of bastard feudalism, baronial blood feuds, and local land rivalries to weld the opposing sides into something resembling conflicting parties encompassing the entire kingdom. By 1460 the disease had infected some forty-nine of the existing sixty titled families of England, but even so, it is dangerous to overestimate the strength of, or loyalties for, dynastic affinities. Barons chose their roses not out of allegiance to York or Lancaster but out of hatred for one another. Lord Bonville was a Yorkist because the earl of Devon was a Lancastrian, and it was sufficient cause for Bonville to switch his allegiance when Devon became a Yorkist. From the start, self-interest, self-aggrandizement, and self-esteem in an age that glorified warfare, condoned violence, and accepted barons as the natural rulers of society were more potent forces in setting baron against baron than any overriding sense of dynastic principle.

In 1460 the predicted event finally happened: Richard, duke of York, gave up any pretense of ruling through a puppet sovereign and claimed the throne as his legal birthright (see genealogical chart, page 62). This was the signal for civil war in earnest. At Wakefield in December 1460, a Yorkist force, which had in part been disbanded during a Christmas truce in the hostilities, was annihilated. The duke was killed, his battered head capped with a paper crown, and mocked as a "king without a kingdom." His second son, Edmund, earl of Rutland, died allegedly at the hands of young Lord Clifford, whose father had been killed at St. Albans. The story that when Rutland begged for his life, Clifford coldly answered "by God's blood, thy father slew mine, and so will I do thee and all thy kin!" is too good to be true, but it contains a grim truth: on both sides vengeance was the order of the day. Three months later, York's eldest son, Edward, earl of March, and now the Yorkist claimant to the throne, had his revenge. Together with his cousin Richard Neville, earl of Warwick, Edward inflicted a crushing and bloody defeat on Queen Margaret's Lancastrian host. On March 29, 1461, at the Battle of Towton, ten thousand men are said to have died in a conflict fought in a blinding snowstorm, and the flower of the Lancastrian nobility perished while floun-

---

[2]Ever since Shakespeare, the Wars of the Roses have been the subject of endless fiction and scholarship. The most balanced historical accounts are J. R. Lander, *The Wars of the Roses* (1965), and C. Ross, *The Wars of the Roses* (1976). David R. Cook's short *Lancastrians and Yorkists: The Wars of the Roses* (1984) and more recently A. J. Pollard's *The Wars of the Roses* (1988), are both excellent. A. Goodman, *The Wars of the Roses: Military Activity and English Society, 1452–1487* (1981), discusses the impact of the wars on society.

The Execution of the Duke of Somerset   "On both sides vengeance was the order of the day." *(The Mansell Collection)*

dering in the icy waters of Cork Stream, a tiny brook swollen by the winter rains and snow.

The price of victory had been heavy, but the results were ephemeral. Edward IV had earned himself a crown, and he would shortly track down his Lancastrian rival Henry VI and place him in quiet abdication in the Tower of London. Unfortunately, however, Margaret of Anjou had escaped capture. She fled to France, where she spent her time teaching her son, the Prince of Wales, "nothing else but cutting off heads or making war." Of more immediate consideration, the young monarch soon learned that he ruled not by the grace of God but by the power of his cousin the earl of Warwick, the kingmaker, who seemed, in the eyes of one observer, "to be everything in this kingdom."

Edward IV was nineteen, handsome, self-indulgent, and self-serving, and in the end both king and kingmaker realized that "it is a matter of being either master or varlet." The crisis came to a head in 1464 when Warwick decided on a French alliance. Peace with England's ancient enemy would destroy the hopes of the Lancastrian exiles and secure conditions necessary to the growth of trade; but amity with France was unpopular, unhistoric, and unheroic, and not to the liking of King Edward.

The treaty with France was to be secured by the marriage of the king to a Gallic princess, but Warwick's designs were blasted and the kingmaker publicly humiliated when Edward calmly announced to his council that he was already secretly married to Lady Elizabeth Woodville. The

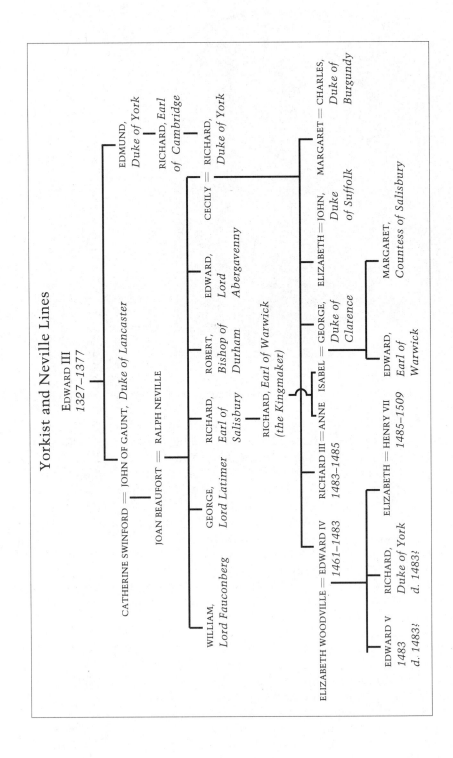

Yorkist and Neville Lines

EDWARD III
1327–1377

CATHERINE SWINFORD = JOHN OF GAUNT, *Duke of Lancaster*

EDMUND, *Duke of York*

RICHARD, *Earl of Cambridge*

JOAN BEAUFORT = RALPH NEVILLE

RICHARD, *Duke of York* = CECILY

WILLIAM, *Lord Fauconberg*

GEORGE, *Lord Latimer*

RICHARD, *Earl of Salisbury*

ROBERT, *Bishop of Durham*

EDWARD, *Lord Abergavenny*

RICHARD, *Earl of Warwick (the Kingmaker)*

ELIZABETH WOODVILLE = EDWARD IV *1461–1483*

RICHARD III = ANNE *1483–1485*

ISABEL = GEORGE, *Duke of Clarence*

ELIZABETH = JOHN, *Duke of Suffolk*

MARGARET = CHARLES, *Duke of Burgundy*

EDWARD V *1483 d. 1483?*

RICHARD, *Duke of York d. 1483?*

ELIZABETH = HENRY VII *1485–1509*

EDWARD, *Earl of Warwick*

MARGARET, *Countess of Salisbury*

new queen and her family, at least in the eyes of the old nobility, were social and political nonentities who had little to their credit except incom-
parable good looks and equal ambitions. Mistress Woodville had been
married to Sir John Grey, a staunch Lancastrian who had died of his
wounds following the second battle of St. Albans, and she had had two
sons by him. Edward IV married not only a complete family but also a
veritable dynasty, replete with five Woodville brothers and as many sisters. The new queen's sisters were quickly matched with the most elevated blood of the realm, while the thrice-married duchess of Norfolk, a
rather dressy dowager of well over sixty, was wed to the twenty-year-old
John Woodville, the queen's brother. As an ultimate insult to ancient lineage and baronial exclusiveness, Elizabeth's father was granted the title
of Earl Rivers. Warwick and the old nobility were disgusted, their feudal
feelings shocked by the promotion of such "new and strange men."

The kingmaker's foreign policy received its final blow when Edward
concluded an alliance with France's traditional enemy, the duchy of Burgundy, and married off his sister Margaret to Duke Charles of Burgundy.
Insulted and slighted, Warwick turned to Louis of France to help him
destroy his ungrateful monarch. A diplomatic revolution followed, in
which Louis XI, that master of Renaissance intrigue, engineered and financed the ultimate moral bankruptcy of the English nobility. In 1469
Yorkist Warwick and Lancastrian Margaret of Anjou patched up their historic feud. It was a bitter pill for the queen to accept as an ally the man
most responsible for the defeat of her dynasty. When Louis XI suggested
that her son Edward marry Warwick's younger daughter, she cried out,
"What! Will he [Warwick] indeed give his daughter to my son, whom he
has so often branded as the offspring of adultery?" Politics, however, triumphed over moral outrage, and the two children, one aged thirteen, the
other ten, were duly pronounced man and wife. The queen and the earl
were joined in this political misalliance by George, duke of Clarence, the
mercurial and covetous brother of Edward IV. He married Warwick's elder daughter, and in the fall of 1470 the kingmaker, the disgruntled duke,
and the militant queen declared the doddering Henry VI to be rightful
king of England. In September they invaded the realm; Edward fled to
Burgundy; and Warwick triumphantly entered London, reinstating Henry
on his shaky throne. The restored monarch, however, was too confused
to realize what had happened and sat "amazed and utterly dulled with
troubles and adversities."

Warwick had achieved a staggering victory, but it proved more fleet-
ing than any he had ever won before. The Lancastrian lords refused their
support even though the earl was now backing a Lancastrian monarch;
the populace demanded peace and the restoration of royal authority, not a
continuation of baronial misrule; and Edward, who had escaped to Burgundy, was planning his revenge. By March 1471, he was back in England
at the head of a tiny army. Instantly, Warwick's grand design collapsed,
and old enemies as well as erstwhile friends rallied to Edward's banner.
At the Battle of Barnet, fought in the midst of a dense fog, friend could

not be distinguished from foe, and the dying "looked up for heaven and only saw the mist." Richard, earl of Warwick, aged forty-three, fell trying to escape, and Edward IV, having triumphed over the real strength of the Lancastrian forces, defeated the queen a month later at the Battle of Tewkesbury. Margaret was captured and her son killed in, or possibly murdered after, the battle. With the Lancastrian Prince of Wales dead, Edward IV now had no reason to keep the father alive, and on May 23, 1471, in the fiftieth year of his life and the forty-ninth of his reign, Henry VI died in the Tower of London "of pure displeasure and melancholy."

Edward IV (1471–1483)

It is customary to end the Wars of the Roses with Edward's victory at Tewkesbury in 1471, for henceforth he ruled as the undisputed master of the realm, and England experienced the blessings of that essential element of good government — a strong sovereign. Edward's reign possessed a Janus quality: it looked back to the overindulgent days of Henry VI, when the king's bounty generated not loyalty but bitter factional rivalry, and it looked forward to a generation when the crown became the font of justice and the beneficiary of economic forces that helped to swell its resources and, therefore, its patronage and prestige. The new king's personality seemed to match the two faces of his reign, for Edward was indolent, dissolute, and addicted to long bouts of inactivity, and he succeeded in eating, drinking, and wenching himself into the grave at the age of forty. On the other hand, he looked and at times acted the perfect king. Golden haired and charismatic, he stood 6 feet, 3½ inches tall. He never forgot a face, acquainted himself with every aspect of his government — especially the financial details — knew the worth of his servants, and politically could be both astute and ruthless.

A kingly façade may have been Edward's greatest personal asset, but a full treasury was even more important in maintaining his rule. Inheritance and confiscation went a long way to rectify the deficit in the king's finances. As his father's heir, Edward could call upon the immense resources of the Yorkist lands; and the bloodbaths of Towton, Barnet, and Tewkesbury had at least one beneficial result: the king was able to repossess the confiscated estates of the fallen Lancastrian nobility, which helped to free him from parliamentary grants and interference. At the same time, the slow economic recovery of the kingdom and more efficient (critics would say more ruthless) methods of collection yielded increased revenues from the crown lands and export and import duties. Edward was in fact the only English sovereign since Henry II to die solvent: by 1483 his cash income had risen to over £90,000 — almost double his predecessor's revenues. But it is important to note that this sum fell far short of Edward III's income, which during the 1350s had reached a high of £157,000.

In government the king turned away from the aristocracy and sought the support of men of middling social position: knights, lawyers, clerks, and merchants. Instead of favoring the ancient organs of state — the exchequer, the treasury, and the chancery — he relied on the more intimate instruments of government — the royal council and household — where his influence made itself more readily felt, and where he could maintain stricter control over crown property and income. In the northern shires, royal authority was enforced for the first time in decades when his brother Richard, duke of Gloucester, was given the title of Lord Lieutenant in the North. New life was infused into the law in 1462 when Edward sat in person on the Court of King's Bench and later accompanied his judges in their perambulations about the kingdom. Unfortunately, however, when Edward unexpectedly died on April 9, 1483, twelve years of strong Yorkist rule proved insufficient to secure his line from destruction because, like Henry VI, Edward failed to raise the crown above court politics and family disputes.

From the moment Warwick the kingmaker died at Barnet, the Yorkist family became embroiled in a dispute over the spoils. Both Edward's brothers, Clarence and Gloucester, had married the earl's daughters, and each determined to deprive the other, as well as Warwick's widow, of as much of the earl's lands as possible. Fraternal avarice and competition were resolved when Clarence overstepped the limits of family decency. Having tried his hand at treason for a second time, he was executed in 1478. Woodville greed and Edward's willingness to gratify it, however, proved more destructive. Edward's support of his wife's family seems to have been a calculated risk: It created a court faction that reached out into the shires, permitting the king to counterbalance local baronial influence and enforce royal law throughout the realm. His most successful use of the Woodvilles occurred in Wales. There he introduced direct rule by creating his elder son Prince of Wales and establishing at Ludlow Castle a council and household for the young boy under the direction and management of his son's uncle, Anthony Woodville, Earl Rivers. Unfortunately, such a policy had a disastrous backlash. The king's generosity antagonized the older nobility: It associated the crown with a single court faction, conjured up memories of Suffolk's political corruption and pernicious influence over royal policy under Henry VI, and created the political crisis that at Edward's death eventually led to the destruction of his dynasty.

Edward V (April 9–July 6, 1483)

The dead king's successor was his twelve-year-old son Edward, the product of that hated Woodville marriage whose relatives seemed to crop up everywhere. It is often argued that popular fear of further misrule and civil war under yet another minority made it possible for Richard of Gloucester to seize his nephew's throne. In fact, the brevity of young

Edward V, Almost a King　This eighteenth-century etching catches the pathos of a child-king who was deposed even before he was crowned. *(Mary Evans Picture Library)*

Edward's reign is merely further evidence of the destructive influence of rival lordships and affinities when they clashed over the control of a hapless child-king.

The duke of Gloucester, Edward IV's younger brother, has come down in history as Richard Crookback — malevolent and crooked in both body and soul. The Shakespearean portrait is a stranger, however, to the historical man. Gloucester had been the faithful servant of his brother and the successful bastion of royal authority in the turbulent northern shires, where he watched the Stanleys and Percys as closely as the Scots. By right of blood and experience, Richard was the natural choice as protector for his brother's son, but he knew the office would never be granted to him by a Woodville-controlled council. To make matters more difficult, he also had to reckon with a twelve-year-old king who had been brought up by Woodville aunts and uncles and who would come of age within four or five years. At best, Gloucester's term of office as protector would be brief, and anything he did in 1483 to destroy the Woodvilles could be undone or, worse, revenged four years hence. With prompt action and fair words, he seized the young monarch, imprisoned most of his Woodville relatives, and proclaimed himself protector. In the fifteenth century, the price of political failure was death; the Woodvilles and their allies would have destroyed Gloucester had they been astute enough to do so, but once Richard controlled the machinery of government, their life expectancy was not long. The young king's Woodville uncles, Earl Rivers and Richard Grey, quickly paid with their lives for being on the losing side.

Richard III "Edward IV's younger brother has come down in history as Richard Crookback — malevolent and crooked in both body and soul." *(National Portrait Gallery, London)*

Then Richard of Gloucester fulfilled the legendary role of the wicked uncle. In uneasy league with yet another descendant of Edward III's fecundity — Henry, second duke of Buckingham, himself a potential heir to the throne should the Yorkist line terminate — Gloucester seized the crown from his young nephew. On June 22, Edward V was declared a bastard; on July 6, the duke mounted the throne as rightful heir to his brother; and a year later, the young prince, along with his ten-year-old brother, conveniently vanished, some say murdered, in the Tower of London.

Richard III (1483–1485)

Murder has magic and can transmute the most sordid politics and vicious designs into grand tragedy. The disappearance of the little princes has inspired endless detective research, journalistic speculation, and partisan efforts to whitewash Richard III.[3] The primary suspect for murder, however, remains Richard III, who continues to be the legendary villain and

---

[3]Richard III and the mystery of the little princes continue to capture both the literary and historical mind. C. Ross, *Richard III* (1981), is the best biography, but see also P. M. Kendall, *Richard III* (1955); R. Horrox, *Richard III: A Study of Service* (1989); M. Bennett, *The Battle of Bosworth* (1985); and P. W. Hammond and A. F. Sutton, *Richard III: The Road to Bosworth Field* (1985). A highly readable survey is G. St. Augyn, *The Year of Three Kings, 1483* (1983). Shakespeare's *Richard III* remains the supreme fictional representation, but see also J. Tey, *The Daughter of Time* (1953), an intriguing detective story about the murder of the princes.

who certainly had motive, means, and opportunity. No matter where the ultimate responsibility lies, the timely disappearance of the two princes proved once again the inadequacies of a political system in which murder supplied the only answer to an ineffectual monarch, be he an irresponsible Richard II, a saintly Henry VI, or a child Edward V.

Murder failed to make Richard's throne secure, and the forces of violence and hatred that had dethroned Henry VI raged unabated under the Yorkist dynasty, especially now that Richard III had deposed his royal nephew. The new king reaped the harvest of usurpation: he could trust no one. Even his closest allies were suspect, and Buckingham was executed only four months after the reign began for having played again, this time unsuccessfully, at kingmaking. No matter how hard the new king tried to restore the luster of the crown by carrying out his brother's policies with vigor, an important percentage of his kingdom regarded him as a traitor and murderer. Not even the extensive feudal affinity that he had built in the north of England as lord lieutenant, nor his lavish redistribution of first Woodville and then Buckingham properties, could create a firm political base on which to foster the personal loyalty necessary to maintain his rule. In the south of England, he never won the hearts of his subjects; he remained a usurper in their eyes. Where forced loans extracted from wealthy subjects had been termed "benevolences" under Edward IV, under his brother they were branded "malevolences." Even fate seemed to turn against Richard, for in April 1484 his only son died. Throughout 1485 exiled Lancastrians were strengthened by banished Woodvilles and disgruntled magnates who had failed to gain from Richard all that they felt should be their due. By the spring of 1485, intrigue and avarice had done their work, and the throne of England was once again staked on the throw of the military dice.

The Battle of Bosworth Field

With the death of Henry VI and his son in 1471, the Lancastrian line had run dry. As one contemporary put it, "No one from that stock remained among the living who could now claim the crown." The Lancastrian faction remained, however, and it searched for a true and rightful claimant to the throne. The desperate plight of the Lancastrian position was revealed when the mantle of party authority fell to Henry Tudor, earl of Richmond, whose birthrights and claim to the crown were twice tainted. Henry's Plantagenet blood came from the wrong side of the blanket; his mother had been a Beaufort, the great-granddaughter of John of Gaunt by his mistress Catherine Swinford, whose children had been legitimized but barred from the succession by act of Parliament. His father may also have been born out of wedlock: Edmund, earl of Richmond, was the product of the union of Catherine, widowed queen of Henry V, and a clerk of her wardrobe named Owen Tudor; the precise legal status of their relationship has never been established.

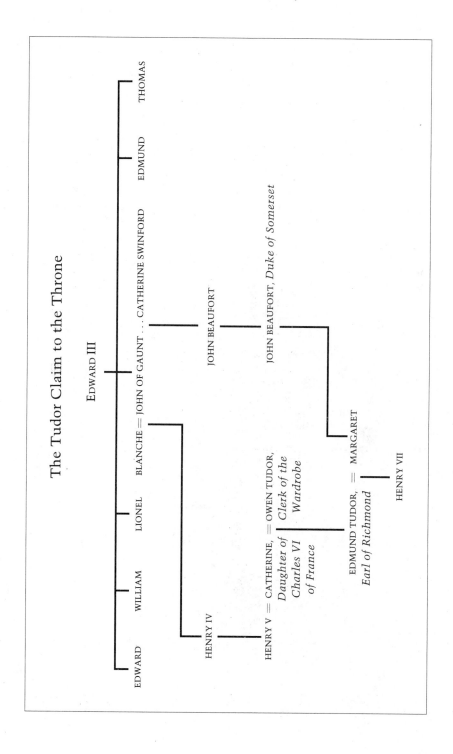

The Tudor Claim to the Throne

EDWARD III

EDWARD   WILLIAM   LIONEL   BLANCHE = JOHN OF GAUNT . . . CATHERINE SWINFORD   EDMUND   THOMAS

HENRY IV

JOHN BEAUFORT

HENRY V = CATHERINE,   = OWEN TUDOR,   JOHN BEAUFORT, *Duke of Somerset*
Daughter of   *Clerk of the*
Charles VI   *Wardrobe*
of France

EDMUND TUDOR,   = MARGARET
Earl of Richmond

HENRY VII

Henry Tudor made one of the most reckless gambles of history: on August 2, 1485, he landed at Milford Haven in Wales with nothing to his credit but a doubtful claim to the throne and possibly 3,000 mercenary troops paid for with French gold. Of Welsh stock, he drew support from his native Wales, but even so the army that met Richard III on August 22 on the high ground two miles from the market town of Bosworth was smaller and far more desperate than its opponents. Tudor historians to the contrary, neither God nor righteousness prevailed. Richard III was left dead on the field of battle, his white rose trampled underfoot by the forces of Lancaster, because key magnates deserted their king at the crucial moment, and because Lord Thomas Stanley and his brother William maintained the doubtful tradition of kingmaking by standing aside to equalize the military balance between the armies. The nobility as a whole took the position of "a curse upon both your houses."

A Man of War   "It is usual to dismiss the wars as the unsavory but exclusive pastime of the great nobles who, like college football teams, fought ferocious and not very effectual battles with their paid, liveried retainers." *(Reproduced by permission of the Trustees of the Wallace Collection)*

Bosworth Field augured nothing but continued civil strife. If the past was any mirror for the future, the future looked bleak indeed for Henry Tudor, who now styled himself King Henry VII. England had experienced eight monarchs in eighty-six years, and simple mathematics indicated that the new sovereign might reign for a decade at most. In fact, the first ten years seemed proof of the prophecy that Bosworth was simply another swing of the pendulum in the vicious game of factional feuding, for Henry fought yet another pitched battle to save his crown and had to execute two pretenders to his throne. Few would have predicted that fate would allow him a second decade or that those years would see relative security and prosperity.

Between 1455 and 1471, thirteen battles were fought during the Wars of the Roses, and if the dates are pushed forward to include the year 1487, at least two more engagements must be added to the list. It is usual to dismiss the wars as the unsavory but exclusive pastime of the great nobles who, like college football teams, fought ferocious and not very effectual battles with their paid, liveried retainers. Philippe Comines, chronicler and statesman of fifteenth-century France, noted with considerable envy that in England "no buildings [were] destroyed or demolished by war and there the mischief of it falls on those who make the war." But the horror that the memory of those years could engender in the minds of later generations makes it difficult to believe that the Wars of the Roses were simply a matter of a Lancastrian unicorn and a Yorkist lion noisily prancing up and down the land. Thirty-eight peers were killed or executed as a consequence of those wars. Nearly four hundred landowners lost their estates, some permanently, others for varying periods of time, for having picked the wrong color rose. At Ludlow in 1459, a Lancastrian army so sacked the town that "men went wet-shod in wine, and then robbed the town and bore away bedding, clothes, and other stuff and defouled many women." The Wars of the Roses were associated in the popular mind with violence, anarchy, and corruption. Whether the civil wars caused lawlessness and embezzlement in government or whether bastard feudalism and royal incompetence produced both is unimportant. To sixteenth-century eyes, aristocratic irresponsibility and civil discord were intimately linked, and that association became the greatest single political asset bestowed upon the new Tudor dynasty.

In 1485 the standards of the age were still medieval. Henry V, *sans peur et sans reproche*,[4] remained the heroic model and pattern for all that society deemed best in life and death. Henry VI was the last king-saint in English history; that he was incompetent was less important to contemporaries than that he was pious. The economic and intellectual background, however, was changing. The successful king would soon replace the devout sovereign in popular esteem, and the solvent monarch would

---

[4]Without fear and without reproach.

garner more honor than the heroic. Henry VII was no messianic states-man, no gifted governmental architect guided by the image of a future monarchical absolutism. He was no better and no worse than the fourth Henry; both were hardworking, careful, and unobtrusive sovereigns who sired sons more glamorous but not necessarily more successful than themselves. But while the first Lancastrian struggled and ultimately failed to rebuild royal authority or to control the forces of dying medieval-ism, the first Tudor succeeded because time and tide were on his side.

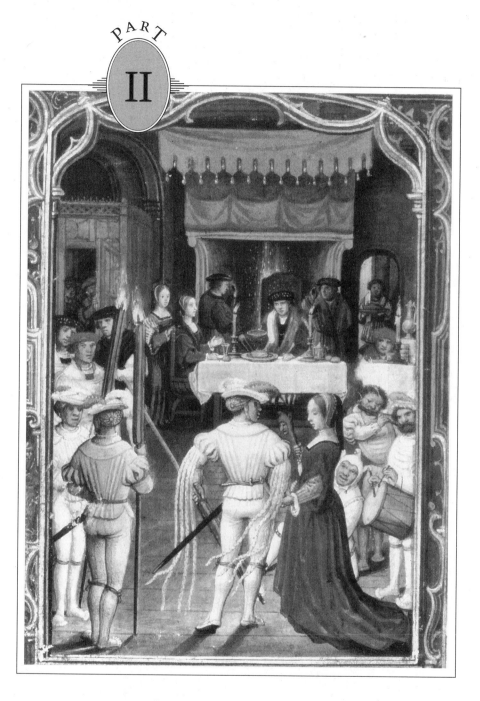

Rebuilding
Society, Tudor Style

1485 to 1547

On preceding page: MINSTRELS ENTERTAINING AT A FEAST
From the *Book of Hours of the Blessed Virgin. (British Library, London/ Bridgeman Art Library, London)*

CHAPTER 4

Economic Resurgence and Social Change

The historian of the fifteenth century confronts a paradox: the generations of the Lancastrian kings were archaic and medieval, but they were also forward looking and modern. The pious peasant, the indolent cleric, and the disorderly baron were part of a receding feudal profile; the clothier and the financier, the explorer and the religious reformer, the humanist and the landed country gentlemen belonged to the image of the future. The era, however, was not the product of a polarity between the old and the new, not a matter of "either/or," but instead a balance between "more or less." Hope and depression, chivalric posing and Machiavellian calculation, peace and war, laity and clergy, feudal loyalty and capitalistic self-interest existed side by side. Often one part of the dichotomy was happily unaware of its opposite; sometimes the tension between the two grew unbearable; but always the fifteenth-century individual was more or less a composite of all elements.[1]

Prosperity

As the fifteenth century gave way to the sixteenth century, new impulses and new ideas were stirring. The day was dawning when a Venetian ambassador would admire the wealth and power of the first Tudor monarch, and another foreigner would remark that in England yeomen ate as well as gentlemen, and nobles rivaled European kings in the lavishness of their tables. The duke of Buckingham fed two hundred guests in his great

---

[1] In addition to the works cited in Chapter 2, see F. Caspari, *Humanism and the Social Order in Tudor England* (1954); L. A. Clarkson, *The Pre-Industrial Economy in England, 1500–1750* (1971); J. Thirsk, *Tudor Enclosures* (Historical Assoc. Pamphlet No. G. 41, 1958) and *Economic Policy and Projects: The Development of a Consumer Society in Early Modern England* (1978); D. C. Coleman, *The Economy of England, 1450–1750* (1977); E. Kerridge, *The Agricultural Revolution* (reprint, 1967); and P. Clark and P. Slack, *English Towns in Transition, 1500–1700* (1976). The best social and economic interpretation is A. J. Slavin, *The Tudor Age and Beyond* (1987), which covers the period between the Black Death and the death of Elizabeth I. Two recent studies are important for this chapter and the entire Tudor period: R. Helgerson, *Forms of Nationhood: The Elizabethan Writing of England* (1992), and M. K. McIntosh, *A Community Transformed: The Manor and Liberty of Havering 1500–1620* (1991).

Tattershall Tower The halfway point between a medieval castle built for defense and a Tudor manor house built for light and gracious living. *(National Monuments Record)*

hall on Christmas Day; Sir Edward Montague, a mere social upstart, dispensed food to twelve hundred who begged at his door; and the duchess of Norfolk customarily sat down to a table set for twenty and served as her first course two boiled capons, a breast of mutton, a piece of beef, seven chevins (fish), a swan, a pig, a quantity of veal, two roast capons, and a custard. The bounty of the rich man's kitchen was an economic necessity, for everybody from the household staff to the beggars in the street ate the crumbs from his table. Although the methods of distribution were unjust by modern standards, there was enough food for all. The pastures were rich, and the fields were "fat, fruitful and full of profitable things."

The land lay green and pleasant, and as the country slowly recovered from agricultural depression and bubonic plague, the horse, costly to feed but efficient to work, replaced the cumbersome ox. Although sheep runs and wheat fields pushed deep into virgin timber, England remained in the year 1500 a realm rich in the most essential of all medieval resources — woodlands. The ancient forests of Epping, Sherwood, and Arden afforded a plentiful supply of ribs, planks, and masts for a growing navy and an expanding merchant marine, the lumber to construct the jerry-built houses of the exploding city of London, and the charcoal for the furnaces of the ironsmiths. Shrinking timber stands might at some future date confront the kingdom with an acute shortage, but for the moment they meant prosperous farmlands and successful commercial enterprises.

Another sign of prosperity was an expanding population. Before the Black Death in 1348–1350, the population may have exceeded 5 million; the plague may have reduced it to as low as 2 million. By 1470, despite still terrifying mortality statistics, optimism — that most mercurial of all social-psychological elements — was in the air, and the kingdom had started down the long path of demographic recovery. The population may have reached close to 2.5 million by 1525, over 4 million by 1600, and well over 5 million by 1700. Population figures in an age blissfully free of statistical exactitude are understandably vague, but the results were everywhere evident. More mouths to feed, more backs to clothe, more vanities to satisfy, and more homes to construct meant busy artisans, eager merchants, and an insatiable commercial appetite. Wool chapmen skipping from shop to shop "as if they were at leapfrog," tradesmen as active as "dancing galliards," and scavengers and apprentices, weavers and dyers, all "as busy as county attorneys" pleading cases in the shire courts — these were the dominant pictures throughout most of the sixteenth century, for England in 1500 stood on the threshold of three generations of unprecedented economic prosperity.

Of all the new impulses in late medieval society, the strongest was the growing export of woolen cloth. England had long served as Europe's most important source of raw material — tin and grain; lead and leather; and, above all, raw wool and unfinished cloth. The lord chancellor sat on a wool sack, the crown lived off the tax on the export of wool, merchants grew fat from its sales, landlords rented pasture lands for sheep runs or raised their own flocks, and one thankful beneficiary of the "golden fleece" wrote

> I thank God and ever shall,
> It is the sheep has paid for all.

By the middle of the fifteenth century, the emphasis had shifted from the export of raw wool to the manufacture and export of broadcloth or unfinished woolen fabric. The change simply enhanced the profits and importance of the trade because the demand for English woolens continued to expand as the European market recovered from the ravages of war and anarchy.

Slowly, painfully, but irresistibly, economic prosperity brought political, social, and moral revolution. The harbingers of change were the gentlemen sheep raisers, the urban cloth manufacturers, and the Merchant Adventurers who supplied the continent with English woolens. Demand stimulated supply, but large-scale production was possible only after fundamental organizational changes. The manufacture of woolen cloth could not be fitted into the rigid and fragmented guild system of the

Sheep Shearer at Work
" 'I thank God and ever shall,/It is the sheep has paid for all.' " *(North Wind Picture Archives)*

medieval past. Sheep raising on the farm, carding and spinning in the cottage, weaving and dyeing in the town, and storing and exporting to foreign markets required careful synchronization of time and material.

Eventually there evolved the coordinator or clothier who bought raw wool in large quantities, delivered it to the spinners, transported the yarn to the weavers, and carried the finished product to the drapers and merchants to be sold. The fifteenth-century clothier soon became the prototype of the modern industrial entrepreneur, supplying raw material and transportation, paying wages on the basis of piecework or by the hour, using the farmer's wife and child as sources of labor, and avoiding the older towns with their hampering guilds and trade restrictions. Occasionally, such organizers took the final step and brought the weavers together under a single roof, converting their own homes into nascent factories where the weavers became their hired servants. Sometimes they rented looms to craftsmen, who lost their independent status as artisans and became industrial sharecroppers. Whatever the organizational method, it brought spectacular economic rewards. Thomas Paycocke of Coggeshall could afford to found a magnificent chantry for the sake of his commercial soul and the souls of his parents, his wife, and his father-in-law. John Winchcomb, better known as Jack Newberry, refused a knighthood, preferring to "rest in russet coat, a poor clothier to his dying day," but he could afford to entertain Edward IV at his urban home. Merchant John

Fortey aptly represented himself on his funeral brass as standing with one foot on a sheep, the other on a sack of wool.

Paycocke and Winchcomb were clothiers and incipient industrialists; their mercantile counterparts were the merchant princes of the city of London, who lived by the verse:

> Some men of noble stock were made, some glory in the murder blade;
> Some praise a Science or an Art, but I like honourable Trade.

Commerce, if organized on a large enough scale, was not only honorable but also immensely profitable. The cloth merchants of London aimed at the formation of a commercial cartel. They organized themselves into a corporate fellowship known as the Merchant Adventurers and maintained a monopoly of trade with Antwerp. Provincial merchants were driven into joining or into bankruptcy, and in the end the Adventurers made good their legal claim to a monopoly of the cloth trade between England and the Netherlands. They received official recognition in 1486, and with each passing year, their influence was more keenly felt. Largely on their recommendation, Henry VII negotiated in 1496 the trade treaty known as the Intercursus Magnus, easing the commercial restrictions that had limited the lucrative London-Antwerp mercantile axis. Finally, in 1497 the Merchant Adventurers were granted the coveted right to impose a fee on all newcomers who hoped to poach on their trade monopoly with Antwerp.

Inflation

As clothier and merchant enlarged their remunerative web of trade, all England was caught up in the larger pattern of European and world commerce. Inflation, that unseen economic monster with an insatiable appetite, devoured fixed incomes and savings, wiped out ancient debts, and injected new life into the economic sinews of society. Between 1500 and 1540, prices doubled, and during the next twenty years, they doubled again. Wheat in 1450 still cost what it had in 1300; a hundred years later the price had risen threefold. By 1600 the general price level had increased fivefold; fifty years later it had reached a factor of six. The late-medieval man confronted a crisis as baffling, as mystifying, and as misunderstood as the Black Death. The feudal world had assumed that war, plague, and famine stemmed from God as retribution for the sins of man, and so it had blamed economic distortion and rising prices on human avarice and sin. The sixteenth century was still sufficiently close to its medieval and Christian heritage to seek an explanation for economic evil in man, not in social systems. The corruption of Eve and the fall of Adam, and all the sin that subsequently infected the world, not the malfunction of God's perfect society, spawned economic evil and the high cost of food. Social critics such as Sir Thomas More spoke against the greedy hoarders of grain who held out for famine prices and against the grasping landlords who pushed up rents or converted wheat fields into sheep runs, thus producing food shortages and higher prices. The lust for lucre, the vanity of courtiers, and the greed of parvenus were the culprits of economic life. Fashion demanded that "whole estates" be worn on a courtier's back, and when Sir Nicholas Vaux willingly paid £1,000 for a suit, social critics understandably jumped to the conclusion that vanity was forcing up the cost of living.

Scarcity, especially a growing shortage of food and land caused by an expanding population, not vanity, was the real culprit in producing inflation. Not until 1574, however, did Europe awake to the realization that high prices had nothing directly to do with human greed and pride. Jean Bodin, the French political philosopher, was one of the first to realize that a new and impersonal factor had begun its work: gold and silver were suddenly abundant. In the fifteenth century, Europe's scarcity of precious metals began to abate. New silver mines were found in central Europe, and new sources of gold were discovered in western Africa. The supply became a flood when in 1545 the Spanish stumbled on the silver mines of Bolivia. By 1572 the world's output of silver was six times what it had been at the turn of the century. As the mineral wealth of the Americas poured into the European market, it drove down the value of money, reduced the purchasing power of traditional coinage, and pushed up the relative cost of services and supplies.

Modern economic theorists, with evidence developed from the twentieth century's experience with runaway inflation, have suggested that population pressure and the abundance of cheap money do not by themselves explain such a price rise during the 150 years between 1500 and 1650. The very forces that prepared England for its industrial takeoff in the early nineteenth century were responsible for skyrocketing costs. Three factors were operating: (1) greater occupational specialization; (2) startling expansion of urban life, whereby the number of towns with over 3,000 inhabitants increased fivefold; and (3) the speed with which money changed hands in a century during which the volume of goods marketed may well have tripled. In short, prosperity and the growing complexity of society generated the inflationary pressures that transformed Tudor England.

Despite the false simplicity of economic determinism, it appears that a growing population, inflated prices, and an insatiable demand for consumer goods, especially wool, were reversing the social and economic cycle that had prevailed before 1460. They transformed the early fifteenth-century pattern of land plenty, labor shortage, and high wages into land hunger, labor surplus, and rising rents. Behind the changing economic design loomed the millions of sheep, which outnumbered humans by three to one. To the social critics of the age, sheep were devouring the realm, eating up fields that had once grown wheat, pushing back the forests, depopulating the countryside, and creating hunger and unemployment. With wool in incessant demand, the lord of the manor discovered that lands for which he had once been unable to find renters or laborers could now be converted into sheep runs. A single shepherd and his dog were all the labor required; the sheep did the rest. Once the landlord was liberated from a scarcity of labor and assured of a market for wool, the value of his land soared. In the midst of land hunger, landlords cast covetous eyes on the common lands of the manor and sought ways of modifying the ancient land tenure. Two paths lay open to them: break the medieval system of community rights to the fruits of the manor and enclose the commons, or evict peasants who could not prove their historic title to the land.

Enclosures

The ease with which the lord could enclose land or raise rents to keep abreast of inflation depended on local conditions and the nature of the prevailing tenure. Freehold land controlled by the freeholders of the manor and demesne land, which to all intents and purposes had become a form of private property owned by the lord of the manor, presented no problems. Short-term leases could be renegotiated as inflation took its course, and freehold and demesne fields, often scattered indiscriminately throughout the manor, could be brought together into a consolidated unit by buying up adjacent strips and by growing hedges and digging ditches to mark property lines. Once enclosed, such property could be turned into sheep runs or farmed more efficiently without regard for the communal customs of the manor. This kind of enclosure caused relatively little social disturbance and, although the lord of the manor had the most to gain, freeholders, wealthy peasants, and even enterprising copyholders were eager to convert their arable strips into consolidated and workable farming units.

What produced a howl of social indignation was the lord's efforts to enclose all or a portion of the common land and to evict peasants who held their property either by copyhold tenure or by the custom of the manor. The division and enclosure of the common pasture spelled economic ruin for many villages and for peasants who held little arable land but who survived by pasturing their few cattle, sheep, and swine on the communal lands. Even more serious than the destruction of the commons was the inability of many peasants to withstand the lord's legal and economic encroachment on their rights and tenures within the manor. By one of the most ironic twists of history, the peasant's hated "copy," preserved in the manor court and recording the conditions of servitude by which the land was held, suddenly became in the sixteenth century his best defense against eviction or increased rents. The copy stated the fixed fees and financial obligations owed to the lord, but in an era of inflation such obligations tended to become more and more nominal. Consequently, the lord hoped to claim copyhold property as demesne land, so that he could raise rents at will. If the peasant could produce no proof or copy of his tenure, he found it difficult to defend himself at law.[2] Where a copy existed and rents were fixed, the lord nevertheless had other means of coercion. He could arbitrarily raise the heriot, or death tax. If the copyholder's descendants could not pay the tax, the land reverted back to the lord of the manor. Where the peasant held tenure simply on the unwritten custom of the manor, he was even more at the mercy of the lord. Although in theory both historic, unwritten tenure and copyhold tenure were protected in the king's courts, neither of them successfully withstood the pressure of landlords determined to enclose land and raise rents by abolishing the manor court, which embodied the collective memory of the community. Whatever the ethics involved, inflation, eviction, enclosure, and a booming trade in wool introduced a revolution in rents. Land in Yorkshire that had leased for four pence an acre in the fifteenth century rose to nine pence by 1548, to two shillings and four pence by 1621 (and, for the record, to twenty-two shillings and seven pence by 1930).[3]

The extent of enclosure and peasant evictions is difficult to estimate. Accurate statistics were scarce, popular indignation profuse. Possibly not more than 3 percent of the land was enclosed during the sixteenth century, but to contemporaries the legion of evicted and dispossessed peasants seemed dangerously large. The presence of able-bodied paupers in Tudor society caused great consternation. Charity was meant for the infirm, the malformed, and the helpless, not for the economically unemployable. The existence of an army of lusty beggars in a century that lacked adequate poor relief or police control was deeply frightening to government magistrates and property owners. The records indicate that between 1455 and 1607, only 516,573 acres of land in thirty-four counties were enclosed, or 2.76 percent of the total, and that fewer than 50,000 persons were evicted from their property. The most disturbing aspect of the land revolution, however, was not acreage statistics, nor even the existence of a vagrant and unemployable labor supply, but the introduction of what was feared most — change. New names, new methods, new blood broke the static timelessness of village life. Suddenly, the oldest peasant families found themselves dispossessed and landless. The ancient equality of the medieval manor, in which the economic status of the lord had not been far removed from the cottager and copyholder, was collapsing. Exactly how far the process could go was dramatized at the manor of Apsley Guise, where in 1275 each peasant had held equal holdings of approximately fifteen acres. By 1542 four lucky and hardworking farmers held sixty acres or more; only three tenants still possessed their original fifteen acres; and all the rest had been forced to give up substan-

---

[2]One of the reasons many tenants in the sixteenth century could claim no copy was that their ancestors had broken into the manor court and destroyed such records during the Peasants' Revolt of 1381.

[3]There were 12 pennies to a shilling.

tial portions of their holdings. It seemed grossly unjust and against all proper proportion in the divine plan that the rich should be getting richer and the poor, poorer. As one poet put it:

> The poor at enclosing do grutch
> Because of abuses that fall.
> Lest some man should have but too much
> And some again nothing at all.

Like so much historical change, enclosure and the agricultural and economic purpose that stood behind it were misunderstood by both contemporaries and later historians. Enclosure was only the visible and highly controversial tip of an agricultural revolution that helped to create the affluence of the Tudor period and explain its ability to feed and clothe a population that grew by one-third during the century. The productivity of Tudor agriculture was vastly increased by the introduction of two relatively new techniques — the cultivation of "floating" meadowland and "up and down" farming. Floating entailed using low, wet meadows to grow winter hay, which tripled the yield of higher, drier fields and produced spring grass a month earlier. Henceforth, it was not necessary to slaughter animals during the lean months of March and April, herds were larger both in numbers and in animal weight, and there was more fertilizer to further enrich the soil.

Up and down agriculture, or alternating land between wheat and pasture, achieved the same end: larger, fatter herds and more food for both human and beast. Whereas the older medieval system had kept crop and pasture fields separate, periodic alternation improved and enriched the soil, increasing the yield and making the land easier to till. The statistical results were startling: pasture acreage used for wheat yielded twice what land permanently used for tillage had done in the past, and the crop was one-fourth as expensive to grow. In other words, although agricultural land shrank because of the demand for wool, the yield per acre drastically improved, making possible a better-fed working population in 1640 than in the so-called golden age of the peasantry during the 1450s.[4]

The Age of the Gentry

The new relationship between land and labor, the steady rise in prices and the relative fall in wages, the growing tension between landlord and peasant, and the mounting wealth of city merchants and Essex clothiers produced more than extremes of beggary and opulence; they changed the social and political face of England. The age of the gentry was beginning; the future belonged to the landed country gentleman and his blood cousins in oligarchy: the merchant, the lawyer, and the parish rector. Not until 1689 would the landed gentry come of age, but already in 1500 the

---

[4]A. J. Slavin, *The Tudor Age and Beyond* (1987), pp. 26–29; 35.

indispensable conditions for their moral and political ascendancy were taking shape. The fifteenth-century esquire and knight of the shire were changing from impoverished and litigious proprietors, ready to fish in the muddy waters of baronial feuding, into the backbone of Tudor respectability. The secret of change was wealth. Enclosure and eviction, rising prices in the wool market, and increased profits to be had from agricultural production gave the country gentleman the means to finance his new status consciousness, while his newfound prosperity created the need for political security and tranquility in which to enjoy the fat of the earth.

Money and political influence, not blood and social origins, were the dominating themes of the sixteenth century. The landed country gentleman and the city merchant lived by the commercial rule that "conscience is a pretty thing to carry to church" but he who "pursueth it in a fair market or shop may die a beggar." Past knavery was soon forgotten when it earned social respectability for even the basest family. The merchant adventurer, the clothier, and the landlord had the means, the desire, and the opportunity to manufacture the tokens and emblems of social position. The sixteenth century became, *par excellence,* an age of heraldry, and pedigrees were carefully recorded in the College of Arms. For the historian, the visitations of the Garter King of Arms, by which the authorities checked into economic and historic claims to gentility, serve as invaluable sources of social history, but they often read like genealogical fairy tales in which imagination and artistry are more evident than truth. The privilege of bearing heraldic arms was limited to those "of good name and fame and good reknown" and to those who could show a yearly rental of ten pounds. Money and influence could conjure up and legalize the most pretentious heraldic claims, and Russells and Guildfords, Cecils and Cavendishes, Pagets and Cromwells sought to obtain by wealth and marriage the symbol of social preeminence — the right to a heraldic pedigree sanctioned by the College of Arms. In fact, political influence carried more weight than gentle origins in persuading the College to sanction what it must have suspected to be the sheerest genealogical fabrications.

The economic and blood ally of the landed country gentleman was the city merchant, united by a two-way traffic in trade and land, and in sons and daughters. Land was the mark of respectability; trade and law, although tolerated if practiced on a grand enough scale, stood as poor relations. Merchants and lawyers were quick to buy estates not only because land was profitable but also because it brought social recognition. Conversely, the sons of landed families went into trade and married the daughters of rich merchants who could sweeten the odor of their tawdry social origins with fat dowries. Landed squires, urban lawyers, and merchant princes were upper-middling people, but they were distinctly not, if they could help it, of what is described today as the middle class. The standards and aspirations of the age were landed and aristocratic. Second sons of country gentlemen might move to town and even turn to trade,

Simon Eyre, Fifteenth-Century London Alderman "Merchants and lawyers were quick to buy estates not only because land was profitable but also because it brought social recognition." *(Guildhall Library, City of London)*

but their spiritual and social souls belonged on their fathers' estates and, as quickly as they could manage it, either through sharp practices or sharp marriages, they returned to their natural habitat. So also did the merchant. The draper Thomas Cony of Bassingthorpe commenced his career with a commercial income of £200. At his death sixty years later, he was worth £450 from land and had cut his ties with the wool business. By changing the source of his income, Cony expected to alter his social status.

The day would come when a peer might marry an alderman's daughter (1597), but for most of the sixteenth century the nobility left the commercial matrimonial field to the country squires. This did not mean that the peerage was untouched by the commercial spirit or left trade entirely to middling gentlemen and upstart merchants. The successful man — be he a member of the noble elite or of the gentry — went in for raising rents, enclosing lands, and dabbling in trade. Howards and Herberts,

Staffords and Latimers owned ships and iron mines and speculated in commerce. Peers may have declined to enter the countinghouse or the parlor of the commercial sort, but they were perfectly willing to take their 15 percent and to profit from the new impulses of the century.

The Education of the Gentry

The gentry, in their newfound social consciousness and economic prosperity, began to send their sons to college. Whether the quest for learning was a symptom of deliberate social exclusiveness or a sign of the new intellectual forces of the century is anybody's guess, but in education and in the "New Learning," the landed gentleman, the merchant, and the lawyer found a badge and an intellectual rationale for their social and economic position, which was even more important than carefully designed pedigrees. Heraldic devices were part of lesser men's efforts to ape their feudal predecessors and social superiors; education set the gentleman off from the old feudal nobility. As a result, Oxford and Cambridge were transformed from medieval seminaries for clerics into Renaissance schools for gentlemen.

In the past, learning had been the preserve of ecclesiastics, and the feudal knight had regarded formal education with scorn, preferring to "hunt and blow a horn, leap over lakes and dikes, setting nothing by politics." The feudal squire learned a way of life, but he rarely received academic training. He was taught to sing and dance and compose on harp and virginal, to speak well, and to move with grace and ease. He learned to ride and hunt, to hawk and fight. His education prepared him for a military existence in which the highest ideals were those of chivalry and his greatest obligations were to his lord. All this he learned in the entourage of kings and barons, not within the cloistered confines of Oxford and Cambridge.

The new students of the sixteenth century sought a formal academic education of the mind rather than training in the physical and social graces of society. By accident or by that curious tendency of men and women to discover what they need to survive, gentry status-consciousness found in humanism an educational creed to its own tastes. The Renaissance spirit, which came to be called in northern Europe the "New Learning," moved slowly northward from Italy, breathing the warm air of intellectual criticism and curiosity into the chilly climes of sterile scholasticism. Secular in mood, slavishly classical in form, and essentially skeptical in spirit, the New Learning laughed at the old ways as the "grossest kind of sophistry" and claimed that rhetoric, history, and the classics were the new gods of the educational world.

In Italy, humanistic education was geared to training men so that they could attain their fullest potential, and the man who could do anything was viewed as the highest achievement of individualism. In England, aristocratic education had a more social and practical end. The study of human affairs as revealed in the "Poets, Orators and Historians" of the classical world captured the essence of sixteenth-century education. Sir Thomas Elyot's *The Governour* (1531) and Roger Ascham's *The School Master* (1570) set the educational aspirations and methods of Tudor England. Training of the mind was to be undertaken not so much for the sake of the individual as for the benefit of the state. In the university the young gentleman was expected to learn "to be a most loyal servitor of his prince" and to serve the body politic "in Parliament, in council, in commission and other offices of the commonwealth." The rights of blood and gentility to a high position in society were never denied, but the medieval notion of a divine right of aristocracy that demanded a share in government gave way to the idea of a moral obligation on the part of an educated gentry, eager to dedicate its talents to the kingdom. The changing state of affairs was even recorded in statute when Parliament noted that "the wanton bringing up and ignorance of the nobility" had forced "the prince to advance new men" who could serve him. A successful and parvenu Tudor crown needed the support and the brains of equally successful and upstart clothiers, lawyers, and landlords. The fact that Henry VIII took as his second wife a young lady whose great-grandfather had been a merchant and lord mayor of London, and whose father was a country gentleman, may indicate that the Tudor dynasty had grown so secure by 1533 that it could afford to go slumming, but it also signifies the speed with which commercial elements were achieving respectability and the economic and social importance of the gentry.

The Nation-State

Education was to be dedicated to the service of the state, not to God, and in this transfer of purpose resides one of the most momentous of all intellectual and political revolutions. Service to the state is predicated on the idea of statehood and the existence of a social body that has outgrown its feudal, corporate, and fragmented nature and has evolved into a nation. The forging of political unity and the transforming of a medieval realm into a modern nation were largely the result of the strong-arm tactics of the great Tudor monarchs, but spiritual nationalism — a sense of oneness and Englishness — was far advanced before the first Tudor seized the crown at Bosworth Field.

Even today, it is said that every Englishman's class is branded on his tongue; in the fifteenth century, it might be added that his geographic as well as his social origins were indelibly imprinted upon his speech. But the indispensable condition of nationhood — linguistic unity — had developed far enough by 1400 so that the babble of innumerable tongues had surrendered to a single dominant speech: that of English as spoken in the neighborhood of the city of London. The conquered tongue of the Anglo-Saxon, much modified and corrupted, had triumphed over Norman French, and possibly nothing better signifies the growing exclusiveness, national consciousness, and sense of separation from the European and continental community than the victory of native English over alien

French. By the fourteenth century, Chaucer was writing in English, and French had ceased to be the sole speech of polite society, although the upper classes tended to remain bilingual. Cases in the sheriff's court in London were pleaded in English in 1356, and six years later Parliament decreed that all lawsuits presented to the royal courts should be conducted in the native tongue. That peculiar English pride in speaking no language save one's own was already manifest in 1404, when a knight and a doctor of law were sent as ambassadors to France and both admitted: "We are as ignorant of French as of Hebrew." By the reign of Henry V, the kings of England considered English their mother tongue, and "learned, unlearned, old and young, all understood the English tongue."

The King's English, richly intermingling Saxon and French, might never have become the common tongue of the realm if not for William Caxton and his printing press, established in 1477 "at the sign of the Red Pale" in the royal borough of Westminster. Caxton was a wool merchant turned savant who joined the service of Edward IV's sister, Margaret, duchess of Burgundy. Inspired by the Renaissance atmosphere of the city of Bruges, "the Florence of Flanders," and encouraged by the duchess, Caxton put aside his wool ledgers to translate into English the *Recueil des Histoires de Troye.* He did not, however, take kindly to the fate of the medieval copyist whose eyes were dimmed from "over much looking on the white paper" and, like any astute businessman, he sought some faster and easier means of disseminating his translation. On a business trip to Cologne in 1471, Caxton encountered an extraordinary device for "putting in enprinte," and he immediately set about mastering the new art of printing with movable type. Six years later, he moved his press from Flanders to Westminster and published the first book ever to be printed in England — *The Dictes and Sayengs of the Philosophres* — translated by no less a person than the king's brother-in-law, Earl Rivers. Perhaps one hundred works came off Caxton's press: not limited editions designed for monks and princes, but relatively cheap volumes for all who loved Chaucer's *Canterbury Tales,* Boethius's *Consolations of Philosophy,* Lydgate's *Temple of Glass,* or Malory's *Morte d'Arthur.* It was a difficult job, as the printer confessed, "to please every man because of diversity and change of language"; but Caxton's English, his choice of "old and homely" words, became familiar to every literate Englishman.

English in the fifteenth century dominated but did not monopolize. The people of County Cornwall still spoke a variant of their ancient Breton tongue; inhabitants of Yorkshire, although they claimed that their guttural sounds were English, were incomprehensible to natives of Kent; and so tenaciously did the Welsh cling to their Celtic speech that Queen Elizabeth felt it necessary to learn that language. But the growth of a single medium of expression, the increasing reference to English as the mother tongue, and the dying use of French and Latin signaled evolving national cohesiveness. The day was not far off when an archbishop of Canterbury, who was no longer appointed by a foreign and Italian-speaking pontiff, would remind his countrymen that strength lay in national unity. "It is an easy thing," Thomas Cranmer warned, "to break a whole faggot when every stick is loosed from another." Bishop Edmund Bonner asserted that "in matters of state individuals were not to be so much regarded as the whole body of the citizens." Once the English became conscious of a sense of Englishness, once they transferred their loyalty from locality and estate to realm and state and began talking about England as that "blessed isle," a sentiment had been set loose that would destroy the last shreds of lingering medieval internationalism. English became the means by which Cornishmen and Yorkshiremen alike could express their loyalty to the land, and once the new Tudor monarchs were able to associate themselves with the Englishman's love of England, then they had become, as one contemporary noted, not only kings "to be obeyed" but also idols "to be worshipped."

The Heart of the Realm

Although England was becoming a land dotted with small urban communities, the center of the Tudor melting pot, the grotesque and growing heart of the realm, which conservative social critics complained was devouring the rest of the body politic, was the city of London. In 1335 the city had possessed three times the wealth of any other community in the kingdom; by 1520 the ratio was fifteen to one and still widening. Although the size and influence of the metropolis upset the political sensibilities of Tudor theorists, London nevertheless inspired immense pride in the loyal Englishman who exclaimed: "What can there be in any place under the heavens that is not in this noble City either to be bought or borrowed?" London was indeed the "store house and mart" of all the world. The metropolis and its suburbs housed the royal court and the courts of law, and by the second decade of the sixteenth century the offspring of the gentry were crowding into the Inns of Court or law colleges for a year of what might be described as postgraduate work. Knowledge of the law and the ways of the city was an indispensable attribute to a landowning element that regarded litigation almost as a pastime. There, in the borough of Westminster, resided His Majesty's High Court of Parliament, and, as the century progressed, the agitation on the part of country gentlemen to participate in the legislative destinies of the nation and to share in the responsibilities of government became a demand that Tudor kings found it expedient to heed and that Stuart monarchs ignored at their peril. From the prostitutes practicing their trade at the Cardinal's Hat and the Swan to the magnificent royal mansion at Whitehall in Westminster, London encompassed every variety of Tudor subject. Gentleman and varlet walked side by side, and the ancient barriers and feudal privileges retreated before the violence and opulence of urban life.

To many Englishmen, London was cancerous, evil, and seditious, and its denizens so fickle that "one moment they will adore a prince and the next moment they would kill or crucify him." Nevertheless, the city held the key to England and to Tudor authority. An overgrown provincial town of possibly 50,000 in 1500, a century later London had grown into a metropolis of close to 200,000 with an annual growth rate averaging 17 percent, about ten times that of the population increase of the rest of the realm. Early in the sixteenth century, the city became the political counterbalance to the feudal northern shires. With each passing decade, the political and economic scales dipped more heavily in favor of the city and the south of England. The Tudors were secure on the throne as long as they held captive the hearts of Londoners. In London the crucial audience for Tudor pageantry resided, and it was there that the drama of Tudor history would unfold.

CHAPTER 5

Old Bottles, New Wines: The Reign of Henry VII

Fashions in history are as unpredictable as tastes in women's clothing. Why flat chests and short skirts should appeal to one generation and accentuated breasts and long skirts prove attractive to another is no whit more comprehensible than why Henry VII should be the perfect "new monarch" to Victorian historians and a medieval relic to modern scholars. Along with such terms as *Lancastrian constitutionalism* and *Tudor despotism*, the *new monarchy* has gone out of fashion. Sometimes historians deny newness to Henry VII on the grounds that he was nothing but an efficient emulator of his Yorkist predecessors, Edward IV and Richard III. At other times, scholars push newness forward into the reign of his son Henry VIII and leave the first Tudor behind as a medieval relic. Historians, however, occasionally sound like Humpty Dumpty: A word means just what they choose it to mean — "neither more nor less." This being the case, the term *new monarch* as applied to Henry VII is not without justification.[1]

The New Monarchy

Since 1399 Plantagenet heirs had been feuding over the royal patrimony of the murdered Richard II. In 1485 a usurper and a Welsh foreigner snatched the coveted crown from them. Henry Tudor's Celtic blood and distaff pretensions to the throne of England were no match for the legitimate claims of the surviving Plantagenets, and the arena still teemed with competitors who lacked nothing but military might to make good their titles. There were the five daughters of Edward IV; his grandson Henry Courtney, marquis of Exeter; plus the de la Pole descendants of his

---

[1]The expression *new monarchy* seems to be making its way back into respectability: see A. Goodman, *The New Monarchy, England, 1471–1534* (Historical Association Studies, 1988). The best modern research on the early Tudors is C. Coleman and D. Sarkey (eds.), *Revolution Reassessed* (1986). The source of much of the reassessment remains G. R. Elton, *The Tudor Revolution in Government* (1953). Henry in his fifteenth-century setting is treated in J. R. Lander, *Crown and Nobility, 1460–1509* (1976) and R. A. Griffiths and R. S. Thomas, *The Making of the Tudor Dynasty* (1985). Useful biographies are S. B. Chrimes, *Henry VII* (1972); M. V. C. Alexander, *The First of the Tudors* (1980); and A. Grant, *Henry VII* (1985).

Bust of Henry VII, by Torigiano   "If novelty of blood and doubtfulness of title confer newness, then the first Tudor qualifies as a new monarch." *(Victoria & Albert Museum, London)*

sister Elizabeth. Equally dangerous were the children of George, duke of Clarence: the ten-year-old earl of Warwick and Margaret, countess of Salisbury. Less direct but more legitimate than Henry VII stood Edward Stafford, third duke of Buckingham, a descendant of Edward III through his youngest son (see genealogical chart, page 95). If novelty of blood and doubtfulness of title confer newness, then the first Tudor qualifies as a new monarch.

Medieval historians never tire of noting that Henry VII did little that his great feudal predecessors had not done or had not aspired to do. Henry II and Edward I had aimed at financial solvency, the enforcement of law, and the exercise of royal authority without the interference of greedy magnates and moralizing ecclesiastics. If the first Tudor had a conscious model from which to draw political inspiration, it was the image of a strong feudal king. Some rather peculiar things occur, however, when sovereigns begin to emulate history. The first Tudor may well have thought of himself as a feudal king and may have seen himself as conforming to the "true" medieval tradition, but this did not make him a medieval monarch. His very success prevented it. He introduced into the ancient feudal formula the one ingredient that had been lacking — efficiency. In doing so he transformed the medieval forms into something new and modern. Opportunistic, changeable, cunning, brutal, and always practical are the adjectives that best suit the Tudor dynasty. The enforcement of law was more important than legality; the king's will was of greater concern than political theory; and the duties, not the rights, of subjects were proclaimed in every royal edict. The institutional bottles remained centuries old, but a new and heady wine was being poured into them, a vintage nourished by the bright sun of economic expansion and social dynamism. Success filled the air; and as the cautious clothier and the hard-headed landlord prospered, so also did Henry VII.

The Succession Secured

Victory at Bosworth Field on August 22, 1485, won a crown for Henry Tudor, earl of Richmond, but the new king was soon to learn the truth of the Machiavellian axiom: "There is nothing more difficult to plan, more doubtful of success, more dangerous to manage than the creation of a new system . . . for . . . the nature of people is fickle and it is easy to persuade them of something but difficult to keep them in that persuasion." The first step in keeping unreliable barons and doubtful friends in line was to secure the succession.

Henry VII outraged the theory of legitimacy and insulted the memory of Edward III by claiming the throne by lawful descent, but he also emphasized that the crown had been won by force of arms, which, although not exactly legal, was obviously a sign of God's will and favor. The "disposition of God" could only be "known by manifest, certain and authentic revelation," of which victory in battle presumably provided the surest indication. As proof of divine sanction, Henry announced that his reign had commenced on the day before Bosworth Field, a date that resolved the dilemma facing the new reign: how to attaint[2] for high treason loyal Yorkists who had fought for Richard, their liege lord and lawful king. In official parlance Richard III was styled "King in deed but not of right." A new Parliament was summoned for November 7, 1485, which dutifully acknowledged God's will and Henry's position as king and obediently referred to the victor as "our new sovereign lord, King Henry." Parliament did not, however, confer regal authority on the conqueror; this, Henry maintained, had already been achieved by military triumph at Bosworth Field.

God's will and Henry's title to the throne still had to be defended against a multitude of real and mythical claimants. One of the foremost contenders, Elizabeth of York, Edward IV's eldest daughter, was removed from the list by marriage to Henry himself. The murder of Edward's sons, presumably by their uncle Richard III, was a blessing to the new sovereign for it left no direct male Yorkist heir except the ten-year-old earl of Warwick, who was promptly ensconced in the Tower. The descendants of Edward's sisters and daughters remained a plague, but only the de la Pole family were serious contenders, and they were hunted down and exterminated.

More difficult by far were two legends against which Henry had no defense: the persistent story that the two little princeling sons of Edward IV had not been murdered but had miraculously escaped, and the equally strong belief that the child earl of Warwick was still at large, claiming his

---

[2]To sentence to death by act of Parliament.

rightful title as the legitimate Edward VI. Despite the parading of the real and incarcerated earl of Warwick and the assurance that a wicked uncle had in fact dispatched both Edward V and his little brother Richard, the myths persisted and became the center for Yorkist conspiracies and artful impersonations. Less than two years after the victory at Bosworth, Yorkist and baronial discontent rallied to the banner of a young boy by the name of Lambert Simnel, who proclaimed himself the authentic and liberated earl of Warwick. Ireland and Burgundy became the haven for exiled Yorkists and the springboard for hopes of restoring the true dynasty. Led by John de la Pole, earl of Lincoln, and manned with Burgundian and Irish mercenaries, the white rose of York made a desperate bid to capture the throne. At the Battle of Stoke on June 16, 1487, Henry Tudor was again victorious; the earl of Lincoln was killed; and Simnel was captured, pardoned, and demoted from a potential king to a scullery boy in the royal kitchen where, by dint of hard labor, he earned the rank of king's falconer.

Impersonating monarchs was not over. Four years later, in 1491, Richard, duke of York, the brother of the murdered Edward V, suddenly reappeared in the person of a young and handsome Flemish lad of seventeen who was blessed with a regal appearance and a facile mind. Perkin Warbeck stands as historic evidence not only of the imaginative mentality of the age but also of the reality that legendary tales of royal pretenders are nourished by a single element of truth: that people believe what they want to believe. Warbeck, or the rightful Richard IV (depending on the color of one's rose), was recognized in the courts of Vienna and Burgundy, where the emperor Maximilian proclaimed him lawful king of England and the duchess of Burgundy accepted him as her nephew. Fortunately for Henry Tudor, this elegant mountebank was a better impersonator of royalty than leader of men. For six years Warbeck maintained his act and involved braver men in treason. In the end he was captured in an abortive invasion of England in 1497. Again the king showed surprising mercy and allowed the imposter to live. Ultimately, however, suspicion and insecurity corroded mercy. Under pressure from the most Catholic majesties of Spain, who refused to marry their daughter Catherine of Aragon to young Prince Arthur until "not a drop of doubtful royal blood" existed in England, Henry Tudor resorted to judicial murder. He lured Warbeck and the real earl of Warwick into treason by arranging their escape from the Tower. They were quickly apprehended, and in 1499 both men were executed in their twenty-fifth year. The earl, befitting his Plantagenet blood, died by the axe; Warbeck was hanged by the neck.

By the very nature of kingship, the elimination of rival contenders to the throne through exile, battle, or execution became the foundation of government policy, for in sixteenth-century monarchy there was no place for legal opposition. The individual who attracted political support to himself, whether through blood like the earl of Warwick or through wealth and power like the kingmaker, had to be destroyed. This policy of extermination did not die with the first Tudor. Anyone unfortunate

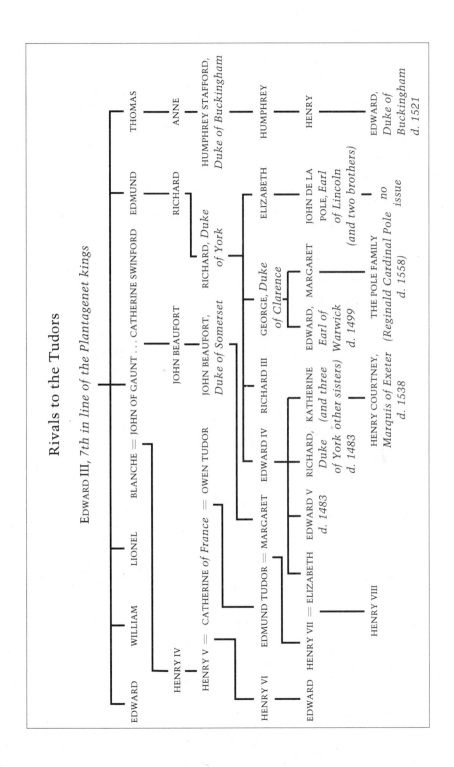

Rivals to the Tudors

EDWARD III, 7th in line of the Plantagenet kings

enough to be tainted with royal blood learned to step warily and lived constantly beneath the shadow of the sword. The duke of Buckingham lasted only until 1521. The sister of the young earl of Warwick — Margaret, countess of Salisbury — was executed in 1541, and her descendants were systematically harried out of the land and destroyed. By 1525 the curse of Edward III's fecundity had worn itself out, the Plantagenet line was all but extinct, and the Tudors had become the primary possessors of royal blood. Dynastically, Henry VII did his job well. Not only did he destroy his rivals, but also his queen gave birth to eight children, of whom four lived to adolescence and three passed on the united blood of York and Lancaster to their descendants. Arthur, the elder son, died of consumption in 1502; Henry, the second son, ascended the throne in 1509; Margaret married James IV of Scotland and became the link through which the Stuart dynasty succeeded the Tudors in 1603; and Mary, the youngest child, wedded her brother's close friend, Charles Brandon, duke of Suffolk.

The secret of political power and the security of the throne entailed more than seizing the crown, eliminating rivals, and propagating the regal race. If Henry VII's subjects were to stay in the proper "persuasion," the new king had to offer them more than royal bratlings; he had to achieve governmental solvency and enforce the laws of the realm. The power of money and the effectiveness of the king's courts were the pillars on which Tudor security rested.

Financial Solvency and Fiscal Feudalism

The fifteenth century had revealed something that might be described as the anatomy of usurpation. The successful contender to the throne had to be lavish with his promises, assuring reformation to reformers and offering the hope of gain to all who hungered for land, title, and position. If the royal aspirant had the good fortune to survive the field of battle and become a king, he had to make good the fair and easy pledges that he had so generously bestowed to win allies. "Friends" had to be rewarded, potential rivals bought off, enemies defeated. In the end, the spoils of victory were consumed, and the new monarch found himself dependent on the bounty of those mightier than he. This had been the fate of the Lancastrians, and this might have happened to the Yorkists had not Edward IV brought with him the immense private resources of his clan. With Edward's elevation to the throne in 1461, the richest magnate of the realm became king. When the kingmaker was finally destroyed in 1471, the crown fell heir to many of the Neville properties. Long before Henry VII "inherited" his kingdom, the financial recovery of the monarchy had commenced. Edward IV had brought not only new estates to the crown but also more efficient administration of the royal domain. At the same time, his customs receipts had profited from the revival of the wool trade with Europe.

The Exchequer at Westminster "The power of money and the effectiveness of the king's courts were the pillars on which Tudor security rested." *(E. T. Archive)*

The new Tudor monarch simply outdid his Yorkist predecessors. Henry's first move was to use Parliament as the legal instrument to ensure the crown's ancient possessions and to confiscate the estates of Yorkist adherents and add them to the crown lands. Legislation was also passed restoring to the king all properties lost by the crown as far back as the days of Edward III. If power is related to finances, Henry VII started his reign as secure as Edward IV had ended his. Income from crown lands in 1485 totaled £29,000, which was probably more than Edward had been able to extract. By the end of Henry's reign in 1509, land revenues had reached £42,000; the profits of the duchy of Lancaster had increased from £650 to £6,500; and income from the customs, reflecting the growing prosperity of the century, had risen to an annual average of £40,000.

If Henry VII thought in medieval terms, he at least did so in an effective fashion. He viewed the historic income of his crown as no more than his just desserts, assets for which he should have neither to beg nor to bargain. Feudal kings had traditionally lived off rents from royal estates, revenues from the customs, fees from the administration of justice, and moneys extracted on the basis of a vassal's duty to his overlord. The last two sources had been sorely depleted, as weak and vacillating kings had allowed royal law courts to fall into disrespect and had let slip their feudal rights. The Tudors aimed not so much at destroying medieval feudalism as at adapting it to the financial needs of the new dynasty. Henry demanded his feudal rights, particularly those involving money payments, and this insistence earned him the reputation of a miser and extortionist. Despite the unpopularity of his fiscal policies, Henry at least realized the medieval dictum that kings should live on their own incomes.

The price that society paid for such financial solvency was the exercise of a variety of fiscal feudalism whereby the sovereign extracted from his subjects the last measure of his historic rights. In 1504 he demanded two feudal aids, the first when his eldest daughter married James of Scotland and the second for the knighting of his son Arthur. The artificiality of the demand was apparent from the start; Arthur had been knighted fifteen years before and had been dead two years. Moreover, Parliament voiced the sentiments of most landowners when it offered Henry £40,000 on condition that he refrain from searching the records for the exact obligations of ancient land tenures. Resisting a revival of feudalism was difficult, however, because military land tenure carried with it endless responsibilities that the crown could transform into a lucrative source of income. As late as the middle of the sixteenth century, Sir Thomas Smith could still write that "no man holdeth land simply free in England but he or she that holdeth the crown of England; all others hold their land in fee." The king's feudal tenants-in-chief owed a form of inheritance tax known as "relief"; if they were minors, they became wards of the crown and their lands passed into the temporary possession of the government; and if a tenant died without heirs, the land reverted to the king. All these policies had their roots in ancient obligations based on the military nature of feudalism, and they operated at every level of the feudal structure.

Wardship, for instance, was an understandable condition because the overlord had originally given the land in return for military service. If his vassal were a minor and unable to fulfill his military duties, it was only natural that the fief should be returned to the lord until the vassal came of military age and competence. Relief, aids, wardship, and the like were terms governing the relationship between any lord and his vassal; but the king, as the greatest lord of them all, derived the most profit.

All these feudal liabilities were legal, but most of them had been ignored or disobeyed for a century or more. In reviving them, Henry VII demanded nothing more than his own, and he systematically went about inquiring into the conditions of landholdings throughout his kingdom. If he could prove that a man held his land as a knight's fee originally presented to him by the king, then Henry exacted his feudal due. A year after he became king, Henry established a commission to inquire into land tenure, and the crown began to scrutinize the *inquisitiones post mortem* (inquests after death) of its subjects to determine the extent and nature of their estates. As a further safeguard to the crown's feudal incomes, Henry's son insisted in 1536 on legislation known as the Statute of Uses to prevent landowners from escaping relief or wardship by legal trickery. Landowners in Parliament protested so vociferously, however, that the crown decided to compromise. By the Statute of Wills in 1540, it allowed those who held their property by knight's service to bequeath two-thirds of their land without obligation and subjected only one-third to the burdens of wardship.

Justice and piety were the two attributes of medieval kingship most highly esteemed. Piety was free, but justice had the added attraction of being profitable. Use of the king's courts was a privilege, not a right, and to start the machinery of justice, a sizable fee had to be paid. More profitable, but less certain, were the fines levied as punishment by the king's courts. With his eye on the exchequer, Henry VII tended to chastise his wayward subjects with the economic whip more than with the executioner's blade. Barons who indulged in treason or broke the many laws against livery, powerful men who tried to subvert justice by bribing or intimidating judges and juries — the crimes of maintenance and embracery — and merchants who evaded governmental regulations and customs duties, all paid for their transgressions with their moneys, not their lives. The story that Henry, while on a social visit to the earl of Oxford, extracted £10,000 for a technical breach of law against the keeping of liveried retainers is probably apocryphal, but the king's words are symptomatic of the spirit of his reign. As he was leaving, Henry turned to his baronial host and allegedly said, "My lord, I thank you for my good cheer, but I may not endure to have my laws broken in my sight: my attorney must speak with you."

A final source of income that reflected the growing strength of the government was the collection of benevolent loans extracted from those most able to pay — wealthy individuals and corporations. The royal tax collectors confronted both rich and poor with the dilemma known as

Morton's Fork. The victim was persuaded to pay if he were wealthy and lived lavishly, because high living was obviously proof of the ability to contribute generously to the king. He was equally persuaded to part with his money if he lived in poverty because this presumably was evidence of frugality and the existence of savings, a portion of which should be donated to the support of the kingdom.

Even in diplomacy, concern for the welfare of his exchequer was paramount in Henry's calculations. Early in the reign, he revived the Yorkist policy of friendship with the Habsburg interests in Europe because he valued the goodwill of whoever controlled the markets of the Lowlands and could threaten the crown's revenues from the export duty on woolen broadcloth. Similar fiscal considerations stood behind the marriage of Henry's eldest son, Prince Arthur, to Catherine, the daughter of Ferdinand and Isabella of Spain. The match was first proposed in 1488, but the children were young, Spain wanted to see whether the Tudor line would survive, and both Henry VII and Ferdinand required time to settle the most important element of all — Catherine's dowry. By 1496 the terms of marriage had been hammered out and the dowry was set at 200,000 crowns. Five years later the wedding took place, and within five months Arthur was dead and Catherine a widow in a foreign land. Although Henry grieved for the loss of his son, he had no intention of losing his daughter-in-law's dowry as well; and after two more years of bargaining, in 1503 Catherine was betrothed to young Prince Henry, six years her junior. For diplomatic reasons, the Spanish princess had to wait still another six years before the fateful marriage finally took place.

In war as well as in diplomacy, Henry realized a profit. England joined Spain in 1489 in a conflict designed to prevent France from absorbing the duchy of Brittany, and the king was quick to use the expenses of sending an army to France as an excuse for extracting £100,000 from Parliament. Henry made noisy military gestures to satisfy his ally and to allay parliamentary suspicions about the purpose for which its grant was being spent. In December 1492, however, he was delighted to sign the unheroic yet extremely lucrative Treaty of Etaples, by which he agreed to put aside his claim to the French throne in return for a handsome monetary tribute paid by the kings of France.

When the first Tudor died, he had accomplished a revolution in finances. Computations place the royal income in 1485 at £52,000; twenty-four years later it may have reached as high as £142,000, but £113,000 is probably more accurate. The Venetian ambassador correctly analyzed the transformation when he wrote home in 1500 that England was "perfectly stable by reason, first of the King's wisdom whereof everyone stands in awe; and secondly on account of the King's wealth." Henry VII had rectified one essential set of statistics: economically speaking, there were no more overmighty subjects. The king was immeasurably the wealthiest individual in the realm, and Sir John Fortescue's formula that monarchs should be twice as wealthy as their greatest subjects had

Coiners at Work   "Money could buy power and enforce a grudging respect." *(North Wind Picture Archives)*

been put into effect many times over. Henry Tudor as a landlord was worth £42,000 annually; his nearest rival could scarcely muster £4,000.

The Resurgence of Royal Authority and the Rule of Law

The wisdom of the king amounted to more than a deep regard for pounds, shillings, and pence. Although money could buy power and enforce a grudging respect, the traditional role of kingship — the source of its esteem — resided in the position of the monarch as supreme judge and administrator of the realm. The crown was regarded as the fountainhead of justice and the wellspring from which flowed "a flood of all that is good or evil." Evil lay in inactivity; if Henry were to fulfill the proper role of kingship, he had to enforce his laws on both great and small, insisting that the machinery of government operated without respect to rank or person. No Tudor was deliberately a revolutionist, and neither Henry VII nor his son desired the destruction of the old governmental or social system. Instead, both endeavored to harness it and to use the existing structure. They sought to convert feudal barons into domesticated peers who regarded themselves as servants of the state — not independent leaders of society — and to transform the structure of government from a preserve of aristocratic privilege into an effective instrument of royal authority. The task involved neither the annihilation of the nobility nor the creation of new organs of government. The secret lay in making the inherited system operate efficiently for the benefit of the crown.

Henry VII summarized the problem that confronted him at the commencement of his reign when he summoned the peers of the realm and required them to swear not to shelter felons, not to impede or ignore royal writs, not to corrupt or intimidate juries, not to maintain private armies of indentured retainers, and not to sanction riots and foster violence. He had to impress on a hierarchically structured society that "it was not fit that private men should carve out their redress which way they list" and that "obedience is the best in each degree." In this task the king benefited immeasurably from the extinction of the old nobility during the Wars of the Roses, which had so reduced their ranks that only eighteen barons were called to Henry's first Parliament. The nobleman, be he Yorkist or Lancastrian, who gave faithful service to the monarchy, irrespective of the man who wore the crown, was rewarded; the magnate who continued to play the risky game of kingmaking was destroyed. It was no accident that Thomas Howard, earl of Surrey, who had fought for Richard III at Bosworth Field, was freed from the Tower in 1491 and his lands restored, while Sir William Stanley, whose timely betrayal had won Henry the battle, was executed for treason four years later. The former had accepted and was willing to live by the axiom: "What pleaseth the prince hath the force of law"; the latter hearkened back to an older generation of nobility that had no place in the Tudor world.

Henry's relations with his great magnates were complex and ambivalent: He distrusted them — the vast majority had remained dangerously neutral during the crisis of Bosworth Field — yet he needed them because local government and law enforcement depended on their cooperation. Noblemen such as George Neville, fifth Lord Abergavenny, although he committed treason and consistently violated the king's statutes against the unlawful retaining of armed servants and tenants, nevertheless regularly sat on the Commission for the Peace for the county of Kent. Neville's influence was essential to the peace of the shire, and when he was dropped from the commission, local violence erupted; yet his influence also protected one hundred of his retainers who terrorized large parts of the county. The government had to devise a way of rendering him impotent while retaining his services for both peace and war. Consequently, when Abergavenny was found guilty in 1507 of retaining 471 armed men, he was fined the enormous sum of £70,550. The amount was preposterous, but it placed the nobleman under the control of the government. Neville, in a series of agreements known as "recognizances," acknowledged his debt to the king and agreed to pay in recompense £5,000 over a period of ten years. Even £500 a year severely strained his resources but did not drive him to desperation and treason, while the threat that the original fine and total debt might someday be called ensured his loyalty in the future. By the end of the reign, the nobility had come under tight financial harness. Two-thirds of them had been forced to enter into recognizances with the king, some of which he demanded as guarantee for proper performance of duty, others simply as insurance for good behavior as interpreted by the monarch.

The first Tudor had the financial wherewithal to purchase a standing army in the style of European sovereigns. He chose not to; yet rebels had to be chastised, the realm defended, and wars fought. The two hundred yeomen of the guard established early in his reign as a personal bodyguard for the king served as mere window-dressing to royalty, hardly an effective weapon of coercion. Henry VII had no use for expensive merce-nary troops; he preferred the historic system of recruitment by which the great magnates armed their own tenants and placed them at the service of the crown. The problem was to limit the system of recruitment to the king's command. This was done by the use of Commissions of Array, ap-pointed by the king for each county and composed of notable personages of the shires who were ordered to arm a prescribed number of men at their own expense. Private liveried armies were illegal, but noblemen who failed to raise their quota were brought before the king's Star Cham-ber to explain their delinquency. Lord William Howard, for example, al-though he complained bitterly about the cost, was commanded to raise one hundred men-at-arms and thirty archers for the king's use. As long as such troops were at the king's command and not under oath to some no-ble lord or wearing his livery, they constituted an effective fighting force with which to secure the crown and defend the realm.

At law the most glaring needs were neither new statutes nor new courts but the "just execution of laws, reformation of faults, giving out of commandments," and impartial justice. For the past one hundred years, justice had been forfeited to influence. The aristocracy had exercised a form of judicial patronage in which local concerns prevailed over royal interests, money over legality, force of arms over the evidence, and baro-nial privilege over the crown's right. Humble folk either did not bother to take their grievances to the law or, if they did, took them to the man who could control the outcome of the case. Common law could no longer fur-nish protection. It had become rigid and archaic, ponderously slow and intricately technical, and the bastion of wealth and influence. Only the rich could afford it, and the common law, depending as it did on juries, was constantly exposed to bribery and intimidation.

Common law was not the only kind of justice available to English-men. The king, who was the wellspring "of all that was good or evil," could hear complaints and administer justice directly or through his council. His decisions were not hampered by juries, precedents, or legal technicalities. Royal justice tended to be commonsense justice, and lesser people found swift, impartial, and equitable decisions whenever they brought their pleas to the king or his council. Such law, sometimes called "equity law," was inherent in kingship, and the king's council could administer justice in its master's name. The Court of Chancery en-forced equity law, and by 1485 it had become a venerable division of gov-ernment; but Chancery had the disadvantage of being restricted to civil cases. Although the court increased in stature and in business under the Tudors, a pressing need for some competent organization to hear crimi-nal cases remained. Men were urged to bring their grievances directly to the sovereign, and the lords of the council began to reserve certain hours of the day and a particular location in the king's palace at Westminster to hear criminal disputes. They met in the Star Chamber, and, as the years passed, many of the king's servants came to specialize in such criminal cases, and their meetings assumed the name of the Court of the Star Chamber. Under Henry VII, the court never became visibly separate from the rest of the council; but after 1509 it took on "great augmentation and authority," joining the Court of Chancery as an instrument by which the baronial few as well as the common multitude learned "obedience."

As Henry knew, obedience was the daughter of respect for royal authority. A proper and humble regard for the king's will could be cultivated by maintaining a deep financial distinction between the sovereign and his subjects, and it could be fostered by making the king's courts havens of justice. The most effective method, however, lay in brutally insisting on the supremacy of law in every corner of the realm. The legacy of the medieval past had been a kingdom divided into semi-autonomous franchises, such as the episcopal palatinate of Durham, the duchy of Lancaster, and the Welsh Marches, where border lords paid scant heed to the king's writs and clung tenaciously to their cherished liberties. Under the first Lancastrian king, the duchy of Lancaster had been absorbed into the royal domain; but even as late as 1534, twenty-five years after Henry VII's death, it was still being said of Wales that "the king's rights are attacked by all manner of liberties, his felons and outlaws are clothed and maintained by stewards and bailiffs of these liberties, so that his process has no place and his laws are not dread." The first Tudor did his best to curb the independence of these ancient franchises by creating the King's Council for Wales and the Marches, but he left it to his son, Henry VIII, to bring the king's law into the Welsh mountains. In 1536 Parliament finally passed legislation "making the laws of Wales the same as those of England" and reorganizing the 136 lordships of the Welsh Marches into five new shires under royal law and administration. The only peace that could now be broken was the king's peace, the only justices were royal judges, and the only right to pardon a crime was the king's right.

Destroying provincialism proved easier than curbing baronial privilege. The lesson of equality before the law had to be drilled into a peerage that for four centuries had happily operated in the tradition of feudal independence and private law. The old nobility had to learn that the king's servant, no matter what his degree, had "a sufficient warrant to arrest the greatest peer of this realm." With calculated cruelty, the Tudors insisted that the great should be humbled while the weak, protected by the mantle of royal authority, should inherit the earth.

Long after Henry VII's death, his son was still carrying on his father's policies. In 1541 Henry VIII struck straight at the heart of feudal exclusiveness when a member of the baronial elite was hanged by the neck as a common criminal. The case involved one of the most cherished of all feudal prerogatives — hunting rights. Those who harked back to the carefree days of the previous century, when nobles were laws unto themselves, felt reluctant to give up hunting at their pleasure in the countryside. As the concept of private property grew more common, the exercise of this right became increasingly difficult. The crisis came to a head when young Thomas Lord Dacre of the south and his brother-in-law, John Mantell, together with fourteen of their friends, were accused of murder. The young gentlemen, in the language of their indictment, had illegally conspired "how they might best hunt the park" of Nicholas Pelham "with dogs and nets and other engines." They had "bound themselves to slay any of the king's lieges who might resist them in their illegal purpose." When Pelham's men tried to stop them, one of his servants was fatally wounded, and the culprits, ranging from a lord to a Sussex yeoman, were arrested, indicted, and sentenced to be hanged.

Since Lord Dacre was a baron of the realm, his trial could not take place in a court of common law but had to be handled directly by the king's council. Dacre insisted that the killing had been accidental and demanded a judgment by his peers. The young man was wealthy and had influential friends at court, and one member of the council, Lord Cobham, was "very stiff and vehement" in refusing to view the affair as anything more than a high-spirited escapade on the part of a band of well-connected delinquents. The council persuaded Lord Dacre to give up his demand for a trial, and "upon hope of grace" confess his guilt and throw himself on the king's mercy. Henry VIII was unforgiving, and the terrible sentence was executed. The court and feudal society shuddered at the spectacle of a rich and socially respectable young blade being treated as if he were a common cutpurse and murderer. In shocked words, the Spanish ambassador reported that Lord Dacre had been hanged from "the most ignominious gibbet, and for greater shame dragged through the streets to the place of execution, to the great pity of many people, and even of his judges, who wept when they sentenced him, and in a body asked his pardon of the king." The aspect of the tragedy that provoked the most astonishment was that only Dacre and Mantell with two of their closest friends were executed, while the others were granted the king's pardon. The moral was perfectly clear: if the English lived under a single law, then it was a denial both of God and monarchy to assume that the estate of nobility could claim exemption or operate as a law unto itself.

The Art of Government

Under Henry VII and his son, a new attitude of mind was at work, a fresh approach to government that had little to do with victory on the battlefield or the death of kings. Statecraft had a long way to go before it evolved into the science of the modern bureaucratic state, but by 1509 in England, and earlier in Italy, government had come to be regarded as an art in which men made a conscious effort to calculate policy and to act accordingly. The ends of diplomacy were to be measured by material benefit, not spiritual or chivalric aspirations. The amoebalike quality of the medieval past, in which little or no distinction existed among the legislative, executive, and judicial aspects of government, was slowly giving way to a more precise notion of governmental function.

The most celebrated expression of the new spirit pervading both the courts of kings and the mansions of merchants was the publication in 1516 of Sir Thomas More's *Utopia*. In part a medieval dream reflecting the perfect harmony of monastic life, in part a fantasy inspired by the discovery of the New World, and in part a learned joke in which Sir Thomas indulged in the fiction of chamberpots made of gold and children playing marbles with precious gems, *Utopia* above all else applied reasoned thought to the problems of good government. It was based on the idea that humanity, by the application of reason, could construct a perfect society. More's *Utopia* was here on earth and was the work of human beings; now men and women no longer had to wait for heaven and the operation of divine grace to achieve peace and happiness.

The accomplishments of Henry VII were a far cry from the reasoned society outlined in More's *Utopia*, but at least Henry "was not afraid of an able man" and he "was served by the ablest men that were to be found, without which his affairs would not have prospered as they did." The secret of effective government lay not as much in the existence of strong kings as in the presence of able councillors: men dedicated to the single ideal of serving their master. New and strange men in government were not unique to the Tudor dynasty. The same complaint had been directed against Henry II, Richard II, and Edward IV. What set the first Tudor apart from his predecessors was the mentality of those who surrounded him. Chastened magnates sat on the royal council by invitation, not by divine right. Literate and educated ecclesiastics traditionally had served as the prop and stay of governments, which tended to flounder in the hands of warrior kings and illiterate peers, but the single-hearted service that Bishop Fox offered Henry VII was different both in kind and in degree. Fox, it was said, "to serve the king's turn would agree to his own father's death." The bishop was first the king's servant and only second an official of the church, owing obedience to God and to a foreign pope. Bushy, Green, and Scroop were the creatures of Richard II, as Empson and Dudley were the servants of Henry VII, but Plantagenet favorites and Tudor workhorses differed fundamentally. Richard's humble councillors were hardworking, loyal knights of the shire. Henry VII was surrounded by men who embodied in their careers the three new influences beginning to predominate in most sixteenth-century states: strict attention to administrative and fiscal detail; a conscious desire to increase efficiency; and a growing appreciation that government, though it operated in the king's name, had a life and spirit of its own.

The art of government, the Renaissance mind as applied to the problems of administration, belonged to no single innovator or individual genius. Henry VII was well served, and much that was branded as avaricious during his reign in fact represented only the efforts of his officials to introduce order and logic into the chaos of medieval government. Sir John Lovell and Sir John Heron, the king's treasurers, worked out a relatively rational system of fiscal collection, appropriation, auditing, and disbursing. Sir Richard Empson and Sir Edmund Dudley, those hated legal advisers to the monarch, earned their evil reputations not so much because they were unscrupulous as because they were highly efficient. In the sixteenth century, however, the king's government was only as good as the monarch himself, and it was Henry's own vigilance, energy, and constant labor that gave life and direction to his reign.

The traditional image of the king is of a man, slight of build, sallow of face, and sparse of hair, who felt more at home in the countinghouse than in medieval armor. But Henry, it should also be remembered, won his crown in a fair fight on the battlefield, and one chronicler acknowledged that "his mind was brave and resolute and never, even at moments of the greatest danger, deserted him." Tudor England had great difficulty with Henry's personality, and it may not be a coincidence that Shakespeare never wrote a play about him. A sovereign who acquired a reputation for avarice; who meticulously initialed each page of his financial ledgers; who covered four folios of one of his treasurer's account books with his own figures; and who rejoiced in converting Utrecht guilders, Flemish pounds, and Venetian ducats into "good sterling" was hardly a subject of great interest to a dramatist. Only later, in the seventeenth century, was the king praised as a sovereign of unusual ability and character who gave himself unstintingly to the affairs of state.

Whatever the monarch's many failings in the eyes of traditionalists, who viewed kingship in terms of Henry V and Agincourt, Henry Tudor possessed two qualities that ensured success in an age of new monarchs who practiced Machiavellian diplomacy and financial extortion. He paid close attention to administrative detail and was immensely hardworking, "so that no one dared to get the better of him through deceit and guile." When he died in 1509, in the fifty-third year of his life and the twenty-fourth year of his reign, almost everyone, except possibly the small cadre of administrators over whom he had complete control and through whom he ruled, gave a great sigh of relief and looked to a brighter future. But that future shone bright in large measure because Henry bequeathed to his son something unique in English history: a safe throne, a full treasury, and a prosperous realm.

The Smell and Flavor of the Kingdom

The writing of history, like the painting of a picture, seeks to trick the eye into seeing something that is not there: an intelligible shape and an aura of sensibility. The art of government, with its emphasis on reason and calculation, was little more than a flitting smile on the face of Tudor England, which remained far more medieval than modern in its conception of the universe and its view of the purpose and structure of society. The Tudor cosmos was tidy, sensible, and psychologically satisfying. Every part fitted together to create a universe in which men and women were the most important actors, earth was the center of the stage, and God was the producer, playwright, and director. Sixteenth-century men and women were placed securely in the middle of an immense sphere,

Title Page of Robert Fludd's *Tomus Secundus de Supernaturali, Naturali, Praeternaturali Microcosmi Historia, 1619*
"The Tudor cosmos was tidy, sensible, and psychologically satisfying." Man is shown at the center of the universe with the four earthly elements — fire (cholera), air (sanguis), water (pituita), and earth as the central sphere. Outside the domain of man rotate the spheres of the heavenly hierarchy: angels through seraphin. God the creator is represented as a blast of light at the top and outside the final circle.

looking upward from a central position toward the inner surface of the universe. Like the layers of an onion, the firmament moved outward in a series of revolving crystalline spheres to which were attached various celestial bodies. There were eleven circles in all, starting with the moon and progressing outward to include the five planets and the sun. Next came the sphere of the starry firmament, then the "orb of heaven" with its complex celestial hierarchy, followed by the invisible "circle of the Prime Mover," which caused all heavenly movement. The final ring was "the eleventh heaven . . . the habitation of God and His angels." Such a cosmos was warm, friendly, and filled with the music of the spheres. As viewers looked upward on a starry night, their minds moved away from this earth — the black pit of all depravity — to the perfection and eternal light of God's domain, and they knew that out there in the firmament resided the ultimate truth about creation.

The universe possessed both spiritual and physical meaning, for it served as the theater in which men and women enacted the drama of their salvation, choosing either good or evil, heaven or hell. Every event — from the birth of Siamese twins or the appearance of shooting stars to hailstones that destroyed the harvest — betokened God's purpose and signified some celestial clash between the soldiers of God and those of Satan. The macrocosm and the microcosm of existence were meshed in a divine web that extended from the butterfly to God, from human society to the kingdom of the angels, for all things in heaven and earth were linked to an endless "chain of being."

Tudor political science was equally teleological, egocentric, and anthropomorphic. God had created in heaven a divine hierarchy of archangels and angels; and here on earth he "had assigned and appointed kings, princes, with other governors under them, in all good and necessary order." The state was far more than a collection of political institutions, social divisions, and economic activities; it was a living organism composed of obedient, loving, and right-minded men and women who lived with one another in concord and Christian harmony. The favorite political metaphor was the body politic, consisting of "the heart, head, hands and feet." The heart was the prince; "as all wit, reason, and sense, feeling, life, and all other natural power, springeth out of the heart, so from the princes and rulers of the state cometh all laws, order and policy, all justice, virtue and honesty, to the rest of this politic body." The head, with its eyes and ears, was comparable to the natural leaders of society, the aristocracy and the gentry. The hands were artisans and warriors, and the feet belonged to "the plowmen and tillers of the ground, because they, by their labour, sustain and support the rest of the body." True beauty in such a political organism consisted of "due proportion" within the system, so that each part knew its proper place and function. The kingdom in theory was "held together by natural affection," every individual "loving one another as members and part of one body."

Tudor cosmology and political theory were intelligible, ordered, harmonious, and inspired by God. Social reality, in contrast, boiled with cruelty, violence, and suffering. Men were generally as quick to anger as to love, and no one, not even the clergy, walked unarmed at night. Unlit streets and the king's highways were the haunts of criminals — disabled soldiers, debtors, starving peasants, professional assassins, and an army of outcasts for whom society felt no particular responsibility. In London a rudimentary police force of 240 constables could do little but make frightful examples of those luckless enough to be caught, or answer the shouts of the victims with the words: "God restore your loss; [we] have other business at this time." The degree of violence is difficult to judge. In terms of recorded felonies, the sixteenth century may have been as safe as the twentieth. Under Elizabeth the documented average yearly crime rate stood at 20 per 10,000 people in the turbulent shire of Essex, while in 1965 the rate for all England reached 95.4 per 10,000; but modern means of crime detection and thoroughness of recording make these comparisons meaningless. Certainly, contemporaries thought there was "no country in the world where there are more robbers and thieves than in England," and although the actual number of homicides may have been low, the incidence of rioting, feuding, brawling, and thieving seems to have been extremely high. Moreover, the number of apprehended criminals who slipped through the law's net and escaped punishment entirely was inordinately great. More serious, crimes of bodily violence — such as rape, murder, and manslaughter — were, at least in Essex, highest among the gentry, that element of society not only the most lethally armed but also in theory the most politically responsible.

In contrast to law enforcement, law enactment was detailed, ferocious, and ritualistic. With a fine appreciation that the punishment should fit the crime, the law prescribed that traitors be drawn to the gallows on a sled, hanged, and cut down alive, castrated, disemboweled, decapitated, and quartered. Poisoners were boiled alive, witches and heretics burned at the stake, and murderers hanged in chains until dead. A Tudor execution, as the following figures indicate, was a carefully staged public spectacle in which the condemned was the principal actor on whom the government was ready to spend a great deal of money. In an era that counted fifty shillings a yearly living wage, it cost fifteen shillings, eight pence to hang the traitor Frair Stone:

for half a ton of timber to make a pair of gallows for to hang Friar Stone	2s. 6d.[3]
to carpenter to build them	16d.
to laborer to dig holes	3d.
to men who helped set gallows up	7d.
for drink to them	1d.
carriage of timber to the Dungeon	4d.
for a hurdle	6d.
for load of wood and horse to draw him to Dungeon	2s. 3d.
to 2 men who set the kettle & parboiled him	12d.
to 3 men who carried his quarters to the city gates and set them up	13d.
halter to hang him	1d.
2 halfpenny halters	1d.
sandwich cord	9d.
for a woman to mind the kettle	2d.
executioner's fee	4s. 8d.

The most common engine of justice was the gibbet, and any theft over one shilling could be punished by hanging. Lesser offenses war-

---

[3]The letter *s* stands for *shillings*, *d* for *pence*. The quotation is in Terence Murphy, "The Maintenance of Order in Early Tudor Kent: 1509–1558" (unpubl. Ph.D. diss., Northwestern University, 1974), from Canterbury Cathedral Library MSS, F/A/13ff. 69d–70.

Tudor Justice — Prisoners in Lollard Tower, 1555
"The stocks were reserved for drunkards, rioters, name-callers, bawds, and scolds." *(Mary Evans Picture Library)*

ranted lesser but almost as unpleasant consequences. Fraudulent merchants and slanderers were chastised on the pillory — there the culprits were forced to stand, neck and wrists pinioned, and, on occasion, their ears nailed to the board behind their heads. The stocks were reserved for drunkards, rioters, name-callers, bawds, and scolds. False jurors were forced to ride "with their faces to the horses' tails" and paper caps on their heads; the village ducking stool was kept for gossips and scandalmongers; and public whipping was the customary method of discouraging idleness and prostitution. The law was without pity, but so also was life. "At any season," lamented Bishop Fisher, there were "beggars or poor folks that be pained and grieved with hunger and cold lying in the streets." Although Fisher preached compassion, it was difficult to feel much pity when every city had its share of those who lacked "their arms, feet, hands, and other features of their bodies." Life was an agony of itches, toothaches, gout, bladder stones, ulcers, and sores, and everyone walked in dread of the plague and smallpox. The torment of the traitor's death had to be set against the agony of the soldier whose bravery had brought him to the operating table to face the surgeon's saw without benefit of anesthesia, or that of the lover whose delights were more than repaid by the horrors of uncontrollable syphilis. Death in one grisly guise or another was everywhere. The only thing that made life endurable and explicable was the knowledge that nothing existed — suffering, love, disaster, good fortune — that did not somehow fit into the pattern of God's ultimate design.

6

This Realm of England Is an Empire

When Henry VII died on April 21, 1509, two men fell heir to his authority: his eighteen-year-old son, Bluff King Hal, and Thomas Wolsey, the child of an Ipswich butcher. While the young monarch cut royal capers, spent his father's treasures — which were not as large as legend pictures them — and enjoyed the role of a lavish and athletic prince graced with inexhaustible charm and a magnificent physique, the business of government was quietly and efficiently assumed by an extremely talented churchman.[1]

King and Cardinal

At thirty-four Thomas Wolsey was a man of extraordinary energy and ambition, and the offices of church and state were lavished on a servant who relieved his sovereign of the burdens of kingship. From a minor cleric, Wolsey rose to be archbishop of York in 1514, lord chancellor and cardinal legate of all England in 1515, and papal legate for life in 1524. For a time it seemed as if the realm possessed two kings — one in blood and name, the other in ability and fact. The cardinal exercised an authority that no medieval monarch had wielded: as lord chancellor and cardinal legate, he united in his ample person the spiritual and temporal powers of the realm. His residences at Hampton Court and York Palace housed an entourage of four hundred courtiers and servants who waited upon his

---

[1]The works, both good and bad, on the reign of Henry VIII are legion. The following is a small sampling of the controversy surrounding Henry VIII as a human being. A. F. Pollard, *Henry VIII* (1902), is a classic and the starting point for any study of the king's character. G. R. Elton's view is best read in "King or Minister?: The Man Behind the Reformation," *History 39* (1954) and *Henry VIII: An Essay in Revision*, Hist. Assoc. Pamphlet no. 51 (1962). H. F. M. Prescott, *The Man on a Donkey* (1952), is a brilliant historical novel in which Henry is cast as the villain. The most recent treatments are J. J. Scarisbrick, *Henry VIII* (1968); L. B. Smith, *Henry VIII, The Mask of Royalty* (1971; new ed. 1982); and David Starkey's *The Reign of Henry VIII: Personalities and Politics* (1986), which looks like a mini-coffeetable publication but is filled with the most recent scholarship on the subject. The best general study of the period is G. R. Elton, *Reform and Reformation: England, 1509–1558* (1977). The most recent biography of Wolsey is P. Gwyn, *The King's Cardinal: The Rise and Fall of Thomas Wolsey* (1990). On Henry's wives, see A. Weir, *The Six Wives of Henry VIII* (1991).

pleasure; and although the ancient nobility hated him for his pride and humble birth, they nevertheless danced to his lordship's fancy. The cardinal's legatine authority brought papal power directly into England; both the archbishop of Canterbury in his palace and the simple monk in his monastery were subject to his scrutiny. As lord chancellor, Wolsey made the Court of Chancery and the Star Chamber the core of his temporal authority, shaking the great barons "by the ear" and teaching them respect for the king's law. Long before the real king claimed plenary power over his subjects' souls as well as their bodies, the great cardinal had marked the way.

The secret of Wolsey's success stemmed from neither his spiritual nor his secular offices; it rested on his understanding of Henrician politics and his ability to manipulate the king. Indeed, the major issue throughout Henry's entire reign centered on the question of responsibility: who made policy — monarch or minister? Today, most historians would agree that policy belonged to the king but its implementation to the minister, whose freedom of action was so great he could at times shape and direct policy. In the cardinal's case, his great talent lay not only in his ability to relieve his master of the wearisome details of government but also in his realization that a successful minister had to control three sources of political authority: (1) the king; (2) the court — especially the privy or secret chamber, whose members waited upon the sovereign and which was headed by the groom of the stool; and (3) the council, directed by the lord chancellor, the lord privy seal, the lord treasurer, and the principal secretary. During the height of Wolsey's success, 1515–1527, the cardinal dominated all three sources of power.

Wolsey's major interests were directed more toward diplomacy than toward reform within the church, and in his young master he found a student eager to step out onto the continental stage and make England's weight felt in the diplomatic balance of power. Young Henry, with his golden-red beard and angel's face, was the hope of philosophers, the friend of scholars, the image of physical perfection, and the pride of England. The whole world — especially the nobility whom Henry VII had so thoroughly chastized — rejoiced "in the possession of so great a prince," and all things suddenly seemed "full of milk, of honey and of nectar." In the words of the Venetian ambassador, the king united "such corporal and mental beauty as not merely to surprise but to astonish all men." Although he spent his patrimony and turned the chilly court of the first Tudor into a glittering palace of dance and music, the prince carried out at least one of his father's deathbed wishes: in 1509 he married the twenty-four-year-old Catherine of Aragon. The new queen had been a friendless and penniless exile in England ever since the death of her first husband, Prince Arthur, in 1502. Whether a frail boy of fourteen and a Spanish lass of fifteen were ever active in the connubial bed will never be known. Years later, when the question had vital importance, Catherine swore that the marriage had never been consummated and that Henry was free of sin in marrying his brother's widow. Certainly, the young

Henry was fond of his Spanish wife, if not especially faithful. Catherine did her best: she produced three stillborn children, two infants who died within the month, and the princess Mary. The birth of the princess in 1516 gave new hope to the royal couple. They were both young, Henry said, and "if it was a daughter this time, by the grace of God the sons will follow." That God's grace might not be forthcoming was a possibility that the king would not consider; he was far too concerned with feats of war to worry about such an improbability.

The Lessons of Diplomacy

War and diplomacy were the last aspects of sixteenth-century society to divest themselves of the language and mentality of the medieval past. The old confusion between war and peace prevailed, the goals of diplomacy were rarely commercial or economic, and war was still viewed as a glorious end in itself and not as an instrument of foreign policy. The moment that an eighteen-year-old sovereign replaced an elderly and parsimonious parent on the throne of England, it was to be expected that he would cast his eyes toward Europe and join the noisy and complex game of continental diplomacy in which the dramatic, the magnificent, and the romantic had more weight than the practical, the calculated, or the profitable. Young King Henry entered the European arena because he was "not unmindful that it was his duty to seek fame by military skill," and because he wanted to "create such a fine opinion about his valour among all men that they would clearly understand that his ambition was not merely to equal but indeed to excel the glorious deeds of his ancestors." Chivalry may have languished in the dark attic of the exchequer, but it remained very much alive in the banqueting halls of kings.

The admiration of all was devoutly to be wished, but the opinions that counted most in diplomatic circles were those of two rival princes — Francis I, the Most Christian King of France, and Charles V, His Most Catholic Majesty of Spain and Emperor of the Holy Roman Empire. Both sovereigns were young and came to power within seven years of Henry's succession to the crown. The three enjoyed a boisterous and chivalric rivalry. It was indicative of the intimate nature of international relations that, when Francis ascended his throne, Harry of England should have immediately inquired of the French ambassador whether the new king had a well-turned leg. When the ambassador admitted that his sovereign's legs were "sparse," Henry proudly indicated his own thigh and boasted, "Look, here! And I have also a good calf to my leg."

Despite a shapely limb and a full treasury, Henry was at a disadvantage when it came to European war and diplomacy. Compared to France and Spain, England was weak in wealth and population, and hovered on the periphery of the diplomatic arena. Henry could not strike at France without risking Scottish invasion through the back door. Nor could he antagonize Spain, for Emperor Charles V was also archduke of Burgundy and lord of the Low Countries, where English wool found its way into the

Henry VIII   *(National Portrait Gallery, London)*

Francis I   *(John G. Johnson Collection, Philadelphia)*

Charles V   *(Museo del Prado, Madrid)*

The Diplomatic Triangle   "The three [sovereigns] enjoyed a boisterous and chivalric rivalry."

European market. In the costly rivalry between Valois France and Habsburg Spain, England lay geographically far removed from the central attractions — Milan, Venice, Naples, and the Papal States. Italy was the courtesan of the European community of nations, and the younger powers fought in a noisy and ostentatious fashion for her manifest charms if doubtful virtues. The young princes of Europe had learned to tax their subjects, and they hastened to send their armies into Italy to plunder or purchase the art and luxury of the Renaissance. Henry VIII had the money to buy his way into the diplomatic game, but he could enter the Italian scene only by proxy.

Henry VIII's first taste of foreign politics was disagreeable but salutary. In 1511 he entered the Holy League of doubtful name to help the Roman pontiff hold the balance of power between Spain and France. England, Venice, Spain, and the papacy confronted the aggressive actions of the French in Italy. English troops were sent into southern France, where they promptly got sick on green wine, mutinied, and returned home without orders — hardly the heroic picture the young king had in mind. The following year, Henry went in person to earn military renown in France, and in August 1513 at the Battle of the Spurs he succeeded in defeating a French army. More enduring and possibly even more glorious, despite the king's absence, was the victory over the Scots that his soldiers won in September 1513 at Flodden Field. Ten thousand of the king's enemies are said to have fallen there, including James IV of Scotland, while the English, led by the earl of Surrey, lost fewer than three hundred men. It is little wonder that contemporaries felt divine intervention to be manifest in such a feat, and Queen Catherine promptly wrote her husband in France to ensure that he offered thanks to God. Henry may have been irritated at a deity who sanctioned such a marvelous victory in his absence, but he did the gentlemanly thing and rewarded Surrey with the dukedom of Norfolk.

The war with France was punctuated by the usual broken promises, diplomatic turncoats, and bad feelings among the erstwhile allies. In the end, Henry and Wolsey found it to their advantage to make peace with France and to marry off the king's youngest sister, Mary Tudor, to Louis XII. The marriage was a mere diplomatic escapade, for Louis was sixty, his English wife eighteen, and the French king survived only three months of wedded bliss. In 1514 dynastic rivalry intensified with the accession of Francis I, who commenced his reign with a major bid for French hegemony in Italy. At Marignano in 1515, Francis crushed the armies of the duke of Milan, and all of northern Italy lay prostrate before him. The Battle of Marignano badly upset the diplomatic balance, and Cardinal Wolsey began to worry lest the Roman pontiff become a French chaplain and the church be brought captive a second time to Avignon. The diplomatic scene changed again in 1516 with the appearance of the third of the princelings of Europe; Charles, duke of Burgundy, "void of all excess, either of virtue or vice," became king of Aragon and Castile. Wolsey quickly allied England to the new master of Spain, at the same

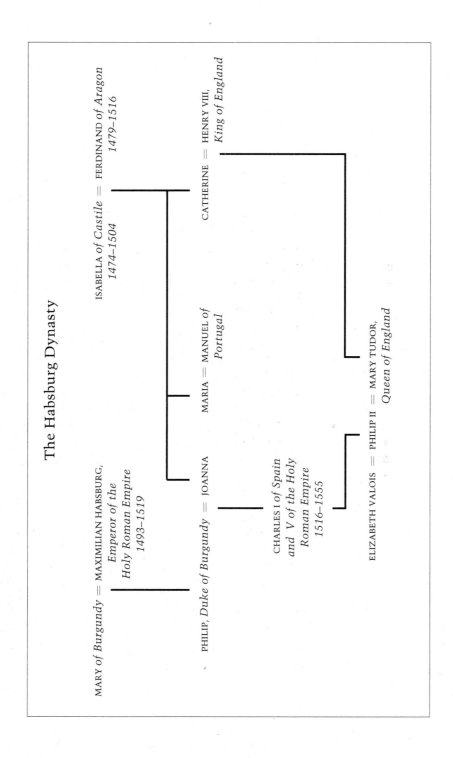

The Habsburg Dynasty

MARY of Burgundy = MAXIMILIAN HABSBURG, Emperor of the Holy Roman Empire 1493–1519

ISABELLA of Castile = FERDINAND of Aragon 1474–1504 · 1479–1516

PHILIP, Duke of Burgundy = JOANNA

MARIA = MANUEL of Portugal

CATHERINE = HENRY VIII, King of England

CHARLES I of Spain and V of the Holy Roman Empire 1516–1555

ELIZABETH VALOIS = PHILIP II = MARY TUDOR, Queen of England

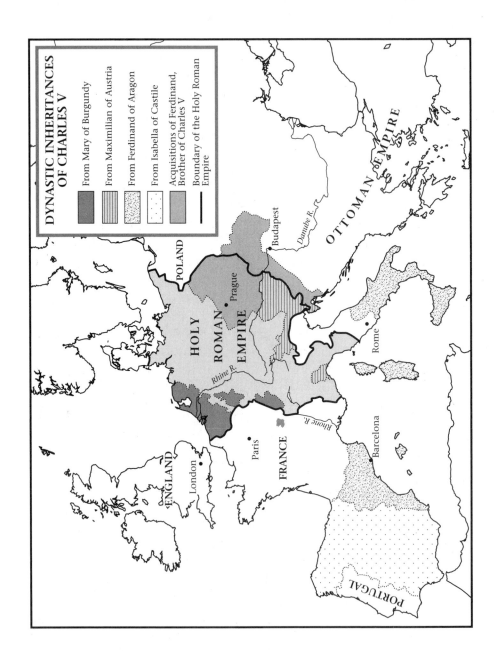

DYNASTIC INHERITANCES OF CHARLES V

From Mary of Burgundy

From Maximilian of Austria

From Ferdinand of Aragon

From Isabella of Castile

Acquisitions of Ferdinand, Brother of Charles V

Boundary of the Holy Roman Empire

OTTOMAN EMPIRE

POLAND

Budapest

Danube R.

HOLY ROMAN EMPIRE

Prague

Rhine R.

Rome

Rhone R.

ENGLAND

London

Paris

FRANCE

Barcelona

PORTUGAL

time joining the pope and the emperor Maximilian of Germany in an effort to curb French pretensions in Italy. When Maximilian died in 1519, however, any idea of countering the French menace was put aside, and the three royal gentlemen of Europe competed loudly for the imperial election and title. Charles, as the late emperor's grandson, was the inevitable winner, and suddenly the immense power of Spain, the Holy Roman Empire, and the Lowlands, together with the Spanish gold and silver of the New World, were united in a single person.

Despite the dangerous preponderance of power in the emperor's hands, Wolsey and his king continued to favor an imperial alliance. In part the decision reflected economic necessity, for Charles could terminate English trade with the Lowlands at will; in part it was habitual, because no one could remember a time when England had not waged war with its long-standing enemy France; in part it was dynastic, for the new emperor was the nephew of Henry VIII's wife, Catherine of Aragon; and in part it was personal, because Charles dangled the bait of a papal election before the covetous eyes of Cardinal Wolsey and his ambitious master. Consequently, in 1522 England found itself again at war with France, but the hollowness of English diplomacy was revealed three years later when it became apparent that a victory for the emperor was tantamount to a defeat for England. In 1525 at Pavia, Charles destroyed a French army and took captive the Most Christian King of France. Italy, and for a moment all Europe, fell before the emperor. England sank from its position as the fulcrum of the European balance of power, to the level of a second-rate principality that was suffered but not seriously considered by the imperial leviathan. The realities of power became obvious in 1527 when imperial troops, sent to Rome to remind His Holiness that he was no longer a French flunkey but a Spanish chaplain, mutinied and sacked the holy city. The situation for Wolsey was serious in the extreme; just when his spiritual master had become the helpless prisoner of Charles's troops, his royal master demanded something that only the emperor or an independent pope could grant: an annulment of his marriage to his fat, sterile, forty-two-year-old wife, Catherine of Aragon.

The King's Great Matter

It is unnecessary to enter into the debate over the king's motives in ridding himself of his Spanish wife and marrying Anne Boleyn.[2] Suffice it to say that almost everyone agreed that the kingdom needed a male heir to secure the succession. Henry may indeed have been sincerely pricked in his conscience because Catherine had been his brother Arthur's wife. The king had violated a clear biblical prohibition with which not even a pope could dispense. But his purpose may also have been considerably

---

[2]Interest in and reevaluation of Anne Boleyn has been intense in recent years. See Eric Ives, *Anne Boleyn* (1988), and R. M. Warnicke, *The Rise and Fall of Anne Boleyn* (1989).

Anne Boleyn, Second Queen of Henry VIII
"His [Henry's] conscience . . . 'crept too near another lady' of the court who refused to become his mistress and who held out for marriage and a crown." *(National Portrait Gallery, London)*

more biological than spiritual; his conscience, in the words of Shakespeare, had "crept too near another lady" of the court who refused to become his mistress and who held out for marriage and a crown. Only three points are beyond dispute. First and most obvious, Henry wanted to marry Anne Boleyn, and to do so he needed an annulment, which only the pope could grant. Second, the succession was endangered by the existence of a legitimate female heir, the princess Mary, and an illegitimate male heir, the duke of Richmond. Finally, the king confronted an inescapable diplomatic dilemma: his wife's nephew was the most powerful sovereign in Europe, and the pope dared not antagonize the man who controlled the silver mines of Peru, the markets of the Netherlands, the military might of Spain, and the destiny of Italy.

In 1527 Henry was in no hurry and was content that Wolsey should accomplish the annulment through the usual diplomatic and military means. The pope first had to be rescued and freed so that he could grant a legal annulment. The only way to achieve this feat lay in alliance with France and war with Spain — but such a policy lasted only as long as there was reasonable expectation that the emperor could be defeated in battle. By the summer of 1529, any such hope had become a figment of the cardinal's desperate imagination, and evidence was mounting that Henry would never get his annulment through the normal channels. Caught between a rebellious king of England and an adamant emperor, the pope procrastinated. He refused to grant Wolsey authority to decide the annulment case in England, but he sent Cardinal Campeggio to open hearings. By late spring, however, Clement VII had decided to "live and die an imperialist," and he dispatched secret orders to Campeggio to "decide nothing, for the emperor is victorious and we cannot afford to provoke him." In July Campeggio commended Henry's case to Rome. The court's ultimate decision became a foregone conclusion when, in August, France and Spain signed the Treaty of Cambrai, leaving Italy to Charles, and Wolsey to face his outraged master. Henry's reactions were ruthless and immediate. Cambrai was signed on August 3, 1529; the cardinal was jettisoned on October 9; and by November Henry had taken the first hesitant steps toward breaking the ancient and constitutional ties with Rome and establishing an independent Church of England.

Wolsey had served his master sufficiently well. In the end, however, the authority that he prized the most — his legatine powers stemming from the spiritual core of Christendom — destroyed him, for suddenly his enemies remembered that his office of papal legate blatantly violated the ancient Statute of Praemunire, which outlawed the acceptance of direct papal jurisdiction in England. For all those who hated him, this fact was enough. The king was no sentimentalist, either. Once the cardinal lost his usefulness, he was without defense, and Henry allowed the law to operate, even though he himself had broken it by sanctioning Wolsey's legatine authority. Had not death intervened, Wolsey might have had to face the charge of high treason.

The king was justifiably perturbed by the course of events. Anne Boleyn continued to refuse him the full enjoyment of her charms, the pope showed every sign of denying his annulment, Charles V remained the obstinate defender of his aunt's marital rights, and Henry still needed a legitimate male heir. This last was the rub that made it impossible for him to listen to the various compromises presented by a pontiff frantic to please both king and emperor. Clement offered to grant a dispensation sanctioning the union of legitimacy and illegitimacy through the marriage of Princess Mary to the king's bastard, Henry Fitzroy, duke of Richmond; he urged Henry to take Anne as his mistress and promised to legitimize the children born out of wedlock; he tactfully suggested that Catherine retire into a nunnery, thus allowing him to permit Henry to remarry; he even toyed with the notion of sanctioning bigamy. But all of these fertile, if questionable, schemes fell afoul of the king's conscience and his determination that his offspring be unimpeachably legitimate. To achieve this end, he needed a legal annulment of his marriage and a legal wife, and these Clement was unable to give.

With Wolsey and his legatine powers gone, Henry sought some new authority to carry out his wishes, and in November 1529 the Reformation Parliament was summoned. The body that met was unprecedented: it lasted seven years; enacted 137 statutes, of which 32 held vital national significance; and exercised an influence in the affairs of God and church that no feudal Parliament had ever dreamed of claiming. The divine and absolute authority of King in Parliament was called forth, and the law, as willed by Henry and proclaimed by Parliament, became "a never erring judge" — the instrument of revolution by which the medieval church was swept away.

In November 1529, there was no real thought of risking a permanent break with Rome, but Parliament, restless in its anticlericalism, seemed to Henry a useful cudgel with which to belabor the pope and possibly frighten that unhappy ecclesiastic into a more amiable frame of mind. In 1530 Parliament enacted a series of statutes aimed at the more obvious clerical abuses. The Mortuaries Act and Probate Act were passed, limiting a lucrative source of ecclesiastical income from the probate of wills and the arranging of funerals. The following year, the king turned on Convocation, the assembly of clergy that served as the church's equivalent to Parliament, and threatened to lay the entire church under ban of outlawry for having violated the Statute of Praemunire in recognizing Wolsey's legatine powers. The threat sufficed to persuade the church to part with £119,000. More important, it supplied the lever by which Henry forced Convocation to acknowledge him as the church's "singular protector, only and supreme lord, and as far as the law of Christ allows even supreme head." In angry silence, bishops and priests submitted, and Archbishop Warham, in presenting the new title, wisely decided to accept silence as the equivalent of assent.

With the church thoroughly intimidated and the potential authority of the king as spiritual as well as temporal leader of the realm acknowledged by Convocation, the government struck at the nerve center of the papacy — its sources of revenue. In the first Statute of Annates of 1532, Parliament gave the king authority to abolish the traditional payment to the pope of the first year's income of all newly installed bishops. Unfortunately, His Holiness remained more frightened of an emperor in his backyard than of a king in distant England, and Henry became convinced that he would have to procure his annulment in defiance of the pontiff. Moreover, patience and time were running short, for Anne Boleyn had finally been lured into the king's bed. In September 1532, she was made marchioness of Pembroke, with an annual income of £1,000; three months later she was pregnant; and on January 25 she was secretly married to the king. If Henry were to be saved from bigamy and his heir born on the right side of the blanket, less than eight months remained in which to divorce Catherine of Aragon.

Chance played into the king's hands, for in August 1532 Archbishop Warham died. Unexpectedly, Henry appointed in his stead an obscure forty-three-year-old Cambridge don who had first come to the monarch's attention for his strenuous, if scholarly, defense of the King's Great Matter, as the struggle for an annulment was termed in academic and diplomatic circles. Both as a man and as one of the heroes of the English Reformation, Thomas Cranmer is difficult to judge, if only because he eventually proved the most timid, backsliding, and reluctant martyr ever to face the stake. Cranmer united a rare literary talent, which could capture in prose the emotional intensity of religion, with a political naïveté that once led Henry to shout out in exasperation: "Oh Lord God! What simplicity have you" to permit every knave and enemy to take advantage of you? Yet the new archbishop's simplicity was his greatest asset, for he alone of the king's servants earned his master's love, and although in theology he shortly passed his sovereign by, the two agreed on one vital tenet: Henry, not the pope, spoke for God.

In the royal mind, the relationship between Henry and his deity was elementary; in return for a punctilious fulfillment of his religious obligations, God rewarded him with material success and eternal salvation. Should such blessings be withdrawn, then Henry assumed that he had inadvertently sinned, had somehow failed to carry out the exact religious formula, and therefore had earned God's wrath. When Catherine failed to secure the succession with a male heir, the king searched his conscience for the source of such divine anger and discovered in Leviticus the terrible warning that "if a man shall take his brother's wife, it is an unclean thing . . . ; they shall be childless" (20:21). God had long ago passed sentence on that marriage, and it was up to Henry to right the wrong and appease his deity, so that he might once again merit all the good things that heaven could bestow. Others might suffer from a sense of their own inadequacies and endure a feeling of sin and undeservingness, but Henry remained serene in the citadel of his faith — as a man, as a Christian, and as a king, he knew God to be his ally. He treated his heavenly partner as he did his earthly colleagues; he expected God to live up to His duty and fulfill His side of the bargain by presenting the king with what he most desired: Anne Boleyn and a legitimate son.

The moment that a frightened and demoralized pope sanctioned the appointment of Thomas Cranmer as archbishop, clerical reformation moved swiftly into ecclesiastical revolution. Before any annulment granted by the archbishop's court could be permanent, the queen's right of appeal to Rome had to be denied. This could be achieved only by cutting the constitutional links between England and the papacy. Therefore in April 1533, one month after Cranmer's installation, Parliament somewhat hesitantly obliged the king by enacting a statute of simple name but of momentous implication — the Act in Restraint of Appeals. By a stroke of the legislative pen, Parliament decreed that all spiritual cases "shall be from henceforth . . . definitely adjudged and determined within the king's jurisdiction and authority" and "not elsewhere." A month later Henry appeared before a tribunal, whose authority now stemmed from the crown, to hear sentence delivered by an archbishop of his own selection. To no one's surprise, the king's marriage to Catherine was declared null and void, and Henry was able to present Anne Boleyn to the world as his lawful wedded wife. When on June 1, 1533, Anne was crowned queen, the final step in a carefully calculated plan was completed. Henry and his ministers had done their best to ensure a legitimate male heir; the rest was up to God and Anne Boleyn, both of whom signally failed in their duties. To "the great shame and confusion of physicians, astrologers, witches, and wizards, all of whom affirmed that it would be a boy," the child who was born at three in the afternoon on September 7, 1533, turned out to be Elizabeth Tudor.

The Royal Supremacy

Henry was outraged that he should have been made ridiculous in the eyes of Catholic Europe. He had risked his crown and endangered his soul, and all he got for his efforts was yet another useless daughter to complicate the succession. A certain amount of consolation could be taken, however, in the knowledge that the child was healthy and the mother fertile. God would not forever withhold His favor; and in the meantime Elizabeth's rightful claim to the throne had to be protected, the break with Rome completed, and Englishmen "reeducated" on the subject of religious and political truth. In the process, a new and pregnant theory of kingship was articulated. During the spring, the king was given authority to make all clerical appointments; a second Statute of Annates severed the financial ties with Rome; papal revenues were redirected to the king's treasury; the pope's name was stricken from the English church's service; and in November 1534 the constitutional revolution was solemnized by the Act of Supremacy, which acknowledged that Henry Tudor was "Supreme Head of the Church of England." The saving phrase, "as far as the law of Christ allows," on which Convocation had insisted four years earlier, was quietly omitted. God and Caesar were joined, and the medieval tenet that divine law stood higher than either man or society vanished when Henry VIII monopolized all secular and spiritual jurisdiction.

More revolutionary yet, the crown was voicing a new perception of its functions and responsibilities. Medieval kings had served as "keepers of the peace and referees of civil behavior"; Henry had now become "the ideological vicar" of his kingdom whose duty was to mold public opinion and root out political and religious error.[3] The government demanded something more than simple obedience to the law. By the Act of Succession of March 1534 and the Act Against Papal Authority of 1536, the crown required all ecclesiastical and state officers down to the level of the village constable and priest to approve openly the break with Rome, to accept Henry's marriage to Anne as "undoubted, true, sincere and perfect," and to take an oath to "repute and take the King's Majesty to be the only Supreme Head in earth of the Church of England." To refuse, to say "that they be not bound to declare their thought and conscience" was high treason. As Sir Thomas More complained to his daughter, a subject was no longer "bounden to the keeping" of the law; he now must "swear that every law is well made." A year later More's fears were realized: "We

---

[3]Christopher Duggan, "The Advent of Political Thought-Control in England: Seditious and Treasonable Speech, 1485–1547" (unpubl. PhD diss., Northwestern University, 1993), p. iv. For the quotations that follow, see pp. 215, 217, 261.

be commanded by the holy Scripture," wrote one of the theorists of Henry's revolution, "to love, to obey and honour our prince not only outwardly in our bodies but also inwardly in our hearts, without any dissimulation or feigning." Conformity of mind now joined control of the body as instruments of state security and unity.

The doctrine of royal supremacy signaled the ultimate destruction of the monasteries. International monastic foundations were an anomaly within a national church, and the crown soon viewed them as seminaries of "factious persons" who recognized at heart, if not at law, an authority higher than that of the state. They constituted a sort of sixteenth-century fifth column and posed a danger to the new ecclesiastical regime. For centuries bishops and archdeacons, almoners, and even simple priests had been in fact, if not in theory, servants of the crown, and the secular church had been the competent and complacent scullery maid of kings. But the monasteries and nunneries were different. They lived by their own rules, they were often exempt from episcopal discipline, and they traditionally advocated papal authority as a convenient balance to prying bishops and interfering monarchs. Although they bowed to the royal supremacy, they did not accept it in their hearts; as one inmate confessed, he acknowledged the king "as supreme head for fear" but "could not find in his conscience" to believe it. A little conscience could be a dangerous thing, and the government decreed that monks and monasteries, nuns and nunneries should go.

The destruction of the monasteries was financially lucrative as well as politically expedient. Between 1536 and 1539, those "putrefied oaks," as one contemporary called the monastic foundations, were cut down, and land worth nearly 2 million pounds was nationalized. In eradicating the monasteries, the state violated divine and human law, for by confiscating nearly one-fourth of all arable land in England, it accomplished, as Bishop Bonner complained, the shameless "breaking of the dead men's testaments, and their most godly intents and ordinances." Godliness, however, was forced to retreat before financial and political need. The treasures of the first Tudor had been consumed by the wars and diplomacy of the second; the royal coffer stood empty; and Parliament, although willing to bless ecclesiastical revolution, as usual hesitated to grant taxes. With the destruction of the monasteries, Henry's income almost doubled, making him one of the richest sovereigns in European history. If he and his children had succeeded in retaining the monastic loot, the English crown might have been assured a sufficient revenue, free of parliamentary purse strings; in that case Parliament might never have found the instrument with which to transform the monarchy into the servant of the landed classes. For better or for worse, however, Henry, his son, and his daughters had to sell the profits of the Reformation, and the monastic lands passed out of the hands of the crown. Country gentlemen who served well the Tudor dynasty profited the most, but merchants, lawyers, corporations, and well-to-do yeomen were all quick to purchase monastic estates from a government that faced bankruptcy.

The legend of a "golden shower" of lordships thrust upon a glutted market at bargain prices has been modified by modern economic research. Evidence indicates that the estates and manors of the monasteries were sold by a government determined and usually able to get a good price. Some property doubtless went to deserving Tudor workhorses and key officials of the shires, but the bulk was sold to pay for the king's wars and foreign policy. The effect, either intentional or accidental, was to commit the governing elements of the realm to the idea of a national church. Although the transfer of the monastic wealth to these groups ultimately destroyed the Tudor monarchy by depriving the crown of an independent landed income, it ensured the permanent triumph of the Reformation, for the most important people in the realm now had a vested interest in protecting property that a return to papal Catholicism might jeopardize.

The man who engineered the break with Rome, and who understood far better than the king the parliamentary means by which the old ecclesiastical constitution was being replaced, was Thomas Cromwell, son of a brewer and blacksmith who had been known for his drunkenness, disorderliness, and illegal commercial practices. In a short but feverish career, Cromwell tried soldiering in Europe, banking in Italy, marketing in the Netherlands, and practicing law in London. After Thomas Wolsey's fall from grace in 1529, Cromwell soon replaced the cardinal as Henry's chief minister, becoming principal secretary in 1534, vicar general in 1535, lord privy seal in 1536, and the architect of the new sovereign and theocratic state. Coldly factual and analytical, Cromwell belonged to that variety of councillor who saw government in terms of efficiency and effectiveness. He endeavored to construct a rational structure of government from the chaos of feudal privilege and overlapping medieval jurisdictions. His fiscal system was indicative of his tidy and categorical mind. For each kind of royal revenue, a separate office was assigned, five courts or departments in all — the Exchequer to collect parliamentary grants and income from the customs, the Court of General Surveyors to administer all crown lands except the duchy of Lancaster (which had its own collecting agency), the Court of Augmentation to administer and milk monastic property, the Court of Wards to oversee the crown's feudal income, and finally the Court of First Fruits and Tenths to administer church revenues. In a possibly more enduring move, Cromwell in 1538 ordered every parish priest to keep a register of births, baptisms, marriages, and deaths. What had stood in the past as a spiritual obligation on the part of the church now became a secular requirement mandated by the state. The vicar general assured a worried kingdom that the government did not intend to use the information to plan further taxation but to avoid "sundry strifes, processes and contentions rising upon age, lineal descents, title of inheritance, legitimation of bastardy, and for the knowledge whether any person is our subject or no." The age of statistics had dawned; knowledge was now viewed as power; and incidentally an in-

Thomas Cromwell, by Hans Holbein the Younger "Coldly factual and analytical, Cromwell belonged to that variety of councillor who saw government in terms of efficiency and effectiveness." *(Copyright the Frick Collection, New York)*

dispensable reservoir of information had been created for later social historians.

Whether the king or his minister inspired the Reformation in England remains one of the most baffling questions of the reign. The two men, one looking as much like an aging professional athlete as a king and the other more like a publican than a vicar general in matters spiritual, embodied different sides of the same coin. Henry "beknaved" his chief councillor twice a week, but Cromwell kept "as merry a countenance as though he might rule all the roost." And rule the roost he did, for Thomas Cromwell became the indispensable technician of the English Reformation, the man who phrased the key statutes that tore apart Christendom, who hammered out the details of the break with Rome, who organized the destruction of the monasteries, and who above all could operate in the new world of rival political and religious factions that emerged once the marriage crisis destroyed Wolsey's monopoly of power. From 1527 on, court and council were torn by the growing discord of factional warfare that reached new levels of bitterness the moment Anne Boleyn won the king's heart, and normal political infighting was joined with the ideological debate over religion.

The king's first great minister, Cardinal Wolsey, had been a priest and a papist; Cromwell was a lawyer and an M.P., whose encyclopedic mind and mastery of parliamentary techniques made possible the king's supremacy. The vicar general, however, was never more than the brains behind the king; unlike the esteemed cardinal, he was no *alter rex*, and Henry himself supplied the willfulness and drive that sustained the revolution. It was accurately stated that the king was determined to "show his absolute power and independence of anyone."[4] Henry's independence could not be relied on, however, for it could prove both capricious and brutal. No one was safe, and both Cromwell and Anne Boleyn played at the risky game of court and religious politics and eventually ended on the scaffold, partly because of bad luck, partly because of factional war, but primarily because of Henry's unpredictable "absolute power and independence."

The new church that was forged in the heat and terror of court and council politics and the bitter struggle between religious conservatives and radicals remained Catholic and orthodox in every particular save one — it was English and Henrician, not Roman and papal. The man who assumed the mantle of ecclesiastical authority was no heretic. In his own estimation, Henry warranted the title of Defender of the Faith as much in 1534 as in 1522, when a grateful pontiff had bestowed the dignity in acknowledgment of the king's diplomatic support and his vigorous attack on Martin Luther. The church needed liberation, not reform, and Henry's ordained task was to free it from the devilish and foreign ministrations of a petty Italian potentate. The king's loyal subjects remained "obedient, devout, catholic and humble children of God." Canon law still had validity in English courts; the rights and authority of the ecclesia to excommunicate remained; and the church continued as an ordained and privileged institution with power to censor opinion, shape the minds of Christians, dictate morals, and, if necessary, withhold the keys of paradise from those judged unworthy of God's salvation.

Henry had "destroyed the Pope but not popery," and ardent reformers, who demanded that the Supreme Head "get rid of the poison with the author," suspected with some justification that "the rich treasures, the rich income of the church, these are the gospel according to Harry." Although "zely people" found the king a sore trial, Henry himself was supremely confident that his religious *via media*, or middle way, was pleasing to God. The structure of his church, which reflected both the spirit of a generation that thought in hierarchical terms and the will of a consummately egotistical sovereign, was depicted in a woodcut showing Henry sitting in his majesty with the hand of God bestowing upon

---

[4]The best summary of the controversy over who planned and directed the Reformation can be found in Chapter 5 in Rosemary O'Day, *The Debate on the English Reformation* (1986). The classic biography of Cromwell is R. B. Merriman, *The Life and Letters of Thomas Cromwell*, 2 vols. (1902). The best modern account is G. R. Elton, *Reform and Renewal: Thomas Cromwell and the Common Weal* (1973).

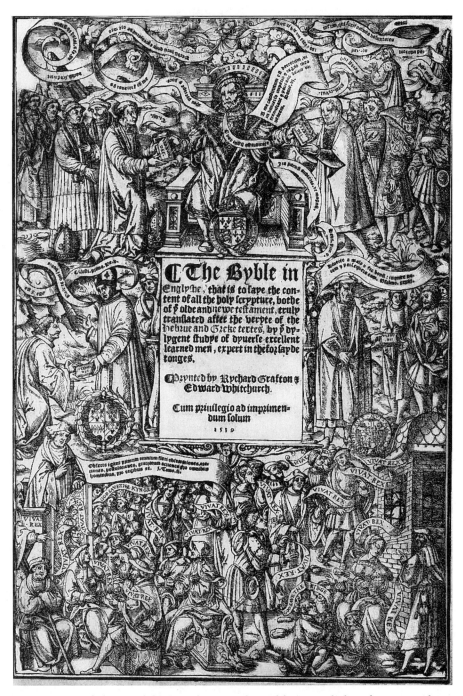

Frontispiece of the Tyndale Translation, *The Byble in Englishe,* of 1539   "The laity . . . loyally reciting: 'Vivat Rex.'" *(Reproduced by permission of the British Library)*

him the Word of God. At his feet in humble supplication kneel the arch-bishops, bishops, and ministers of the church, respectfully listening to Henry's interpretation of God's Word. At the bottom of the picture stand the laity, obediently accepting their faith from on high, believing what those in authority tell them, and loyally reciting: "Vivat Rex." The "wine of obedience" and the "fatness and substance of religion" were carefully equated in a church that remained authoritarian to its core.

Although the church continued to be largely Catholic and unre-formed, the state did not. The Reformation in England called forth the modern leviathan, the sovereign national state. What Henry II had tried, the eighth Henry achieved: the subjugation of an international priestly order that adhered to a spiritual and legal jurisdiction outside of and above the crown. The Act of Supremacy not only gave the monarch the authority of the pope but also expressed a political creed that smashed once and for all the essential international duality of medieval Christen-dom. That Caesar had won over the bishop of Rome in the struggle to monopolize God's representation on earth was nothing new. Caesaropa-pism had existed for centuries in the eastern half of the Roman Empire. What was unique was the organ through which Caesar voiced his will. As the pope spoke through and for the international medieval church, so now the king spoke through and for the state. As the church could not err, so now the state claimed infallibility. The English people were con-fronted with the "new found article of faith" that a statute made by the authority of the entire realm could not be thought to "recite a thing against the truth." The nation-state, above which no power stood higher and which could make or unmake truth on the grounds of *raison d'état* (reason of state), was heralded in the preamble to the Act in Restraint of Appeals. The text read: "This realm of England is an empire . . . governed by one supreme head and king," and the monarch is imbued with "ple-nary, whole and entire power, preeminence, authority, prerogative and jurisdiction to render and yield justice and final determination to all manner of folk."

Such was the story of the King's Great Matter and the break with Rome. Two questions, however, remain. How did Henry get away with a revolution that involved a nationalization of property unparalleled in Eu-rope until the Russian Revolution, that shocked the sentiments of possi-bly two-thirds of the English population, and that defied the sensibilities of all Christendom? And how did he exercise his new authority of "Pope, King, and Emperor" in England?

CHAPTER 7

The Floodgates of Reformation

If there is a lesson to be gleaned from history, perhaps it is the recognition of the perversity of casual relationships. It is astonishing in the extreme that the rage of spiritual battle known as the Reformation should have had its English inception in diplomacy, not psychology; in the accident of marriage, not the design of heaven; in the war of political factions, not the hearts of believers; and in the court of kings, not the house of God. Across the channel in Europe, the anguish of souls in mortal fear lest they fall into eternal damnation led such men as Martin Luther to regenerate and revolutionize the ancient church. When the medieval ecclesia would not or could not give them the spiritual aid and comfort for which they clamored, they turned their backs on Rome, defied its anathemas, and set about constructing for themselves a new and deeply personal spiritual edifice in which they could find contentment. In England the constitutional cart came well before the spiritual horse. Only after an act of state established the church did the floodgates open and a spiritual reformation begin that continued unabated until 1660.[1]

The fact that the English Reformation commenced as a revolution of legal forms and not of religious content goes a long way toward explaining why Henry VIII succeeded in bringing the old church to heel. The break with Rome involved few fundamental doctrinal or ceremonial changes. Except for omitting the name of the pope in their prayers, the English continued to pray and kneel, to worship and think in the old familiar ways. In fact, quite possibly in the more distant shires, humble folk were unaware that any reformation had taken place at all. For the moment at least, Henry had achieved the impossible: he was like "one that would throw down a man headlong from the top of a high tower and

---

[1]The best discussion of the English Reformation remains A. G. Dickens, *The English Reformation* (1964), but his interpretation must be carefully balanced with G. R. Elton, *Policy and Police, the Enforcement of the Reformation in the Age of Thomas Cromwell* (1972); J. J. Scarisbrick, *The Reformation and the English People* (1984); C. Haigh, *The English Reformation Revised* (1987) and his *English Reformations: Religion, Politics, and Society Under the Tudors* (1993); and P. Collinson, *The Birth Pangs of Protestant England* (1988). A splendid summary of the debate over the Reformation can be read in Rosemary O'Day, *The Debate on the English Reformation* (1986). In the Bibliography see "Religious History" for a listing of the many specialized recent works on the Reformation.

bid him stay when he was half way down." Catholicism without the pope was the king's religious solution, a *via media,* or middle way. The chronic problem of the last twelve years of Henry's reign was how to prevent an ecclesia of his own creation from falling further into Protestant heresy or sliding back to Rome.

Debate over the Reformation

There are three ways of looking at the English Reformation. First, it can be viewed as an act of governmental coercion. Religious change was forced onto the kingdom by a willful sovereign and a small court faction of evangelically inclined reformers led by Thomas Cromwell and Anne Boleyn. The realm after all had long since disowned Lollardy, was opposed to the new-fangled Lutheran ideas from across the channel, and was perfectly satisfied with the religion of the past. Second, the Reformation can be perceived as a spiritual and institutional upheaval that had been centuries in the making and that the king took advantage of to cast off Catherine of Aragon and marry Anne. Third, it can be seen as evidence that religious apathy ran rampant, that the spirit of martyrdom in the old church had died generations earlier, and that the vast majority were willing to accept the claims of their king when he said he spoke for both God and his subjects. Like most historical arguments, the truth is not monogenic — all three views are correct depending on which factors are emphasized.

The Reformation in England was certainly an act of state; without Henry's determination to be rid of his first wife, even at the price of a constitutional break with Rome, Protestantism might never have triumphed. Without statutes written in blood, the realm might never have accepted Anne as its queen, Henry as its Supreme Head, or the destruction of the monastic foundations as an act of reform. Had not this government-inspired revolution occurred piecemeal — no one step sufficiently outraging the vast majority of subjects to warrant outright armed rebellion — there might have been no Reformation. The coercion school insists that what little anticlericalism actually existed was directed at individual clerics, not against the concept of a sacerdotal priesthood. Whoring, pluralist priests made excellent propaganda, and Protestant polemists grossly exaggerated their numbers. In short, a responsive, compassionate church, neither institutionally rigid nor spiritually sterile, still maintained its hold on the hearts of the overwhelming majority of the kingdom as it had done in the fifteenth century (see pages 43–45). The driving force, then, for religious change came from (depending on one's preference) either Henry's willfulness or Cromwell's cleverness.

If the coercion interpretation sees the Reformation as an "event," the evolutionary school views it as a "process"[2] that placed the roots of

---

[2]R. O'Day, *The Debate on the English Reformation* (1986), p. 143.

change in the distant past. Such a view relates religious need to social and economic changes, insists on the connection between Lollardy and Protestantism, and links Henry VIII with Henry II. In nationalizing the church, Henry did little more than give statutory recognition to the reality that time and history had passed the old ecclesia by, making possible what Henry II had failed to achieve in his controversy with Thomas à Becket in the twelfth century — the creation of an English ecclesia dominated by the king, not the pope. As a vast, ponderous, and conservative body, heavy with vested and corporate interests, the church of the early sixteenth century was the institutional incarnation of dying medieval cosmopolitanism. Kings and representative bodies had begun to forge special geographic preserves for their own laws and jurisdiction, transforming feudal kingdoms into nation-states and shattering the emotional and cultural unity of Christendom. The international church had lost touch with a generation that was turning away from the seamless cloak of Christ. God was becoming French or English or German; and his vicar in Rome was finding it increasingly difficult to speak so many languages.

From the fourteenth century on, it is argued, Englishmen had been growing resentful of the papacy and of the international character of the church. They darkly suspected that their interests and their taxes were being sacrificed to the aspirations of a foreign potentate residing in Rome. In 1417 the pontiff, Martin V, bestowed a cardinal's hat on Bishop Beaufort of Winchester, the richest subject of the English crown and the half-uncle of Henry V. The pope failed to inform the English king of his decision, and Henry V angrily told his uncle that if he accepted the cardinal's hat, he would have no bishopric to go with it, for he would be deprived of his diocese. Not until 1427 did Beaufort attain the coveted title, and his promotion was bitterly resented by the laity and nobility, who feared that he might support the interests of Rome in preference to those of England. Antiforeign feelings were running so high by the sixteenth century that the stolid English duke of Norfolk informed Cardinal Wolsey, on the occasion of his appointment as papal legate, that he gave not "a straw" for the cardinal's legatine and foreign powers but that he honored him because he was archbishop of York and cardinal within the English church, "whose estate of honour surmounteth any duke now being within the realm." A subject was to be known by his rank within the English hierarchy, not by some intruding authority from abroad.

By the early years of Henry VIII's reign, all the signs pointed to a major crisis brewing between church and state. In 1514 public opinion became so inflamed against clerical pretensions that Richard Fitzjames, bishop of London, had to seek protection for his chancellor, who had been accused of murder. The case involved one of the most tragic mysteries of Lollard persecution. On the morning of December 4, 1514, Mr. Richard Hunne, merchant-tailor and suspected heretic, was found hanging by the neck from a beam in his prison cell. Ecclesiastical officials dismissed his death as suicide committed by a dangerous and deranged heretic, and a court of three bishops and twenty-five lesser clerics decreed that his body be burned. Public reaction was immediate and portentous. It was said that Hunne's arrest for Lollard heresy was nothing but a punishment inflicted on a man who had refused to give up his dead child's winding sheet as a burial fee to the local priest. A coroner's jury, far from accepting the story of suicide, returned a verdict of willful murder against Hunne's jailor and the bishop's chancellor, Dr. William Horsey. By English custom, Horsey would have stood trial before the king's court, but his benefit of clergy would have protected him from any sentence handed down by a secular tribunal. To protect his chancellor from an irate London jury, Bishop Fitzjames called on the king to prevent the trial. The prelate appointed Richard Kidderminster, abbot of Winchcombe, to preach in Convocation a reminder that trying a cleric in a royal court went contrary to the law of God, to the liberties of the church, and to a recent papal decree claiming that benefit of clergy exempted all priests in holy orders from any contact with secular authority. Kidderminster's sermon produced an uproar, and Parliament petitioned Henry to allow a public hearing on the principle of benefit of clergy. The king himself presided and, although the regal theologian remained a loyal and dutiful son of the church, there could be only one decision in such a clash between royal and papal claims. "Kings of England," Henry pronounced, "have never had any superior but God alone." When the young king became Supreme Head of the Church of England in 1534, he simply gave title to what he and his whole generation had known for twenty years.

The insistence by an international ecclesia on a double standard — one for clerics and another for laymen — might have been accepted had not the church exposed itself to the charge of corruption. *Corruption* is an explosive word meaning different things to different people. Is the unchaste priest as corrupt as the judge who accepts a bribe? Is the student who cheats to be compared with the merchant who knowingly sells impure drugs? Was the church of pre-Reformation England as corrupt as righteous reformers claimed? Was it, in fact, a bedlam of fornicating clerics, proud prelates, and unclean ritualists? The heart of the question is a matter not so much of comparing degrees of depravity as of establishing some standard of judgment. The medieval church had aimed high; it had claimed to be the possessor of a better way of life, and men and women tended to judge it in terms of that ideal. The evolutionary explanation of the Reformation maintains that, although the sixteenth-century church may have been no more corrupt than in the past, the laity's expectations of priests and prelates had become higher and its views more critical.

Had Henry faced either an ecclesia with nothing to lose but its spiritual existence or a church backed by the respect of the laity, he never would have risked the break with Rome. Possibly, he would not have even thought of it and would have immediately executed Cromwell as a dangerous and perverted radical instead of waiting seven years. Concern for religion was not lacking, but respect for the old forms was obviously waning when Erasmus could write to an English bishop in support of the

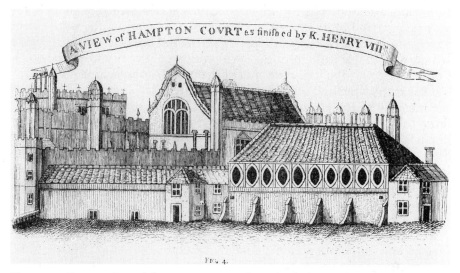

FIG. 4.

Hampton Court   One of the sumptuous palaces built by Cardinal Wolsey and later taken over and rebuilt by Henry VIII. *(North Wind Picture Archives)*

argument that "the expenses laid out on a monastery had better been bestowed on the poor."

As it was, the image of the ecclesia presented to both king and subject depicted Cardinal Wolsey loitering in his lordships and embodying in his person the most invidious clerical abuses. At the apogee of his power in 1527, besides serving as cardinal and papal legate, he was bishop of Winchester, archbishop of York, and abbot of St. Albans, the richest monastery in England. His ecclesiastical revenues approached £10,000, while the profits of justice and the gratuities and pensions presented by foreign princes and humble supplicants in his Court of Chancery raised the total to the princely sum of £50,000 per year. Here, indeed, stood a magnate of the church who would ultimately have to answer for the sin of avarice. Busy with the burdens of state, the cardinal never visited any of the dioceses of which he was bishop, and only at the end of his life did he travel northward for the first time to his archdiocese of York. His legatine authority from Rome gave him the means to sweep clean the ecclesiastical stables, but a man who was in the pay of both France and Spain could hardly be expected to take seriously the abuse of simony.[3] The priest who sired a son and a daughter did not feel obliged to enforce the church's laws of celibacy; the prelate who built sumptuous mansions fit for kings (both York Palace and Hampton Court were taken over by Henry VIII) scarcely had time to relight the dying embers of spiritual zeal within the church; and the man who left the cure of souls to vicars and

---

[3]The sale and purchase of church offices.

suffragans was in no position to criticize his ecclesiastical colleagues for absenteeism and pluralism. Worse, Wolsey used his legatine powers not to reform the church but to extend his personal control, building a vast structure of jobbery, the profits of which flowed into his silken pockets. The cardinal was the living symbol of the proud, unpreaching prelate.

For many men and women, the old church, the Roman church, was the memory of the great cardinal; and the bishop of Rome was nothing more than a Wolsey writ large without the redeeming quality of being English. If the heart of the ecclesia had turned to gold and its soul had been consumed with greed, it is little wonder that few men could be found to defend it. England remained deeply religious but vocally anti-clerical. A Supreme Head in Westminster Palace could be no worse than a cardinal legate in York Palace or a pope in Rome. Moreover, the royal prince was not to be judged by the same standards as the spiritual father. The Supreme Head could not be accused of pluralism, simony, absenteeism, and immorality. Henry made no pretense of a higher way of life. Papal bastards remained the scandal of Christendom, but royal escapades into infidelity neither shocked Christian sensibilities nor weakened respect for the crown. Henry was a man of the world, not of God, and he made no hypocritical claims to a more moral existence.

Signs that the church was faltering in its leadership and losing its hold over the laity were everywhere manifest. In 1510 Dean John Colet decided to place the management of St. Paul's School under the guardianship of London businessmen and not in the hands of the clergy. There was, he said, "nothing certain in human affairs, yet he found the least corruption" in men who lived without hypocrisy by the standards of this world. The same doubts were evident in the economic decline of the monasteries. In Norfolk, Yorkshire, and Buckinghamshire, the capital wealth of the religious foundations between 1480 and 1540, a period of considerable inflation, increased by only 1.13 percent, not enough to offset the normal depreciation wrought by fire, decay, and inefficiency. In Norfolk only £136 or 2.6 percent of the monastic revenues went into the distribution of alms, and in Yorkshire the figure had fallen to less than 0.14 percent. When one of the essential spiritual justifications for monastic establishments was limited to such minimal sums, many laymen began to look elsewhere for other means of fulfilling their charitable aspirations.

A decline in monastic endowments can be attributed, as the coercion school maintains, not to a decline in faith but to a change in taste — establishing chantries and building parish churches intensified, interest in monasteries flagged — but what most convinces the evolutionists that something was wrong with the church is the presence of men and women, righteous in their spiritual strength and adamant in their stand against evil, who saw the Reformation as more than the removal of the pope's name from the liturgy and of the lead from the roofs of monasteries. If the coercionists are correct in viewing the old church as healthy and soul-satisfying, why then the persistence of a small but determined

Lollard underground? Why the magnetic appeal of Martin Luther's revolutionary ideas, which were spreading rapidly at the two most sensitive points of Tudor society — the universities and the court?

The answer offered by the evolutionists is that, throughout Europe and England, the faithful were searching for a sense of spiritual security in the midst of worldly uncertainty. As the zeal of the old church declined and its leadership lagged, the medieval ecclesia could no longer offer the spiritual solace that those of tender conscience so ardently sought. The prescribed formula — a balance between faith in divine grace and good works, whereby the faithful strove to attain salvation — no longer offered certain men relief from sin and the hope of paradise. In Germany Martin Luther in his despair hurled inkpots at the devil and practiced his monastic calling until he was warned that his health could be endangered by such ceaseless prayers, vigils, and mortification of the flesh. "If ever a monk got to heaven by monkery," Luther confessed, "it was I." In England, too, a Cambridge scholar sought to find spiritual comfort by following the rules of prayer to the very letter. Little Thomas Bilney, because "our Lord doth bid us when we will pray to enter into our chamber and shut the door," thought it "a sin to say his service abroad and always would be sure to have his chamber door shut" when saying his matins. But Thomas Bilney could no more shut the door on his doubt and sense of guilt than Martin Luther could close his mind to the same dread, the terrifying fear that he did not deserve God's mercy.

The similarity between the religious anxiety of an English Cambridge student and a German Augustinian monk indicates the general failure of the old forms and rituals, which waxed all the more luxuriant as inward worship and conviction waned. The resemblance between their solutions is equally symptomatic of the universal appeal of the reformed faith; both Luther in his monastery and Bilney in his college turned to the Bible. Quite independently, they stumbled on a profound truth: in hopelessness lies the seed of new promise, in despair is found new consolation. Luther read, "The just shall live by faith"; Bilney read, "It is a true saying, and worthy of all men to be embraced, that Christ Jesus came into the world to save sinners." Suddenly, both Bilney and Luther discovered that it was not necessary to warrant salvation. God's grace stood above justice. No amount of striving, no number of good works, could earn a Christian a place in heaven, for God's mercy saved even the undeserving. Faith and faith alone could move mountains and save sinners, and the reformers of the sixteenth century were above all else men of uncompromising faith.

Doctrinally, the reformed faith stemmed from Luther, but historically the memory of John Wycliffe and his army of simple Lollard followers helped to set the emotional stage in England. Although the fifteenth-century church had in part succeeded in purging the kingdom of overt heresy, it had not been able to fill the void in Christians' souls. During the 1520s, the Lutheran heresy found a receptive audience, especially among Cambridge undergraduates gathered at the White Horse Tavern,

Martin Luther Burning the Papal Bull   "During the 1520s, the Lutheran heresy found a receptive audience, especially among Cambridge undergraduates gathered at the White Horse Tavern, where new ideas were discussed and debated." *(North Wind Picture Archives)*

where new ideas were discussed and debated. Whether Lutheran tracts made converts, or whether dissatisfied but deeply religious and questioning minds like Bilney's discovered for themselves the same wonderful experience that had thrown "open the doors into paradise" for Martin Luther is unclear. Certainly, for the English and for the Germans, Paul's words of encouragement to sinners became "a gate to heaven" and the source of their spiritual strength. For those who found "marvelous comfort and quietness" of soul in Scripture, a profound sense of God's infinite mercy was sufficient to sustain them. They needed neither church nor cathedral, neither image nor ceremony, to fortify them in their conviction. Fervent reformers had no need of a mediator between God and man other than Christ. For the likes of Bilney and Luther, faith alone redeemed them in the eyes of God and inspired them to the Herculean task of living the righteous life. "No man," said the reformer John Hooper, "can possess the joys promised in the gospel, but such as study with all diligence to live after the gospel." This was the inner spirit that three centuries earlier had led men into the monasteries and had persuaded them to give their blood in defense of the church; in the sixteenth century, this passion provided the dynamism that urged them to reform the world.

Although Henry neither approved of the Protestant creed nor liked such "zely people," he well knew their value as militant storm troopers in defense of the royal supremacy. If the king's supreme headship was not to "lie post alone, hidden in the acts of Parliament and not in the hearts of his subjects," he had to turn to those who regarded the political gains of a break with Rome as only a first step toward the spiritual triumph of hurling the pope and all his doctrines out of the realm. Religious radicals quickly became the dangerous but essential allies of the monarchy, and throughout the land they trumpeted the evils of the pernicious doctrines of the bishop of Rome. By 1536 the Church of England and especially the episcopal bench were heavily populated with zealous exponents of royal supremacy, who urged that constitutional revolution by act of Parliament pave the way for spiritual revolution by act of faith.

The third and final interpretation, although it draws from both the coercionist and the evolutionary schools, sees the Reformation as neither an event nor a process. Instead, the third school poses a series of questions. If the early sixteenth-century ecclesia was so robust, why were so few martyrs willing to die for their faith when the crisis of conscience came? If the process of long-term institutional and spiritual change was so profound, why did Protestantism spread so slowly among the public, and why did the new faith's final victory have to wait until well into Elizabeth's reign, possibly as late as the 1570s? The answers to all these questions have to do with religious apathy and the growing Erastian belief that matters of doctrine were best left to the monarch to decide. The evidence is murky and difficult to find, but two points seem clear. First, the largely bloodless nature of the English Reformation can be seen as the product of religious indifference on the part of men and women content to leave decisions of faith to the crown. Historically, the blood of the martyrs had sowed the seed of the early church; self-sacrifice and suffering had been the soul of the old ecclesia. When the spirit of martyrdom died, so died the medieval church. Statistically, the break with Rome, the jettisoning of Catherine of Aragon, the enactment of the royal supremacy, and probably even the destruction of the monasteries would have been voted down resoundingly in a democratic election. Tudor England fervently believed, however, that the better part of society was more capable of leadership than the "more part," and neither part cared enough to defend to the death the institutions of the past. Archbishop Warham was no Thomas à Becket, and the "better part" of the realm concerned itself more with preserving its skin than its soul, and had more interest in the citadel of man than in the City of God. The English, one and all, knew well the adage "Power is present, holiness hereafter."

The second factor to which the apathy school points deals with declining church attendance. This newly researched subject seems to provide evidence not only that the Reformation may have had its roots in religious indifference but also that this apathy was greatly magnified by the

Reformation itself.[4] If we can believe later Elizabethan Puritan ministers, there was mounting outrage that so many — especially the young — preferred the pleasures of the tavern to the spiritual food of the parish church. It would seem then that as the century wore on, Tudor England increasingly bred men like Sir Richard Riche, a devoted government workhorse who perjured himself at the trial of Sir Thomas More, attended to the torturing of Protestant Anne Askew, became a hot gospeler under Edward VI, and returned to the religion of his youth with Catholic Mary, founding a boys' school so that future generations could be brought up in the true faith. He finally resumed his Protestant creed under Elizabeth and personally destroyed the popish ornaments with which he had endowed the chapel of his school. Sir Richard and his generation were content to bend with the variable wind of government policy and political expediency. They agreed with the old gentleman who argued that it was "safest to be of the religion of the king or queen . . . for he knew that he came raw into the world," and counted it folly "to be broiled out of it."

Apathy and expediency were later dignified by the political philosophy of Erastianism. The sovereign who had assumed the papal tiara as well as the royal crown could denounce those who defied his doctrine even more effectively than could the Roman pontiffs; and the Tudors elevated political obedience into a creed sanctioned by God, legalized by statute, and enforced by the engine of the state. The question of whether the king was beyond law and protected by the divinity that "doth hedge a king" involved a political and theological issue left in studied vagueness. Only one consideration prevailed: obedience to the king. "Let no man think that he can escape unpunished that committeth treason, conspiracy, or rebellion against his sovereign lord the king; though he commit the same never so secretly, either in thought, word or deed." Bishop Richard Sampson stated the Erastian gospel of obedience in its most succinct form when he wrote, "The Word of God is to obey the king and not the bishop of Rome."

Acts Written in Blood

Henry could not depend solely on religious apathy to protect his church or on the earnest exponents of religious change who felt close upon them the joys of salvation and the fires of damnation. He knew the truth of the political dictum: "Horror waits on Princes," for "out of subjects' fear groweth Princes' safety." The king was fearful for his own safety as well as that of his church, and he agreed with Bishop Gardiner that "it is better for edicts to be written in blood than in water." The instruments of terror forged to strike fear into the hearts of subjects and to hold the

---

[4]R. Whiting, *The Blind Devotion of the People: Popular Religion and the English Reformation* (1989).

timid to a proper respect for the new church were twofold: the Act of Succession passed in March 1534 (see page 124) and the Act of Treason enacted in December of the same year. The first was essentially a loyalty test; the second vastly extended the meaning of treason to include the malicious wishing, willing, or desiring the king's death by word or deed, calling him a heretic, tyrant, or usurper, or seeking to deprive the royal family of "the dignity, title or name of their royal estate." The most famous of Henry's subjects to fall victim to these statutes was Sir Thomas More.

When Wolsey fell from grace in 1529, More succeeded him as lord chancellor. The appointment was heralded as the dawn of a new era in which the philosopher-statesman would guide the realm toward a utopian existence, for Sir Thomas More was England's most distinguished scholar and humanist. As the king moved closer to revolution, his new lord chancellor grew increasingly alarmed and finally resigned his office in May 1532 on the pretext of ill health. As far as More was concerned, the principle at stake was not the king's marriage, nor even the defiance of Rome, but his own unwillingness to acknowledge the state as the be-all and end-all of human existence. For More the realm, the crown, Parliament, and even the law were subject to the common conscience of all Christendom. In annuling his marriage to Catherine and separating his church from Rome, Henry violated the unity of Christendom, the common heritage of western Europe. "I cannot perceive," More wrote in

Sir Thomas More "For More the realm, the crown, Parliament, and even the law were subject to the common conscience of all Christendom." *(The Granger Collection)*

1534, "how any member thereof may without the common assent of the body, depart from the common head." A thousand years and more of history became for Sir Thomas sufficient proof that God's Word was indeed enshrined within the body of the old church. More's view was medieval and historical, and it ignored the new impulses of nationalistic fragmentation and the realities of Machiavellian politics. Many men must have felt as More did, but few died for such a philosophical and historical concept. Most agreed with the worthy dame Alice More, who scolded her husband when she visited him in the Tower: "I marvel," she said, "that you, that have always hitherto [been] taken for so wise a man, will now so play the fool as to lie here in this close and filthy prison and be content to be shut up among mice and rats, when you might be abroad at your liberty."[5]

A determined minority enforced a religious, political, and economic revolution, and scholars still debate the extent and danger of the conservative reaction. The opposition was not limited to Sir Thomas More, Bishop John Fisher, and a handful of monks, all of whom were executed in 1535–1536. It was endemic throughout the land as the habit of obedience and respect for established authority deteriorated in the wake of an officially sponsored revolution. The government's response was swift and brutal. Between 1532 and 1540, some 489 were accused of overt rebellion, of whom 266 were executed, 23 fled, 23 were acquitted, 96 were pardoned, and 39 had their cases dropped. In addition, 394 other Englishmen were investigated for treason by word; of these 63 were executed, 14 acquitted, 12 pardoned, and 184 dismissed before their cases came to trial. Revolutions inevitably exact a high price, and, judged by the bloodbaths of modern times, the break with Rome cost surprisingly little in terms of human blood. Nevertheless, the memory of those 329 souls executed for treason remained the underlying element of the Reformation, for as Bishop Bonner confessed, "Fear compelled us to bear with the times, or otherwise there had been no way but one." That one way was the path of martyrdom. Bonner and his colleagues learned their lesson well when in 1540 they were presented with the proof that Henry's *via media* would be written in blood. In that year, three Catholics were butchered as traitors for questioning the royal authority in matters spiritual, and three Protestants were consumed in the fire as heretics for questioning the tenets of the catholic Church of England. The French ambassador was aghast at such terrifying justice and wrote, "It was wonderful to see adherents to the two opposing parties dying at the same time, and it gave offense to both."

---

[5]The bibliography on More, the humanist, the martyr, the statesman, and the social scientist, is mountainous. A start can be made with R. W. Chambers, *Thomas More* (1948); J. H. Hexter, *More's Utopia: The Biography of an Idea* (1952); R. Ames, *Citizen Thomas More and His Utopia* (1949); A. Fox, *Thomas More, History and Providence* (1982); R. Marius, *Thomas More, a Biography* (1984); and L. L. Martz, *Thomas More, the Search for the Inner Man* (1990).

In maintaining Catholicism without the pope and in demanding that the man cast down from the high tower stop halfway, Henry confronted a serious dilemma: was not the pope's doctrine the pope? Was not all that had been sanctioned and exploited by the papacy corrupted and desecrated through that association? If the pope had been proved false and satanic, how could Englishmen be sure that such an antichrist had not also been leading them into damnation by preaching a false doctrine about such matters as purgatory, the sacrificial mass, and the veneration of saints and images? "The pope's doctrine is the pope," said William Turner to Bishop Gardiner, "and ye hold still the pope's doctrine, ergo ye hold still the pope." Henry VIII had no intention of accepting the doubtful logic of such a syllogism or of permitting impudent inquiry as to whether "the state of our religion" after 1,500 years "be established in mere idolatry." The *via media* of Catholicism without the pope faced peril from both the right and the left, and after 1536 the government was absorbed in closing the floodgates of change and in enforcing the royal supremacy on a people deeply troubled by growing religious dissension and bitterness.

The Pilgrimage of Grace

The first shock came from the right. In the late summer of 1536, Lincolnshire and Yorkshire rose against a Tudor regime that had encroached on the ancient privileges and provincialism of the feudal north and against a Tudor church that had callously torn asunder the corporate unity of Christendom. In Yorkshire the rebels called themselves the Pilgrims of Grace and placed badges on their arms depicting the five wounds of Christ. For a moment it appeared that the life expectancy of the newborn national state would be short, for the rebellion seemed capable of reaching London. Fortunately for Henry's government, the two uprisings were badly coordinated. Moreover, the rebels knew better what they did not want than what they hoped to achieve. The pilgrimage was essentially the culmination of widespread antagonism to every aspect of the Tudor regime. The badge of religion produced the appearance of unity, for all malcontents could unite in defense of the monasteries and the old church. Beneath the surface, however, divergent social interests weakened the pilgrimage and gave the government time to arm. The old feudal nobility, men who lived in the tradition of the Nevilles and the Percys, were aggrieved that their family prerogatives and ancient privileges were being infringed upon by a professional bureaucracy in London, which had established a district office in the northern shires — the King's Council for the Northern Parts. The Northern barons and gentry complained that their traditional right to be represented on the king's council was being usurped by commoners and parvenus, and that a blacksmith's son held sway where once nobles of ancient lineage had guided the realm and advised the king. Lesser folk were agitated by high taxes, and the peasants felt themselves threatened by the steady encroachment of enclosures, which the government would not or could not prevent.

Henry VIII in Later Life   "The King's wrath is death." *(Reproduced by permission of the British Library)*

The immediate cause of the Pilgrimage of Grace was the publication in July 1536 of the Ten Articles. Of all the Henrician religious formulas, these missives reflected most strongly the growing influence of reformers frantic to purge the church of both pope and popery. The articles cut the traditional seven sacraments to three, and accepted Protestant ideas about the uselessness of prayers for souls in purgatory. One of the most persistent demands of the rebels was the return of the missing four sacraments. Henry was merciless in his handling of the Pilgrimage; his vanity was outraged by "rude commons of one shire" and the "most brute and beastly of the whole realm," who had dared to defy God's viceroy on earth and had failed to learn the truth of the dictum: "The King's wrath is death."

The monarch, however, was not blind to the dangerous discontent behind the rebellion. The moment that it was crushed, he turned to the question of religious uniformity, for now that he had assumed the authority of the bishop of Rome, he was responsible for the faith of his flock. Three turbulent years passed, however, before the king's heavy hand made itself felt, years during which "simple loving subjects" spent their time "arrogantly and superstitiously" debating theological niceties and religious novelties with ever-increasing vehemence in taverns and alehouses. When one impassioned but impractical reformer could advocate the reading of Scriptures in a brothel, while an equally dogmatic defender of the old faith wanted to see the heads of all the reformers impaled on stakes, it was obviously time for the Supreme Head of the Church of England to speak out so that his obedient subjects might know the truth and live in concord and quiet. The difficulty was that diplomatic and marital problems continued to bemuse and befuddle the purity of religious policy.

Religion, Matrimony, and Diplomacy

England's only allies were the Lutheran princes of Germany but, as long as the stubborn and historic rivalry between Valois France and Habsburg Spain dragged on, Henry judged his crown and his supremacy relatively secure. Unfortunately, the diplomatic kaleidoscope continued to shift with senseless regularity, and at home the threat of disputed succession continued to hang over the kingdom. Anne Boleyn had produced a future queen, but the princess Elizabeth in many sensitive minds remained a child of sin and bastardy. Worse, Anne failed to fulfill her obvious wifely and royal duty by presenting the king with further live children. Whether Henry again cast his eye on a lady of the court or whether, having risked so much for a male heir, he determined to try again is not clear; but once the king had set his mind on a new wife, he called upon the ever-efficient Cromwell to resolve his problem, and Anne's destruction followed with terrifying speed. On January 8, 1536, Catherine of Aragon finally died, and Henry, dressed in brilliant yellow, celebrated the occasion with a festive ball. The old queen's death signaled the demise of the new queen.

With both wives dead, Henry could remarry and no one could claim the union illegal or the results born in sin. Within three weeks fate struck Anne the final blow — she delivered a dead baby on January 29. By May she had been accused of high treason and adultery, and on May 19 she was executed.

For Anne, Henry had performed miracles, taming the ancient and arrogant church and transforming a medieval dragon into a modern pet; but marriage to the lady had proved to be neither fruitful in the bedchamber nor tranquil in the parlor. Anne Boleyn was a better mistress than queen, and she allowed the breath of adultery to touch her married life. The charges of adultery and incest with her own brother were patently false, but the queen on occasion had acted with indiscretion, and she soon learned that in royalty a double standard existed. Kings could cut extra-marital capers with impunity, but queens could not be touched by even a hint of infidelity, lest the legitimacy of their children be placed in doubt. Eleven days after Anne's execution, on May 30, 1536, Henry married once again. This time he chose Jane Seymour, who fulfilled her nuptial vows to be "bonair and buxom in bed and at board." Although she died from the consequences, she gave birth on October 12, 1537, to the future Edward VI.

With Anne Boleyn dead and the succession secured, it seemed that the king might be able to settle the religious issue to his liking — in a highly orthodox fashion. In May 1539, Parliament was called upon to fulfill the ultimate logic of the English Reformation. For the first time in history, the faith of the kingdom was determined by the authority of the sovereign national state in the guise of statutory law. The Act for Abolishing Diversity of Opinion reavowed transubstantiation,[6] communion in one kind, celibacy of the clergy, private masses, and auricular confession. All five points had been issues of growing controversy. Each was decided in a strongly Catholic manner and accepted by a realm that was still overwhelmingly conservative and that viewed the bill as the "wholesomest act ever passed."

Conservative and orthodox as these measures were, they did not stand alone, nor could they be divorced from diplomatic considerations. The Act of Abolishing Diversity of Opinion remained largely unenforced during the period when it was wise for England to appear less Catholic and more Lutheran. Throughout 1539 Henry was alarmed by the thought of diplomatic isolation and by the possibility that France and the emperor might patch up their ancient feuds and turn on the schismatic enemy, England. For the moment, the danger was so great that conservatism in religion was put aside, and the king allowed himself to be stampeded into an alliance with the Lutheran princes of Germany and marriage with Anne of Cleves in January 1540. The instant, however,

---

[6]The doctrine that the bread and wine used in celebrating the mass actually change into the body and blood of Christ even though their appearance remains the same.

that Francis and Charles proved that they disliked one another more than they disliked their cousin Henry, the king returned to the conservative position. In July Thomas Cromwell paid with his head for having dragooned Henry into the German marriage alliance with Anne of Cleves. His mistake was not simply a diplomatic one, for if any man symbolized the forces of change and reformation, it was the king's vicar general in matters spiritual. Consequently, when Henry determined on orthodoxy in religion, his minister was sacrificed to satisfy the conservative party. Within days of Cromwell's death, Anne of Cleves was divorced and became instead Henry's "loving sister." On July 28, 1540, the king married Catherine Howard, the protégé of the conservative faction at court. Mistress Catherine lasted eighteen months and left at her execution nothing but a broken, white-haired sovereign of fifty-two, who had grown suddenly old from the knowledge that his vivacious teenage wife, the apple of his elderly eye, was not, after all, "a rose without a thorn." Catherine proved to be no virgin before her marriage and a dangerously silly, if not overtly adulterous, woman afterward. She paid for her carefree delinquencies with her life in March 1542, and a law was passed making it illegal henceforth for a maiden who was not a virgin to wed the monarch, a limitation that, the French ambassador acidly noted, excluded most of the ladies of the court.[7]

The concluding years of Henry's reign were taken up in warring with France and Scotland, prescribing religious truth for his subjects, marrying a respectable widow who could double as nursemaid for an unpredictable and increasingly difficult old man, and preparing for the day when the king must die. In Catherine Parr, Henry found his most dutiful, if least romantic, spouse; and in war he sought distraction from the afflictions of old age — gout, obesity, an ulcerated leg, and general weariness. Again the king's forces triumphed, and at the Battle of Solway Moss in November 1542, English troops routed the army of yet another Scottish sovereign. James V died, it was said, of shame at the behavior of his soldiers. He left behind him a six-day-old heiress, Mary Queen of Scots, Henry VIII's grandniece and the lady whose manifest charms, questionable intrigues, and legal claim to the Tudor throne bedeviled both Scottish and English history for most of the century. In France between 1543 and 1546, Henry was also victorious, but his military efforts ultimately had but one lasting consequence: the expenses of war forced him to part with a substantial portion of his monastic riches, which were snapped up by those harbingers of a future political system, the landed country gentlemen.

In religion, as well as war, the aging monarch exercised his will, but the results were equally ephemeral. In the *King's Book*, published in 1543

---

[7]Henry's many wives can be neatly recalled to mind by reciting the following:

Divorced, beheaded, died;
Divorced, beheaded, survived.

Mary   *(National Portrait Gallery, London)*

Edward   *(Royal Collection Enterprises Ltd.)*

and carefully scrutinized by the royal eye, the Supreme Head of the Church of England presented his final opinion on religious matters. The new document was largely Catholic in creed and antipapal in sentiment, and it placed heavy emphasis on obedience. The proper role of Christians living in this world, as far as Henry was concerned, was to live "soberly, justly and devoutly." The king reminded his people that God "hath ordered some sort of men to teach others, and some to be taught," and that the surest way to heaven lay along the path of obedience to "such order as is by us and our laws prescribed."

Religious sobriety lasted only as long as the king, and the *via media* of a Catholic church without the pope came to an end almost the moment that the huge and bloated sovereign died on January 28, 1547. Henry left behind him subjects of many minds who, oddly enough, had one thing in common — they had loved this bulging bully of a king, whose single redeeming quality of great personal magnetism had held both Catholics and Protestants loyal to his person. Neither that godly imp Edward VI nor his neurotic half-sister Bloody Mary was ever able to

The Three Children of Henry VIII "The time to worry had arrived, for a new generation was about to take control."

Elizabeth *(The Lord Chamberlain's Office)*

command the same devotion. Henry's church, the anomaly of a Catholic ecclesia to which had been grafted the royal supremacy, ultimately rested on the king's massive personality. Now, in the new year of 1547, a child-king sat on the throne. During Henry's lifetime, men of conservative inclination, like Bishop Gardiner, had feared "not these fond malicious follies" of the Protestant reformers, but "when those that now be young shall . . . win a contempt of religion," then was the time to worry "what is like to ensue thereof." In 1547 the time to worry had arrived, for a new generation was about to take control.

Uneasy Equilibrium

1547 to 1603

On preceding page: THE SPANISH ARMADA OFF THE ENGLISH COAST   By Cornelis Claesz vom Wieringen (detail). *(E. T. Archive)*

CHAPTER **8**

The Little Tudors

That serene and invincible prince, Henry VIII, was dead. Most of his political life had been consumed in begetting a legitimate heir. In the winter of 1547, the moment of truth arrived: could the monarchy that he had sacrificed so many lives and consciences to secure and the church that he had created withstand the crisis of succession when a boy and two women stood in line to inherit the crown? What followed proves two interrelated, if somewhat contradictory, propositions: that the secret of efficient government in the sixteenth century depended heavily on the personality, adaptability, and forcefulness of the sovereign, and that the Tudor state was surprisingly resilient and capable of surviving in rapid succession first a Protestant child-king, then a middle-aged Catholic queen, and finally another female ruler in the person of Elizabeth Tudor. Henry's religious settlement was destined for a generation of frantic and sometimes bloody fluctuation, but in England there emerged no wicked and usurping uncles, no overmighty magnates who could seize the throne in their own right, and no successful rival claimants to the crown who could use the war of opposing truths to overthrow the Tudor dynasty. Most subjects remained loyal to the children of the old king, even when they or those who spoke for them introduced policies that a sizable majority of the kingdom opposed.

The Lord Protector[1]

The succession of that godly imp, the nine-year-old son of Jane Seymour, had been established by parliamentary statute in 1543 and by his father's last will and testament. Henry bequeathed the crown imperial first to Edward, then to his daughters Mary and Elizabeth, and finally to the offspring of the marriage of his sister Mary and his old friend Charles Brandon, duke of Suffolk. Significantly, the children of his elder sister

---

[1]D. M. Loades, *The Mid-Tudor Crisis, 1545–1565* (1992), is an excellent survey of the period. W. K. Jordan, *Edward VI*, 2 vols. (1968, 1970), is the best study of the king and his reign. Northumberland, Paget, and Somerset have attracted considerable scholarly attention. See B. L. Beer, *Northumberland* (1974); S. R. Gammon, *Statesman and Schemer: William, First Lord Paget, Tudor Minister* (1974); M. L. Bush, *The Government Policy of Protector Somerset* (1975); and D. E. Hoak, *The King's Council in the Reign of Edward VI* (1976).

Margaret, who had married James IV of Scotland, were not included in the succession. Henry's testament was more than a bequest; it was a constitution. The ferocious personality of the old sovereign was replaced by a council of sixteen "entirely beloved councillors" who were empowered to govern the realm during the young king's minority, and Edward was strictly enjoined by his father never "to change, molest, trouble nor disquiet" his legally appointed advisers. More remarkable still, the autocratic old monarch named no single man to rule the kingdom but instead imposed a strict majority rule on a council of regency, composed of absolute equals. Henry's purpose is in doubt, but he had good cause to fear that once the dark shadow of his own authority had vanished, the regal sapling would bend beneath factional intrigue and religious strife. The Tudors had come to the throne in the wake of the deaths of the two Yorkist princes murdered, according to sixteenth-century historians, by their uncle and protector. It remained to be seen whether sixty-two years of Tudor rule had sufficiently revitalized the crown so that it could withstand another Edward and another minority.

The dead lion was no match for the live jackals. Within four days of Henry's death, his will was violated, his most dire pronouncements were ignored, and the young king's uncle Edward Seymour was elevated by the council to the office of lord protector and governor of the king's person. Most men agreed that a protectorate was "both the surest kind of government and most fit" for the commonwealth, and that no man had a better right to the office of lord protector than the new king's uncle, who was now created duke of Somerset. It was by no means certain, however, whether even a protectorate could replace the prestige of royalty and give direction to a country suddenly liberated from the will of a despotic monarch and beset with a host of political, diplomatic, religious, and economic problems.

The keystone of Tudor governmental structure lay in the existence of an active royal authority that could determine policy and fill the bureaucracy with vitality. Devoid of leadership, the Tudor regime tended to rot; the medieval tradition that government offices were more a private sinecure than a public trust and that royal finances served more as a personal source of profit than a governmental responsibility still thrived in such places as the Exchequer, the Chancery, and the Court of Augmentations. Personal loyalty to the monarch, heavily fortified with fear of the king's wrath, had instilled a reasonable degree of honesty into Henry's government. Respect for the old king had derived from an almost atavistic fear that Henry, as God's lieutenant on earth, could scrutinize and root out the secret treason hidden in the reaches of a subject's heart, and on the conviction that the wages of disobedience were the soul's damnation. In puny contrast, Seymour was simply the king's maternal uncle, merely a man of "fit age and ability" to rule in Edward's stead. No Tudor blood coursed through his veins, no divinity graced his person, and respect for his office was solely contingent on his personal ability to win esteem and exercise leadership.

The Tudors: 1485–1603

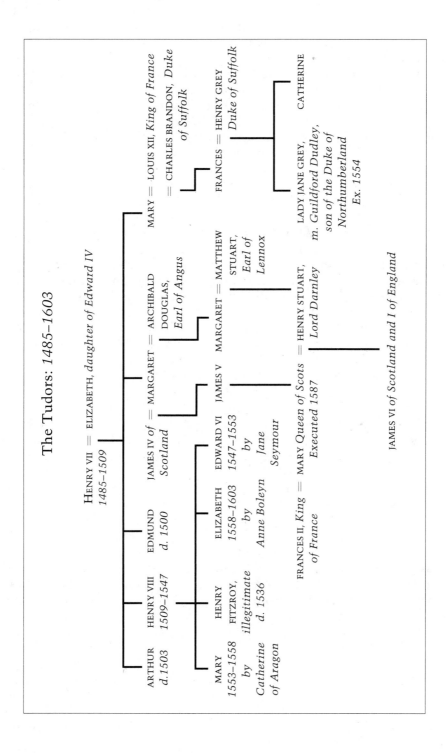

In theory the authority of the Tudors stemmed from God, but in reality their power rested on the cooperation of subjects who were constantly bullied and cajoled but who always could be inspired by the presence of the king. Henry once called himself "a father and nurse to his subjects," and in a way all the Tudors regarded themselves as governmental nannies appointed by a higher authority to rule, but ultimately dependent on the devotion of the children in the nursery. Henry, on occasion, could become almost oriental in his aversion to his rebellious and thankless subjects, whom he threatened to make "so poor that they could not have the boldness nor the power to oppose him." Yet for all his grumbling, the old king had relied on their goodwill. No Tudor possessed a standing army or the usual instruments of coercion; Henry knew that when the chips were down, he held power and sovereignty, as Erasmus sagely remarked, "by the consent of the people." He may have scolded and even shocked his subjects, but he rarely forced them to do what was not already in their hearts.

With Henry gone, the duke of Somerset stood *in loco parentis* (in place of a parent). Unfortunately, for the endurance of his rule, the new lord protector proved himself a man of mercy but not of tact, and a far better soldier than politician. The protectorate was totally divorced from the symbol of regality, and it never capitalized on the loyalty and allegiance owing to the prince who sat on the throne. Unwilling to rule by the heavy hand of tyranny, and innocent in his belief that reason and goodwill were sufficient instruments of government, Seymour sanctioned disobedience, permitted corruption in government, and failed to stifle the strident voice of factionalism.

If Edward VI's reign indicates that the Tudor regime floundered when deprived of a popular, vigorous, and divinely ordained leadership, the period also reveals another facet of sixteenth-century life: that discord was anything but dead. Although the structure of Tudor government may have withstood the passing of an autocratic and divine prince and his replacement by a protectorate of human contrivance, it could not resist the encroachment of political and religious factionalism. The ghost of feudal feuding had never been permanently laid to rest, and it tended to reappear in different guise. The overmighty magnate of the previous century was no more dangerous to the well-ordered kingdom than the country gentleman of the sixteenth century, bent on the enclosure of land, or the London clothier, greedy for further profits in the booming wool trade. The proud prelate who had once claimed the special sanction of God was no more difficult to handle than the earnest reformer willing to sacrifice state and church, concord and obedience, to achieve the kingdom of heaven on earth. The spirit of feudal anarchy would not be buried permanently until a single political-religious faction had won complete control of government and society. Two generations of Stuart ineptitude, six years of civil war, two decades of republican interregnum, and a Glorious Revolution would have to pass before a single element — the landed country gentleman in league with the city lawyer, the town merchant, and the country parson — managed to establish firm oligarchical rule.

The Failure of Foreign Policy: France and Scotland

The new protector faced problems that stemmed from a combination of his own personality, the uncertain nature of his office, and the economic and religious burdens bequeathed to him by the old king. The most immediate troubles of the new reign concerned matters of foreign and military policy. The last years of Henry's rule had seen wars with France and Scotland that had not been permanently concluded on the king's death. The lord protector quickly proved his worth by smashing the Scottish forces at the Battle of Pinkie in September 1547. The victory was never followed up, however, and Somerset's handling of diplomacy revealed a basic flaw in his character: He could conceive but never execute; he could start but never finish. The protector lacked the essential characteristics of any ruler who must act as his own prime minister — attention to detail, careful planning, and endless hours of crushing labor. Instead, he was a genial and politically naïve gentleman, whose training and experience were largely military. Thrust into high office by the accident of marriage, he ruled over a government composed of office-seeking suitors, unscrupulous and land-hungry colleagues, and puritanical and militant religious reformers. He lacked both the ruthlessness and the political finesse to control such a wolf pack. He allowed the fruits of victory at war to wither away and did nothing to prevent the young princess of Scotland, Mary Queen of Scots, from being sent to wed the dauphin of France, thus joining in marriage England's most dangerous enemies. In his handling of France, the same fatal weakness prevailed. Somerset did little to prevent the outbreak of hostilities in 1549; he did nothing to strengthen the defenses of English holdings along the French coast; and his religious policy at home antagonized the emperor, the only man in Europe who could have helped in a war against France. The lord protector never realized that Protestantism in religion necessitated peace with France at any price; and, conversely, that friendship with the emperor required caution and orthodoxy in religion.

Religious Turmoil

The duke of Somerset's religious inclinations are difficult to gauge because conviction, either in religion or in politics, was not a strongly developed quality in any of the Edwardian ministers of state. Whatever his personal faith, the lord protector associated himself with the reforming party, and he opened up the court and the king's schoolroom to the Protestant creed. The young king had been brought up by tutors already tainted with reforming ideas, who had not dared influence their royal protégé during his father's life; but once Henry was dead, they transformed

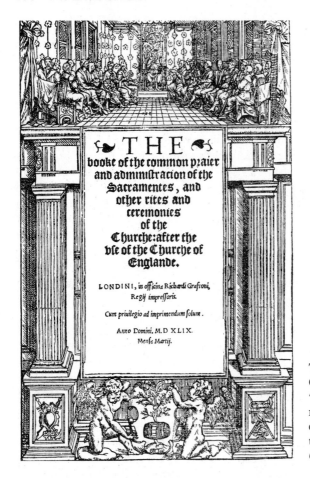

The First Book of Common Prayer, 1549
"Although a literary masterpiece, [it] turned out to be a religious catastrophe." *(The Mansell Collection)*

Edward into a thorough-going, unremitting radical. The moment the new government repealed the Henrician treason and heresy laws in November 1547, England became a haven for continental heretics, and the clamor for religious reform rose to deafening proportions. The heart of the theological controversy involved the ancient ceremony of the Eucharist, and every alehouse and tavern, pulpit and street corner, became the forum for a debate in which all was either "as black as pitch, vice, abomination, heresy and folly" or "fair roses and sweet virtue."

Somerset reacted to the mounting discord by reestablishing spiritual conformity slightly to the left of the old Henrician *via media* and concocting a religious formula that would be sufficiently broad to satisfy all but the militant extremes in both the Catholic and Protestant camps. The crucial question centered on the nature of the mass: Was it a miraculous ritual in which the bread and the wine were actually transformed into the body and blood of Christ, whose sacrifice was reenacted each time the ceremony was performed, or was it a commemorative service in which no change occurred except in the hearts of the communicants and which only brought to mind Jesus' sacrifice for humanity? The new Prayer Book of 1549 offered a simplified version of the ancient liturgy and a verbal revision of the Eucharist that deliberately left the exact nature of the mass in doubt. For a moment it seemed as if the Prayer Book, which was predominately the work of Archbishop Thomas Cranmer, might become the basis for a new religious settlement. Even the conservative and outspoken Stephen Gardiner, bishop of Winchester, announced his compliance, pointing out that the book was capable of a Catholic interpretation. Therein, however, lay the trouble, and the radical reformers were disgusted by a settlement that so openly threw "ambiguous expressions before posterity." In the end the Prayer Book, although a literary masterpiece, turned out to be a religious catastrophe; and the humane Act of Uniformity, enacted to enforce it, proved totally ineffectual. Protestants continued to clamor for further reformation, and peasants in the southwest of England rose up in revolt, calling for a return to the good old days of Henry VIII.

Economic Trauma and Social Upheaval

Had religion stood alone without the coincidence of economic crisis, the lord protector might have managed to ride out the storm of contention and rebellion. Two interlocking economic forces, however, reached their apex during Edward VI's reign — inflation and prosperity. The flood of specie pouring in from the New World during the decade of the 1540s nudged prices up. But the cost of war during Henry's final years, along with his debasement of the currency, plus the velocity of monetary circulation in the wake of commercial expansion, touched off an inflationary cycle that strained the Tudor economy beyond endurance. During the last years of Henry's reign, the government extracted approximately £650,000 from direct taxation, another £799,310 by selling monastic lands, and some £363,000 by reissuing the coinage. Even these unheard-of sums, however, failed to meet Henry's military needs, and he left his son a deficit of £75,000. The pressure of debasement and the cost of war doubled prices between 1547 and 1549. By August 1551 there was so much debased coinage in circulation that the council was forced to establish the value of a silver shilling at six pence, half its original value but approximately its true silver worth. Individuals who found their coins suddenly devalued by half suffered severely, for the government made no effort to exchange worthless currency for sound coins; it could not have afforded to do so. Pensioners and schoolmasters, landlords and clerics, all trapped by fixed and customary rents, and government officials dependent on the historic fees of their office faced economic annihilation. As a way out, landlords turned to the enclosure of lands (see pages 80–83); government minions, to corruption; pensioners, to patronage; and schoolmasters and clergymen, to vocal but ineffectual complaint.

Debasement of the coinage produced the added hysteria of economic boom because English woolens could be purchased in Europe with uncorrupted specie at bargain prices. The woolen industry grew monstrously. The livelihood of possibly one-third of the population depended in some fashion on the manufacture and export of woolen cloth; and the entire economic health of the realm was at the mercy of a foreign market exposed to the vagaries of world commerce, dynastic wars, and the caprice of princes. By 1549 the howl of protest from peasants being evicted by merchant landlords and gentlemen farmers, who were anxious to profit from the unprecedented expansion, began to meet a receptive response among a small and idealistic group of men at court known as the commonwealth faction. Joining economic conservatism and religious radicalism, the commonwealth men were impassioned and doctrinaire exponents of an organic, balanced, and self-sufficient body politic in which famine prices, capitalistic greed, enclosures, and a swollen wool trade dependent on a foreign market had no place. Economic and religious reformers agreed that avarice and idolatry must be banished from the realm. Bishop Hugh Latimer spoke most loudly for outraged economic justice and religious righteousness, railing against proud and unpreaching prelates in their cathedral palaces, rent-raising landlords in their lordships, and profit-taking merchants in their countinghouses: "You landlords, you rent-raisers, I say you steplords, you unnatural lords, you have for your possessions yearly too much."

If Latimer was the propagandist who struck at the moral decay of the kingdom, John Hales in the House of Commons was the political theorist who hit directly at wool merchants and enclosing landlords. He challenged the authority and endangered the economic well-being of the group who monopolized the Commons and who filled the offices of justices of the peace throughout the shires. That the lord protector was himself a commonwealth man is most unlikely, but he gave his blessings to Hales's Subsidy Act of 1548 and the Enclosure Commission of the same year. The first decree was a levy on sheep aimed at shifting the tax burden to those most capable of paying and at rectifying the widening imbalance of an economy in which farmlands were giving way to sheep runs. The second decree was a moral crusade to enforce already existing but largely ignored legislation against the enclosure of land, and to ensure that enclosing landlords pulled down their hedges and returned their stolen acres to the village commons. The two measures were disastrous to Somerset and the commonwealth party, for they not only antagonized the landed and mercantile classes but also inspired the "poor commons" to revolution. When Latimer preached that landlords and rent-raisers had "yearly too much," he inadvertently sanctioned the demands of peasants who bitterly resented the actions of the rich in raising rents and enclosing the commons. At the same time, the appearance of the Enclosure Commission during the summers of 1548 and 1549 gave the peasantry the idea that the "Good Duke" was their guardian angel and would approve their taking the law into their own hands.

In the summer of 1549, Somerset's theological and economic policies sparked Catholic religious revolt in Cornwall and Devon, and Protestant economic sedition in Norfolk. The Devon uprising was in the best tradition of provincialism and instinctive reaction to change, but Ket's Revolt, as the Norfolk rebellion was called, smacked of religious communism, something that struck fear into the ruling classes. "It is not agreeable with the Gospel," stated one champion of the underprivileged, "that a few persons shall live in so great abundance of wealth and suffer so many of their Christian brothers to live in extreme poverty." A scared but determined gentry struck hard at such advocates of a social system that directly opposed the Tudor doctrine of political, social, and economic inequality and hierarchy. Both revolts were promptly put down with sufficient ease to make one wonder whether the importance and strength of the commonwealth appeal for social and economic equality rests more in the mind of the twentieth-century historian than in the public consciousness of Tudor England. In the eyes of landlords and merchants, however, the duke of Somerset was responsible for governmental ineptitude, mismanagement, and policies that seemed to have led directly to social and religious rebellion. In a palace revolution in October 1549, he was arrested and deprived of office; two and a half years later, he was executed on a trumped-up charge of treason. His real crimes, however, had been his popularity with the unwashed multitude of Tudor society and his mishandling of the affairs of state.

The Wicked Earl

The man who engineered the protector's destruction was his one-time colleague-in-arms, John Dudley, earl of Warwick. The reign of Edward VI is usually presented in terms of stereotypes — Catholic versus Protestant, idealist versus realist, the good duke versus the wicked earl. Somerset has had his impassioned apologists, but almost no one has ever had a kind word to say for Warwick. He assumed power not so much by talent as by default, and he brought to high office both the strength and weakness of the military mind. He preferred action to inaction, he was always willing to gamble on luck if he could not think of a ready solution, and he constantly took the shortest route to a given objective regardless of the consequences.

Uniting a highly developed instinct for political survival with an absolute determination to establish himself and his family as one of the great landlords of the realm, Dudley headed a governmental faction consisting of earnest Protestant reformers and unscrupulous court elements who coveted the wealth of the church. These strange political bedfellows had but a single creed in common — that clerical wealth and lordships were harmful to God's church. The earl never took the office of lord protector. Instead, he assumed the title of duke of Northumberland and ruled through his influence over the twelve-year-old Edward, who was declared by law to be of age and who was allowed to go through the pretense of ruling, sitting in the council, and being consulted in weighty matters of state. The way to the king's heart was financial — he was given control over his privy purse, something his uncle had never seen fit to do. In his own eyes, Edward had come of age, and Northumberland assiduously fostered this notion; Somerset, to his cost, had continued to regard his nephew as a small boy scarcely out of the nursery.

Purifying the Church

As early as 1547, the Spanish ambassador noted that a royal commission was sent out to inspect all English bishoprics and had orders to "examine the clergymen and inquire into their knowledge, manner of life and income." He concluded that it "may well turn out that the question of income is the principal one." The truth of his prophecy was soon revealed. The attack on church property commenced under the lord protector with the destruction of the chantry lands, but this was a policy left over from the previous reign and followed logically from Reformation theology. The case against the chantries was clear: chantry priests, who prayed for souls who had not managed to make it into heaven but had achieved that level between hell and paradise known as purgatory, had lost their spiritual reason for being. The estates that financed such superstitious practices deserved to be confiscated and put to more secular and political uses. Full-scale plunder of the ecclesia, however, did not get under way until the rise of Northumberland. The Henrician bishops had for the most part been allowed to retain their offices under Somerset, but after the lord protector's fall in October 1549, the surge of religious revolution quickly swept them off the episcopal bench and into the Tower as disobedient subjects of the crown. They were replaced by men who advocated high thinking and simple living for the episcopate. At a vastly reduced income, Nicholas Ridley followed Edmund Bonner in the see of London; John Ponet succeeded Stephen Gardiner in the richest bishopric in England, accepting a government salary of £1,300 in lieu of his predecessor's episcopal income of £3,000; and Coverdale of Exeter managed with £500, one-third the usual revenues of the see. The plunder of the bishoprics peaked in 1551 when Tunstal, bishop of Durham, was deprived of his office. No one was appointed in his place, and the revenues of his diocese were swallowed up by Northumberland.

Religious radicals gladly returned the church to its primitive poverty, but they were shocked that religious reform should provide the cloak behind which avarice and economic greed could operate. On the other hand, the Northumberland gang was fully aware that doctrinal purification was a necessary prelude to territorial looting. They, therefore, supported the extreme Protestant position that the mass was a commemorative service, that priests were biblical and moral teachers, and that the church should be returned to its original ceremonial purity. By the new Ordinal of 1550, the divinely ordained priest became a parson appointed by government patronage, and in 1552 a revised version of the 1549 Prayer Book ended any pretense at compromise with Catholicism. The clergy were required to wear plain surplices at mass instead of ornate

Catholic robes, stone altars were pulled down to make way for movable wooden communion tables, and household bread replaced the consecrated wafer. In the same year, a second Act of Uniformity passed, which, unlike its predecessor of 1549, threatened the most dire punishments for nonconformity and nonchurchgoing. The government seemed determined to chastise moral turpitude in humble folk, even if it condoned corruption in high office.

Kingmaking

From the start Northumberland tried to conceal the partisan and factional nature of his government with the pretense that young Edward had come of age. The king had grown from a small and impish lad, who always did his best and thanked his tutors for telling him his faults, into a precocious and rather terrifying young man obsessed with a royal sense of duty and a strait-laced Puritan conscience that would never allow him to "set light God's will" merely for the sake of expediency. Edward's governors had done their work well and had shaped the Tudor clay into the image of an Old Testament prophet — upright and just but devoid of humanity. At sixteen, Edward died in the odor of biblical sanctity. "O Lord God," he cried, "save Thy chosen people of England. O my Lord God, defend this realm from papistry, and maintain Thy true religion."

Edward's approaching death produced a dynastic and religious crisis that remains to this day one of the most baffling episodes of the sixteenth century. Northumberland has been pictured as the evil duke who had no intention of leaving the defense of God's chosen people to the deity. The traditional explanation is that he had tied his political star to a frail and consumptive boy. When in January 1553 Edward's doctors told him that the king had "a tough, strong, straining cough" and was pining away, Northumberland realized that he could save the "true religion," not to mention his own neck, only by barring the succession of Catholic Mary and launching forth on the risky game of kingmaking. By law, by blood, and by rightful inheritance, Mary Tudor stood next in line to the throne, but she was a Catholic and a woman. Northumberland persuaded the dying king to devise a new order of succession whereby both Mary and Elizabeth were declared illegitimate and the crown was willed to Lady Jane Grey, Henry VIII's grandniece, a fervent Protestant and, most important of all, Northumberland's daughter-in-law. With a certain amount of judicious rephrasing of Edward's "Device for the Succession" and a great many threats, the duke bullied the judges into accepting the change and cajoled the council into acknowledging Lady Jane as Edward's lawful heir. All this maneuvering was done in the nick of time, for on July 6, 1553, Edward died, his sputum "livid, black and fetid," his feet swollen, and his body smelling "beyond measure."

More recently, another interpretation has emerged that casts the duke in the role of a confused, desperate, and ailing politician confronted with a dying but religiously fanatical sovereign who demanded that his

Lady Jane Grey   "The crown was willed [by Edward VI] to Lady Jane Grey, Henry VIII's grand-niece, a fervent Protestant and, most important of all, Northumberland's daughter-in-law." *(Mary Evans Picture Library)*

"chosen people of England" be saved from his papist sister and her sa-tanic horde. Northumberland faced an impossible situation: browbeat the council into accepting Edward's own device for changing the succes-sion and thereby commit treason in the eyes of the Catholic majority of the country; or do nothing, permit Mary to succeed to the throne, and thereby install in power a lady who regarded him as the leader of every-thing she most detested.

Whoever was responsible, the plot to divert the succession was short-lived. At the crucial moment, the duke was overcome with a strange and fatal lassitude. Probably he was ill, possibly he sensed the futility of his desperate plan, for he failed to take the one step that might have ensured the success of his scheme: he allowed Princess Mary to slip through his fingers and proclaim herself the rightful queen of England. Northumber-land had also reckoned without one vital factor — loyalty to the Tudor line as well as to the crown. The days of kingmaking had ended; most people felt satisfied that Mary was a Tudor, and very likely a large major-ity were delighted she was Catholic. Her faith, the confusion surround-ing her legitimacy, even her sex, were of no consequence compared to the fact that she was her father's daughter and had been bequeathed the crown imperial by parliamentary statute and the old king's will. Almost without dissent, the kingdom rallied to her, Northumberland's army melted away, the council acknowledged her as queen, and the duke humbly apologized for having defied the divinity of Tudor monarchs. In nine days the reign of Lady Jane Grey was over.

Mary Tudor (1553–1558)

The new queen had endured disgrace, humiliation, submission, headaches, fits of melancholia, and palpitations of the heart. She had suffered a surfeit of stepmothers, some callous, some silly, some abusive. What Mary could not forget, however, was the knowledge that she had betrayed her mother's memory and the church that had upheld the legitimacy of her birth. Unlike Bishop Fisher and Sir Thomas More, she had hesitated and at her father's command had taken the Oath of Supremacy. Now, as queen, she was determined to do penance for that moment of weakness and to turn the clock back to those golden days when her mother had reigned as undisputed queen of England, her father had been a dutiful and loyal son of Rome, and Mary herself had danced at court, fresh-faced and free of troubles.[2]

For all her many redeeming qualities, which led contemporaries to judge her "a prince of heart and courage, more than commonly is in womankind" and modern historians to describe her as "the most merciful of all the Tudors," the queen at thirty-seven was an anachronism. Time had passed her by. She passionately sought to return her errant and unhappy land to the bosom of a church that bore little resemblance to the ecclesia of her youth. The corrupt and comfortable papacy of Clement VII had died in the fury of religious wars, and by 1553 both Catholics and Protestants denied absolutely the argument that no matter what their religious creed "men who live according to equity and justice shall be saved." The light laughter of Erasmus's humanism and the tolerance of More's *Utopia* had no place in the stern world of Cardinal Caraffa, who, as Inquisitor-General of the Roman Inquisition, had advocated "burning men as well as books," and who now wore the papal tiara as Paul IV. The ranks of Catholicism had closed: either one was counted among the true believers or one belonged to the devil's camp. Religious strife, persecution, and atrocities on both sides had polarized the two faiths, engulfing any middle ground where men of moderation might seek understanding and accord. The hopelessness of Mary's vision of a world sans heresy, sans doubt, and sans discord was evidenced by the sterility of her means: her fruitless marriage to Philip of Spain, the use of fire to purge her church of error, and her dependence on ecclesiastics even more out of touch with reality than she was. Nevertheless, it is

---

[2]The classic work on Mary remains H. F. M. Prescott, *Spanish Tudor* (1940), revised as *Mary Tudor* in 1952; but see also D. Loades, *The Reign of Mary Tudor* (1979) and *Mary Tudor: A Life* (1989). The revisionist school is summarized in R. Tittler, *The Reign of Mary I*, Seminar Studies in History, 1983.

just possible that she might have succeeded had her kingdom not staggered under poor harvests, disease, inflation, and a losing war, and had a benevolent deity seen fit to allow her a longer reign — she was given just over five years. Mary, indeed, fulfilled her epithet: "daughter of misfortune."

The fervent welcome accorded Henry VIII's Catholic daughter convinced her that the past could be resurrected and the Roman church restored. At first the queen's policy followed the cautious lines laid down by Stephen Gardiner, the wily bishop of Winchester, who had exchanged the cold stone of a prison bench for the lord chancellor's soft woolsack. Four years of imprisonment under Edward VI had left their mark, but in 1553 Gardiner still remained more a politician than an ecclesiastic, more a governor of men than a healer of souls. Both he and Emperor Charles V cautioned Mary to go slowly; the Reformation would have to be unmade as it had originally been made, legally by act of Parliament. For the first years of Mary's reign, all sides practiced tolerance and rehabilitation. Only Northumberland and two of his closest colleagues lost their lives for playing at kingmaking; the queen's council was enlarged to include all important men of moderate faith and politics; and distinguished Protestants were allowed, and on occasion even encouraged, to flee the realm. (The duchess of Suffolk took five weeks to make her way from London to Gravesend.) The church was purged of its married clergy, but if Protestant parsons quietly put away their wives, they were allowed to serve as priests in parishes where their lapses into sin were unsuspected. Finally, in October 1553, an obliging House of Commons reversed the annulment of Catherine of Aragon, absolved Mary of bastardy, and repealed the Edwardian Reformation. Catholicism without the pope was reinstated, but further than this Parliament would not go, and Mary had to live with her satanic title of Supreme Head of the Church of England. She even found it necessary to exercise its hated authority to cleanse the church and reintroduce the old ritual.

Two barriers blocked the path to reunion with Rome: opposition to Mary's marriage to Philip of Spain and the fear that spiritual absolution might entail the return of the monastic lands. On the first point, the queen remained adamant, proving that she had both her mother's Spanish pride and her father's savage willfulness. Against her councillors' advice, her Parliament's determined opposition, and her country's dislike of "proud Spaniards or strangers," she set her aging heart on Archduke Philip, heir to the Habsburg domains and the son of her mother's champion, the emperor Charles V. "She would," as she informed her Commons, "choose as God inspired her," and on July 25, 1554, Philip became king of England by grace of his marriage to Mary Tudor.

On the subject of the church lands, Mary was less firm and more politic. She accepted the argument of expediency: guaranteeing the riches of the church to their secular owners was a small price to pay for the spiritual salvation of her realm. Only after property owners in both the Lords and the Commons had been assured on this point did Parliament in November and December 1554 repeal the Act of Supremacy, petition for reunion with Rome, reinstate the old heresy laws authorizing the crown to enforce orthodoxy with fire and sword, and lift the ban of treason against Cardinal Reginald Pole, who brought back with him to England the pope's absolution for twenty years of schism and heresy. Even more than his cousin the queen, Cardinal Pole represented the past. For over a generation, he had suffered exile and privation as a consequence of both his faith and his blood, for Reginald Pole was not only the leading English Catholic prelate but also the grandnephew of Edward IV and one of the last remaining Yorkist claimants to the English throne. Spiritually as well as dynastically, he belonged to an England that was vanishing.

Sedition and Heresy

Pole arrived in England, as he said, "not to destroy, but to build; to reconcile, not to condemn," but both queen and cardinal "with bitterness of heart" soon discovered that heretical opinions everywhere ran rampant, and that a policy of love and moderation only encouraged the devil to greater acts of sacrilege. By the end of 1554, it was becoming painfully apparent that papal absolution had brought not blessed relief from sin but further sedition.

Even before Pole arrived, the government had been presented with a clear lesson in the dangers of trying to turn back time. In her determination to marry Philip of Spain, Mary had blinded herself to the disappearance of those diplomatic and economic considerations that had originally produced the Anglo-Spanish alliance under Henry VII. The collapse of the wool trade with Antwerp in 1551–1552, although it spawned poverty and depression, had liberated England diplomatically from dependence on the foreign power that controlled the Low Countries. Spain, with its disciplined legions of tough Castilian peasants and its golden treasures plundered from Mexico and Peru, was becoming the military leviathan of Europe and the champion of resurgent Catholicism. English merchants who encountered Iberian maritime and commercial power in the Mediterranean and Caribbean began to wonder whether Spain, not France, might be the real enemy.

The English were notoriously uncivil to foreigners, and when Philip's emissaries, sent to settle the treaty of marriage, made it clear that they regarded England as a pestilent land of heretics and barbarians, anti-Spanish feeling erupted into rebellion. In January 1554 three thousand Kentish men rose against the threat of a Spanish king and a popish mass, and marched on London. Their leader, Sir Thomas Wyatt, was a gentleman of parts, and his presence was a dangerous indication that the rebellion was no aimless agrarian revolt or a senseless explosion of class hatred and revenge. The natural leaders of Tudor England as well as the many-headed multitude concealed treason in their hearts and, had London been less loyal, Wyatt more swift, or the queen less resolute, Mary might have lost her throne. As it was, the magic surrounding the Tudor dynasty held firm. The queen was magnificent; she stayed on in London, and with the usual Tudor flair for words rallied the city to her defense. "What I am," she cried, "ye might well know. I am your queen, to whom at my coronation . . . you promised your allegiance." Therefore, "good subjects, pluck up your hearts, and like true men, stand fast against these rebels." When Wyatt swept up to Ludgate, he found it closed, held by men loyal to the Tudor line. Without the city, the rebellion withered and died. Wyatt knew full well the penalty for unsuccessful treason and paid the price. But two others also paid with their lives for his ill-starred venture: less than a week after Sir Thomas entered the Tower, Lady Jane Grey and her husband, Guildford Dudley, walked out to their execution. The princess Elizabeth fared better. She also was a threat to her sister's crown and church, but Mary's reluctance and King Philip's caution saved her, even though Bishop Gardiner begged to be given authority to gather evidence of her treason and complicity in the Wyatt rebellion.

When Mary exhorted her brave Londoners to stand fast, she had also told them that should she "leave some fruit of my body behind me to be your governor," she trusted that such a blessed event would be of great comfort to the realm. In this expectation Mary reckoned without a virulent and vocal minority of Protestants who had the audacity to nail to the palace gate the defiance: "Will you be such fools, oh! noble Englishmen, as to believe that our queen is pregnant; and of what should she be, but of a monkey or a dog."

The Smithfield Fires

The futility of turning back the hands of time was revealed in the misguided conviction that the old church could best be served by fire and brimstone. Patience, forbearing, and loving understanding had proved their uselessness when confronted by obstinate heresy and sedition. Safe in Geneva — the haven of exiled Protestants from every kingdom in Europe — John Knox, that Moses of Scotland, thundered dreadful curses against women in regal office, declaring Mary "a wicked woman, yea a traitoress and bastard" and encouraging the English to cast out the Jezebel. At home the godly translated his advice into action: a priest had his nose cut off, and rebels set a church in Suffolk on fire while mass was being celebrated inside. Wyatt's rebellion and the actions of Protestant extremists seemed proof that heresy and treason marched hand in hand and that heretics waited impatiently to overthrow those two bastions of all good government: law and religion.

Had Mary burned fewer heretics and hanged more traitors, she might never have earned the censure of later generations. The judgment of history has rested on a somewhat doubtful distinction: bloody is the sovereign who sets fire to men's bodies to cleanse their souls; politic is the monarch who hangs and mutilates to preserve the state. Mary, however,

The Execution of Thomas Cranmer   "The futility of turning back the hands of time was revealed in the misguided conviction that the old church could best be served by fire and brimstone." *(The Mansell Collection)*

thought otherwise; she deemed it worthier and better for her future reputation that it be known and recorded that Archbishop Cranmer died for his heresy to God rather than for his treason to her throne. Toward rebels, the queen showed herself unusually merciful; toward subjects disobedient to God she could administer only justice, which clearly stated that such obstinacy deserved death at the stake. Except for the handful of Protestant leaders who died early in 1555, it is difficult to fix the responsibility for burning close to 300 men, women, and children. Currently, it is fashionable to depreciate the horror by presenting the sorry statistics of persecution elsewhere in Europe — 6,000 heretics burned in the Low Countries by Charles V, almost as many executed in France by order of Francis I and his son Henry II, 800 witches burned in Savoy, 199 sorcerers punished in Venice, and under Elizabeth I of England 125 persons tried for witchcraft and 47 executed. The ugly figures merely indicate that the sixteenth century reviled heretics and sorcerers as murderers of the soul who deserved death just as surely as criminals who destroyed the body. Some authorities place the blame on Bishop Bonner of London, others prefer Cardinal Pole or the queen, and still others speak of the spirit of an age that accepted it as a "work of cruelty" against both God and man to nourish heretics within the commonwealth.[3]

Wherever the ultimate responsibility may lie, the immediate decision in 1555 rested with Stephen Gardiner, who argued the belly wisdom of his old master, Henry VIII: that laws enacted in blood endured longer than those written in ink. The lord chancellor always had more interest in outward political obedience than in inward spiritual conformity, and he reasoned that the agonizing spectacle of men dying by slow fire would destroy the religious ardor of even the most courageous and render them obedient. He sensed that the Protestant radicals were in a state of disarray. Protestantism, associated as it was with plundering of the church and economic greed, seemed to be morally and spiritually bankrupt. Moreover, God had obviously expressed his disapproval of the reformers under Edward by permitting that Protestant Joshua to die young and by replacing him with a Catholic queen. Finally, Gardiner was convinced that the majority of the kingdom remained loyal to the old faith.

The first martyrs were a select half-dozen who were sacrificed to politics, not God. Cranmer, Ridley, Hooper, Latimer, and two others were ordered to face the fire in the expectation that they would fail to play the man, or that the sight of their suffering would discourage those of weaker spirit. In adopting such a policy, Gardiner proved to be as unrealistic as his queen. He totally underestimated the spiritual strength that led martyrs to endure with a smile the torments of the stake, in preference to risking their immortal souls in the agony of everlasting damnation. "Wily Winchester" could never comprehend the words of Dr. Rowland Taylor, who rushed to the fire exclaiming, "Now I know I am almost at home . . . and I am even at my Father's house!" Far from frightening lesser men, the sight of such conviction encouraged those of weaker hearts to become martyrs.

Within the year Gardiner sickened of the Smithfield fires and died questioning the wisdom of enforcing heresy laws at the stake. Once the flame had been lit, however, it was difficult to put out. During Wyatt's rebellion, a number of religious prisoners in the Marshalsea had been offered a chance to escape; but they had refused their freedom, stating that "as we came in for our consciences, and [were] sent hither by the council, we think it good here still to remain till it please God to work our deliverance . . . ; whether it be life or death we are content." In the face of such Protestant obstinacy, a kind of administrative exasperation set in. Spiritual conviction lay beyond argument or reasoning. The law required that such folk be destroyed, and in lieu of any other solution, there was

---

[3]The question of ultimate responsibility remains open. See W. Schenk, *Reginald Pole* (1950); P. Hughes, *The Reformation in England,* vol. 2 (1954); and D. M. Loades, *The Reign of Mary Tudor* (1979). Whatever one's religious preference or historical favorite, John Foxe's Book of Martyrs (*Acts and Monuments,* 1563) remains the classic and impassioned account of the Protestant tribulations.

Philip and Mary, by Hans Eworth "Mary's marriage was as sterile as her religious policy." *(By kind permission of the Marquess of Tavistock and the Trustees of the Bedford Estates)*

nothing to do but proceed with the grisly policy of purging the kingdom with fire. If, as is sometimes said, "sterility was the conclusive note of Mary's reign," it lay primarily in the dreadful truth that nobody was able to think of anything but the stake as a way of handling heresy.

Mary's marriage was as sterile as her religious policy. The union had grown out of the queen's determination to recapture the past, and out of Charles V's willingness to sacrifice his only legitimate son to a middle-aged spinster for the sake of Habsburg diplomatic policy. In the century-old Habsburg-Valois rivalry, the entrance of England into the Spanish imperial fold completed the encirclement of France and ensured the vital sea link between the emperor's most valued possessions — Spain and the Netherlands. From Charles's dynastic view, the marriage served a crucial purpose; from Philip's more intimate perspective, the union was something less than a success, and Spaniards blatantly wondered what their king could "do with such an old bitch" who was ten years his senior. Although Philip did his father's bidding, he felt that "it would take God himself to drink of this cup," and, despite the queen's prayers, he remained in England for only a year and a month. He returned to Mary only once again, in March 1557, to claim his reward: England's participation in the most recent flare-up of hostilities between Spain and France. In

June, against the advice of her council and the threats of the pope, who had allied himself with France and excommunicated her husband, Mary dragooned her reluctant kingdom into a war for which it felt no liking and for which it was financially and spiritually unprepared. The ultimate fruit of her marriage was not the child for whom the queen had shed so many tears and offered so many prayers, but the loss of Calais, the last English possession on the continent.

The final verdict on a woman who was deeply compassionate but who died branded with the epithet of "Bloody" was passed by the English chronicler Ralph Holinshed when he said that the queen had not "the favor of God, nor the hearts of her subjects, nor yet the love of her husband," and therefore God had sent her a short reign. She died on the morning of November 17, 1558, just twelve hours before Cardinal Pole. Mary had grown old, sick, and disillusioned in the struggle to make a vision come true. The dream had turned into a nightmare, and her stout subjects greeted the news of her death with jubilant ringing of bells and blazing bonfires. The prayer book that had been her constant companion was found to be tear-stained at the two places where her failure had proved most complete — the prayers for the unity of her church and for women bearing children.

The fifteenth century had been plagued by Plantagenet fertility; ironically, the sixteenth suffered from Tudor sterility. The offspring of lusty King Hal seemed lacking in the crucial qualities of survival: good health and fecundity. Henry's sons — Edward VI and Henry Fitzroy — both died of consumption in their teens; now Mary had perished childless and unmourned at forty-two. It only remained to be seen whether the last of the old monarch's children, the princess Elizabeth, would fare any better.

CHAPTER 9

Elizabeth of Good Memory

The role of womankind in sixteenth-century Europe was perfectly clear; in sermon, book, and Bible it was stated that women were frail, foolish, and inferior. Their ordained function was to bear children "till they die of it; that is what they are for." Without doubt God had created man to rule, and it was a wife's duty "if she saw her husband merry, then she was merry; if he were sad, she was sad." In 1558 this secure order of things was upset by an abundance of ladies who failed to fit the conventional pattern. In France, England, and Scotland the realms were afflicted with what John Knox called that enormity of nature — "the monstrous regiment of women." It was against all human and divine law that "a woman should reign and have empire above men." Yet Mary of Guise served as regent of Scotland; Catherine de Medici would soon become regent and queen mother of France; Mary Stuart ruled as queen of Scotland; and Elizabeth Tudor succeeded her sister on the throne of England. No one questioned that such an unnatural and undesirable situation would create discord, inconstancy, and civil strife. The regent of Scotland died in the midst of civil war; Catherine de Medici bequeathed to her heirs a kingdom convulsed by religious conflict and human atrocities; and Mary Stuart perished on the execution block. Only Elizabeth proved an exception to the rule, and Englishmen were quite certain that the cause lay with the special interference of God and the divine genius of their sovereign lady.[1]

Elizabeth I (1558–1603)

"Vain but acute" was the judgment passed by one observer of the new queen. Her vanity was forgiven as one of the natural weaknesses of her

---

[1] J. E. Neale, *Queen Elizabeth* (1934), remains an aging classic. E. Jenkins, *Elizabeth the Great* (1958), and P. Johnson, *Elizabeth I: A Study in Power and Intellect* (1974), are modern efforts to improve on Neale. L. B. Smith, *Elizabeth Tudor: Portrait of a Queen* (1975), is a short biographical essay. Equally short and topically organized is C. Haigh, *Elizabeth I* (1988). The most recent work is A. Somerset, *Elizabeth I* (1991). By far the best political study of the reign is W. T. MacCaffrey's trilogy: *The Shaping of the Elizabethan Regime* (1968); *Queen Elizabeth and the Making of Policy* (1981); and *Elizabeth I: War and Politics 1588–1603* (1992). Two new studies are useful: S. Bassnett, *Elizabeth I: A Feminist Perspective* (1988), and M. Perry, *The Word of a Prince: A Life of Elizabeth I from Contemporary Documents* (1990).

sex; her acuteness was regarded as a gift from heaven usually reserved for men. Whatever the role of the deity in the making of a queen, Elizabeth at twenty-five proved an experienced student of political survival in an age that had seen her mother executed for adultery, her uncle for incest, and her cousin Lady Jane Grey for treason. Under Edward VI she had romped with the lord protector's brother, Thomas Seymour, only to discover that his favors were given with calculation and his motives touched with treason. Under Mary she had bent with the papal wind but found that her mere existence posed such a threat to her sister's throne and faith that she could not blame Mary if, out of state necessity, she had demanded the death of her Protestant sister. If Elizabeth had not served such an exacting apprenticeship and been fortunate beyond expectation, she, as well as Lady Jane Grey, might have written on a prison wall: "To mortals' common fate my mind resign; my lot today, tomorrow may be thine."

Hard work, an infallible political instinct, and innate Tudor tact and sleight-of-hand saved Elizabeth from the common fate reserved for female rulers. The planning and labor that went into her coronation showed that from the start she appreciated that the love of her people was the surest bastion of her throne, and she carefully cultivated it by every kind of artistry and pageantry. On January 14, 1559, the eve of her coronation, the queen officially entered the city of London at the head of

Elizabeth I, by an Unknown Artist "Vain but acute." *(National Portrait Gallery, London)*

an immense procession. Elizabeth spared no cost — silks for livery and banners, timber for the seats in Westminster Abbey, delicacies for feasting important guests, food to be distributed among the poor, and even the fee to be paid the astrologer royal for setting the most favorable day for the crowning — all were financed with a single purpose in mind: to disperse the gloom that had settled on a country humiliated in war and floundering in spiritual and financial bankruptcy for almost a decade. The cost totaled well over £16,000 but was worth every penny.

Elizabeth needed every advantage she could scrape together, for it was anyone's guess whether a Protestant princess in a still largely Catholic realm could attract the support necessary for a long and prosperous reign. What Englishmen desired most was strong, vigorous, and secular leadership devoid of fanaticism and passion. They sought in Gloriana, as her people came to call her, a monarch who could curb factions, quiet discord, and present herself as the symbol of unity to which they could sacrifice their lives and give their hearts. The old king had achieved this unity by elevating the crown, through his personal magnetism and the ferocious laws of Parliament, to a point above party and politics. Elizabeth was her father's daughter — athletic, red-haired, autocratic, and vain — but she added a new element to royal leadership: a genius for courtship and coquetry. She wooed and won her people, transforming subjects into lovers who sought "Sweet Bessy's" hand. "Elizabeth of Good Memory" built no empires, nor sought to bring heaven to earth, but in a halting, vacillating, and often infuriating fashion, she solved the three most pressing problems of the early years of her reign: she put out the spreading fires of religious hysteria, she secured the realm in a world filled with women rulers and religious frenzy, and she redeemed England's confidence in itself and in Tudor government.

The Elizabethan Religious Settlement

Like her sister, Elizabeth was the victim and product of the past. She could not permit her kingdom to remain within the papal fold without admitting her mother to be a whore and herself a bastard unworthy of inheriting the throne. Unlike Mary, however, she sought neither to vindicate the faith of her childhood nor to prove her mother right. Instead, the new queen was a *politique*, a firm believer that religion should be an instrument of state and a compartment of life, not the end of government or the whole of human existence. As the daughter of Anne Boleyn, she had little choice — she embodied the hope and inspiration of English Protestantism — but within those limits she endeavored, not always successfully, to walk a delicate tightrope. She tried to convince the Catholic world of her religious orthodoxy, she struggled to win the support of the clergy as well as the laity and to ground her church on a broad parliamentary consensus, and she sought to make her royal prerogative in matters of ecclesiastical government as extensive and secure as possible.

In reconstructing the church, Elizabeth could depend on three sources of support. First and possibly most important was nationalism, now heavily tainted with the dislike of anything Spanish. Second was the acceptance of Erastianism, the belief that a loyal subject should leave matters of faith to the wisdom of the sovereign. Third was the existence of a wide base of religious opinion ranging from still staunchly antipapal Henrician Catholicism to radical Protestantism, all of which would underwrite some sort of ecclesiastical compromise. A fourth current also ran in the queen's favor: the widespread acceptance of *adiaphora*, the argument that, except for certain fundamentals, there existed in religion a wide area of "things indifferent" that could be safely left to time, expediency, and the queen's prerogative to determine. This last element would provide the unexpectedly firm sand upon which Elizabeth's religious settlement was based. Everything from issues of ceremony and clerical attire to questions of precise theological interpretation and ecclesiastical organization were set aside, at least for the moment, in an effort to achieve as wide a base of agreement as possible on the two crucial pillars of the Elizabethan settlement — the revival of the royal supremacy and the conversion of the Catholic mass into a Protestant communion service. Unfortunately for the new queen, these two together were unacceptable to a Catholic minority in the House of Commons and a majority in the House of Lords, where the Marian bishops dominated. In the end the government achieved a settlement, partly by intimidation, partly by compromise, and partly by astute politics, but it had to jettison any hope of consensus that included the Marian clergy.[2]

To a man, the spiritual peers took the position that "whatsoever is contrary to unity is schism" and that "it is the same thing, as far as schism is concerned, to do a little or to do all." Unlike their Henrician predecessors, the bishops adamantly opposed the royal supremacy and a second break with Rome, and they unanimously voted against a return to the Edwardian Prayer Book of 1552. Two astute compromises, however, won over a majority of the lay peers. For those Protestants as well as Catholics concerned about whether a woman was "qualified by God's Word to feed the flock of Christ" and could assume the title of Supreme Head of the church, the more equivocal name of Supreme Governor was devised. At the same time, the 1552 Prayer Book was amended to soften its Protestant severity, and ambiguous wording was introduced, which once again allowed the communion service to become a mass for those who viewed the Eucharist as a sacrificial ceremony and not simply a remembrance of Christ's sacrifice. After three attempts, an acceptable supremacy bill passed in April 1559. It was followed by a new Act of Uniformity, which passed the Lords by a majority of three, giving teeth to the Prayer Book and enforcing right thinking throughout the land.

---

[2]The best treatment of the religious settlement is N. L. Jones, *Faith by Statute: Parliament and the Settlement of Religion, 1559* (1982).

Extremists in both camps complained; the Marian bishops resigned their dioceses, and religious radicals protested against a compromise that so obviously smelled of political expediency rather than God's holy Word. The advocates of the "perfect school of Christ," however, received a partial victory; four years later in 1563, Convocation passed the Thirty-Nine Articles, which were and have remained unequivocally Protestant and strongly Calvinistic.

Elizabeth's settlement did in part have its desired effect: It dampened the fire of religious bigotry. It did so for two reasons. The queen's religious solution rested on the sound psychological principle that in England Catholics were better losers than Protestants. The old church, Mary's resurrected ecclesia, lacked the spirit of martyrdom and came to heel almost without a fight. Quietly and without fuss, the Marian bishops resigned their sees and were replaced by middle-of-the-road Protestants. Few priests stood firm — only 189 out of 9,000 refused to take the new Oath of Supremacy — and fewer still of the Catholic laity placed devotion to the pope above patriotism and duty to the crown. In contrast to Mary's handling of Protestants, Elizabeth chose to treat unrepentant Catholics not as religious martyrs, determined to supply the seed for a new and militant church, but as traitors who acknowledged an allegiance to a foreign potentate. Equally important, the principle of *adiaphora* lulled the Protestant radicals into a false sense of security. They had won the substance of the battle against Rome, and they were now content to wait to abolish the forms, the ceremonial "livery of antichrist" that continued to pollute the true church. The formula of "things indifferent" became all things to all people, for if matters of religion were indifferent, almost anything could be either removed or continued. Too late, the radicals learned that their queen was determined that her settlement, once established, should be final, authoritative, and grounded on her own divine and royal prerogative. She alone spoke for God, and the religious history of her reign witnessed a prolonged duel waged between those who would purify her church of all "popish rags" and a sovereign determined to keep her church as she had conceived it — comfortable, reasonably tolerant, and generally popular.

Religion and Diplomacy (1558–1572)

Human contrivance had again established the Word of God. Equally significant, the religious settlement, at least in its early stages, had been enacted solely by laymen, without the consent of a single cleric in the House of Lords or in Convocation, and no one in 1559 felt optimistic that the queen's solution would endure. Even ardent Protestants were sufficiently cautious to protect themselves from having ejected the pope, institutional bag and spiritual baggage, from the kingdom. They legislated that any "matter of religion or cause ecclesiastical" enacted by Parliament was not to be "adjudged at any time hereafter to be any error, heresy, schisms or schismatical opinion." What Mary's Parliament had done to Edward's Protestant legislation could be done to Elizabeth's reforms by some future representative body reflecting the will of yet another sovereign. It was all very well to hope that Catholics would be graceful losers and dutiful subjects; God's church and its royal champion, the Lady Elizabeth, still had to defend themselves against formidable foreign enemies.

Mary Tudor had died just in time to leave her sister the thankless task of concluding a losing war, acknowledging the loss of Calais, and facing Henry II of France who, it was said, bestrode England, "having one foot in Calais and the other in Scotland," where a regent ruled in the name of the French king's daughter-in-law, Mary Queen of Scots. The Treaty of Cateau-Cambrésis in April 1559 brought peace to Europe by ending three generations of Habsburg-Valois rivalry, but it also left Henry II of France and Philip II of Spain free to turn their energies to exterminating heresy in Europe. Henceforth, the soul's salvation, not dynastic ambitions in Italy, became their avowed diplomatic aim.

The death of Mary Tudor had proved a blessed liberation for Philip; it freed him to again settle his diplomatic affairs by marriage. He might have been a more serious suitor for Elizabeth's hand had not peace with France involved his marriage to Elizabeth Valois, the daughter of Henry II. His marriage by proxy in July 1559 had a fateful and unexpected consequence. During a joust in honor of his daughter's wedding, Henry II was mortally wounded. Within ten days the king was dead, and France fell prey to a three-way struggle among the ducal and militantly Catholic family of Guise, the dowager queen Catherine de Medici, and the Protestant house of Bourbon. A leaderless France nominally ruled by the ailing fifteen-year-old Francis II produced a diplomatic revolution. Spain, overnight and almost by default, was transformed into the Catholic colossus of Europe, and France was exposed to a generation of leaders who regarded the voice of religious conscience as an adequate guide to domestic and international affairs.

Everywhere in Europe, religious passions and hysteria were on the increase. In Rome, the Vatican breathed the extravagant air of the Counter Reformation. The new spirit was symbolized in the terrifying and apocryphal words of Pope Paul IV: "If our own father were a heretic, we would carry the faggots to burn him." Paul would have had no difficulty in detecting error even in his own father, for in 1563 the Council of Trent concluded its lengthy labors and presented the Catholic world with an authoritative pronouncement on what the faithful were to believe. The supremacy, but not the infallibility, of the pope was proclaimed, and the papacy found in the new order of the Society of Jesus a champion of its authority and an instrument with which to revitalize the ancient faith. The Jesuits were the shock troops of Rome, militant and singleminded believers in a variety of Catholicism that left no room for doubt or uncertainty, no place for discord or disobedience. The new soldiers of the church, led by their spiritual general Ignatius Loyola, viewed the world as torn between the forces of Satan and the disciples of God, and they called on men and monarchs to work for "the greater glory of God." Militant, crusading, and convinced, Catholicism went on the march, undoing the work of heretics, rewinning lost souls, saving whole kingdoms from damnation, throwing back the Turkish infidel, and yearning to win England again for the Catholic fold.

The Jesuits ranked as the elite of the Counter Reformation, infusing it with leadership and inspiration; but Spain regarded itself as the chosen instrument of the deity and custodian of the priceless treasure of spiritual liberation. From 1545 on, the prodigious riches of the silver deposits of Peru and the loot of the Incas financed the men and arms dedicated to destroying the godless. In 1559 the trumpet to bring down the Protestant walls of Jericho was tuned and ready; but Philip was by nature cautious, preferring peace to war, marriage to battle. He waited to see whether Elizabeth could be lured into an alliance with Catholic Spain or whether she would prove her birthright and relapse into religious error. Even after the publication of the Prayer Book and the Act of Supremacy, Philip manfully restrained any impulse to chastise his sister-in-law. Protestant Bess seemed preferable to the leading Catholic claimant to the Tudor throne, Mary of Scotland, who, although of the proper faith, was married to the dauphin of France. Only when the Spanish king became convinced that the reconquest of his own heretical subjects in the Lowlands was impossible as long as they were receiving encouragement from Protestant England did he sound the blast for her destruction.

The first victim of fanaticism was France, where the monarchy had slipped into incompetence, and the kingdom was torn by Catholic bigotry, unbending Protestant self-righteousness, family feuding, provincialism, privilege, and aristocratic ambitions. Following each other in quick and dissolute succession, the last three Valois kings personified the unhappy condition of France. The sick and insipid Francis II died within the first year of his reign; Charles IX proved to be a dissolute young prince who ran the gamut of vices, both natural and unnatural, but managed to survive until 1574; and the last and most intelligent of the Valois, Henry III, chose to play the vicious fop, ruling over a "court of silk and blood" and a realm that despised his cynicism and perversity. Nine civil wars in forty-two years engulfed the land. The wars were fought in the absence of any effective form of central government and in the presence of abundant moral and political corruption. Frenchman butchered Frenchman as an act of Christian piety, and, in 1572, on St. Bartholomew's Day, some 2,000 to 3,000 Huguenots were massacred in Paris. The Protestant world was horrified, and England shuddered at the thought that there but for the grace of Elizabeth lay slaughtered English Protestants.

With civil war raging in France, England reaped the diplomatic harvest. On the debit side, the war upset the balance of power, leaving Spain the unrivaled giant of Europe and the leader of the Catholic crusade. No longer was it possible to ensure England's safety through the time-honored policy of playing off Valois France against Habsburg Spain. On the credit side, a prostrate France torn by domestic strife could not join

St. Bartholomew's Day Massacre, Paris, 24 August, 1572   "Frenchman butchered Frenchman as an act of Christian piety. . . . The Protestant world was
horrified, and England shuddered at the thought that there but for the grace
of Elizabeth lay slaughtered English Protestants." *(Mary Evans Picture Library)*

Spain in a religious war against England. For a time, Elizabeth and her
council toyed with the possibility of open intervention in France in
the hope of recovering Calais; and in 1562, by the Treaty of Hampton
Court, the queen promised the French Protestants 100,000 crowns and
an army of 6,000 men in return for the port of Le Havre. The city proved
an easy gift to receive but a difficult one to keep. Within the year, French
Protestants and Catholics had again made peace, and Catherine de Medici was encamped in front of Le Havre with an army 40,000 strong. The
English defense was neither long nor glorious, and Elizabeth learned
that it was dangerous and expensive to concern herself with the domestic
affairs of a foreign power. Moreover, the Spanish menace had grown so
acute that England could no longer indulge in the luxury of war with
France. The new situation was reflected in the Treaty of Blois of 1572, by
which England and France pledged themselves to mutual defensive assistance. Although Anglo-French relations remained fretful throughout the
century and Elizabeth sent troops to help French Protestant rebels, three
centuries of rivalry had ended. Elizabeth herself never forgot nor forgave
the loss of Calais, but England learned to live without its continental port, and the approaching battle with Spain, for spiritual and national survival more and more consumed English energies.

John Knox and Mary Queen of Scots

English meddling in the affairs of other lands proved to be more success-ful in Scotland than in France. The northern kingdom had long been a thorn in England's side, but ever since the death of James V in 1542, the danger had increased, for Scotland had become a province of France, strategically located at England's back door. The regent was James's widow, Mary of Guise, sister of the most powerful nobleman in France. The child-queen of Scots had been sent to Paris to be educated in French ways and to marry the dauphin, and French culture and interest prevailed in Edinburgh.

James V, despite the advice offered by Henry VIII that defiance of the Vatican would open up the monastic lands to the Scottish crown, had re-mained loyal to Rome. The Church of Scotland needed reform far more than did the English ecclesia. Nevertheless, James had been unmoved be-cause Scottish clerics tended to be useful and worldly prelates, and be-cause he could bestow ecclesiastical estates and offices as rewards for po-litical loyalty rather than for service to God. After James's death in 1542, the situation began to change. With the growth of French influence at court, God-fearing Protestant preachers were able to pose as true Scottish nationalists working to liberate the church from the hands of a godless foreign power.[3]

After a prolonged and tumultuous sojourn, first in Frankfurt and Geneva and then in England, John Knox, the irascible member of God's elect, returned home from exile in 1559. He brought with him a species of Protestantism peculiarly congenial to the restless and rebellious hearts of highland lairds who coveted the lands of the church, hated the regent for exercising royal authority, and hoped to rid the kingdom of French domination. What particularly appealed to their clannish souls was Knox's militant assurance that it was the duty of "nobles and estates to be as bridles to repress the insolvency of your kings." Even before Knox arrived, Scottish nobles, wise in the ways of feudal anarchy, had joined in defense of God's Word and their own treasured independence by forming the Congregation of the Lord, part an army and part a covenant of the faithful. By the summer of 1559, the Protestant clans had launched a full revolt against the regent, and in February 1560 Elizabeth reluctantly al-lowed herself to become embroiled in the expensive and risky policy of fostering revolution across the border. She had no other choice: the Lords of the Congregation were consistently defeated in battle; Mary Stuart, who in 1559–1560 was already queen of Scotland and queen consort of France, was advertising her claims to reign as queen of England as well;

---

[3]For information about the Scottish Reformation, see Ian Cowan, *The Scottish Reformation* (1982); G. Donaldson, *All the Queen's Men: Power and Politics in Mary Stewart's Scotland* (1983); M. H. B. Sanderson, *Mary Stewart's People* (1987); and J. Kirk, *Patterns of Reform: Continuity and Change in the Reformation Kirk* (1989).

and French troops were pouring into Scotland in support of the regent. For Elizabeth, intervention in Scotland was not so much a matter of defending the Protestant faith as of preserving her own throne. Helped by English soldiers and pounds sterling and by the death of Mary of Guise, the Protestant faction finally triumphed. By the Treaty of Edinburgh, signed in June 1560, French troops were withdrawn, and England and Scotland joined hands for the first time in three hundred years. Not even the arrival of Mary Stuart the following year to claim her Scottish inheritance could undo the links that the Protestant faith was forging.

With the death of Francis II in December 1560, seventeen-year-old Mary Stuart faced the doleful prospect of leaving the center of Renaissance culture for the bleak hills of Calvinistic Scotland. Like Elizabeth, she was a monarch without a spouse; but, unlike the English queen, Mary made matrimony the center of her life, not the instrument of her rule. She sought and found romance in a fashion that elevated the sordid career of one of history's most capricious females into something approaching classical tragedy. Deeply religious but devoid of moral restraint, Mary Stuart combined the granite stubbornness of her Scottish blood with the coquetry of her French upbringing. She was the most fatally charming and dangerously idiotic of her ill-starred Stuart dynasty. She sought to win back her heretical and rebellious kingdom by tact and feminine charm, and for a time she listened to the warning administered by Preacher Knox when she asked him whether he thought "that subjects having power may resist princes." "If the princes exceed their bounds" was his dour answer. It was not her Catholicism, however, but her dynastic ambition that was the queen's undoing, for Mary refused to ratify the Treaty of Edinburgh, which required her to renounce her rights to the Tudor throne. Indeed, to strengthen that claim, she married on July 29, 1565, her cousin Henry Stuart, Lord Darnley, a grandson by a second marriage of Mary's own grandmother, Margaret Tudor. Darnley was a vicious and effeminate young man, and ultimately the match resulted in double murder and the loss of her throne;[4] but the child of Mary Stuart and Lord Darnley lived to rule Scotland for thirty-six years and England for another twenty-two.

Mary's marriage lasted scarcely nineteen months. It was destroyed by her husband's hatred for his wife's Italian and very private secretary, David Riccio, whom Darnley killed in a jealous rage. In revenge Mary connived at and possibly arranged the murder of her husband on February

---

[4]The romance of Mary Queen of Scots and the controversy surrounding her involvement in the murder of her husband have produced a veritable library of works. Possibly the three best older biographies are T. F. Henderson, *Mary Queen of Scots* (1905); Andrew Lang, *The Mystery of Mary Stuart* (1901); and Antonia Fraser, *Mary Queen of Scots* (1969). Since they present different views, they should be read together. The most modern scholarship is best read in the introduction to M. Lynch, *Mary Stewart, Queen in Three Kingdoms* (1988), and J. Wormald, *Mary Queen of Scots: A Study in Failure* (1988).

9, 1567. She then ran off with his murderer, James Hepburn, earl of Both-well. Catholics and Protestants alike were aghast at adultery and murder in a queen, no matter how young and charming, and the streets of Edin-burgh resounded with the cry "Burn the Whore." In June she was seized and shortly forced to abdicate in favor of her thirteen-month-old son. A year later she managed an utterly romantic escape, but within the week she was defeated in a final effort to win back her kingdom. To escape re-newed imprisonment or worse, she fled to England, where she became Elizabeth's difficult and unwanted guest for the next nineteen years.

Throughout Mary Stuart's hectic reign, Elizabeth had made it clear that as long as she could secure her northern frontier, she preferred her legitimate, although Catholic, cousin to any Protestant rebel. Even after Mary's imprisonment and abdication in 1567, Elizabeth sought her restoration; and during the years that the Stuart queen was her guest in England, Gloriana treated her as the rightful sovereign of Scotland. Only after Mary had entangled herself in the designs of Philip of Spain and per-sisted in dangerous intrigues to unseat her Tudor cousin did Elizabeth finally settle her diplomatic relations with Scotland. By the Treaty of Berwick in 1586, she entered into a defensive alliance with her northern neighbor; recognized James as lawful king; granted him a handsome pen-sion; and, although she never expressly said as much, let it be known that Mary Stuart's son was the heir to her crown.

Mary of Scotland's career epitomized the wisdom of Gloriana's deci-sion to remain single. Maidenhood proved to be Elizabeth's surest diplo-matic weapon and her greatest domestic anxiety. Abroad she used the prospect of marriage to bait her diplomatic hook, and she allowed herself to be courted by almost every eligible crown prince of Europe. At home, however, almost everyone regarded an unmarried queen as unnatural and dangerous to the realm. A husband and an heir were supremely impor-tant, but no one, least of all Elizabeth, could decide on an appropriate spouse. The Scottish ambassador struck at the core of the problem as far as Gloriana was concerned when he tactlessly but astutely told her that "ye think that if ye were married, ye would be queen of England, and now ye are king and queen both. Ye may not suffer a commander." Elizabeth's "stately stomach" regarded marriage as incompatible with sovereignty, and she chose the risky path of spinsterhood. In doing so, however, she exposed England to the terrible possibility of civil and religious war, for as long as Elizabeth remained single and childless, Catholic Mary Stuart was her legal heir. In 1562 the queen hovered on the threshold of death with smallpox; and, when she recovered, she was boldly told that "the want of your marriage and issue is like to prove . . . a plague" upon the land. Elizabeth remained unmoved, and when Parliament begged her to name a husband, she tartly replied, "I will not in so deep a matter wade with so shallow a wit." Clearly, the queen considered Parliament pre-sumptuous and unworthy to discuss the question of a monarch's mar-riage and nuptial bed. Her own wit told her that it was politically safer and diplomatically wiser to remain single. Dangerous as a maiden and childless queen might be, a royal lady who lost her independence and created a rival political power through marriage — as Mary Stuart had done — would be even more disturbing. Elizabeth preferred to keep the world and her subjects guessing and to play the delightful game of coquetry. She flirted with — and possibly she loved — Robert Dudley, earl of Leicester, but she never forgot that the people of her kingdom were the principal audience of her courtship. "Do not upbraid me with miserable lack of children," she implored her Parliament, "for every one of you, and as many as are Englishmen, are children and kinsmen to me."

The Elizabethan Body Politic[5]

In the clash between the queen and her loyal Parliament over the question of marriage, Elizabeth articulated a political creed that became the basis of her domestic policy: she would set her own house in order without the advice or interference of overmighty magnates or presumptuous commoners, and she would rule as master in that house. The first step in revitalizing the body politic was the selection of councillors congenial to a sovereign who was secular in spirit and politic in thought and who demanded that she alone monopolize the stage of royalty and receive the accolades of her loving people. The queen chose moderate, hardworking men who were content to remain behind the scenes, arranging the pomp and circumstance of monarchy and managing the drudgery of government. In politics, Gloriana turned to William Cecil who, like Elizabeth, had been a Henrician under Henry VIII, a Protestant under Edward VI, and a nominal Catholic under Mary. He was first the queen's principal secretary and finally, in 1572, her lord treasurer, and upon him Elizabeth conferred one of the few new peerages of her reign.[6] He became Lord Burghley, "a great heretic, and such a clownish Englishman," it was said, that he believed "that all the Christian princes joined together are not able to injure the sovereign of his country."

In religion Gloriana placed her new church in the cautious care of Matthew Parker, archbishop of Canterbury, whose wife offended the queen's sense of clerical propriety but whose conservatism and loyalty more than compensated for his being married. In finance, she turned to William Paulet, marquis of Winchester, her lord treasurer until his death

---

[5]Essential to an understanding of the Tudor body politic are L. Stone, *The Crisis of the Aristocracy, 1558–1641* (1965); C. Morris, *Political Thought in England, Tyndale to Hooker* (1953); and E. M. W. Tillyard, *The Elizabethan World Picture* (1934), which should be read along with D. K. Shuger, *Habits of Thought in the English Renaissance: Religion, Politics, and the Dominant Culture* (1990).

[6]Anyone interested in the queen's great minister should read C. Read's two studies: *Mr. Secretary Cecil and Queen Elizabeth* (1955) and *Lord Burghley and Queen Elizabeth* (1960). B. W. Beckingsale, *Burghley* (1967), is a good short biography.

William Cecil, created Lord Burghley " 'A great heretic, and such a clownish Englishman' . . . that he believed 'that all the Christian princes joined together are not able to injure the sovereign of his country.' " *(North Wind Picture Archives)*

in 1572, and to Sir Thomas Gresham, an expert in international finance. With unerring political sense, Elizabeth perceived that only a solvent monarchy could win popular support, and she began the long, painstaking task of rebuilding the nation's credit. The job was not easy. Her sister had bequeathed an empty treasury, a debt of £227,000, an unstable currency, and a costly and futile war. Elizabeth's own adventures into France and Scotland were not cheap: They involved selling £90,000 worth of crown lands and borrowing £247,000 from the continent. Yet the queen's government managed somehow to perform a fiscal miracle. The debased coinage was withdrawn and a new currency issued, which improved the foreign rate of exchange and netted the government a profit of £45,000. The debt was then paid off, and Elizabeth's credit rose to the point where she could borrow in the Netherlands at 8 percent interest, while Philip of Spain had to give 16 percent. By 1562 the crown, for the first time since the days of Henry VII, lived on its own historic sources of income — about £250,000 in all — with only minimal help from Parliament.

In setting her house in order, the queen unconsciously followed the political mentality of her age, which was soundly authoritarian in its social, religious, and political prejudices. Society was an organic and hierarchical whole in which obedience to legal authority became "the glue and solder of the public weal, the ligament which tieth and connecteth the limbs of this body politic each to the other." Monarchy gave

Queen Elizabeth in Parliament   "When Elizabeth sat in the midst of her Lords and Commons, and legislation was enacted by the whole Parliament, then the government spoke in the name of all subjects." *(The Mansell Collection)*

the kingdom its unity and leadership, and Elizabeth told her Parliament that "it is monstrous that the feet should direct the head" and "no king fit for his state will ever suffer such absurdities." The crown, however, existed only in confederation with a myriad of local and regional interests, classes, and corporations. Guilds, towns, and shires recognized their subordinate position within the state, yet each was conscious of its own identity and stubbornly retained a high degree of independence of action. In such a scheme of things, the parts as well as the totality claimed divinity. Elizabeth, by necessity, was a divine-right monarch, "the life, the head, and the authority of all things that be done in the realm of England." The queen, however, could not monopolize divinely ordained authority, for in the sixteenth century, the right to rule at every level of society stemmed solely from God. In a sense, a religiously articulated constitutionalism existed, in which every element of the body politic was expected to cooperate but could also claim a hearing. Consequently, the highest institution within the realm was that organ that could speak for all interests in the commonwealth — King in Parliament.[7] When Elizabeth sat in the midst of her Lords and Commons, and legislation was enacted by the whole Parliament, then the kingdom spoke in the name of all subjects. Parliament was the "highest and most absolute power of the realm" because "every Englishman is intended to be there present . . . from the prince to the lowest person in England."

Not only was King in Parliament the highest authority of the land, but in that body the crown also found its greatest bulwark against rebellion. The Spanish ambassador spoke the truth when he said of Henry VIII that he "always fortified himself by the consent of Parliament." Royal caprice was translated into statute. Should rebellion arise, it would not be against the king alone but against the will of King, Lords, and Commons as embodied in law. The Tudors required no standing army. They had no need to rule in "the French fashion," for the will of God and the monarch were enshrined in acts of Parliament. On one point, however, Elizabeth was adamant: The controlling mind within that mystical union of crown and Parliament belonged to the queen.

All the Tudors took pains to retain the initiative in the lawmaking process, and Elizabeth scrutinized each aspect of the legislative machinery. From the molding of public opinion to ensure the election of "godly and Christian men," to the writing of bills and their passage through Parliament, the crown supervised every step of the process and endeavored to influence the mind of its faithful Commons. No dynasty was ever more solicitous of the good opinion of its subjects or more conscious of the need for a proper frame of mind within the realm. Governmental paternalism by public connivance and acclaim was the Tudor goal. Indeed, the art of propaganda and the deliberate manipulation of public opinion had their birth in the sixteenth century. Pamphlets and official versions of almost every historic event of Gloriana's reign were distributed for home and foreign consumption. Elizabeth's public relations man and keeper of the public conscience was her principal secretary and lord treasurer, William Cecil, whose spies sounded out popular sentiment and whose instruments shaped it. Even the works of Shakespeare were read and censored by the master of the revels, and his deletions and alterations can be read to this day.

If loyal subjects failed to send right-minded representatives to Parliament, the government could exercise pressure, although it rarely tampered openly with elections. As part of their political patronage, the great lords all had "pocket boroughs" that looked to them for favor at court, and the voters often left one of the two names on their election forms empty to be filled in by their patron. In controlling the peers and bishops of the realm, Elizabeth in effect held reign over a sizable proportion of the personnel of the lower house.

---

[7]Possibly the phrase should be *Queen in Parliament,* but the sixteenth century tended to think of royalty in masculine terms, regardless of the sex of the sovereign.

Once in London and at Westminster Palace, landed gentlemen, county merchants, and city lawyers, although they quickly grew wise in parliamentary precedent and procedure, needed guidance and had to be on occasion severely scolded if a turbulent assembly of rowdy provincials was to be transformed into a legislative body. As late as 1581, it was necessary to teach the house polite manners, so that at the end of the day Commons would "depart and go forth in a comely and civil sort" and not "so unseemly and rudely to thrust and throng out as of late time hath been disorderly used." The speaker of the house and the privy councillors were the queen's instruments of discipline. The speaker was a royal appointee who controlled the timing of bills, curtailed debate, and passed judgment on a close vote between the ayes and the nays. He was held strictly accountable for a properly cooperative house, and one speaker was told by an Elizabethan privy councillor, "You, Mr. Speaker, should perform the charge Her Majesty gave you at the beginning of this Parliament, not to receive bills of a nature which is not pleasing to Her Majesty."

The ultimate source of parliamentary leadership was the queen's Privy Council, many of whose members sat in the House of Commons. They worked through "men of business" in the lower house who were clients of the crown and could be depended on to translate government policy into law. As long as members of the council were experts in procedure and precedent, drafted and piloted legislation, coordinated the labors of Lords and Commons, and determined the subject, length, and direction of debate, the House of Commons filled the role assigned to it in the divine order of things: the docile, silent, and obedient junior member in the triumvirate of Crown, Lords, and Commons, in which the queen was very much the senior partner.

The Privy Council was more than the monarch's voice in Commons; it was the mainspring of Tudor government and the channel through which direction and inspiration were infused into the body politic. Although it spoke solely in the queen's name and in theory acted only on matters brought to it by the sovereign, the council in fact was the administrative ruler of the realm and helped the sovereign to determine national policy. A Tudor sovereign was only as good as his council, and was dependent on it for accurate information and efficient execution of the royal will. The queen's council handled foreign affairs, either writing or drafting official communiqués to foreign powers. It issued proclamations on every facet of Elizabethan life, appointed local officials in the queen's name, and had constant contact with the most detailed aspects of provincial affairs. The price of wheat, the level of wages, the drainage of rivers, the apprehension of criminals, the construction of bridges — nothing was too slight or too important for the council's consideration and action. Together, the queen and her Privy Council formed the head and heart of a commonweal in which some were born to lead, others to follow, and all to obey divinely constituted authority.

Beneath the council was a salaried bureaucracy of scarcely 500 persons. The secretariat numbered no more than 15; the treasury, which included customs officials and exchequer clerks, amounted to possibly 265; the judiciary managed with a staff of 50; and the various regional agencies — the duchy of Lancaster, the earldom of Chester, the councils of Wales and of the North — completed the list with a staff of 145. Possibly another 500–600 of the king's servants administered the crown lands. In all there was only one salaried royal official for every 3,000 subjects, a ratio that contrasted markedly with France's 1:400 relationship. This happy scarcity of bureaucrats in Tudor society did not mean that the English were blessed with less government than other countries. Quite the contrary; Elizabethan paternalism and control over the common folk were brought directly into the shires by a regiment of unpaid amateur officials and by the political philosophy of the age, which taught that the ownership of land carried a responsibility for leadership and a duty to serve the crown. Whether or not the 5,000 natural leaders of society actually held title as justices of the peace, lord lieutenants of the counties, sheriffs, chief constables, or commissioners of the sewers, they were expected to preserve order throughout the realm. At the apex of the ruling classes stood the 60 or so peers of the realm, worth anywhere from £20,000 to £100,000 in land and capital assets; at the bottom of the governing pyramid were the provincial merchants, lesser country gentlemen, government clerks, and city lawyers, most of whom possessed at least £50 a year and many of whom, especially as the century wore on, received a great deal more in rents, fees, and gratuities. The group was financially and socially privileged, and enjoyed the choicest plums of office and patronage in return for single-hearted service to the throne.

Of all the unpaid government officials, the 740 or so justices of the peace played the most important and effective role. The J.P.'s were chosen from among men of birth and breeding by the Privy Council; they were often members of the House of Commons, and combined knowledge of law with understanding of local conditions. From 40 to 70 justices were appointed in each county, and they united the judicial and administrative functions of government. Except for major crimes, they handled local justice, often hearing complaints and handing down punishment in their front parlors. Administratively, they acted as the eyes, ears, and hands of the Privy Council, informing the government of such local crises as floods and famines, fixing wages and watching over the needy of the parish, supervising weights and measures, and auditing the accounts of the overseers of the poor. They ultimately had responsibility for the collection of parliamentary taxes and, along with the lord lieutenants, supervised the defenses of the shire and raised troops in time of emergency. Overworked and conditioned to ruling, the J.P. was the indispensable unit of Tudor government, and both queen and council took pains to ensure his loyalty and efficiency.

The presence of unpaid local officials raises a critical debate. Did justices of the peace, sheriffs, deputy lord lieutenants, and lesser county and parish officials fit neatly into the Tudor-Stuart political metaphor of the organic body politic? Did they maintain a distinction between their own "fond fancies" and the sovereign's fatherly decisions, and did they act as the nervous system by which the will of the head — king, council, and Parliament — reached the foot and was translated into administrative reality in the shires? Or did they function independently, establish their own priorities, resent royal interference, drag their feet, return false reports, and harken to local interests, not to the concerns of the kingdom? Put differently, is the proper model for studying Tudor-Stuart England the image of a unified totality directed from the top, all its parts endowed with a sense of responsibility for the whole; or is it a "federation of semi-autonomous republics" whose sense of shire identity far exceeded their loyalty to king and kingdom, and their powers of disruption such that "a revolt of the provinces" could later topple the Stuart government?

The controversy is complicated and unresolved because both models are probably correct. Under Elizabeth, J.P.'s were selected carefully, even though the social demand for the office was so great that in some counties the number of justices doubled or even tripled, and the Tudors constantly increased the burden of public responsibility on them. By the end of Gloriana's reign, it was estimated that 306 of the statutes of the realm required J.P.'s to ensure their enforcement, and when the judges of the assizes went out on circuit, the queen's council systematically instructed them on the needs of royal government and ordered them to report on the effectiveness of individual J.P.'s. But Elizabeth, her Privy Council, and her prerogative courts of Star Chamber and High Commission did not expect J.P.'s to be the equivalent of French intendants — paid servants of the crown in the provinces. Not only was the J.P. unsalaried, but also his authority in the shire was in part independent of the crown; it stemmed from two other sources — his status in the community as a gentleman with economic means, social connections, and ancient lineage, and his position as the father and head of his own family. Government, therefore, was a cooperative venture shared by a series of overlapping — sometimes competing, sometimes complementary — authorities, and it is wise to remember that, although the crown's voice carried great weight, it had to speak in harmony with other, lesser voices.

Two examples suffice to reveal the complexities of Tudor-Stuart local administration. While on circuit in Norfolk in 1583, Elizabeth's Assizes judges ordered the imprisonment of leading Puritan clergy and removed two Puritan J.P.'s from office. The central government flexed its muscle in this way despite the warning given by a delegation of the most influential county gentlemen that the queen's judges shared "only equal authority" with the local gentry and should handle "triffling matters [such as religious conformity] more kindly" — in other words, to the liking of the local authorities. Elizabeth could make her will fully felt in the shires, but two generations later in the same county of Norfolk, Charles I discovered that he could not. His high church archbishop learned that Puritan clergyman Samuel Fairclough could not be persuaded to appear before the archbishop's court even when that body came directly into his parish. Fairclough always had an excuse: He was forever suffering from a fall from his horse. He successfully defied the king's ecclesiastical authority because he could rely on his patron and protector, Sir Nathaniel Barnardiston, one of the richest men in England on whom the crown depended for effective government in the shire.

In short the local gentleman magistrate could be on occasion a surprisingly free or surprisingly servile agent, depending on local circumstances and royal policy. He had to walk a treacherous line between loyalty to locale and conscience and duty to king. Under Elizabeth and James, most gentlemen struck a balance, one loyalty reinforcing the other. Under Charles, that balance became increasingly difficult to maintain; and one of the basic assumptions of Tudor-Stuart government — that crown and local gentry should cooperate to ensure stability and government in the shires — began to collapse. Unlike Charles, Elizabeth made the system work because the queen and her council sensed the threefold secret of political success: first, the importance of maintaining respect for government and of encouraging the habit of obedience among the leaders of society as well as the multitude; second, the guiding through Parliament of legislation agreeable to the ears of M.P.'s who often turned into J.P.'s when they returned to their shires; and third, the binding of the financial and social aspirations of the ruling elite to the throne by the judicious distribution of court, county, church, and military patronage. More than her religious settlement, more than her diplomatic victory in Scotland, more even than her triumph over Spain in the years to come, Elizabeth's greatest accomplishment was her success in infusing her government and her realm with the confidence, pride, and energy that sent Drake around the globe (see page 207), led Raleigh to plant nations in the wilderness of the New World (see page 247), and inspired Shakespeare to eulogize

> This royal throne of kings, this scepter'd isle,
> This earth of majesty, this seat of Mars,
> This other Eden, demi-paradise,
> This fortress built by Nature for herself
> Against infection and the hand of war,
> This happy breed of men, this little world,
> This precious stone set in the silver sea,
> Which serves it in the office of a wall
> Or as a moat defensive to a house,
> This blessed plot, this earth, this realm, this England.
>
> *Richard II*, act 2, sc. 1

The Theory of Paternalistic Government

The queen depended for her magic on loyalty to herself and to "this blessed plot . . . this realm, this England," but her ministers also worked hard at maintaining a paternalistic concept of government that sought to keep all her subjects in social harmony and economic accord and to protect the poor from the predatory impulses of the rich and powerful. The usurer, the profiteer, and the capitalist wrought as much destruction on society as the irresponsible baronial magnate; economic individualism presented as great an evil as the political individualism of a willful Essex who placed pride above obedience (see page 225). The Tudors and early Stuarts harbored an essentially medieval economic outlook, decrying cutthroat competition and expounding strict government regulation of all aspects of economic life, to achieve an ordered, fixed, and stable society and a fair living for all. Their motives were not so much economic as political; the healthy body politic was that commonwealth in which all elements prospered according to their station, and wise councillors knew that obedience and respect on the part of the common sort depended in large measure on full bellies and fat children. The evicted tenants of "progressive" landlords, the starving and homeless victims of land enclosures, and the jobless textile workers and miners posed dangers to a kingdom devoid of police force or standing army. William Cecil voiced the haunting fear of all men of substance, and acknowledged the hard pragmatic foundation on which Tudor economic policy rested, when he wrote that trade, both foreign and domestic, was the salvation of the realm. Once trade was curtailed, he explained, subjects "must either perish for want or fall into violence to feed their lewd appetites with open spoil of others, which is the fruit of rebellion."

Medieval social theory had advocated the twofold doctrine of economic and moral justice for all and competition for none so that the kingdom might not suffer from outrageous prices and shoddy goods, and individuals might escape the sins of avarice and usury. By the sixteenth century, the same creed, divested of much of its religious trappings, still held true. The fair price was no longer a moral issue, but regulation remained the order of the day. Tudor economic control was not yet synonymous with the mercantilism of the second half of the seventeenth century, for no Tudor or early Stuart sovereign ever consciously associated state regulation with economic power. Instead, the ideal remained the medieval one of achieving an ordered and static class structure by guaranteeing a fixed labor supply, discouraging social mobility, and curtailing economic freedom. Such a code was anticapitalistic to its core. It opposed economic individualism, industrial growth, free enterprise, unrestrained competition, and the absolute freedom of employer and employee to contract on the basis of the worker's skill and the demand for what he could produce.

The crown regulated for "the general good" of the kingdom. The Privy Council, which had once spent its time scrutinizing the liveried servants of great peers, now directed its labors at relieving the consequences of unemployment in the cloth industry, helping wounded war veterans, issuing zoning proclamations, enforcing health and sanitation regulations, and protecting lesser merchants and artisans from their more predatory colleagues. An early Stuart council branded the ribbon-making machine as a "devilish device," and an engine for manufacturing needles was suppressed as dangerous to the king's interests, "spoiling and maiming his subjects." Wages and working conditions were inspected and controlled, justices of the peace were ordered to buy wheat in periods of scarcity and to sell it below cost to prevent famine, and they were told to prevent employers from firing their workers during times of economic distress.

The Statute of Artificers (Apprentices) enacted in 1563 enshrined the Elizabethan concept of an ordered society and reflected the basic social premises of Tudor paternalism. It postulated the social and moral obligation of all men and women to toil, and it assumed the existence of "degree, priority, and place" as the natural order of a divinely ordained hierarchical society. Town and country, court and shire, agriculture and industry were seen as separate but interrelated parts of the body politic, and the statute sought to preserve the balance between these parts by legislating against occupational and geographic mobility. A seven-year apprenticeship was required for everyone who engaged in any trade, even agriculture. The working day was set at twelve hours during the summer and daylight during the winter. Deference, regulation, and immobility, however, had their compensation. If no servant could "depart from his master, mistress, or dame before the end of his or her term" of service, no servant could be fired without cause. And "if any such master shall misuse or evil intreat his apprentice, or the said apprentice shall have any just cause to complain," the apprentice could have his case heard by a justice of the peace, who would "by his wisdom and discretion take such order and direction between the master and his apprentice as the equity of the cause shall require." The justices of the peace not only inspected and controlled the conditions of labor but also regulated the wages of "artificers, handicraftsmen, husbandmen, or any other laborer, servant, or workman." The protection offered the worker was in large measure a spinoff from the statute's main purpose of safeguarding the interests of the employer, but it did acknowledge the obligation of the "better part" of society to respect the rights of the "more part." The act remained on the law books for 250 years and was not repealed until 1813, when the concept of the body politic and the doctrine of paternalism gave way to a more atomized view of society and to the free operation of the laws of supply and demand.

The Statute of Artificers sought to control only the employed. The unemployed — the victims of famine, pauperism, and economic dislocation — were not officially recognized as the responsibility of the state for another 38 years. Poor relief had been traditionally viewed as the responsibility of the individual — the giving of alms benefited the donor's soul and paved the way to heaven. When Elizabeth's government reluctantly assumed responsibility for the alleviation of poverty, a giant stride was taken in the development of the secular, bureaucratic, modern state. After 1590 England stumbled through a generation of economic recession during which the peasantry came close to starvation. The need for charity on a national scale was manifest; but the church, divested of its riches during the Reformation, was helpless in the face of unemployment, progressive malnutrition, famine, and rioting. Only the state had the means to handle poverty on such a scale and, with the Elizabethan Poor Law of 1601, the crown for the first time seriously and systematically entered the field of social welfare. It used the ancient ecclesiastical unit of the parish as the basic administrative division for poor relief, and appointed overseers of the poor to administer charitable funds raised by local taxes on all property holders.

Far more important than the actual dispensing of charity by state officials was that a government contrived by man had accepted not only the philosophy that all Christians had a duty to labor but also the corollary that everyone had a right to work. The parishes were ordered to provide work for the unemployed, aid for the sick, protection for the aged, and punishment for those who preferred begging to an honest day's work. The doctrine behind state control of wages and prices and the relief of human suffering was not the theory of the modern welfare state. Instead, it rested on the logic that if God ordained every man and woman to live without envy or malice in that station into which they had been born, then society could not risk revolution by allowing the victims of economic dislocation, human greed, and natural calamity to die miserably in their peasant hovels. Some help, if only reluctant and minimal, had to be offered; and even a Parliament monopolized by property owners, taxpayers, and employers realized that poverty presented too ominous a social danger to be ignored. The natural leaders of the body politic by necessity had to accept the political and economic responsibilities of their birth and fortune and give their time to government and their money to the relief of the poor.

Life at the Bottom: Law Enforcement and the Family[8]

Mention of royal authority as it permeated downward into the shires and of Tudor-Stuart theories and practices of paternalism fails to capture the realities of life that existed for 90 percent of the population. The justice of the peace and the overseer of the poor viewed society from the top down; a very different perception of life appears when it is perceived from the bottom up. For most people, the parish — some 9,400 in all — not

---

[8]The two best social surveys are J. A. Sharpe, *Early Modern England: A Social History 1550–1760* (1987) and K. Wrightson, *English Society, 1580–1680* (1982). Crime and social control are best studied in J. A. Sharpe, *Crime in Early Modern England* (1984); R. Houlbrooke, *Church Courts and the People During the English Reformation 1520–1570* (1979); M. Ingram, *Church, Courts, Sex and Marriage in England 1570–1640* (1987); and C. Herrup, *The Common Peace: Participation and the Criminal Law in Seventeenth-Century England* (1987). For the family, see M. Anderson, *Approaches to the History of the Western Family 1500–1914* (1980); R. Houlbrooke, *The English Family 1450–1700* (1984); M. L. King, *Women of the Renaissance* (1991); A. Fraser, *The Weaker Vessel: Women in 17th-century England* (1984); and L. Stone, *Family, Sex and Marriage in England, 1500–1800* (1977).

the county formed the jurisdictional unit where governmental, social, and economic discipline made itself most immediately felt. The shires' assizes, presided over by the king's judges on circuit twice a year, and the courts of quarter and petty sessions, controlled by the local justices of the peace, kept a sharp eye on potential violence in a society that had no standing army and permitted the widespread possession of weapons. Nevertheless, most interpersonal strife and violation of what the village regarded as acceptable moral and civil behavior was handled either directly by the village constable — who was not so much a modern policeman enforcing "state law" as a "village headsman" responsible for defusing conflict before it exploded into crime — or they were sent to the manorial, borough, and church courts. In the Lancashire manor of Prescott during the 45 years between 1615 and 1660, only 23 cases of assault were recorded in the court of quarter sessions, but 1,252 inhabitants were cited before the manor court for the same offense. The typical parish miscreant who came before the local courts was in trouble for swearing, adultery, fornication, scandalous words, illegal business practices, failure to attend church, drunkenness while in church, fighting and quarreling with his neighbors, refusing to pay church rates, cutting down trees without permission, leaving ditches unrepaired, or obstructing roads with dunghills.

Law enforcement was the watchword of good government, but the Tudor-Stuart magistrate also knew that the well-disposed mind and heart proved a far more effective instrument of social control than the whip, the stocks, the prison, or the gallows. The key to the well-ordered commonwealth, the social and governmental unit that embodied and symbolized the kingdom, was the family, because it was here that every subject of the crown learned how to live in what historians refer to as a deference society. The principles of the Tudor-Stuart body politic — respect for and obedience to one's betters — were learned at home, for the family, held together by the divine authority of the husband and father, was seen as the kingdom writ small.

The family had three distinct but overlapping functions. It formed a biological, security, and jurisdictional-ideological unit. As a means of legitimizing procreation, the family reflected the demographic realities of early modern England. Marriage came late in the sixteenth century — aged 27–28 for men, 25–26 for women — thereby slowing the population growth far more severely than disease, economic hard times, or famine. Seventy percent of the kingdom lived in the nuclear, two-generational household (not the multigenerational, extended family), which contained on average only 4.75 individuals: husband, wife, and two to three children. Labor was cheap and plentiful. Thirteen percent of the population was in service, and 29 percent of all households hired one or more servants who started working in their early teens and served for ten to fifteen years before marrying and establishing their own households. On average, five to six children were born to the typical family, but only half survived, and three-fourths of all marrying males had no living father at the time of their weddings, two statistics that starkly reflect the death toll wrought by diphtheria, influenza, dysentery, measles, smallpox, scarlet fever, typhoid, whooping cough, syphilis, and the plague, to name but a few of the killers that beset the family. Fifteen percent of all children died in their first year; another 10 percent did not make it to their tenth birthday. Only those who managed to reach age 30 could expect to approach 60, a statistic that explains why only 8.4 percent of the population in 1551 was over threescore years. Death did for the union of husband and wife what divorce achieves today — a high rate of multiple marriages. The average union lasted only 17 to 20 years. Indeed, one-fourth of all people marrying in the seventeenth century had been married at least once before, a figure that gives poignancy to Cinderella's plight with her stepmother and stepsisters.

Security was the main purpose of the family: the cooperation of husband and wife in a precarious economic system that required both to work, and the protection of the young. For the poor, children could be either a heavy economic burden — thus the early age they were sent off into service — or an economic necessity as supplementary labor in the family business and as support for their parents in old age. Children for the political elite, however, provided the essential means for securing the family inheritance and passing down economic and political power — in the form of land — through the generations. In wealthy families marriage was a carefully monitored business concern in which land, dowries, and social status could override romance and any "chemistry" between bride and groom.

Within the family unit, the husband was, at least in theory, the undisputed head. In reality, however, husband and wife generally operated as a team grounded on love, respect, and mutual affection. The family, according to William Gouge, the seventeenth-century London clergyman who penned *Of Domesticall Duties*, formed a unit "wherein man and wife are after a sort even fellows and partners." The fifth commandment — honor thy father and mother — was unquestioned, and fathers held responsibility for the good disciplining of their children, servants, or any lodgers and apprentices that lived under their roofs. The consequences of juvenile disobedience were not pleasant, and it was asserted that "the eye that mocketh at his father and despiseth to obey his mother, the ravens of the valley shall pick out and the young eagles shall eat it." Fortunately for the father, his authority did not stand alone. It was reinforced by the schoolmaster, the magistrate, and the parson — all of whom were equally responsible for transforming the family into "a school wherein the first principles and grounds of government and subjection are learned." Only the cooperation of all varieties of authority could safeguard the body politic from the devil's devices, could curb crime — always known as the wages of sin — and could secure the kingdom: the family writ large.

Seadogs, Style, and Schooling: Culture in Renaissance England[9]

No one has yet come forth with an adequate explanation of Renaissance England, where human magnetism and daring seemed unlimited; where the brevity and suffering of life engendered not despondency but the determination to excel in all manner of things — in literature, in feats of navigation and endurance, in philosophy, and even in saintliness and fiendishness. No one has explained what trick of sociological legerdemain produced the magic of Will Shakespeare (1564–1616), the intellectual daring of Francis Bacon (1561–1626), the genius of Christopher Marlowe (1564–1593), Ben Jonson (1573?–1637), and Edmund Spenser (1552–1599), or the insatiable dream that led Sir Walter Raleigh (1552?–1618) at the age of forty-two to seek the legendary land of El Dorado. What created the dynamic self-confidence that induced Drake, Gilbert, and Grenville to risk their lives for God and queen? Sir Humphrey Gilbert (1539?–1583) was last seen returning home from his ill-starred effort to colonize Newfoundland. Seated in the stern of a tiny cocklecraft in the midst of a North Atlantic storm, he serenely soliloquized: "We are as near to heaven by sea as by land." Sir Richard Grenville (1541–1591) in the *Revenge* took on the entire Spanish Atlantic fleet and had to be forcibly restrained from ordering the powder magazine of his ship blown up to prevent the ignominious loss of one of her majesty's warships. He could not be stopped, however, from toasting the Spanish captain and then, according to legend, committing suicide by eating the goblet as his horrified captors looked on. Sir Francis Drake (1540?–1596) was incredibly vain, but for once vanity and achievement marched hand in hand in a naval hero who regarded it as his divine mission personally to punish Philip II for his perfidy to God, to England, and to Sir Francis Drake! His name alone — the Spanish called him *El Draque*, "the dragon" — was said to have been worth the mightiest galleon in the queen's navy. All three of these intrepid seadogs had their answer to Raleigh's proud challenge: "What shall we be, travelers or tinkers, conquerors or novices?"

Other lands and other centuries have had their demigods, but Elizabethan England was unique in that the heroes of the mind and pen paralleled the deeds of conquerors; in fact, on occasion they were one and the same person. The poet John Donne (1573–1631) went voyaging in 1596 with Lord Admiral Howard, Raleigh, and the young earl of Essex on their triumphant attack upon Cadiz. Sir Walter Raleigh, in the midst of military, commercial, and governmental enterprises, found time to compose some of the finest verses of the century; other professional soldiers also

---

[9]See three surveys on education and literacy: D. Cressy, *Literacy and the Social Order: Reading and Writing in Tudor and Stuart England* (1980); M. V. C. Alexander, *The Growth of English Education, 1348–1648: A Social and Cultural History* (1990); and N. Orme, *Education and Society in Medieval and Renaissance England* (1988).

Hardwick Hall, Derbyshire   Built 1590–1597 in the new lantern style to be viewed from a distance, its myriad windows sparkled in the sunlight by day and glowed with torchlight by night. "In one way or another, the heroes of the sixteenth century regarded themselves as on display." *(Aerofilms Library)*

produced quite passable poetry; and Elizabeth herself wrote speeches that might have done credit to Shakespeare. Style, wrote Raleigh, "is the man," by which he meant far more than fashionable clothing. Life for Sir Walter's generation was a play; "it matters not how long the action is spun out, but how good the acting is." In one way or another, the heroes of the sixteenth century regarded themselves as on display — either before God or before history — and Elizabeth spoke both a political and metaphysical truth when she exclaimed, "We princes are set on stages in the sight and view of all the world duly observed."

Life was a "wide and universal theatre," but Shakespeare, Bacon, and Marlowe offered something more than a narrow sixteenth-century script; they voiced ideas that have proved enduring for all people and all times. The great Shakespearean history plays, which open where this text begins, with the deposition of Richard II, provide both a lesson in the judgment of God on a kingdom that had violated the divine order of things and a deeply human study in the relationship of means to ends: when men are corrupt, they debase the most inspired ends; when the ends are ignoble, they destroy the most noble men. Bacon's *Advancement of Learning* and *Novum Organum* are sustained sixteenth-century attacks on medieval scholastic thought, but they also go to the root of a profound intellectual revolution that would eventually overwhelm the western world. Sir Francis advises his fellow Elizabethans that knowledge is power and that if they would learn to generalize and experiment on the basis of empirically proven evidence, they could be as the gods and possess sovereignty over the universe. Power — political, technological, and scientific — fascinated the late Elizabethans, and they were fully aware that the world was their oyster, if only they themselves were not pygmies forever in need of divine guidance. It was presumptuous but understandable that Marlowe's Doctor Faustus should seek to make a pact with the devil to gain a dominion that "stretcheth as far as doth the mind of man." Faustus, however, was justifiably consigned to hell when he listened to the diabolical proposal "Here Faustus, try thy brains to gain a deity." Those who seek to become gods in fact become devils, and sometimes it is not easy to be sure whether an individual like Raleigh was a hero and a genius or, as many of his contemporaries called him, "the greatest Lucifer that hath ever lived in our age."

Economic prosperity, an intense sense of Protestant mission, incredible good luck, and the presence of a sovereign whose personality and showmanship somehow managed to ignite the fire of boundless loyalty in most of her subjects, all contributed to this flowering of mind and spirit, but one element of cultural dynamism deserves special notice — literacy. What playwrights and poet adventurers, essayists and statesmen, philosophers and soldiers had in common was that they could all write the queen's English. More fundamental, they represented the glittering peak of an educational revolution that reached far down into the fabric of Tudor and Stuart society.

Sir Walter Raleigh, by Nicholas Hilliard
"Sometimes it is not easy to be sure whether . . . Raleigh was a hero and a genius or . . . 'the greatest Lucifer that hath ever lived. . . .'" (*National Portrait Gallery, London*)

As in most other revolutions, the velocity and extent of change depend on our judgment and characterization of what came before and on where we look for change. Because our knowledge of literacy is sketchy at best and varies according to the specialist's definition of the term, it is difficult to say whether a literacy rate of 30 percent of the male population, which some experts claim for late Tudor and early Stuart England, constitutes an impressive increase. The rate of change reached undeniable revolutionary proportions, however, among the ruling elite, especially the gentry, which by 1640 was nearly 100 percent literate. The ability to write and the level of poverty tended to be closely but inversely related: possibly 50 percent of the yeomanry but only 10 percent of husbandmen and very nearly 0 percent of agricultural laborers were literate. Townsfolk fared better, wealthy merchants and professionals equaling the gentry, and shopkeepers on average excelling the yeomanry. As one historian has summed up the educational revolution, it "produced not a literate society but a hierarchy of illiteracy which faithfully mirrored the hierarchy of status and wealth."

Historians stand on somewhat surer statistical ground when they measure educational change in terms of the numbers of students and institutions. The old medieval apparatus of education — the parish church school conducted by the local priest and the universities of Oxford and Cambridge — were secularized, humanized, and expanded. Petty (primary) schools and more advanced grammar schools sprang up throughout the kingdom. Between 1560 and 1640, some £293,000 was bestowed on grammar-school education, and by the first half of the seventeenth century, 142 new schools had been founded. By 1630 most market towns had a grammar school, and possibly 50 percent of the parishes of the more prosperous areas of the realm had schools — grammar or petty. Oxford and Cambridge also responded to the new educational demands, servicing 800 students in 1560 and 1,200 in 1630. A year or two at either Oxford or Cambridge or at one of the Inns of Court — the equivalent of today's law schools — became by the mid-seventeenth century the mark of the ruling elite.

Petty schools were in theory open to all, male and female, rich and poor, but education was not cheap; students paid tuition fees and supplied their own ink, quills, and paper. As a result some petty schools did not bother to teach writing. Moreover, many parents regarded education for their daughters as an unnecessary, nay dangerous, luxury, for it simply increased "their tendency to curiosity" and in no way prepared them to be obedient wives. The aim of Tudor primary education was not to train the child in the three "R's" but instead, to "catechize him in religion truly, frame him in opinions rightly, fashion him in behavior civilly." Social and religious indoctrination, not education as we understand it today, was the schoolmaster's purpose, and he sought to drill his pupils "in the knowledge of their duty toward God, their prince, and all other[s] in their degree."

The Schoolmaster His purpose was to drill his pupils " 'in the knowledge of their duty toward God, their prince, and all other[s] in their degree.' " *(The Mansell Collection)*

Grammar-school and university education was almost entirely restricted to the sons, not the daughters, of those in society who had carried off the lion's share of the prizes in life, especially the gentry. In grammar schools throughout the land and to a lesser extent at university, boys were converted into gentlemen who could display the two essentials of gentility and rank: a knowledge of Latin, with possibly a nodding acquaintance of Greek, and training in rhetoric, the queen of all the liberal arts. The educated Englishman was no longer a cleric; he was a J.P., an M.P., a merchant, or a landed country gentleman. For the first time, he possessed the ability to express his religious opinions and economic and political grievances in a fashion that helped to convert political factions held together by patronage into political parties held together by ideas. He could now speak in "generalized constitutional, religious, and philosophical terms."

Lower down the social hierarchy, the expansion of education carried with it equal potential for change. Education may shape the mind and generate right-thinking subjects, but it also opens the mind. Limited as the educational base may have been, it included "middling sorts" of people who were quite capable of reading both for pleasure and for profit. Every year for a few pence apiece, they purchased hundreds of thousands of almanacs and chapbooks filled with romantic tales, sermons, useful domestic and agricultural hints, historical information, and both astro-logical and astronomical predictions — all innocent enough material on the surface but heady stuff for imaginative minds. A publication explo-sion also hit religious literature. A Warrington bookseller who listed the 1,200 items in his bookshop in 1648 stocked Shakespeare and Cervantes, but he also had on hand 110 Bibles and dozens of religious exegeses and devotional works, most of them by Puritans.

Whether the political and social upheaval of the mid-seventeenth century would have been possible without a reading public that had ac-quired the habit of thinking for itself is anybody's guess. As every educa-tor worth a mortarboard knows, it is dangerous to overestimate the im-pact of the educational process, but Renaissance England — the century that produced Shakespeare, Marlowe, Bacon, and Milton — would never have occurred without the quiet industry of a growing number of school-teachers, publishers, and booksellers.

CHAPTER 10

Crisis and Recessional

Sound management and God's special favor saw Elizabeth through the first ten years of her reign; her religious settlement was adopted with surprisingly little opposition and her kingdom committed to a Protestant foreign policy that was as peaceful and economical as the queen could make it. In 1568, however, the situation began to change. The deity showed a depressing tendency to forget his special charge — "God's Englishmen" — and Elizabeth and her council had to work that much harder to guide the realm through rebellion at home and crisis abroad.[1] The same centrifugal forces that were tearing France to pieces began to appear in England, and on the international front, a decade of living in the same world with a touchy and pugnacious Catholic Spain began to strain even Gloriana's diplomatic finesse.

Cold War — Sixteenth-Century Style

Elizabeth had begun her reign as an ally of her Spanish brother-in-law in the conflict against France, and it had been Philip who successfully countered French influence in Rome and guarded Elizabeth against excommunication. The Most Catholic King of Spain preferred upon the English throne a Protestant but independent Elizabeth Tudor to a Catholic but French Mary Stuart. By 1568, however, Philip was beginning to wonder whether he had miscalculated; ten years later he was convinced that he had made a terrible mistake and that someday Elizabeth would have to be destroyed. When Elizabeth ascended the throne, France had been strong and united, Mary Stuart's Guise relatives militantly anti-Spanish,

---

[1] W. T. MacCaffrey, *Queen Elizabeth and the Making of Policy, 1572–1588* (1981) and *Elizabeth I: War and Politics 1588–1603* (1992) are the best general treatments of the queen's middle and later years. The following are a number of books that give a somewhat different flavor to the events of the reign: R. Lacey, *Robert Devereux: The Earl of Essex* (1971); J. Hurstfield, *The Queen's Wards* (1958); L. B. Smith, *Treason in Tudor England, Politics and Paranoia* (1986); A. Esler, *The Aspiring Mind of the Elizabethan Younger Generation* (1966); R. Strong, *The Cult of Elizabeth: Elizabethan Portraiture and Pageantry* (1977); R. B. Wernham, *Before the Armada: The Emergency of the English Nation, 1485–1588* (1966); *After the Armada: Elizabethan England and the Struggle for Western Europe, 1588–1595* (1984); N. Williams, *Thomas Howard, Fourth Duke of Norfolk* (1964); and F. A. Yates, *Astraea: The Imperial Theme in the Sixteenth Century* (1975).

and England weak and struggling under the Virgin Queen. Twenty years later things were markedly different: France had lost its standing as a great power, the Guise family had moved into the Spanish orbit, and England had become the champion of heresy on the continent.

Slowly, the diplomatic friendship between England and Spain cooled into toleration, cold war, and open conflict. From the start, Anglo-Spanish relations were strained by English trading incursions into the Caribbean, which Spain regarded as its special preserve. In 1562 John Hawkins, his ships' holds filled with slaves from western Africa, sailed for Haiti. There he sold his contraband cargo and with handsome gifts persuaded Spanish officials to ignore their own imperial edicts outlawing all trade with foreign powers. Two years later he was back again; this time Cecil, Leicester, and even the queen herself invested in an enterprise that netted the shareholders a 60 percent profit. Hawkins's third voyage, in 1567, fared less well; his squadron of ten ships was set upon by a Spanish fleet, and he was fortunate to escape with two of his vessels.

Just when Spain ordered her colonial officials and admirals to treat Hawkins as a pirate, England decided to give unofficial but vital aid to Philip's rebellious and heretical subjects in the Netherlands. The Dutch crisis proved all-important. Philip's seventeen Dutch and Flemish provinces, part of his Habsburg inheritance, were growing increasingly restless under their Spanish-Catholic overlords. Open rebellion erupted in 1566 when Philip, eager to exterminate the hateful Calvinistic faith, introduced the Spanish Inquisition. The more he tried to suppress heresy and rebellion, the more desperate grew the revolt. England became involved when Dutch heretics in the northern maritime provinces took to the ocean as "Sea Beggars," set on striking a blow for God by destroying Spanish shipping in the channel. Philip called them pirates, but Elizabeth offered them sanctuary in English ports and allowed them to take on provisions and sell their plunder to London merchants. Relations between Elizabeth and Philip came close to open war in December 1568 when a Genoese ship, laden with gold loaned to Spain to pay for the disciplining of the Netherlands, put into an English port to escape the Sea Beggars. Gloriana promptly seized the bullion and renegotiated the loan with the Genoese bankers. An outraged Philip decried the action as blatant robbery. In retaliation he stopped English commerce to the Lowlands, and Elizabeth countered by freezing all Spanish assets in England.

The Northern Rebellion

Just as the diplomatic cold war began to heat up, Elizabeth confronted her first major domestic crises: the arrival of the fugitive Mary Stuart on May 16, 1567, and the rebellion of the northern earls in the autumn of 1569. The Revolt of the North was a lesson in inept timing and evidence of the strength of the Tudor regime. Three divergent grievances coalesced to produce insurrection: feudal sensibilities in the northern shires; dislike for Mr. Secretary William Cecil at court; and the queen's opposition to Mary Stuart's proposed marriage to Thomas Howard, fourth duke of Norfolk. Howard was England's sole remaining duke and the ranking peer of the realm. He was also a cousin to Elizabeth and fancied himself as husband to a queen. He and a number of other peers had determined to destroy Cecil, whom they deemed the source of Elizabeth's anti-Spanish, pro-Protestant foreign policy, and responsible for her interfering and bureaucratic ways in government. Behind Norfolk stood the earls of Northumberland and Westmorland, who harked back to the days of their Percy and Neville forefathers when feudal loyalty to kin and clan spoke louder than allegiance to the crown. The crisis came to a head in June 1569 when Elizabeth threw her support behind her secretary, forbade Norfolk's marriage to Mary Stuart, and ordered him to return to court. The duke elected discretion over valor and submitted, but the northern earls took alarm; they revolted in the name of the true faith and the good old life, both of which were threatened by economic and social change. By Christmas 1569 the last feudal uprising had collapsed, and eight hundred peasants died on the gallows for their loyalty to a code that no longer had a place in Tudor England.

The long-deferred bull of excommunication against Elizabeth was finally issued in February 1570, but papal thunder fell on deaf ears. In England the voice of rebellion was silenced, and abroad both Philip and Elizabeth still hesitated to commit their kingdoms to the ordeal of war. The king of Spain was far too concerned with heresy in the Netherlands and Turkish penetration into the Mediterranean to lend teeth to an otherwise harmless spiritual threat; and Elizabeth, despite the passionate appeals of the war party in her council, had no intention of embroiling England in costly hostilities. Relatively inexpensive cold war was more to her taste.

For all their caution, however, Elizabeth and Philip edged ever closer to armed conflict. Gloriana, despite her barefaced disclaimers, continued to give aid and comfort to Dutch rebels and to sanction English piracy against Philip's treasure fleets. In his turn, Philip encouraged Catholic sedition in England; gave support to Mary of Scotland; and slowly became convinced that he was God's instrument, chosen to rid the world of that archheretic, Elizabeth of England.

Philip II of Spain and His Great Enterprise

On paper Philip appeared far stronger than Elizabeth. He was not only king of Spain but also after 1580 monarch of Portugal, thus uniting the Iberian peninsula and the empires of the New World. In Italy, the duchy of Milan and the kingdom of Naples were Spanish. The western Mediterranean was a Spanish lake from which the Turks were driven after their defeat at the naval battle of Lepanto in 1571. The seventeen provinces of the Netherlands and the county of Burgundy were Philip's birthrights, and the profits from the commerce of Antwerp, the silver of Peru, and the trade of the entire world poured into his capital. The center of this family empire, acquired helter-skelter by the vagaries of death and marriage, was Philip's residence outside of Madrid — the Escorial. Part tomb, part palace, the Escorial reflected the king's literal turn of mind. Built in honor of St. Lawrence, who had been grilled over burning coals, it was shaped in the form of a vast gridiron. There, with the eight coffins of his nearest and dearest, Philip resided, laboring into the long hours of the night over the most intimate details of his empire and allowing no decision, however trifling, to pass uninspected through his cautious hands.[2] Philip and Spain possessed the will to lead the forces of the Lord in a triumphant Counter Reformation, but they lacked the resources and the resourcefulness. The wealth of the Indies flowed into the realm but stayed only long enough to disrupt the Spanish economy, which was still agricultural and medieval, causing inflation and the illusion, not the substance, of prosperity. The real benefactors were the seventeen provinces of the Lowlands, which supplied Spanish armies and navies with the ingredients of war, Iberian aristocrats with luxuries imported from all parts of the world, and Catholic monks with salt herring for their fast days.

At one time, Spanish seamen had known the North Atlantic and the English Channel as well as Hollanders and Cornishmen did. By midcentury, although Spain ruled the oceans of the world, it ranked neither spiritually nor materially as a great naval power. Genoese and Italians, Flemish and Portuguese captained the giant galleons that transported soldiers to fight for Christ and priests to save heathen souls in Mexico and Central America. When the Armada against England finally set sail, its best pilots were Dutchmen. The Spanish commanding officer was Alonso Perez de Guzmán el Bueno, duke of Medina Sidonia, a nobleman of blameless and devout life but of uncertain health who confessed that he had rarely put to sea, easily caught cold, and always became seasick. Spanish military power excelled on land. Its soldiers regarded the navy as an inferior branch of the service, and warships were used as floating platforms for musketeers and pikemen and not as mobile batteries. Its naval tradition and architecture were Mediterranean, and Spanish ship designers built oared galleasses and clumsy, top-heavy galleons suitable to quiet waters but not to the winds and waves of the Atlantic. "To speak the truth," wrote one English naval captain, "till the King of Spain had war with us, he never knew what war by sea meant, unless it were in galleys against the Turks."

The impending struggle with England was intimately linked with Philip's troubles with his rebellious Dutch subjects. In 1576 he decided on a concerted effort to destroy heresy and subdue his provinces. By a

---

[2]The character of Philip II remains baffling. See R. B. Merriman, *The Rise of the Spanish Empire*, vol. 4 (1934); R. Trevor Davies, *The Golden Century of Spain* (1954); J. H. Elliott, *Imperial Spain, 1469–1716* (1963); and G. Parker, *Philip II* (1978).

Sir Francis Drake "The most blatant act of piracy had been Sir Francis Drake's global voyage of pillage and plunder in 1577." *(North Wind Picture Archives)*

policy of force and diplomacy, the king's governor-general of the Netherlands, the duke of Parma, succeeded in splitting the provinces and rallying the southern states to the side of Spain and Catholicism, leaving only the ten northern principalities in revolt. In 1581 the northern states declared their independence, and four years later in desperation they called for English military assistance. As Parma's troops moved steadily northward, Dutch appeals grew more urgent, and finally Elizabeth agreed to send an army of 6,000 soldiers under the earl of Leicester to fight in Holland. No matter how reluctant Philip was to risk war with England, by 1585 he realized that peace and victory in the Netherlands could come only after the English heretics had been destroyed and the realm re-Catholicized. Moreover, Spain had suffered long and patiently the indignity of English piracy on the high seas and the violation of its imperial and commercial monopoly in the Americas.

The most blatant act of piracy had been Sir Francis Drake's global voyage of pillage and plunder in 1577. Of the five ships that left Portsmouth, only the *Golden Hind* returned thirty-four months later, having completed the second circumnavigation of the earth, but the profit was worth the cost. Elizabeth for once was lavish in her praise, England gleeful, and Philip infuriated: English investors, of whom Elizabeth was among the largest, had realized a 4,700 percent profit, entirely at Spain's expense. Worse indignities would soon follow. In April 1587 Drake struck again, this time with twenty-three ships carrying royal troops for the official purpose of "distressing" the king of Spain. The

English fleet attacked the Spanish homeland, burned thirty ships in the harbor of Cádiz, destroyed naval installations, and blockaded Lisbon for four weeks. Sir Francis completed Philip's humiliation by sailing on to the Azores, where he seized a Spanish merchantman laden with treasure valued at £114,000, of which Elizabeth claimed £40,000.

Mary of Scotland and the Menace of English Catholicism

Open war in the Netherlands and on the high seas was complicated by a series of plots and counterplots in England that led to the execution of Mary Queen of Scots on February 8, 1587. For nineteen years Mary Stuart lived in England as an unwanted and embarrassing prisoner, but this confinement did not prevent her from meddling in high treason. Surrounded by English spies, she jumped from one harebrained plot to the next, any one of which would have ended on the scaffold if Elizabeth could have brought herself to execute a cousin who was an anointed queen. Mary never learned; messages continued to flow from her prison in the accustomed manner of cloak-and-dagger drama. Elizabeth's government, if not the queen herself, became convinced that sooner or later, by the law of averages, one of these plots must succeed. Parliament and council implored their queen to exterminate such a "monstrous and huge dragon," and even men of the cloth argued that mercy need not be shown to one who "hath heaped up together all the sins of the licentious sons of David — adulteries, murders, conspiracies, treasons, and blasphemies against God." After months of agonizing indecision, Elizabeth signed the warrant that sent her cousin to the block. In the end she had no other choice, for England faced open war with the man who acknowledged Mary Stuart to be the rightful ruler of the realm and who even talked about making her his wife.

As Spain readied itself for a religious crusade, English Catholics suffered from guilt by association. "No papist," so the equation read, "can be a good subject." During the first years of the reign, Catholics had out of necessity been tolerated — 40 to 60 percent of the country still held to the old faith — but the Northern Rebellion, the papal excommunication of the queen, the threat of invasion, and the intrigues surrounding Mary Queen of Scots forced Elizabeth to adopt a more severe policy. A new spirit of martyrdom was emerging in English Catholicism. More and more, "the cause" received fresh ideas and blood from the continent, where Jesuits, fanatics, and exiles dreamed of a united Christendom in which England would be purged of its Protestant heresy. By 1572 Catholicism was clearly tainted with treason when Mary Stuart and the duke of Norfolk, those two veteran intriguers, were caught up in a plot manufactured out of the optimistic and fertile imagination of Robert Ridolfi, an Italian merchant and papal spy. Ridolfi convinced many people that 10,000 Spanish soldiers were waiting to sail for England and that an equal number of English Catholics were ready to rise up against the queen of

Catholic Priests Being Executed for Treason   "Elizabeth's policy of moderation and toleration collapsed, and the queen found it impossible to resist the demands of nationalists and Protestants determined to exterminate the Catholic menace." *(The Folger Shakespeare Library)*

heretics. The plot came to nothing and Norfolk was executed, but England could not dispel the specter of militant and seditious Catholicism. Fear of Catholic treason was heightened by the arrival of seminary priests trained at the English college at Douai in the Netherlands. They came during the 1570s by the dozens to revive the hope and courage of the faithful. Catholic resurgence received further impetus from the Jesuits under Edmund Campion and Robert Parsons, who were smuggled into England to "confute errors" and to assure Elizabeth's subjects that their primary duty was to the pope and the law of God.

Confronted with such provocation, Elizabeth's policy of moderation and toleration collapsed, and the queen found it impossible to resist the demands of nationalists and Protestants determined to exterminate the Catholic menace. The penalty against saying mass was increased to 200 marks and a year in jail; Catholic priests were imprisoned; and in theory, every Catholic layman faced bankruptcy if he persisted in the errors of his faith. Campion was caught, tortured, and hanged in 1581; and possibly some 200 other seminary priests and Jesuits were executed during Elizabeth's reign. Those who died were hanged and disemboweled as traitors, not heretics. The queen persecuted, but she did so in the name of the sovereign national state, not the true faith. Significantly, she never saw fit to call on God as her ally; nor did she seek to justify her actions as spiritually necessary to her own salvation or to that of her victims.

The Armada

The diplomatic and religious crisis came when the Armada,[3] on which Catholic prayers and Spanish gold had been lavished, finally sailed in July 1588. One hundred and thirty ships weighing 58,000 tons, carrying over 31,000 men and 2,431 cannons, set forth to administer the vengeance of heaven and the censure of the church. The mission of this vast effort was the destruction of a middle-aged female whom the Catholic world branded as "born in adultery, an offspring of incest, a declared bastard," and a sovereign "incapable of lawful succeeding." Officers and men, sailors and soldiers had confessed and heard mass before setting sail. Gambling and swearing were forbidden, and no unclean person was allowed to accompany God's special enterprise. Twenty-one massive galleons, floating fortresses each bearing as many as fifty-two guns, four galleasses, propelled by sail and oar, and some forty armed merchantmen, slow, seaworthy, and hard to sink, formed the fighting core of the Spanish fleet. The procession also included thirty-four fast sloops — the eyes and ears of the navy — and two dozen transports to carry the men and arms dedicated to the Lord's Armada. Philip's strategy was to avoid battle if possible and to send his Armada up the channel to rendezvous with the Spanish forces under the duke of Parma, stationed in the Netherlands. Reinforced with Parma's troops, the fleet would then turn and carry the army up the Thames estuary, and land south of London.

What happened every schoolchild knows — the guns of a larger, better-armed, and more mobile English fleet, two hundred strong and commanded by Drake, Hawkins, and Lord Howard, led the heavy Spanish galleons on a merry chase. What saved England and destroyed the Armada was not so much English heroism — of which there was plenty — but Spanish inexperience at sea, the inability of Philip's fleet to make contact with Parma's land forces, and the winds and waves of the North Atlantic, which swept down on a demoralized Armada and splintered it on the rocks of Scotland, the Orkney Islands, and northern Ireland. Of the one hundred thirty ships that had left Corunna, history records that only sixty crawled home in defeat. Of the rest: ten were captured, sunk, burnt, or driven aground by the English; twenty-three more were vanquished, in the words of one Spanish author, "by the elements, against which valour and human daring are impotent because it is God who rules

---

[3]By far the best modern study of the Armada is G. Mattingly, *The Armada* (1962). See also F. Fernández-Armesto, *The Spanish Armada, The Experience of War in 1588* (1988), and C. Martin and G. Parker, *The Spanish Armada* (1988).

The Arch Royal, the English Flagship During the Attack on the Armada
" 'Twelve of Her Majesty's ships were a match for all the galleys in the King of Spain's dominions.' " *(North Wind Picture Archives)*

the seas"; and possibly twelve others were "lost, fate unknown." How many of the remaining twenty-five reached safety remains uncertain.

Whether accomplished by God or man, the victory was spectacular, and England congratulated itself that "twelve of Her Majesty's ships were a match for all the galleys in the King of Spain's dominions." The Counter Reformation slowed down, Calvinism and the independence of the northern provinces of the Netherlands were ensured, and Elizabeth's "beardless boys" henceforth felt confident that the future and the riches of the New World were theirs. In this, however, the fates reserved a bitter disappointment. Spain learned to defend her empire and to build more seaworthy vessels. The naval war, so brilliantly launched, deteriorated into a costly, endless struggle in Holland, France, and Ireland. At home the kingdom grew restless under the maternal restraint of an aging royal nanny and waited, none too patiently, for the old queen to die.

Puritans and Puritanism

For most Protestants in England, the paramount issues of the reign centered on the Spanish menace from abroad and the dread of Catholic rebellion from within. Even as late as 1589, no one knew exactly how many adherents of the old faith still remained or how many of them were willing to place duty to the queen and country above the voice of inner conscience.[4] Elizabeth saw the situation differently, however. As she had been almost continuously at odds with her privy councillors and Parliaments over the fate of Mary Stuart and the wisdom of a tolerant policy toward English Catholics, so she was at equal odds over what she regarded as the greatest peril to her rule. For her, the ardent and interfering Protestant, better known by the derogatory name of Puritan, who demanded windows into every subject's soul, posed a far greater danger to her religious settlement and her well-ordered commonwealth than obedient Catholics who kept their religious opinions to themselves. What made the Puritans doubly troublesome was that they were well established within the church and well connected at court, and therefore difficult to distinguish from faithful supporters of the established church. Moreover, because they tended to be militantly anti-Spanish and anti-Catholic, they could wrap themselves in the cloak of patriotism and loyalty to their Protestant queen.

The Puritan was first and foremost a Protestant, holding the Bible as the sole source of religious authority and believing in the sanctity of individual interpretations.[5] He held to the doctrine of Calvinist predestination, in which an omnipotent God ordains every aspect of the universe and not a leaf can drop from a tree without His foreknowledge. He believed in election, by which God selects certain of His creatures for everlasting salvation. The church was viewed as the body of the faithful, and ministers were regarded as teachers and expounders of Scripture, not as priests endowed with miraculous authority. Like all Protestants, the Puritans believed that the miracle of salvation came solely through God's grace and through the willingness of men and women to open up their souls and pray for a deliverance that they in no way merited, but that God of His mercy might or might not allow.

What distinguished Puritans from other Protestants was the literalness with which they subscribed to the Protestant creed and the rigorous logic of their approach. No church belief or government policy could be

---

[4]The best work on Catholicism is J. Bossy, *English Catholic Community, 1570–1850* (1975). See also W. R. Trimble, *The Catholic Laity in Elizabethan England, 1558–1603* (1964).

[5]Works on Puritans and Puritanism and the debate over whether Puritans can be distinguished from "normal" supporters of the Elizabethan church, or whether the term *Puritanism* can even be used, are legion. The indispensable starting point is P. Collinson, *The Elizabethan Puritan Movement* (1968), *The Religion of Protestants: The Church in English Society, 1558–1625* (1982), *Godly Rule: Essays on English Protestantism and Puritanism* (1983), and *The Birthpangs of Protestant England: Religious and Cultural Change in the Sixteenth and Seventeenth Centuries* (1988); but see also P. G. Lake, *Moderate Puritans and the Elizabethan Church* (1982). The best review of the literature and the controversy can be read in R. L. Greaves, "The Puritan-Nonconformist Tradition in England, 1560–1700: Historiographical Reflections," *Albion*, vol. 17, no. 4 (Winter 1985), pp. 449–486. For a fascinating case study of Puritanism in action in the seventeenth century, see D. Underdown, *Fire from Heaven: Life in an English Town in the Seventeenth Century* (1992).

accepted unless verified by the Bible. Scriptural silence could not be used to justify human expediency, for "what is not of faith is sin." Puritans tended to be spiritual hypochondriacs who watched out for their souls' health. They were militant in their convictions; and, above all, they possessed the sense of rebirth and conversion that set them above and apart from the rest of humanity. Almost without exception, Puritans had experienced a sense of conversion. They counted themselves members of a spiritual elite endowed with rights and privileges denied to lesser Christians. They served as soldiers of the living Christ, the elect of God who alone in a depraved and degenerate world had experienced a rebirth and regeneration.

Puritans viewed the Bible as the literal mirror of life. Holding up church and state to scriptural inspection, they generally found both institutions woefully lacking in piety and godliness. The trouble with Puritans in the eyes of the established church was their determination to thunder against the evils of society. In the righteous view of Christ's evangels, there was much to criticize and purify, for the world was a wicked place and the devil whistled seductively at unwary souls in every corner — in the alehouse, the theater, the country house, the court, and the bedroom. In a sense, Puritans were deeply medieval, believing that life was a spiritual drama and that the material affairs of today must be judged by the spiritual concerns of tomorrow. They did not dismiss everything cheerful and bright as sinful, for they, too, danced, wined, and laughed — but only if such gaiety sprang from godliness and not from humanity's depraved preoccupation with itself.

Why more of Elizabeth's subjects had grown increasingly fervent in their faith and more militant in their religious opinion in the 1580s than back in the days of her brother Edward is a mystery. Possibly greater literacy and Bible reading had something to do with spreading high-intensity religion. Possibly a deepening sense that the antichrist was about to assault the kingdom stirred religious hysteria and paranoia; only by purging God's citadel of corruption from within could the kingdom be saved from the papal beast without. Possibly it had something to do with the evangelizing success of the reformed faith; in the 1570s and 1580s, Protestant numbers had increased greatly, thereby providing a larger base from which to generate extremists. Certainly both sides began to close ranks, and intolerance and aggression marched hand in hand. The Puritan stood in the same relationship to Protestantism as the Jesuit did to Catholicism. Both served as stormtroopers of their faith, driven on by the voice of passionate conviction; both were utterly uncompromising, placing spiritual values above human prudence; and both viewed religion as the key to life. In this sense Elizabeth would have agreed with James I's witticism, "One puritan presbyter equals one popish priest."

Militant, disciplined, elite, and elected, Puritans saw themselves as separate from the corruption of the world. They were "another people," and they deemed it natural that they should have banded together as an exclusive society of God's saints on earth, determined to reform and improve Elizabeth's religious settlement. They scorned the established church, so infamous in the eyes of God's elect, as a comfortable and confused organization catering to the muddled desires of mild Protestants and apathetic Catholics who placed loyalty above faith and prudence above conviction. Largely Catholic in structure, it substituted a sovereign lady for a pope but retained bishops, archdeacons, ecclesiastical courts, and tithes. Weighed down with sinecures, it was deliberately vague on crucial points of doctrine, and laymen controlled much of its patronage. Elizabeth, the Supreme Governor, was God's lieutenant on earth, but the Anglican episcopate never renounced the idea that, as a divinely inspired organization, it derived authority from God as well as the queen, who appointed its members. Anglicans viewed the Bible as the Word of God, but the Church of England argued that it was not for simple folk to inquire too deeply into such mysteries as predestination or the nature of sin. It was far better and infinitely safer to leave the Scriptures to official interpretation, which tended to be more allegorical than literal. Elizabeth went to great pains to warn her Parliament that it was "overbold with God Almighty" when subjects scanned "His blessed will as lawyers do with human testaments." The presumption, she concluded, "is so great as I may not suffer it . . . nor tolerate newfangledness." The threat of newfangledness lay at the core of the controversy, for Puritans showed a dangerous radicalness in their insistence that the sole purpose of life was spiritual and that the duty of the church was to serve God, not the crown.

The Puritan's sense of urgency was rooted not only in the fear of the Catholic menace but also in the feeling that the godly had been sold a bill of goods in the religious settlement of 1559. Christ's truth had been compromised in the name of expediency and the sophistry of "things indifferent," which had offered radicals the expectation that governmental decree would eventually abolish hateful papal trappings. Twelve years later, they discovered that their queen had every intention of leaving her church exactly as she had "found it at her first coming in." Thwarted by an ecclesia that refused to reform itself, Puritans throughout the 1570s and 1580s turned to the press, the pulpit, and Parliament to persuade Gloriana to accept their vision of the new Jerusalem. In this campaign they had important allies in the Privy Council, in Convocation, and in the episcopate, for all three organizations supported various kinds of moderate reform. The radical clamor, however, did more harm than good because it hardened the queen in her determination to block any change in her religious settlement.

In their attempt to pressure Elizabeth, Puritan extremists found that in parliamentary freedom of speech it had a popular cause and a weapon that might induce the queen to ease her opposition to religious reform. It was the Wentworth brothers of biblical name — Paul and Peter — who led the war for free speech and a purified church. Peter publicized the root of the controversy when he told Archbishop Parker that "we will pass nothing before we understand what it is; for that were but to make you popes." In 1576 he again spoke out against the queen's refusal to allow Parliament to discuss matters of religion, saying that, during the last session of Parliament, God had been "shut out of doors." Next, Paul persuaded Commons in 1581 to hear a godly sermon at the commencement of each daily meeting, but the queen, sensing the righteous Puritan hand of the Wentworths, forbade it.

The crisis came in the Parliament of 1586, when the Puritan faction introduced Cope's Bill and Book, two statutes calling for the abolition of the state episcopacy and the Anglican Prayer Book and for their replacement by a Presbyterian Church and a Puritan creed. The Bill and Book had short shrift with the Supreme Governor, who ordered both withdrawn from Commons. In answer, Peter Wentworth submitted ten articles to the house in which he defended the constitutional privilege of free speech and suggested that anyone who violated the liberties of Parliament was an enemy of God. Inasmuch as it was Elizabeth herself who had infringed on these doubtful rights, Wentworth's words were both blasphemous and seditious. Much to the delight of most of his parliamentary colleagues, he found himself in the Tower of London for his audacity.

The uncompromising opposition of the queen was not the only danger facing the Puritans. Equally serious was their inability to present a united front on the proper organizational structure of God's church. The great majority of Puritans under Elizabeth continued to accept the existing church structure, advocating only that bishops be restricted in their authority and that the doctrine of "things indifferent" argued for greater local autonomy, not for more central control. A minority, however, held out for revolutionary change. Some favored a state church modeled on the Kirk of Scotland in which the queen's episcopate would be replaced by a Presbyterian synod with power to purify the faith, determine doctrine, and appoint parish ministers. An even more radical, almost lunatic, fringe led by Robert Browne and Henry Barrow believed that the godly should covenant together, not on a national scale as the Presbyterians argued, but on a local level, and that each congregation should be free to determine its own doctrine and elect its own minister. The Congregationalists, as they would be called in later centuries, tended to be anarchistic in spirit and democratic in organization. Under the Tudors, however, they were voices crying in the wilderness of an authoritarian age that accepted the principle of religious and political uniformity and that strove to root out any sign of such dangerous dissent.

As the special vessel of God's will and the saintly soldier of His kingdom, the Puritan constituted "a poor security risk." Doubtless God's people were loyal to the queen, but when Peter Wentworth proudly told the House of Commons, "I will never confess it to be a fault to love the Queen's Majesty," he significantly added, "neither will I be sorry for

Queen Elizabeth Sitting in Parliament   "Elizabeth perceived that a community of religious idealists deriving spiritual authority from on high was contrary . . . to the very existence of a monarchy that claimed divinity from God." *(The Bettman Archive)*

giving Her Majesty warning to avoid her dangers." The dilemma was inherent in the Puritan faith. What if the queen rebuked godly council, ignored the truth, and endangered the spiritual welfare of the realm? Worse, what if the crown turned upon the soldiers of Christ, harried them out of the land, suppressed the Word of God, and openly allied with the devil? From 1590 on, this was exactly the problem that the religious radicals faced.

Elizabeth perceived that a community of religious idealists deriving spiritual authority from on high was contrary not only to the political theory of the organic Tudor state but also to the very existence of a monarchy that claimed divinity from God. As early as 1573, the Anglican Church had recognized the threat, and the dean of York Cathedral summed up the inherent danger of Puritanism when he wrote: "At the beginning it was but a cap, a surplice, and a tippet [over which these Puritans complained]; now, it is grown to bishops, archbishops, and cathedral churches, to the overthrow of the established order, and to the queen's authority in causes ecclesiastical." Elizabeth reacted by finding an archbishop who would exterminate an organization that so obviously smacked of treason. Throughout the 1590s her new archbishop, John Whitgift, worked with a will, uncovering secret Puritan presses, crushing Puritan associations, and imprisoning Puritan leaders. He enforced legislation that threatened to exile or execute all who refused to attend Anglican services, who spoke out too loudly against the church's episcopal organization, or who questioned the queen's supremacy. Once the Spanish menace had passed, Elizabeth was convinced that her crown, her supremacy, and the entire theory of Tudor government had far more to fear from Puritans than from Catholics.

The Elizabethan House of Commons

The presence of a handful of religious radicals in the House of Commons, speaking high-mindedly of freedom of speech and debate and trying to legislate a revolution in religion, goes to the root of a historical problem: the proper role of Parliament within the Elizabethan body politic. Until recently, historians argued that the position of Parliament — especially Commons — was changing: Instead of acting as the obedient junior partner in the mystical union of King in Parliament, it started to exert its independence, claiming responsibility to speak for the entire kingdom, and seizing governmental initiative from the queen. In other words, Commons was becoming the organ through which the landed country gentleman could express his views and dominate the government. The lower house was maturing and preparing itself for the revolutionary role that it would later play during the crisis with Charles I. Puritan leadership in the parliamentary effort to persuade the queen to marry, to name a successor, to execute Mary Queen of Scots, to exterminate Catholicism, and to reform her church was seen as proof of a growing spirit of conflict. Only Elizabeth's matchless tact and command of language, by which she sought to defuse and befuddle the opposition, averted a political explosion and open rupture between crown and Commons.

Of all the signs of change, the most obvious was the phenomenal increase in the size of the House of Commons. The Tudors may have been stingy in their presentation of noble titles, but they were lavish in their creation of M.P.'s. While the House of Lords decreased in number throughout the century as a consequence of the removal of the monastic spiritual lords, the House of Commons almost doubled in size. In Henry VIII's first Parliament, 74 knights sat for the 37 shires, and 224 burgesses represented the chartered and franchised boroughs of the realm. As the century progressed, two interrelated movements developed: Landed country gentlemen of the shires violated the historic residence laws and sat for borough seats, and the number of towns holding the right to send delegates to the House of Commons increased. Henry added 14 borough seats[6]; Edward, 34; Mary, 25; and Elizabeth, most prodigal of all, created 62. One element of King in Parliament was obviously growing at an alarming pace, and the older interpretation argues that socially and economically, the Commons, monopolized by the gentry, was becoming a vocal, self-aware, and opinionated group. Politically replacing the Lords in importance, Commons had the potential to seize the initiative from the crown if royal leadership and control faltered.

Such a view, based on the historian's foreknowledge of what would later happen in the seventeenth century, is now unacceptable to most

---

[6]Henry also gave representation to the border shires of Monmouth and Chester (two knights each) and to the six new Welsh shires (twelve knights and eleven burgesses).

scholars.[7] Today historians emphasize consensus and not conflict, cooperation and not confrontation. Parliament is represented as a central
component of political stability. Government policy was discussed, debated, and resolved within a parliamentary forum that included Lords
just as much as Commons and that the Privy Council carefully controlled. Indeed, in the total scheme of government, the House of Lords,
although reduced in size, had considerably more importance than its
lesser parliamentary counterpart. Opposition to the queen, today's scholars argue, was illusionary. No Puritan party existed in Commons, let
alone any spirit of independent action. The sole purpose of Parliament
was to tax and legislate, to remedy deficiencies and redress grievances by
making or occasionally unmaking law. Parliament was an instrument,
not a source, of power. Real political initiative rested with the queen,
with factions within her court, with her Privy Council, and especially
with "the local hierarchies" headed by the great peers and wealthy gentry
who controlled church and state patronage and, therefore, governmental
policy in the shires. When debate and controversy erupted in Commons,
it either reflected disagreement within the Privy Council itself or constituted a carefully orchestrated display organized by members of the
queen's own government, designed to manipulate her into doing the
will of a majority of her Privy Council. The proper study of Parliament
is not crown versus Commons, but instead a prolonged duel between
Gloriana and most of her ministers who pressed her either to change
or to make up her mind. Finally, the extraordinary growth of Commons
is seen no longer as a sign of growing gentry strength and a shift of
the balance of political power, but as evidence of the power and authority of the Tudor throne. Landed gentlemen clamored to sit in Parliament
because it provided the surest and quickest way into the queen's
government.

Adept as Elizabeth was at countering her ministers' maneuvers in
Parliament, she could not totally fulfill her political ideal of as few Parliaments as possible — she was loath to call "the assembly of her people"
except "upon just, weighty and great occasions." Unfortunately, "great
occasions" kept cropping up throughout her reign, and she had to call
upon her people's advice and especially their financial support approxi-

---

[7]The older view of Elizabeth's Parliaments can be read in J. E. Neale's *The Elizabethan
House of Commons* (1949) and *Elizabeth I and Her Parliaments*, 2 vols. (1957). For the
new approach, see G. R. Elton, *The Parliament of England, 1559–1581* (1986); N. L. Jones,
Faith by Statute: Parliament and the Settlement of Religion, 1559 (1982); M. A. R. Graves,
The Tudor Parliaments, Crown, Lords and Commons, 1485–1603 (1985); M. Kishlansky,
Parliamentary Selection: Social and Political Choice in Early Modern England (1986); and
D. Starkey and C. Coleman, *Revolution Reassessed: Revisions in the History of Tudor
Government and Administration* (1986). A review of the debate and the literature can be
read in N. L. Jones, "Parliament and the Governance of Elizabethan England: A Review,"
Albion, vol. 19, no. 3 (Fall 1987), pp. 327–346. Two new surveys that show signs of a return
to Neale's position are T. E. Hartley, *Elizabeth's Parliaments: Queen, Lords and Commons
1559–1601* (1992), and J. Loach, *Parliament under the Tudors* (1991).

mately every three and a half years. Gloriana sensed that it was important not to go to Parliament hat in hand begging for money, and she avoided frequent sessions and requests for subsidies by forfeiting the Stuart future and selling her capital to avoid excessive taxation. War, however, made her insolvent, and in the end she realized that she could not do without the goodwill of that organ of state which paid for her government and her policies. Henry VII had averaged £11,500 annually from parliamentary subsidies. His son's rate rose to £30,000, but Elizabeth's reached £50,000. Consequently, when Commons (which in theory at least initiated all money bills) complained, Gloriana felt obliged to listen, if not necessarily to act.

The Winds of Economic and Intellectual Change[8]

Once the crisis of the Armada and national survival had passed, new and discordant forces emerged that ran counter to the central theme of the Elizabethan political creed: the organic unity of the realm. The foreign menace remained, but it no longer generated the magical response of earlier days. Instead, an aging monarch found herself troubled by economic problems that she little understood, faced with mounting political infighting that she could not control, and enmeshed in an inglorious war in Ireland.

Between 1597 and 1601, a political storm gathered that does not easily fit the model of a cooperative and well-behaved Parliament. In retrospect the crisis was the constitutional tip of a growing economic iceberg upon which some deterministically inclined historians would argue the Tudor-Stuart state eventually floundered. Exercising its historic right to petition the crown to redress grievances, Parliament clamored for the abolition of government-licensed monopolies. In doing so, it unconsciously reflected the new economic and capitalistic impulses of the sixteenth and seventeenth centuries. It also quite consciously raised questions about the value and purpose of Tudor-Stuart paternalistic economic theories and practice, exposing to public debate the crown's historic prerogative right to curb free enterprise and impose economic controls without statutory sanction.

Political theory extolled parliamentary authority on the grounds that the two houses spoke for all interests within the realm. The interest that was growing fastest and transforming the kingdom most rapidly was

---

[8]Works on capitalism and Tudor-Stuart society and economy are legion. The following is a sampling of the best: D. C. Coleman, *The Economy of England, 1450–1750* (1979); L. A. Clarkson, *The Pre-Industrial Economy in England, 1500–1750* (1971); C. G. A. Clay, *Economic Expansion and Social Change: England 1500–1700*, 2 vols. (1984); P. Slack, *Crisis and Order in English Towns, 1500–1700* (1972); L. Cantor, *The Changing English Countryside, 1400–1700* (1987); E. Kerridge, *Trade and Banking in Early Modern England* (1988); and D. Levine and K. Wrightson, *Making of an Industrial Society: Whickham 1560–1765* (1990).

Iron Processing in the Seventeenth Century
"Between 1540 and 1660 England was experiencing major economic changes sometimes dignified with the name 'First Industrial Revolution.' " *(Mary Evans Picture Library)*

that of the entrepreneur and capitalist. Between 1540 and 1660, England was experiencing major economic changes, sometimes dignified with the name "First Industrial Revolution." True trade and industry remained the social inferiors to land and title, and the countenance of the city dweller was described as "a dull plodding face, still looking in a direct line forward," but the direction of that mercantile expression was one of immense expansion. Iron production during the century following 1540 increased fivefold; coal mining rose from 200,000 tons a year to 1.5 million. By 1640 English coal production was three times that of Europe and the truth of John Cleveland's words — "Correct your maps: Newcastle is Peru" — became clear. Spain might possess the wealth of the New World, but England found far greater riches in its own backyard, where the coal mines of Yorkshire kept London hearthfires burning, supplied

East India Company Ships Preparing to Sail   "Spice was more precious than gold." *(National Maritime Museum, Greenwich, England)*

the white heat needed in cannon foundries, converted ore into iron and cane into sugar, and made fortunes for the mine owners.

On the high seas, English shipping doubled between 1570 and 1650, and the largest merchantman afloat during the first half of the seventeenth century was a thousand-ton East Indiaman symbolically christened *The Trades Increase.* Much of this commercial explosion was due to the development of chartered trading companies, of which there were basically two types — regulated and joint-stock. The oldest of the regulated companies was the Merchant Adventurers, first organized in the early fifteenth century, chartered in 1505 by Henry VII, and rechartered in 1564. A governor and twenty-four assistants controlled the company, which had its home office in London and self-governing branches in such provincial cities as Newcastle, Hull, York, and Exeter. By 1600 perhaps two to three thousand merchants, each paying an entrance fee of £200, composed the membership. It was, as one member exclaimed, "the most famous company of merchants in Christendom." Its control was primarily regulatory, and each member was free to sell or buy cloth within the rules prescribed by the company. In contrast, in the joint-stock companies each merchant bought shares and left the buying and selling to officials of the corporation. The Muscovy Company was chartered as a joint-stock organization in 1553 to deal directly with the government of the czars. Each subscriber paid £25, and the company was able to operate, pay its officials, hire sea captains, and purchase Russian furs and grain with a capitalization of £6,000.

The greatest of all joint-stock companies was the East India Company, founded in 1599 and consisting of 24 directors and 218 original subscribers who paid an entrance fee of £50. The company was established on the grandiose notion that England was "the mistress of the ocean, her navies putting a girdle round about the world." In this belief, London financiers and merchants were badly mistaken. The initial impetus for the company had come from the monopolistic actions of the Dutch, who in 1599 boosted the price of pepper from three to eight shillings a pound. Elizabethans depended on heavily seasoned foods to conceal the stench of putrefaction and on spiced drinks to warm their stomachs. Spice was more precious than gold, and the first company ships set sail to the Spice Islands of Sumatra and Java. There they met the Dutch and were promptly evicted; only as second best did the company turn to India, where it established a foothold north of Madras at Masulipatam and then in 1612 a station on the west coast at Surat. India may have been second best, but the value of the company's assets, originally something over £60,000, ballooned to £370,000 by 1660.

In all the new enterprises as well as in the manufacture and the export of English broadcloth (which remained the golden fleece of the economy), entrepreneurs stored away fat profits — the Muscovy Company paid a 90 percent dividend in 1611, and the East India Company earned a 500 percent profit on its investment in 1607 — but even greater quantities went to reinvestment in industry. Coal mining, draining, and digging required vast sums of money as shafts drove deeper and deeper into the earth. The manufacture of soap, bricks, and glass; the refining of salt; and the brewing of beer all demanded capital. One iron smelter employed 4,000 men. At the mouth of the Tyne, where coal was cheap and available, workers produced salt by heating iron pans twenty feet square and five feet deep. Four men were needed to operate a single pan, and by 1589 one producer employed 300 men and had a capital investment of £4,000. Under James I, one London brewer bragged that he was worth £10,000. Despite the sums spent buying noble sons for merchant daughters, purchasing estates and pedigrees, and "ladifying" aldermen's wives, larger amounts were poured back into commerce and industry. As a consequence, by the end of the seventeenth century, England was per capita the wealthiest kingdom in Europe, with the financial strength to play the costly game of continental power politics; to invest in long-term colonial adventures; to pay for its mania for architectural extravagance; and to supply the endless capital needed for the factories, the canals, and later the railroads of the Industrial Revolution.

Merchants may have felt inferior to country gentlemen, but the governors of high finance and the directors of economic expansion amassed enough wealth to ensure themselves a place in heaven by heeding the advice of Bishop Curteys of Chichester, who asked them to "consider wherefore did God give you such great store of riches and large possessions in this life, above your brethren; was it not to do good with them and to help them that have need?" Their answer was overwhelming: between 1485 and 1640, the merchants of the city of London supplied £1,889,211 for charity, or one-fourth of the total contributed by men of substance throughout the realm.

Possibly, mercantile generosity reflected another economic fact of seventeenth-century life: the spectacular growth of London. Elizabethan authorities deplored this grotesque development, which seemed to transform the body politic into a distorted monster with its head out of all proportion to its body, but the city continued to burgeon, both in size and in economic importance. Its consumption of wheat doubled between 1605 and 1661, and by 1600 London merchants monopolized seven-eighths of the cloth trade. At the beginning of the seventeenth century, the population of England and Wales stood in the neighborhood of 4.5 million, and during the century it increased by another million. Impressive as this rate of growth was, London far surpassed it. The city that James entered in 1603 numbered 200,000 souls; by the time the last Stuart died in 1714, the population had reached well over 500,000, and one Englishman in every nine lived within the boundaries of greater London. Since 1500 London had been sucking up great armies of men and women, for whom society felt little social and only slight Christian responsibility, and who died in droves in the plague-infested slums of Westminster and Southwark. Some 40,000 persons perished in the plague of 1603, but still the stampede into the disease-ridden metropolis continued, and any pretense of government zoning collapsed. Once upon a time London had been a city of brick, mortar, and slate roofs; by Elizabeth's death it had become a vast cluster of jerry-built thatched and plastered houses that kept spreading until everything — rats, lice, slums, and palaces — perished in that purging holocaust, the Great Fire of 1666.

The traditional view of a regulated and static commonwealth in which all the queen's subjects lived by "one law, one love and one life, one voice, one heart and one people" would continue to be voiced down to the eve of the Civil War, but the growth of the city of London eloquently testified to the ineffectiveness of laws limiting the movement of labor and the migration of peasants into the city. Far more serious for the future of that paternalistic concept was the mounting criticism in Commons of the queen's prerogative to issue monopolies as a way of regulating the economy. Three kinds of monopolies existed: (1) a grant by the government to some favored individual to break the existing mercantile laws of the realm — for instance, a patent to export or import some restricted commodity; (2) trade monopolies given to privileged companies such as the Staplers, the Merchant Adventurers, or the East India Company; and (3) grants to individuals to monopolize the selling of articles that otherwise would have been exposed to unrestricted competition. As a variant of this last type, some monopolies exploited, for example, the mineral resources or the riches of the New World. In theory, the granting of monopolies protected essential military industries and safeguarded both the producer and consumer from cutthroat competition and shoddy standards of production. All items except the staples of life such as meat and bread were organized and licensed as monopolies, which ran the alphabetical gamut from belts, butter, and buttons to tar, timber, and tobacco, and from beer sold in monopoly barrels and distributed in licensed alehouses to soap manufactured in government factories.

Unfortunately, what started off as government regulation justified by state security and social welfare almost immediately became mired in the profit motive and the financial needs of the government, for monopolies, which were so potentially lucrative to the possessor, could be sold to the highest bidder. The earl of Salisbury netted £7,000 a year in 1622 from his monopoly on silk, and the earl of Suffolk managed to extract £5,000 from soap. By 1630 the licensing and sale of monopolies, which brought in some £100,000 annually, had become essential to the financial existence of the crown and an almost insurmountable barrier to fiscal reform (see pages 234–235).

Increasing criticism of the government's right to issue monopolies to favored courtiers and financial speculators coincided with a decade of hard times. The fat years of economic expansion had ended. In their place came the depressed 1590s, when bad harvests, soaring food prices, peasant unrest, high taxes, and an unprofitable war afflicted the kingdom. Under the circumstances, monopolies seemed unwarranted as a means of protecting the consumer, because they increased the cost of living without achieving a corresponding rise in the standard of production. Worse, the system did not even serve as an effective sales tax, for the crown received only about 12 percent of the increased cost of production. The lion's share went to private owners. The cry went up that the kingdom was being "spoiled, imprisoned and robbed by monopolists," and in 1601 hotheads urged that Commons quit petitioning the queen for redress of such obvious abuses and pass legislation to restrain and regulate the crown's licensing powers. At stake stood not merely the theory of paternalistic government but also the queen's historic prerogative, which stood above earthly criticism, especially by a subordinate Parliament. During the controversy, the Privy Council tried to explain to a Commons filled with landed country gentlemen and wealthy city merchants that the government had the authority to curb free enterprise and impose economic controls at will. Elizabeth's dutiful subjects listened in angry silence to a philosophy at variance with their own thoughts and, when the queen passed through their chamber at the end of the first parliamentary session, the customary greeting — "God bless your majesty" — was half-hearted. Gloriana was deeply alarmed, and she had cause: the essence of her political magic, her personal popularity, had begun to give way before the growing criticism of royal policy. As usual, Elizabeth knew when to retreat. She saved her prerogative from becoming a topic for debate in Commons by promising a complete inquiry into the abuse of monopolies. Nevertheless, by implication a constitutional issue had been raised, one that would find growing support in the generations following the old queen's death: the question of whether crown or Parliament possessed ultimate responsibility for determining state policy and the correction of abuses.

Essex and the Irish Wars

The queen's affairs prospered no better in Ireland and at court than they had in Parliament. Across the Irish Sea, religion, racism, and tribalism plus 10,000 Spanish troops and 100 ships united to spark civil war and rebellion in 1595–1596, a conflict that took eight years to quell. English rule had existed in Ireland since the days of the Norman kings, but early English conquerors had tended to become more Irish than English, and with the Reformation the government in London could no longer depend even on the loyalty of the English Pale around Dublin. In 1596 Anglo-Irish Ireland and tribal Ireland joined in a revolt led by Hugh O'Neill, earl of Tyrone. The uprising cost the queen £120,000 from the sale of crown lands, £2 million more from parliamentary funds, and a debt of £473,000 before Tyrone was captured and English rule of Ireland secured.

A tragic by-product of the Irish quagmire was the destruction of Robert Devereux, earl of Essex, the last of the queen's favorites and the greatest rebel to her crown. Essex had been the darling of the court ever since his arrival in 1586 at the age of eighteen. The embodiment of the Renaissance man, he coveted honor and renown above all else. The earl had been granted military responsibility in France and in the naval war against Spain, where he proved himself better at personal heroics than leadership. Nevertheless, Essex yearned for absolute command, and in 1599 he demanded that Elizabeth allow him to lead an army into Ireland to redeem English honor and crush the Tyrone rebellion. He discovered, like many before him, that the Emerald Isle was a military graveyard for English reputations. Instead of finding glory, Essex revealed his incompetence and latent treason. He came to terms with Tyrone and, in defiance of the queen's express orders, returned to London to justify his actions and excuse his lack of military success.

Throughout her reign, Elizabeth had endured a great deal of youthful insubordination on the part of her favorites and military gallants, for war and the quest for honor were male prerogatives, but Essex's disobedience smacked of sedition. Anyone who touched her scepter courted disaster. Essex was placed under house arrest, deprived of the offices and incomes so necessary to his political power, and was quite deliberately goaded into outright rebellion. In desperation he attempted in February 1601 to raise the city of London against his prince and to stage a palace coup d'état. Elizabeth's throne, even in the winter of her reign, was far too secure for a neurotic nobleman of considerable charm but no common sense to topple, and she "taught him better manners" with the headsman's blade. Essex paid for more than his abortive attempt at

An Allegory of the Vanity of Courtly Life   "The divinity of Elizabeth's rule was finally being called in doubt." *(© Copyright in this photograph reserved to the Ashmolean Museum, Oxford)*

king-making. Two years before, he had questioned the very essence of the divinity of kings. In a clash of wills between himself and his royal mistress, he had voiced the one sentiment that no Tudor sovereign could for long ignore or leave unpunished. Raging with fury, he had written to Sir Thomas Egerton: "What! Cannot princes err? Cannot subjects receive wrong? Is an earthly power or authority infinite? Pardon me, pardon me, my good lord, I can never subscribe to these principles." The words were ominous, for they meant that the divinity of Elizabeth's rule was finally being called in doubt. Spoken by an unstable and churlish Essex, they meant little, and most Englishmen gave a sigh of relief when he was executed in 1601; but Tudor society had heard and recorded his question, although as yet it did not care to give an answer.

Recessional

A world of radical Puritans and capitalistic profiteers was passing the old queen by, and so was time. Old friends and dependable enemies were disappearing. "Her Robin," Robert Dudley, earl of Leicester, died in 1588; Henry III of France and Catherine de Medici, in 1589; Marlowe, in 1593; Hawkins, in 1595; Drake, in 1596; Philip II, in 1598; and her good and faithful servant William Cecil in the same year. An England was emerging that Old Bess neither desired nor understood.

The end came on a cold day in March 1603. She died not so much of old age (she was sixty-nine) as of want of anything for which to live. Death was hastened by melancholy caused by the loss of her last close friend, the countess of Nottingham. Gloriana retired to bed, and turned her face to the wall. Ere she died, however, her chief councillor, Robert Cecil, the son of her old and valued adviser Lord Burghley, confronted the question that Elizabeth had left unanswered throughout her life. For over a year before the queen's death, he had been in secret contact with James VI of Scotland; and when Elizabeth's council asked her to name her successor, it was carefully arranged that she should gasp, "Who should that be but my nearest kinsman, the king of Scots."

Gloriana was gone. In life she had been, as the Spanish ambassador once reported, "much attached to the people and . . . very confident that they are all on her side." Not everyone had favored her politics, but as the ambassador admitted, they were all, Catholic and Protestant, peasant and noble, on her side. Elizabeth had possessed marvelous magic — the affection of her people. Her subjects may have heaved a quiet sigh of relief that their beloved but difficult lady was dead, but the love that they had given her was not easily transferred to the Scottish son of Mary Stuart. As the queen's godson Sir John Harington said, "Now that my good mistress is gone, I shall not hastily put forth for a new master."

A Woman in a Man's World

Elizabeth's reign raises a question: the proper role of women in Tudor England. Women had been queens before but only queens consort, not queens regnant; their power stemmed from their husbands' authority, not their own. Mary Tudor had been an exception, but she had willingly placed her husband's wishes above her own, as a good sixteenth-century wife was expected to do. She had brought England into the war against France as Philip had required, even though the papacy had placed him under ban of excommunication. Elizabeth was different. She remained an unmarried queen regnant, claiming for herself all of the powers that belonged to a man and a prince. For the first time, women possessed real political influence at court, and men had to curry favor among the maids and ladies-in-waiting who controlled access to the queen and her patronage. Elizabeth was no modern feminist; she believed in the traditional subordination of women to men — except, of course, for herself — but she sometimes went out of her way to support her own sex in family land disputes and domestic conflicts.

It is hard to judge the impact that forty-five years of queenly government had on gender relations and wifely behavior throughout the kingdom. As a domestic role model, Elizabeth fitted poorly into the male
ideal. André Hurault, the French ambassador during the final years of the
reign, may have sensed the undercurrent of male restlessness when he reported that, though the queen's government was "fairly pleasing to the
people . . . , it is little pleasing to the great men and the nobles; and if by
chance she should die, it is certain that the English would never again
submit to the rule of a woman." Gloriana's successor was only fulfilling
his regal and masculine duty when he took it upon himself to take
"down high-handed women." He warned his secretaries of state to "be-
ware of trusting their wives with secrets of state" and ordered the pulpits
to "ring continually of the insolencies and impudence of women.[9] England's grief at the death of its queen was heartfelt and many of her subjects did not "hastily put forth for a new master," but the transition from
a Tudor to a Stuart monarch was made more palatable by the knowledge
that the new sovereign was married and had fathered two healthy sons —
a happy return to normalcy and the correct order of things.

---

[9]See Joan B. Goldsmith, "All the Queen's Women: The Changing Place and Perception of
Aristocratic Women in Elizabethan England, 1558–1620 (unpubl. Ph.D diss., Northwestern
University, 1987), for the role of women at Elizabeth's court. The quotations are from pp.
207–208.

The Demise
of the Tudor State

1603 to 1660

On preceding page: CROMWELL AT MARSTON MOOR
Engraving by Abraham Cooper *(Mary Evans Picture Library)*

CHAPTER 11

Straining the System: The Reign of James I

The news of Elizabeth's death and the proclamation of the Scottish king's succession "sounded so sweetly" in James's ears "that he could alter no note in so agreeable an harmony." His entry into his new possession was celebrated by a triumphal march, a thousand strong: "The people of all sorts rid and ran, nay, rather flew" to meet him, "their mouths and tongues uttering nothing but sounds of joy." On both sides expectations ran high. James Stuart looked forward to "the promised land," a kingdom with revenues six times the royal fare offered Scottish kings, and his new subjects, with the experience of the old and cankered queen's declining years much in their memory, saw in James the very model of a seventeenth-century monarch. He was a man wise in the ways of kingship, who, his people hoped, would put an end to a decade of niggardly retrenchment, economic hardship, administrative misconduct, prolonged inglorious war, and bitter court rivalries. A new century was commencing; a new dynasty, blessedly headed by a male — not an old-fashioned and unpredictable spinster who had modeled herself on Henry VIII — had taken charge; peace was about to break out; and almost everyone had ideas about reform in church and state that were dear to their hearts or pocketbooks. The question in 1603 was whether James, in an era of religious sensibilities, continuing economic change, and political tensions, could be all things to all people. The new king certainly tried, and in the attempt he may have committed his gravest mistakes.[1]

James VI and I (1603–1625)

James was England's "new broom," but, like so many household implements, once acquired, it remained in the closet. Largely as a consequence his reputation, especially among historians, has suffered. Although he

---

[1]The best single-volume survey of the seventeenth century is B. Coward, *The Stuart Age* (1980). More detailed but equally good is D. Hirst, *Authority and Conflict: England 1603–1658* (1986). Quite different in emphasis and organization is C. Hill's *The Century of Revolution* (1961). J. P. Kenyon's *Stuart England* (1978) is fast-moving but offbeat, and G. M. Trevelyan's *England Under the Stuarts* (1904) is old-fashioned but beautifully written and still a classic.

James I   "His new subjects, with the experience of the old and cankered queen's declining years much in their memory, saw in James the very model of a seventeenth-century monarch." *(The Granger Collection)*

may have done little to cause the debacle of his son's reign, scholars invariably point out that he did equally little to prevent it. Like military analysts, historians find it easy to be wise and critical after the event, and the traditional picture of James's reign is conditioned by the knowledge that within thirty-eight years of his succession to one of the most stable thrones in Europe, his promised land exploded into civil war. Even more unfortunate for James, he followed a sovereign who has since won almost every critic's heart. The makers of historical reputations delight in pointing out that in contrast to Elizabeth, her Scottish cousin appeared unkingly and ridiculous. Gloriana had driven her councillors to distraction by her disregard for security measures; James, however, was almost pathological in his abhorrence of violence, and he wore an ungainly, quilted, dagger-proof doublet for fear of assassination. The Tudor queen had dazzled England with her innate dignity and consummate showmanship, but the first Stuart was comical in his breeches, "great pleats and full stuffed" pantaloons. Elizabeth had willingly sacrificed privacy to court her people, but James hated publicity; when he was told that he ought to show himself more often to his eager subjects, he inelegantly asked whether as a king he was also expected to "pull down my breeches and they shall also see my arse?" Good Queen Bess had rarely talked about her royal rights but had spoken of her love for Englishmen, whereas James earned the reputation of being "God's silly vassal" for his scholarly insistence on legal prerogative and the divinity of kings. Ever since James fell afoul of the nineteenth-century historian Thomas Macaulay's devastating pen, the first Stuart king has remained in textbooks a sorry excuse for a monarch, "stammering, slobbering, shedding unmanly tears, trembling at a drawn sword, and talking in the style alternately of a buffoon and a pedagogue."

In recent years a kinder, and one suspects more accurate, portrait of the king has begun to emerge, in which much of the blame for failure to reform the Tudor system of government in time to prevent war and revolution has been shifted from the monarch to the system itself. James has been pictured as his motto described him — the "royal peace-maker" whose mission, both at home and abroad, was to foster unity and harmony. Today he is considered "a fundamentally tolerant ruler" whose verbal bark invariably conflicted with his conciliatory and, at times, practical handling of political and religious affairs. James was no stranger to kingship. He had become a king at thirteen months; then a ruler at seventeen years; and on his succession to the English throne at thirty-seven, he was a prince already highly expert in the art of political survival.[2]

James was, without doubt, the most successful of his ill-starred Stuart line. His great-grandfather had been killed at Flodden Field in 1513 at the age of forty. His grandfather, James V, had died of "shame" in 1542 after the Battle of Solway Moss, where a Scottish army, 18,000 strong, had floundered in a bog and surrendered to 3,000 English soldiers. His father, Lord Darnley, had died mysteriously at the hands of his mother's lover; and his mother, Mary Queen of Scots, had met her end on an English execution block. Survival was no mean accomplishment in Scotland, and under the circumstances it cannot be said that James was a royal failure.[3]

In sixteenth-century Scotland, feudal loyalty flourished, religious differences were as much a matter of clan as of creed, and respect for royalty was largely a question of "liberating" the king from some rival faction. The realm was backward and impoverished, and Calvinist minister and highland laird were quite ready to take up arms in defense of kirk and clan. It is small wonder that James VI grew up dreading violence and that

---

[2]D. H. Willson, *King James VI and I* (1956) is an older and unflattering interpretation of the king. Better and more accurate are M. Lee, *Great Britain's Soloman: James VI and I in His Three Kingdoms* (1990), and D. N. Bergerson, *Royal Family, Royal Lovers: King James of England and Scotland* (1991).

[3]For the history of Scotland, see J. Cowan, *The Scottish Reformation: Church and Society in Sixteenth-Century Scotland* (1982); G. Donaldson, *The Scottish Reformation* (1960) and *Scotland Under James VI and I* (1980); and J. Wormald, *Court, Kirk and Community: Scotland, 1470–1625* (1981).

he detested the association of armed men and Presbyterian preachers. Considering the life expectancy of his family and the stultifying education reserved for monarchs who ascend their thrones in infancy, James came through surprisingly unscathed; indeed, during the 1590s, he proved himself the political match of any feudal lord. He successfully frustrated Catholic murder plots and Protestant kidnappings, Presbyterian intrigues and baronial deceits. The influence of the kirk was curbed, a modified episcopacy introduced to govern the church, and the independence of the clans checked. In fact, by 1603 the Scottish monarchy was stronger than it had been at any time during the sixteenth century, and James had justification for voicing exalted notions of the divine right of kings in his scholarly, if impractical, tome *The Trew Law of Free Monarchies.*

The secret of James's Scottish success lay in his ability to balance conflicting interests, to temporize, delay, reward, and detract, but never to drive enemies to desperation or give friends so much power that they could dictate their own terms. Survival, at which James was so adept, rested on the principle of never permitting opponents to find common cause and of rewarding abundantly all who offered their support. James's political training turned out to be both his greatest asset and his most serious weakness when operating within the English scene, for understandably he viewed the problems of his English realm in terms of his Scottish experiences. His education in monarchical survival was magnificent, but his knowledge of English kingship and Tudor government was bookish and often archaic. Although he knew in theory what was expected of him and spoke grandiosely about the divinity of kings — "for kings are not only God's lieutenants upon earth and sit upon God's throne, but even by God Himself they are called gods" — he never fully comprehended how much real power a Tudor sovereign actually possessed.

From the start of his English reign, James felt insecure; as a consequence, he ruled as if he were still in Scotland, surrounding himself as much as possible with Scottish cronies and charming young men beholden only to their royal benefactor. He failed to give support to those councillors who had the imagination and drive to reform the system; he passed out royal largesse as if from a bottomless reservoir of bounty; and he proved unwilling to rock the political and religious boat, "all novelties being," he said, "dangerous as well in a politic as in a natural body."

The Failure of Fiscal Reform

The first year of the new regime established the atmosphere for the remainder of James's twenty-two-year reign. Reform and optimism were in the air, and James called his first Parliament not to milk it of money but "to relieve all grievances of our people." He acknowledged the need for reform and pronounced that "no state either ecclesiastical or civil [exists] whereunto in 40 years some corruptions might not creep." Parliament's grievances stored up from previous reigns were legion. Nevertheless, the two subjects on which reformers waxed most vocal were the old trouble over monopolies (which, despite Elizabeth's promises to alleviate, still brought in thousands of pounds to a select and favored few) and the growing irritation over what is called fiscal feudalism, in particular the abuse of purveyance and the burdens of wardship.

Purveyance stemmed from the military power of the crown, the right to purchase provisions for the military and the royal household at a fixed price, which in an era of inflation was far below the market value of the goods collected. Possibilities for corruption and embezzlement were endless. Provisions could be resold; merchants were blackmailed by purveyors; and commercial interests, especially around London and in coastal areas, found themselves paying for the country's defense and government, while other parts of the kingdom went unburdened.

Wardship was even more widespread and distasteful, especially to the landowning interests. Under the Tudors the crown had begun the systematic investigation of the nature of all land tenure, and no one was safe from the eager eyes of government legal experts eager to prove that a subject's land was held by feudal knight's fee. The earls of Oxford and Essex were royal wards, but so also might be the son of a Middlesex yeoman with his ten acres. By 1540 wardship had become so important to the government that the Court of Wards was established to administer lands held in trust and to direct the education and protect the interests of the ward. The government, however, often sold its rights to favored courtiers and royal officials, who then controlled the ward's marriage, managed his estates, and as often as not left him in beggary. In effect, wardship meant the imposition of a heavy and unpredictable inheritance tax on property or, as the earl of Nottingham said, "the ruin of every man's house once in three descents."

Wardship, purveyance, and — to a lesser extent — monopolies had been and continued to be important sources of royal income; James made it known, however, that he would curb, possibly even abolish, monopolies and would give up purveyance and wardship in return for some kind of regular and predictable annual parliamentary grant. With the crown initiating fiscal reform and responding positively to parliamentary grievances, the way seemed ready for a thorough revamping of the tax structure. Instead of reform, however, within six months king and Commons became entangled in a potentially serious constitutional debate, and James had decided that his English Parliament was no more responsible or useful than its Scottish equivalent north of the border. Part of the explanation for this unexpected development involved basic political emotions — fear and self-interest. Known methods of revenue raising, though corrupt and inefficient, were invariably preferable to unknown and untried devices. James felt irritated that Parliament, after complaining about wardship and purveyance, should shy away from formulating substitute sources of income that could be levied on the kingdom as a whole.

Commons grew equally annoyed with the king. After initiating the reform movement and offering to abandon fiscal feudalism, the crown now began to have second thoughts about giving up nonparliamentary sources of income, which could be increased at will, for a fixed parliamentary grant that only Commons could adjust upward to match inflation. The potential for a future constitutional crisis was clear: The king might lose his independence and become the servant of Parliament, for whoever paid the piper called the tune. Both parties ended by feeling aggrieved, and the conditions for the growth of mutual distrust were established. More fundamental to the explanation were three other entangled and overlapping issues: the state of the crown's finances, the prevailing mentality of early Stuart Parliaments, and James's fatal inability to exercise monetary restraint.

The basic fiscal problem fraught with grave constitutional implications was that Parliament refused to grant the crown enough money to live on and at the same time insisted that the king should take nothing from his kingdom except what Parliament voted. Faced with a representative body that stubbornly failed to put the king's finances on sound footing, the government had no choice but to turn to nonparliamentary sources — especially fiscal feudalism and income from the customs — to pay for the cost of defense, justice, and administration. These actions in turn challenged and placed in jeopardy Commons's claim to approve the imposition of all new tariffs and to raise taxes. The situation was further compounded by three other factors: inflation, which increased the cost of government while it decreased revenues relative to expenses; what Commons regarded as the king's outrageously extravagant lifestyle; and Parliament's inability to conceive of itself as a permanent and equal partner in government responsible for the financial welfare of the kingdom.

James, it is often said, inherited a critical fiscal crisis: a costly war in Ireland inflamed by Spanish money; a debt of £422,000 — over a year's normal income; and an exchequer that had already sold off nearly one-fourth of the crown lands (thereby reducing land revenues from £150,000 to £110,000), and that had failed to keep income from either crown lands or the customs abreast of inflated prices. Among the most pressing matters during the first year of the reign was peace with Spain, which moderate Protestants, overtaxed landowners, and a government with a curtailed income welcomed. Although peace brought immediate fiscal relief, military economies were more than offset by the increased cost of maintaining a sovereign with two sons and a spendthrift wife who in three years spent £4,200 on clothes and baubles. Despite inflated household expenses, Robert Cecil, now the king's chief minister and earl of Salisbury, was optimistic that the crown could live on its own in good medieval fashion if it "modernized" the tariffs on imports and exports. He rewrote the book of tariff rates, which had not been updated since the beginning of the old queen's reign. In addition, he imposed new tariffs on heretofore untaxed goods and increased the theoretical value of commodities used to establish duties in order to conform to inflation, thereby bringing in an extra £6,000 a year.

"Modernization," as so often happens, had unexpected consequences. In 1606 when importer John Bate refused to pay the new duty on Venetian currants, the Court of the Exchequer ruled that all customs were part of foreign policy and came under the royal prerogative. They were not fiscal in nature and therefore required no parliamentary sanction. This decision opened up a source of income that, despite vehement parliamentary protest, the government hastened to exploit. New tariffs on virtually all imports in 1608 yielded £70,000, and by 1630 further increases plus inflation raised the total to £218,000. In a period of three years, the earl raised his master's regular income from £315,000 to £460,000. Unfortunately, even with increased revenues, Cecil failed to balance the budget. By 1610 the annual deficit had reached £50,000, and eight years later the king's debt had risen to £900,000. Clearly, if the crown were to remain solvent, either the cost of government would have to be radically curtailed or Parliament would have to make up the difference. Neither solution seemed possible.

Much of the blame can easily be placed on James, who was forever promising to curb his spending but could not resist the role of prince bountiful. He was anxious never to appear mean, and he regarded the royal treasury as a bottomless wellspring from which to reward and maintain his favorites. James knew full well the wisdom of the sixteenth-century maxim "Bounty is an essential virtue of the king," and royal largesse became the means by which an unknown king sought to build affection and loyalty in the wake of a dead queen who had been notoriously tightfisted in bestowing honors, titles, and incomes. Yet one suspects that James's extravagance had other than political ends. It was a means of advertising his own generosity and importance. As a consequence, the cost of government skyrocketed. In the first four years of his reign, wardrobe expenses quadrupled, and James gave away gifts worth £68,000 and pensions valued at £30,000, and he forgave debts totaling £176,000. By 1619 one-sixth of the king's entire regular income was going to pay for annuities to his favorites and officials. Had most of this largesse remained in English hands, the hue and cry in Parliament might have been considerably less; but of the £90,688 given away in 1611, £67,498 went to eleven Scottish cronies whose loyalty and friendship brought no political profit, at least not in England.

Parliament's argument that its sovereign was wildly extravagant and possessed no sense of economy had substance, but it is doubtful whether even a thrifty Stuart sovereign could have achieved solvency, given the administrative and fiscal corruption that by 1603 had become an essential attribute of Tudor government. Crown officials were hopelessly underpaid, their salaries were frozen in history, and their pay had to be supplemented with pensions and sinecures and by licenses to violate mercantile laws. Sir Robert Aitoun, principal secretary to Charles I's queen, Henrietta Maria, earned an official salary of £100, but he also received annuities and special payments that brought his yearly total to £940. The earl of Salisbury operated on an even grander scale. Besides his official fees, he pocketed as master of the Court of Wards the sum of £3,000 annually and another £1,333 a year from the imposition of duties on silks and satins (profits from which eventually rose to £7,000 a year).

Unfortunately, Parliament could not perceive the fiscal advantages of a system of payments that is easy to brand as inefficient at best and totally corrupt at worst. Moreover, members of Commons were growing increasingly fearful that nonparliamentary sources of royal income might make parliaments obsolete, as was happening on the continent. Both houses resented a government that seemed to turn a deaf ear to the need for administrative and fiscal reform and a king who gave good English money over to Scottish parasites and court toadies.

King and Parliament[4]

Not only did Salisbury find it impossible to balance the king's budget, but he also discovered that it was equally difficult to extract sufficient money from Parliament. The explanation is threefold: (1) James was unable to see the importance of that institution and in his irritation did much that antagonized his Lords and Commons; (2) even in 1603, Parliament still had a profoundly medieval understanding of its proper role in government; and (3) the landed and commercial elites represented by Parliament were extremely reluctant, after a generation of war taxation and during a period of depression and inflation, to introduce any kind of fiscal legislation that might increase their taxes.

In its dealings with the king, Parliament by historic necessity had to operate within a framework that in 1603 no M.P. was yet ready to deny. Parliament served as an instrument of the king, who was "God's anointed, being the head and chief of the whole realm and upon whom the government and estates thereof do wholly and only depend," and without the king's "authority, no Parliament can properly be summoned or assembled." Not only was Parliament an organ of the crown, but the formula also significantly added that a king "ought not to summon his Parliament but for weighty and grave causes." Parliaments, then, were both derivative and essentially temporary, meeting only for emergency reasons. Theoretically, the initiative rested solely with the crown; a meeting of Parliament was, in a sense, nothing more than an extension of the king himself. True, kings did not always get along with their Parliaments,

---

[4]C. Russell's *Parliaments and English Politics, 1621–1629* (1979) and his textbook, *The Crisis of Parliaments: English History, 1509–1660* (1971) have become the new orthodoxy, but the pendulum refuses to remain steady; see T. Cogswell, *The Blessed Revolution: English Politics and the Coming of War, 1621–1624* (1989), and R. Cust, *The Forced Loan and English Politics, 1626–1628* (1987).

anymore than they did with their councils or great barons, and Parliaments were forever complaining. Indeed, the right to complain about the way the king was handling the affairs of state and war was as much an established parliamentary prerogative as the right to levy taxes. Controversy and dispute, however, were conducted within the parliamentary family and in no way involved disagreement over the theory of the constitutional relationship between crown, Lords, and Commons. This awareness of both impermanence and inferiority and the recognition of the rights as well as the obligations of kingship fundamentally conditioned the way in which M.P.'s viewed seventeenth-century politics and responded to the issues of James's reign.

Under the Tudors, the system worked reasonably well. Parliaments were called only for weighty matters concerning such kingdom-wide issues as war, the break with Rome, the succession, and the establishment or reestablishment of the true faith; and Elizabeth had acknowledged Commons's right to free speech but with the significant proviso that such freedom be limited to subjects introduced for debate by her councillors. Under James, the crown's interest in and control of parliamentary procedures became more lax, partly because James was inexperienced with parliamentary techniques and customs; partly because M.P.'s, although acknowledging themselves as servants of and responsible to the sovereign, also felt themselves to be representatives of their constituents in shire and borough. How much of the mounting rift between king and Commons stemmed from royal laxness and how much from a growing spirit of independence on the part of Parliament is difficult to say. During Elizabeth's final years, six privy councillors out of a body of thirteen had regularly sat in Commons. Under James the number fell to three in a council of twenty-three. As a result, the Privy Council began to falter in its most crucial role — it failed to take the initiative in Parliament. There was no one who could present the government's view in debates, let alone control parliamentary machinery. The situation became so serious that one good friend of the crown wrote, "I think the state scorneth to have any privy councillors of any understanding in that house." Speakers of the House of Commons were shouted down by rebellious and bumptious members, privy councillors were hissed when they entered the house, and the ultimate insult came in 1626 when the Chancellor of the Exchequer had to wait two hours for leave to speak. Members of Parliament no longer looked to the crown or asked what the Privy Council thought. Instead they turned to their own leaders and preferred their own opinions to that of the sovereign.

The growing independence of Commons was reflected in the lower house's demand that James officially recognize its claim to decide disputed elections and to judge the legal qualifications of its own members. Early in the reign, Commons made its attitude perfectly clear when it politely but firmly informed the king that "the voice of the people, in the things of their knowledge, is said to be as the voice of God." The phrase "in the things of their knowledge" constituted an important qualification. Nevertheless, King and Parliament were beginning to assert competing rights because James claimed that he alone spoke for the deity. The evidence in the scholarly controversy over whether *conflict* or *cooperation* most appropriately applies to the relationship between crown and Commons is not all in, and what there is of it points in both directions, but Commons seems to have been declaring its right to speak for public opinion throughout the shires of the realm. "If," said one M.P. in 1610, "we should now return into our country with nothing for the good of the commonwealth, they will say we have been all this while like children in catching butterflies."

Commons, with its new sense of assertiveness, could never decide what was good for the entire commonwealth, as opposed to what was good for its various parts. A Parliament that did not complain about wardship, monopolies, administrative malfeasance, court corruption, royal extravagance, and pensions for worthless but insatiably "hungry Scots" was no Parliament at all, for these were the very issues that provoked those whom it represented. A House of Commons that did not protest the extension of tariffs and the imposition of new duties on imports and exports or did not doggedly defend its own perceived historic privileges was not performing according to custom. Nevertheless, M.P.'s found it easier to complain and protest than to act constructively in fiscal matters for two reasons. First, their constituents for years had been successfully avoiding taxation and opposed any extension of the tax burden. This feat had been achieved under Elizabeth in the face of growing crown pressure for money because local tax assessors dropped landlords from the tax lists or grossly underevaluated their estates. As a consequence, a subsidy — a tax on the value of land and chattel — that had yielded during the 1580s £130,000 fell to £55,000 by 1628. As James's reign progressed, a paradox developed: Parliament was paying less than in the past, even though it was voting in more subsidies. Second, by implication, any regularization of the king's income geared to a yearly parliamentary subsidy implied an annual Parliament, and this violated the derivative, temporary, and emergency nature of Parliament's authority and thinking. As a result, fiscal reform in the shape of a regular parliamentary grant in return for the abolition of fiscal feudalism and import-export tariffs floundered in 1604. It would flounder again in 1610 when Salisbury, gambling his entire political credibility with both king and Parliament, proposed the Great Contract, by which the crown offered to give up wardship and purveyance and refrain from extending the customs without parliamentary sanction in return for an annual grant of £200,000. Instead, Parliament continued, as in the past, with stopgap measures, rescuing the government on an emergency basis and often joining its insufficient generosity with demands for monetary concessions and bitter complaints about James's extravagance or his conduct of foreign policy. Commons, however, never offered enough to prevent the crown from developing and exploiting unpopular nonparliamentary sources of revenue that may or may not have been constitutional, depending on one's interpretation of history.

Although Parliament spoke largely in terms of the alleviation of abuses, the friction between king and Commons contained latent, if unappreciated, constitutional issues. In its frustration with James, the House of Commons or one of its committees in 1604 penned a statement of parliamentary rights known as the Great Apology; it included the significant statement that "all experience shows that the prerogative of princes may easily and do daily grow" but "the privileges of the subject are for the most part at an everlasting stand[still]." In the Apology, Commons was complaining about wardship and fiscal feudalism, not expounding the constitutional rights of liberty-loving Englishmen. Impassioned rhetoric, however, is easy to misinterpret; and although nineteenth- and twentieth-century historians may be wrong in viewing the Apology as a prelude to the coming constitutional struggle, it nevertheless dramatized the basic constitutional dilemma faced by both James and his son: Parliament had a choice either to modernize and assume responsibility for financing the crown or to become obsolete and permit the king to raise money without parliamentary consent. Neither choice was acceptable, and as a consequence, the historically indissoluble bonds between the king and his faithful Commons were slowly corroded by the acid of distrust on both sides. Although the year 1604 was a long way from civil war in 1642, in a sense the history of the prewar years should be seen as the steady transformation of parliamentary clamor over perceived governmental abuses and pleas for reform into demands for constitutional change. When that transformation was complete, a totally new and potentially revolutionary situation had emerged.

James had entered the promised land, and he neither understood nor deeply felt the need for fiscal reform. As long as the system generated the wherewithal to gratify his almost pathological need to be generous, he asked few questions and was only mildly irritated by a Parliament that complained vociferously but passed no constructive legislation. Union with Scotland was a reform close to the king's heart, however, and he never totally forgave nor forgot Parliament's failure to accept royal leadership, to put behind it five hundred years of Anglo-Scottish hatred and war, and to create a perfect union between the two nations. A tolerant and educated man, James possessed none of the chauvinistic emotions that ran high on both sides of the border; and he took it as a personal affront when his English Parliament refused to change the name of his kingdom from England to Britain, and thereby acknowledge him as King of a united realm.

"No Bishop, No King"

In one area alone — in matters of religion — James proved reasonably successful in creating harmony and conciliation in the wake of his succession. Even here, however, it is not always easy to separate the king's talent for high-flown polemics and his extraordinary, if at times irritating, gift for the catchy phraseology from what actually occurred in his handling of the established church and his relations with the Puritans. God-fearing Puritans, like almost everyone else in 1603, were optimistic about the new reign and were hopeful that a Scottish king, brought up in a Presbyterian kirk, would be their Moses, leading his people into a Calvinistic paradise. When they petitioned their new prince in 1604 to reform the Church of England, James, in the spirit of reform, met them at Hampton Court and listened to their complaints about the need to abolish papal ceremonies and their pleas for a better-paid, educated, and preaching clergy. James was not impressed; he associated Presbyterianism in Scotland with rebellion, and he found the Church of England very much to his taste, its episcopal organization being peculiarly suited to a divinely ordained monarchy. When Puritan speakers at the meeting overstated their position and raised the specter of a Calvinistic and Presbyterian theocracy in England, James made his position manifestly clear — "I will have one doctrine, one discipline, one religion, both in substance and in ceremony" — and he coldly warned them that Presbyterianism "agreeth as well with a monarchy as God with a devil." Then, in a formula for which he is justly famous, he stated the issue in its most succinct and quotable form: "No bishop, no king."

"One religion" required conformity. Through his newly appointed disciplinarian, Archbishop Richard Bancroft, James demanded that all clergymen of the Church of England not only conform to the Thirty-Nine Articles but also do so willingly or otherwise resign their posts. Elizabeth had weeded out Puritan Presbyterianism in a remarkably thorough fashion, and only 1 percent of members of the clergy found their conscience so tender that they felt obliged to give up their living. Moreover, as the years went by, Puritans discovered that what James refused in theory and in public he was willing to concede in private and through the back door. He appointed good Calvinists to the episcopal bench; he issued the authorized "King James" version of the Bible, for which Puritans had been clamoring, and unlike his predecessor, he refrained, even in his financial desperation, from plundering the church. He even permitted a high level of tolerance within the ecclesia, especially of tender Puritan consciences. Except for a tiny radical minority, his Protestant subjects never regarded James as "soft" on religion. He was viewed as a "godly prince," having achieved a far greater breadth of consensus than Elizabeth had ever attained, and throughout his reign, Puritan religious agitation remained minimal.

The Gunpowder Plot

If the radical Puritans were disappointed in a Scottish monarch who had breathed, but alas had rejected, the pure air of Presbyterianism, English Catholics were equally disappointed in a Scottish king who was the son

The Fate of the Gunpowder Plot Conspirators   "England was horrified to learn of the diabolical conspiracy of the Catholics and their willingness to commit treason. The plotters died horribly for their sins." *(E. T. Archive)*

of the "martyred" Mary Stuart. James, despite his claim of religious tolerance, regarded the pope as the antichrist and the Jesuits as Satan's disciples plotting the overthrow of all Protestant kingdoms. Millenarianism — the belief that Christendom would soon experience the cataclysmic victory of the forces of evil through the murder of the godly and the destruction of the commonwealth before the final triumphant second coming of Christ — was never far below the surface of much of Protestant thinking. The events of November 5, 1605, seemed to give proof that the day of the antichrist might not be far off.

Once peace had been established with Spain, English Catholic extremists could no longer hope for foreign aid in their battle to restore the old faith and proper devotion to the pope. Therefore, a small but strategically placed band of them decided on a "sudden blow" to rid the kingdom of its heretical government. Guy Fawkes and a handful of conspirators planned to blow up King, Lords, and Commons when they met to open the new session of Parliament. Fortunately for James and the Protestant leaders, some plotters were reluctant to incinerate Catholic peers along with heretic peers, so with only hours to spare, they leaked the plan to their Catholic friends who, in turn, informed the government. England was horrified to learn of the diabolical conspiracy of the Catholics and their willingness to commit treason. The plotters died horribly for their sins, but the memory of those gunpowder kegs in the cellars of Westminster Palace never died. Each year the kingdom reminded itself that the papal antichrist could well strike again and celebrated its deliverance by burning Fawkes in effigy, thereby further fanning the fires of anti-Catholicism.

James on His Own

The failure of the Great Contract in 1610 was the turning point of James's reign; thereafter, the responsibility for the king's government slipped from the crown's chief minister, Robert Cecil, earl of Salisbury. Cecil had engineered the succession, and his new master was both grateful to and dependent on Elizabeth's principal secretary, who under the new management became first the earl of Salisbury and then in 1608 lord treasurer. Deformed of body but keen of mind, Cecil was exactly to the king's taste, a servant who relieved his sovereign of the crushing administrative burden of monarchy. Unlike that other relic of the Elizabethan past, the flamboyant and unpredictable Sir Walter Raleigh, Cecil was content to remain in the shadows. Moreover, master and servant agreed on foreign policy — peace with Spain and neutrality in Europe. Much to militant Puritan disgust, Stuart England turned its back on the glorious tradition of Drake and Hawkins and the dream of empire, and in 1604 concluded a peace with its ancient enemy. Both James and his lord treasurer recognized that peace was essential to the survival of the new dynasty. James believed in it out of principle, Cecil out of financial necessity. The old system could be milked with a minimal amount of protest only as long as war did not impose intolerable financial strains and expose the administrative and fiscal rot that had set in. War inevitably upset the terms of the crown's relationship with Parliament and raised grave constitutional issues not only about nonparliamentary taxation but also about the conduct of foreign policy.

Cecil's failure to persuade either his master or Parliament to reform the kingdom's finances destroyed his credibility and usefulness to the king. Between 1610 and his death two years later, Salisbury's influence declined, while those characteristics that would influence the last decade of James's reign grew apace, giving to James and his reign their unsavory reputation. The period was dominated by favorites who had little to recommend them except their good looks and ability to ingratiate themselves, and by increasingly desperate and degrading stopgap fiscal devices to keep the government out of bankruptcy. The king had become addicted to pleasing young men with graceful limbs and fair complexions before he appeared in England; nevertheless, the English court was not prepared for the spectacular rise of Robert Carr, a young and handsome, if not overly intelligent, Scottish pageboy who caught the king's eye when the young man was thrown from his horse and broke his leg during a court joust. From such an unlikely beginning, Carr rose to be Viscount Rochester and to covet the fascinating, but totally unprincipled, Frances Howard, wife of the earl of Essex. With royal connivance and a great deal of faked evidence, the judges were persuaded to grant the countess a divorce, and she married Carr in 1613. As a wedding present, James advanced his handsome sycophant to the earldom of Somerset; congratulations were scarcely over, however, when it was revealed that connubial bliss had been made possible not only by political pressure but also by murder. During the divorce proceedings, it was alleged that Somerset and Lady Frances had first arranged the imprisonment and then the poisoning of Sir Thomas Overbury, one-time confidant and close friend of Carr and a bitter opponent of his marriage. Although James did not attempt to save his favorite (another even more attractive gentleman had already put in his appearance at court) and allowed both Carr and Frances Howard to stand trial for murder, the crown was nevertheless besmirched by association with a scandal that shocked the kingdom. The reputation of the government was further shaken by the revelation that the earl of Suffolk, Frances Howard's father and lord treasurer of England, had been misappropriating funds and accepting bribes.

Not only did scandal smear the name of monarchy, so also did monetary practices that, although profitable in the short run, bequeathed to James's son seriously depleted sources of land revenue and did little to enhance the reputation of the crown in the eyes of its subjects. The selling of crown lands began under Cecil, but on his death, James, who left Salisbury's key offices vacant for years as part of his policy of balancing factions at court, sanctioned the sale of land on a dangerously high level. He divested the monarchy of estates worth £775,000, or about one-fourth of his patrimony, thereby accelerating a trend that had already started under Elizabeth and would eventually prove fatal to the Tudor-Stuart crown. Land, with all the political and social power associated with it, increasingly passed out of the hands of the monarchy and into those of the gentry and nobility. Later, when Charles I had sold acreage worth £650,000 to pay for his early wars against France and Spain, and the Civil War had divested the sovereign of his remaining estates, the king was no longer the greatest landowner in the realm. Lionel Cranfield, Salisbury's eventual successor as lord treasurer, warned James that "in selling land he did not only sell his rent, as other men did, but he sold his sovereignty, for it was a greater tie of obedience to be a tenant to the king than to be his subject."

George Villiers, First Duke of Buckingham "He was tall, athletic, beautifully proportioned, and seductive." *(The Mansell Collection)*

Equally serious was the new policy of converting titles of nobility into marketable commodities. The rank of baronet had purposely been created in 1611 to be sold to the highest bidders; the competition was so keen that a baronetcy went for as much as £10,000, and the sales netted the government the enormous sum of £100,000. James and his son viewed knighthood and the peerage in the same light: 2,600 Knights Bachelor and 126 Knights of the Bath were created, and membership in the House of Lords rose from 59 in 1603 to 121 by 1625, and to 186 under Charles I. Fiscal, not social, pressure lay behind most of these creations, and although it was said that such transactions defiled the flower of nobility, they seemed a small price to pay for such a painless source of income.

As James grew older, he turned more and more for advice and comfort to a new favorite, George Villiers, the threadbare second son of a genteel county family, who would eventually become duke of Buckingham. He was tall, athletic, beautifully proportioned, and seductive, and far more capable than Somerset. "No one," wrote an unflattering observer of court life, "dances better, no man runs or jumps better"; indeed, Villiers jumped in seven years "from a private gentleman to a dukedom," with an annual income of £80,000 at a time when the government was running an annual deficit of £90,000. From James's point of view, Villiers was worth every penny, for he was not only extraordinarily good-looking but also extremely hard-working, and he relieved his prince of the burdens of kingship in a way that no one had done since Salisbury's death.

In one area, however — the colonization of Ireland — the king continued to bestow his time and energy. To appreciate the unusualness of the monarch's interest, the case of Ireland must be set within the wider context of English overseas expansion, which neither James nor his son approved of or fully understood, because so much of it took place without government sponsorship or control.

"No Land Uninhabitable, No Sea Innavigable": *Overseas Expansion and the Founding of Colonies*[5]

Angles and Saxons who swept across the English Channel to conquer Roman Britain; their descendants who unified the island; the Viking "swift sea kings" who harried and plundered the land; and their blood cousins the Normans who conquered and made England their own and who carried Anglo-Norman culture deep into Scotland, Wales, and Cornwall were all explorers, exploiters, and pioneers. The jump across three thousand miles of ocean to a new world was merely the next step in a process that had begun when the first Saxon set foot in Britain.

In the sixteenth century, English eyes and thoughts for the first time looked outward. The glitter of Spanish gold and the legend of a direct sea passage over the top of the world to China and the Orient enthralled the imagination. As early as Henry VIII's reign, the English boasted that "there is no land uninhabitable, no sea innavigable" to those with courage and a sense of adventure; in fact, one of the avowed purposes of the Muscovy Company in 1553 was to discover "how men may pass from Russia either by land or sea to Cathaia [China]." The idea of planting English men and women beyond the seas and the lure of the fabled wealth of imaginary civilizations, where kitchen utensils were forged of gold and grotesquely shaped people had eyes in their shoulders and mouths in their stomachs, had caught men's fancy long before Captain Christopher Newport set sail for Jamestown in 1607.

From the start, English expansion overseas was unique, for the course of British colonization fulfilled Sir Walter Raleigh's prophecy that, despite his failure to establish a colony at Roanoke in Virginia, he would yet live to see the New World "an English nation." The English expected "to plant a nation where none before hath stood." From Maine to Georgia, from Bermuda to the Barbados, from Newfoundland to Ireland,

---

[5]For colonization and overseas expansion, see K. R. Andrews, *Trade, Plunder and Settlement: Maritime Enterprise and the Genesis of the British Empire, 1480–1630* (1984); D. Cressy, *Coming Over: Migration and Communication Between England and New England in the Seventeenth Century* (1987); J. C. McCusker and R. R. Menard, *The Economy of British America, 1607–1789* (1985); and A. N. Ryan, *England's Sea Empire, 1550–1642* (1983).

A Sea Monster   Myriad real and imagined dangers lay in the way of the search for "a direct sea passage over the top of the world to China and the Orient." *(The Granger Collection)*

England exported its peoples and transplanted a living social organism into the wilderness of a new world and across the Irish Sea. As Francis Higginson marveled in 1629, "Those that love their own chimney corner and dare not go far beyond their own towns . . . shall never have the honor to see the wonderful works of Almighty God." The hand of the deity may have been present, but hard economic facts were even more apparent, for neither Puritans nor profiteers, neither pilgrims nor promoters, could have built a temple or a trading post without the wealth of England behind them. The age of colonial expansion was possible because it happened to coincide with an era of capitalistic and industrial growth in which money became available to finance the pioneering energies of the seventeenth century.

The picture, treasured by generations of Americans, of God-fearing pilgrims dressed in "black plug hats — truncated cones with silver buckles — " and piously turning their energies to the creation of a Puritan paradise in "the place that God will show us to possess in peace and plenty" is not strictly true. God's elect not only wore clothing in the height of Stuart fashion but also came to the New World seeking profits

The White Man Encounters the Florida Indians "The dream of profits finally came true when the colonists sent home to England the rolls of dried tobacco leaves smoked by the Indians." *(North Wind Picture Archives)*

of the purse as well as those of the spirit. Colonial settlements were expensive, requiring long-term investments and confidence in the future to realize a return on the original capital outlay. Francis Bacon acknowledged this fact when he compared the founding of colonies to the planting of trees. "You must make account," he said, "to lose almost twenty years' profit, and expect your recompense in the end." The Massachusetts Bay Company spent almost £200,000 during the first decade of its existence; the settling of the Barbados between 1627 and 1629 cost £10,000; South Carolina in 1620 involved an outlay of £17,000 without a penny in return; and the Virginia Company spent £100,000 during the first fifteen years of its uncertain existence, only to go bankrupt in 1622.

Funds on such a scale were originally collected in the expectation of fabulous profits, and colonial investors organized themselves into joint-stock companies in the hope of a quick return on their money. The Virginia Company, chartered in 1606, was founded by merchants from London and Plymouth who had given precise instructions to the 105 hardy souls who eventually landed at Jamestown on May 24, 1607. The company expected the colony to produce "all the commodities of Europe, Africa, and Asia and to supply the wants of all our decayed trades." Besides the establishment of a thriving community, the settlers were ordered to search in their spare time for gold, a northwest passage to China, and heathen souls to convert to Christianity. Unfortunately, this wonderful picture of a bustling community of iron smelters and glass-blowers, tar makers and woodcutters, was never realized. Three thousand miles of chilly water, a death toll that reduced the Jamestown colonists by three-fourths, and the terror of the wilderness smashed the optimistic dreams of London financiers. Two years later, however, stubborn promoters sent out another six hundred settlers, determined this time to "take fast hold and root in the land." They arrived none too soon, for the remnants of the original settlers of Jamestown had abandoned their site before relief arrived. London businessmen poured thousands of pounds into the Virginia adventure only to end up in bankruptcy; but the dream of profits finally came true when the colonists sent home to England the rolls of dried tobacco leaves smoked by the Indians. When Englishmen acquired the habit, branded by James I as "loathesome to the eye, hateful to the nose, harmful to the brain, dangerous to the lungs," the economic salvation of the colony was ensured. Tobacco exports rose from 20,000 pounds in 1619 to 60,000 pounds within five years, and the population of Virginia reached 38,000 by 1670.

The Plymouth settlement, although more godly in its design, was no less commercial in its conception. Mr. Thomas Weston, a London iron-monger, and John Pierce, a London clothmaker, received a patent from the Virginia Company in 1620 to found a neighboring colony. They induced William Bradford and his Puritan band of exiles in Holland to join them in an informal stock company. Cautious men who preferred to invest their riches but not their lives in such a problematic venture were urged to do so at the cost of £12½ per share. More daring investors who actually sailed to the New World were rewarded with two shares for the same price, and settlers who could contribute nothing but their persons received one share apiece for their labor and the risk of their lives. The capital thus raised, as well as all future profits, were assigned to the company for seven years, at the end of which time the venture was to be dissolved and the money divided proportionately among the shareholders. Of the 101 passengers aboard the *Mayflower,* only 35 were Puritans from Holland; the remaining 66 came from Southampton and London. Many of these were the elect of God, but many more were men of Mammon.

Throughout the New World, the English were on the move — some to the granite outcroppings of New England, some to the fisheries of Maine and Newfoundland, some to the red earth of Virginia, some to the Carolinas, some to the garden paradises of the West Indies rich in sugar cane. The trickle of daring souls willing to risk three thousand miles of water and one to two months on the high seas became a flood. In 1630 seventeen vessels carrying a thousand men and women landed in the Boston region; within the year, that number had doubled. By 1634, 4,000 had arrived in Massachusetts, and New England boasted a population of 50,000 in 1675. The city of Boston, the largest town in the colonies, doubled in size every generation: 1,200 in 1640; 3,000 in 1660; and 7,000 in

1690. The total population of the mainland colonies rose to 100,000 by 1650, and possibly 250,000 Englishmen lived overseas by the end of the century.

What induced thousands to leave the comfort and security of their homes for the inhospitable, rockbound shores of New England and the dreadful silence of endless forests is difficult to explain. Of all the great powers, only England exported her people. Spanish imagination was caught by the glitter of gold and the anguish of souls crying out for salvation; France sought trade and raw materials. Only England developed plantations, exported homes and a way of life, and established entire nations in the wilderness. Permanent colonization demanded a type of recruit different from the missionary, the conquistador, or the trapper. It required men, women, and children to build, to toil, and to pray. The Indians, in the eyes of such settlers, were not heathens in need of conversion or even potential assets as trappers of animals, but menaces to the well-being and very existence of the colonists. Long before the advent of the cowboy and the conquest of the prairies, the English colonists believed that the only good Indian was a dead Indian.

The lure that could succeed in the face of disease, famine, and privation must have been prodigious. The Roanoke colony organized between 1585 and 1587 disappeared entirely; at Jamestown only 32 colonists survived out of 105; at Plymouth 50 died within the year, and at one time during the first winter only 7 men were fit to work. Quiet folk were enticed from their homes "to seek new worlds for gold, for praise, for glory." As one Englishman put it, "God sends me to go. If His will be, I shall die, for I had rather die with credit than live with shame." Whether the credit uppermost in his mind was economic or spiritual is immaterial, for the seventeenth century tended to see no distinction between the two. Certainly, the hope of a Garden of Eden rich in profits and in godliness provided a potent motive; but an equally important, if less positive, influence was at work: escape from that ugly trinity — religious persecution, economic exploitation, and social discrimination. England in the first years of the seventeenth century saw itself as overpopulated, overgoverned, and overly corrupt. The godly complained that it was "impossible for a good and upright man to maintain his charge [i.e., social position] and live comfortable," and almost everybody agreed that "we must starve or eat up one another" unless the surplus was sent out to the colonies. In fact, the realm was not overpopulated, merely underemployed. The plague, the jails, and the gallows took their grisly toll, but thousands more remained, unwanted burdens on an already inadequate relief system. The New World quickly became a place to unload the undesirable and unwanted, a haven for all who could find neither religious nor economic comfort in the organic state of the Tudor-Stuart commonwealth. In 1618 a hundred homeless and starving young boys and girls from the slums of London were shipped to Virginia. Jail sentences and capital punishments were regularly commuted to deportation because brawn and muscle, although they might be morally depraved, could yet "yield a profitable service" in the New World where labor was at a premium.

If the common sort were often shipped off against their will, men of substance went forth of their own accord. The hazards of the New World seemed slight compared to the harsh realities of life at home. The dream of a future world in which men and women could live freely "without sergeants or courtiers or lawyers or intelligencers" attracted all who suffered from economic, political, or religious privation. The desire for change, the urge to avoid conditions imposed by the accident of birth, and the demand for free land were motives strange and foreign to the Tudor system, which in the hands of the Stuarts grew increasingly rigid, corrupt, and archaic.

Expansion and the pioneering urge had little place in the Tudor-Stuart governmental scheme. Settlements located in the wilderness and populated with men and women of independent and rebellious spirit did not fit the official picture of a tidy, organic, and static society. Charles I and his archbishop William Laud viewed both the Plymouth and Massachusetts Bay colonies with the deepest misgivings; Puritans may have been good colonists, but they were generally bad subjects. Very early in their history, the New World settlements evidenced a deplorable sense of independence and acquired rights that few Englishmen at home enjoyed. Only ten years after the first settlers landed at Jamestown, Virginians had been awarded the dangerous liberty of holding a general assembly once a year. The Massachusetts Bay Colony soon proved even more rebellious and disobedient, showing little regard for authority when, during the Civil War in England, it announced that "our allegiance binds us not to the laws of England any longer than while we live in England." The pioneers who sailed for America may have "resolved to be Englishmen gone to the world's end," but they shortly discovered that their country was where "the heart and blood are given." A new nation, struggling to shape its own ideals and laws, was born the moment the English turned their backs on the Old World. Their hopes and aspirations, their loyalties and devotion were directed to something new: to "dear New England! dearest land to me."

If so many ventured forth into a wilderness thousands of miles from their chimney corners, still more preferred the shorter trip to Ireland. Of all the colonies, Ireland received the greatest number of immigrants throughout the seventeenth century, was economically the most important, and was the single enterprise in which the crown played a direct role. Except for the colonization of Ireland, the history of England's expansion is one of private enterprise, private funds, and private dreams. Elizabeth and James were largely interested in colonies as possible military bases, bits "in the ancient enemy's mouth." The prospect of revenue, however, always interested the state. The charters of all the early settlements reserved for the crown one-fifth of all gold and silver discovered, and imports and exports to and from the colonies paid a heavy tariff. Except for the profit, the government paid slight attention to overseas development. On occasion, it discouraged it, as when James endeavored to curtail colonization in the interests of peace and trade with Spain.

Ireland became the one exception to the crown's laissez-faire colonial policy. The island was Roman Catholic in faith, tribal in social structure, and only a short sea voyage away. From every point of view, it was ideal for colonization conducted in the name of religion, civilization, and trade. In 1600 the time seemed propitious for the completion of a conquest begun five hundred years before under Henry II. James I accepted the protestantizing and civilizing of Ireland as his special care, and between 1609 and 1625, the crown selected fifty-nine Scottish "undertakers." Each settler was granted anywhere from one to three thousand acres in the county of Ulster on the understanding that he populate his estate with good and godly Presbyterians. Ulster was filled with English and Scottish settlers, and it remains today heavily Protestant and Anglo-Saxon, and a controversial part of the United Kingdom. The policy of fostering English emigration to Ireland continued under the Cromwellian Protectorate, when thousands of English soldiers and immigrants were settled in the wake of Oliver Cromwell's military conquests. There they thrived as the elect of God, ruling over a Celtic and Catholic population who never forgot nor forgave their English overlords.

Foreign Policy and Renewed War with Spain

When the duke of Buckingham became all powerful at court during the early 1620s, he found himself in a position to fulfill a life-long dream — to win for himself renown as a statesman and diplomat and to reestablish England as a victorious international power. Europe in 1618 had exploded into a war that would last off and on (mostly on) for thirty years. The uneasy political stalemate established in Germany during the later half of the sixteenth century when Catholics and Protestants learned to tolerate one another, not out of principle, but out of exhaustion, had broken down. What upset the balance and aroused latent religious bigotry were the actions of Ferdinand of Styria, a crusading Catholic and ardent believer in a centralized and German-oriented Habsburg empire. The Austrian branch of the Habsburg dynasty was to the seventeenth century what the Spanish had been to the sixteenth — champions of a unified, imperial Europe and God's instrument to purge the continent of heresy. The princes of the German empire, however, suspected with considerable cause that when Ferdinand became emperor, the ancient and cherished political liberties of the independent German states, as well as heresy, would be exterminated. War broke out when the Protestant nobility of Bohemia rebelled against their Habsburg and Catholic overlord and elected in Ferdinand's stead Frederick V, elector of the palatinate, the son-in-law of James of England, to be king of Bohemia. James might have prevented a general European war had he been willing to order Frederick not to accept such a risky crown. The king, however, badly underestimated Habsburg family solidarity and mounting religious frenzy, and hopelessly overestimated English influence in the continental balance of power, believing that he could prevent Philip III of Spain from aiding his Austrian cousins. Habsburg vengeance in Bohemia was swift and overwhelming. Frederick became known as the Winter King, so short was his reign; and his own palatinate was overrun by Spanish troops. The Protestant-Catholic balance in Germany was so badly upset that both Denmark and the Netherlands were drawn into the conflict to check Habsburg-Catholic domination. By 1620 the situation had deteriorated to the point that it looked as if Habsburg armies might finally destroy German Protestantism and overrun Central Europe.

In England there was rising religious hysteria, cries of "no popery," a growing demand that James intervene to save Frederick, and mounting pressure to recommence the glorious crusade against Spain. Although the king did not oppose unofficial military aid to his son-in-law, financially and emotionally he hesitated at the idea of war against Spain. The cost of any really effective aid to Frederick — estimated at £900,000 — was prohibitive, and James had no wish to risk his financial well-being on a wild commitment in Germany or to expose himself to further fiscal blackmail by his none-too-loyal Commons. On only one point did king and Commons concur: armies sent to recover the palatinate were expensive. Parliament, however, urged the antiquated and unrealistic strategy of a cheap, profitable, and glorious naval war against Spain and her treasure fleets. As one M.P. inaccurately argued, "England never throve so well as when at war with Spain."

James now faced controversy with his Commons on two counts — money matters and foreign and military policy. Throughout the early 1620s, he roundly lectured Parliament on the true nature of the royal prerogative — matters of peace and war belonged exclusively to the crown and did not concern Commons. Despite opposition, he persisted in a pro-Spanish position. Raleigh was sacrificed to appease Spain and executed in 1619; and in 1623, young Prince Charles and the incurably romantic Buckingham started off for Spain to cement Anglo-Spanish relations. Sporting false beards and riding posthaste for Madrid, they appeared unannounced at the résidence of the Spanish infanta, whom they planned to woo with whirlwind speed and carry off to England in the proper tradition of swashbuckling romance. Things did not turn out quite as anticipated. Buckingham was snubbed by the Spanish court, the infanta was unamused by such juvenile antics and shuddered at the prospect of marriage to a heretic, and the Spanish government refused to budge in its determination to support Habsburg power in Germany and punish Frederick of the palatinate.

Buckingham and Charles returned home humiliated and hotly anti-Spanish, and they promptly stampeded the reluctant and rapidly aging James into war with Spain. For once the king found a "Parliament of love," for in 1624 a majority favored the conflict. James allowed a full debate on foreign policy, and Commons granted him a handsome subsidy. England allied itself with the Netherlands in June 1624, eight thousand men were promised for the recovery of the palatinate, and a small naval expedition was organized to plunder the Spanish Main. As a final step, at Buckingham's passionate urging but against the king's better judgment, negotiations were begun to bring France into the war against the Habsburgs, and arrangements were made for Prince Charles's fatal marriage to Henrietta Maria of France.

In the midst of all these military preparations, James's peaceful reign came to an end on March 27th, 1625, in a more favorable atmosphere than at any time since he had entered his promised land. As in the great days of '88, England appeared to be once again united in a national effort to vindicate the Protestant faith and tweak the king of Spain's nose. Under the first Stuart sovereign and his largely successful policy of letting sleeping dogs strictly alone, the bonds of loyalty and tradition that tied crown, Parliament, and kingdom together in an indissoluble union still held. Respect for paternalism and guidance, though strained, survived, and above all else, enough of the habit of obedience endured so that it is difficult to say whether in 1625 the political, fiscal, and psychological conditions that led to civil war seventeen years later were apparent. Only three jarring notes disturbed the perfect harmony that King in Parliament once again enjoyed: first, Spain in 1625 was no longer the unwary and unprepared colossus of Philip II's day; second, England's new king, Charles I, and the ebullient duke of Buckingham had never tested their competence in battle; and finally, no one knew the cost — financial, psychological, or constitutional — of winning, let alone of losing, a war.

CHAPTER 12

Charles I and the Royal Road to War

There are fashions in scholarship as in dress. Today's scholarly style plays down the color-coordinated designs of determinism and long-term social, economic, and ideological drift and emphasizes the discordant hues and random patterns of short-run occurrences that result from chance and personality operating within an atmosphere of suspicion, paranoia, and misunderstanding. The winner in this shift has been James I; the overwhelming loser, Charles I, whose character and policies are seen as central to what historians as well as contemporaries refer to as the tragedy of "this bloody and unnatural war." In the dreary annals of history, dullness, obtuseness, well-meaningness, and mental rigidity on the part of kings have been the absolute prerequisites to revolution and rebellion. Had Charles been more tactful, more ruthless, even more humorous, he might not have ended his days a sovereign "without state, without honour, without order."[1] Unfortunately, the second Stuart seems to have been designed by God to die on the scaffold, for he made a far better martyr than ruler, and he was venerated far more sincerely in death than in life.

Charles I (1625–1649): A Tidy King

Archbishop Laud had no illusions about his master; he delivered a gentle but devastating indictment when he said that Charles was "a mild and gracious prince who knew not how to be or be made great." Taciturn, se-

---

[1]The most useful single-volume biography of Charles I is P. Gregg, *King Charles I* (1981). See also C. Carlton, *Charles I, the Personal Monarch* (1983); R. Strong, *Charles I on Horseback* (1970); and M. Havran, "The Character and Principles of an English King: The Case of Charles I," *Catholic Historical Review*, Vol. LXIX, April 1983, pp. 169–208. The king is such an elusive character that he is best studied either in detail — C. V. Wedgwood, *The King's Peace* (1955), *The King's War* (1958), *The Trial of Charles I* (1964); and A. Fletcher, *The Outbreak of the English Civil War* (1981) — or through his servants: for example, H. R. Trevor-Roper, *Archbishop Laud* (2nd ed., 1963); C. V. Wedgwood, *Thomas Wentworth, First Earl of Strafford: A Revaluation* (1961); M. Havran, *Caroline Courtier: The Life of Lord Cottingham* (1973); and R. Lockyer, *Buckingham* (1981). See also G. Burgess, *The Politics of the Ancient Constitution: An Introduction to English Political Thought 1603–1642* (1992).

Charles I, by Anthony Van Dyck "Dullness, obtuseness, well-meaningness, and mental rigidity on the part of kings have been the absolute prerequisites to revolution and rebellion." *(Staatliche Kunstsammlungen, Dresden-Gemalde-galerie Alte Meister)*

cretive, and reserved, Charles never achieved the dignity of inscrutable silence; instead, his quietness concealed a stammer in speech and lack of confidence in himself. In his first address to Parliament, he "thanked God that the business of this time is of such a nature that it needs no eloquence to set it forth, for I am neither able to do it, nor doth it stand with my nature to spend much time on words." Although the contrast with his father's garrulous pedantry and academic wit must have been refreshing, it did not augur well for the future that Charles should start his reign by informing his Commons that a divine-right monarch need not explain, let alone justify, his actions.

For all Charles's good intentions and the deadly seriousness with which he approached his office, he was coldly impersonal in his human contacts and rigidly narrow in his moral and intellectual approach to life. He made a virtue of inflexibility and proudly announced that he could not "defend a bad or yield on a good cause." He constantly confused technicality with principle; if he could convince himself of the justice of the technical merits of his position, he was adamant. As the Venetian ambassador pointed out, he sought "to open the entrance to absolute power" with a lawyer's casebook and "the key to the laws." Charles knew the law and every privilege that it conferred on him, but he had no understanding of the true meaning of power. In the face of the inevitable he would yield, but he generally did so with bad grace, contriving to give the impression that his actions were merely a temporary and strategic retreat. He knew not, as one observer noted, the art of pleasing; nor was he "bountiful," being "so constituted by nature that he never obliges anyone, either by word or deed." The root of the matter was that Charles was incapable of engendering trust. In moments of great crisis, he could and did win the affection and self-sacrifice of devoted followers, but his motives seemed to many — both friend and foe — to be unnecessarily secret and, as Cardinal Bagna commented, "beyond guessing."

If Charles had an abiding passion that dominated his personal and political life, it was an obsession for decorum, a fastidious love of order that conformed to propriety and gracefulness. He was a man of exquisite taste: the patron of Van Dyck, Rubens, and Inigo Jones; and the greatest collector of paintings, coins, medals, and *objets d'art* in his day. He strove to turn his court into a microcosm of that idealized and divinely regulated cosmos in which all things had a place and all things knew their place: an ordered perfection that he had inherited from the Tudors and from which strife and disagreement could be banished. The lax and disheveled atmosphere of his father's court, where "fools and bawds, mimics and catamites" had abounded, gave way to a new order and return to hierarchy. The young king reintroduced the ancient household regulations originally laid down under Henry VIII, by which court privileges were carefully related to rank and dignity of office; furthermore, in 1625 Charles spent £10,900 building a high wall around Richmond Park, as if to keep out the sordid world. The project was a profoundly symbolic gesture, for as the reign progressed Charles became more and more isolated from reality, living in a secure fantasy of masques and murals, while outside the walls, the world of Parliament and economic and intellectual change passed him by.

The Spiral of Suspicion

In the light of historical hindsight, the events that led to civil war and revolution seem deliberate and preordained, the result of actions and decisions free of doubt, accident, and confusion. In reality, however, if there is any certainty in the unfolding drama, it is that neither king nor Parliament desired, expected, or had much to gain from war. The behavior of individuals was so varied, contradictory, and obscure that it is impossible to discern any precise pattern based on economic, political, or religious motivation. The seventeen years following the death of James I are a study in confusion in which the only certainty is that a spiral of suspicion between king and Commons began the moment Charles and Buckingham assumed the burdens of government.

Charles began his reign with a lie and a complaint. As Prince of Wales, he had publicly sworn in front of Lords and Commons that should he ever marry a Catholic princess, he would give no relief to English Catholics. As part of the secret marriage agreement with France, however, Charles agreed to educate his children until their thirteenth year as

Henrietta Maria, Wife of Charles I "Although he [Charles] allowed his wife a personal chapel, he sent her large Catholic entourage of ladies-in-waiting back to France." *(The Granger Collection)*

Catholics and to allow his bride, Henrietta Maria, a chapel open to all English Catholics. He also promised that Catholic recusants[2] throughout the kingdom would no longer be persecuted for their faith. He had to break his promise to either Parliament or his wife. In the end he reneged on both parties: he lifted the penal laws against English Catholics, and although he allowed his wife a personal chapel, he sent her large Catholic entourage of ladies-in-waiting back to France. Naturally, both sides were outraged. Henrietta Maria sulked, and Parliament grew so concerned with the rising tide of Catholicism at court and the young king's apparent willingness to support popery, and so irritated at what it regarded as Buckingham's mismanagement of the war effort, that it refused to fund Charles's multipronged military-diplomatic strategy. His plans called for a small expeditionary force in association with the Dutch to regain the palatinate for the king's brother-in-law, the financing of a European alliance against Spain, and a naval raid in the grand tradition of Drake upon the Iberian coast — all at a cost of over £1 million. Charles had some right to be offended; Commons, having urged on the war, voted a paltry £140,000 to pay for it. Worse, it committed the unprecedented act of curtailing the customary grant of "tunnage and poundage," the historic right given to the crown to tax the import of wines and certain other commodities. Traditionally, this right had been given for life at the

---

[2]Catholics who refused to attend the services of the Church of England.

commencement of each reign, but now it was limited to a single year. Charles, who was always touchy about his prerogative powers, took the action as a personal insult. The king was oversensitive but not far off the mark, for the lower house was thoroughly angered by his calm refusal to discuss foreign and military policy and by his demand for money to fight a war that cost far more than Parliament had initially envisioned.

Commons still held to the traditional argument that a king could do no wrong; consequently, it directed its annoyance and suspicions at the duke of Buckingham, who was blamed for the French marriage and the court's toleration of Catholicism. Peeved by the criticism of his favorite and frustrated by Commons's niggardly wartime appropriations, Charles dissolved his Parliament in August 1625, and in the hope of a quick victory and ready plunder, he determined to invest his wife's dowry in an amphibious expedition against Cádiz. The results were humiliating; his troops got drunk on Spanish wine, the royal navy proved totally unseaworthy, and the king faced the prospect of begging Commons for funds to stave off bankruptcy. Although Charles did his best to purge his new Parliament of critics, the removal of old enemies only placed the leadership of the lower house in the hands of Sir John Eliot. The fiery Cornishman from St. Germains fiercely informed Commons that "our honour is ruined, our ships are sunk, our men perished, not by the sword, not by the

Henry, Prince of Wales A drawing by Isaac Oliver. The boy who would have been king had he not died of typhoid at the age of eighteen — Charles's older brother, Henry, Prince of Wales. *(The Mansell Collection)*

enemy, not by chance" but by the criminal negligence of "those we trust." Eliot held Buckingham, as lord admiral, responsible for the Cádiz fiasco, and he commenced action to impeach the duke. An alarming change had taken place in Parliament. Throughout much of James's reign, Commons had stood alone in its demand for the reform of abuses, but by 1625 the monarchy had succeeded in antagonizing the House of Lords by the mercenary sale of titles and by Buckingham's zealous efforts to advance his many friends and greedy relations. Both houses now stood ready to unite against the duke; and in order to save his friend and chief adviser from impeachment, Charles had to dissolve his second Parliament without even having persuaded Commons to grant him tunnage and poundage for a second year.

The king congratulated himself that strong action had saved the day. Eliot was learning better parliamentary manners in the Tower; Commons was packed off home; Buckingham was safe; and Charles had had the pleasure of informing the lower house that he would not tolerate the interrogation of one of his servants, least of all "one that is so near to me." The crown could not survive, however, on constitutional principles alone. It had to have money, and Charles proceeded to collect tunnage and poundage as a prerogative right and to levy the largest forced loan in history. The revenues so raised were gratifying, but the cost in the goodwill of the propertied and mercantile classes was enormous. Seventy gentlemen, of whom twenty-seven were members of Parliament, had to be imprisoned for refusing to contribute to the loan. Five of the prisoners brought action against the crown for arbitrary arrest and sued to be charged or released on grounds of habeas corpus. The "Five Knights' Case" was judged in favor of the government because it was argued that the "special command of the king" was sufficient cause for arrest and imprisonment. Strict legality doubtless lay with the king, but men of property throughout the realm began to wonder whether the decision of royal judges could make executive action either just or legal.

Had Charles been able to prove the vigor of his government by victory in war, he might have managed to muzzle his opponents and exercise his prerogative powers without too much criticism. Unfortunately, in 1627 Buckingham committed the sublime folly of entangling the kingdom in a conflict with France while still at war with Spain. There were substantial reasons for animosity between France and England — historic antagonism, English claims to search and seize French shipping in the channel, and unofficial English aid to French Huguenot rebels. The duke, who assumed full responsibility for the conduct of the war, personally led a fleet of ninety ships and ten thousand men to strengthen the French Huguenot port of La Rochelle. The expedition was bungled from ill-conceived start to ignoble finish, and Buckingham returned home to face Charles's third and thoroughly provoked Parliament.

Sir John Eliot was again in evidence; so was that aging defender of historic law and one-time chief justice of the Court of the King's Bench, Sir Edward Coke. Even more ominous was the presence of another parliamentarian, Mr. John Pym, an aggressive Somerset businessman and former clerk of the exchequer, who shortly became a master of parliamentary techniques and eventually the uncrowned king of Commons. Together they directed the attack against Buckingham and the royal prerogative. Backed by the Lords, they drew up the Petition of Right, a declaration of what both houses felt to be fundamental law, which even a sovereign was expected to observe. Although the petition clearly presented no bid for parliamentary supremacy, it was just as certainly an indictment of the Stuart monarchy, for it listed the four areas in which Charles had endeavored to exercise unlimited prerogative authority. The petition stated that no man should be "compelled to make or yield any gift, loan, benevolence, tax or such like charge, without common consent by act of Parliament" (i.e., forced loans, tampering with the customs, and the illegal collecting of tunnage and poundage); that no man should be imprisoned without published cause (i.e., the Five Knights' Case); that soldiers and sailors should not be billeted on subjects without their consent; and that martial law should never again be used against civilians.

Confronted with a unified and aroused Parliament, Charles had no recourse but to yield in the hope that he could salvage a partial financial victory out of constitutional defeat, and he signed the Petition of Right in 1628. The king did persuade Commons to grant him a subsidy, but the amount was disappointing, and the dismissal of Buckingham from all his offices was made a condition for a new tunnage and poundage act. This last decision proved too much for even an impoverished monarch, so in June 1628 he prorogued Parliament until the next January. Six months of inactivity improved nobody's temper. In August, Buckingham was murdered with a ten-penny dagger by a disgruntled naval officer who had learned much of his politics from Eliot. An incensed Charles held Eliot personally responsible. For its part, Commons was outraged by the king's tactless imprisonment of several of its merchant members for having refused to pay tunnage and poundage charges. The monarch further provoked Puritan opinion by his failure to disassociate himself from courtiers whom the godly regarded as dangerous crypto-Catholics. The religious issue had a particularly explosive impact because Charles had committed his government to a high church position called Arminianism, which emphasized ceremonialism in religious services and deemphasized predestination and the doctrine of the elect. Arminianism advocated an almost Catholic position whereby the church again partially accepted free will and the ability to earn salvation and God's grace.

When Parliament met in January, both Charles and Eliot sensed that the session would be short and stormy. Commons complained about the arrest of its members, popery in high office, and illegal fiscal practices. The king in turn lectured the house on his prerogative rights and its failure to grant him tunnage and poundage. The crisis came in March 1629 when Eliot proposed three resolutions: high churchmen and anyone suspected of popery would be branded as "capital enemies" of the commonwealth, the king's advisers who had urged him to collect taxes without parliamentary consent would be similarly judged, and anyone who paid customs charges would be a betrayer "of the liberties of England." The resolutions were not merely defiance; they were very nearly an invitation to revolution, and Charles had no choice but to order the speaker to rise and dissolve the house. Commons then proceeded to express the new temper of the times: a willingness to use violence. While Eliot's resolutions were being read and voted by the house, the speaker was forcibly held down in his chair by two members who curtly informed him, "You shall sit till we [the Commons] please to rise." The statement was tantamount to mutiny, for it presumed the right of Parliament to prorogue and dissolve itself.

By 1629 it was manifest that the legal bonds uniting King and Parliament into a single and indivisible body had stretched to dangerous lengths. As one seventeenth-century commentator summed up the situation, "I see little hope of any good unless the king and Parliament shall agree, for without that no money shall be forthcoming, and without money nothing can be done." The two sides had reached a stalemate in which the crown could not live on its own, but at the same time it denied a voice in the control of policy to the one really adequate source of income.

Eleven Years of "Brave and Noble Resolutions" (1629–1640)[3]

The dilemma was resolved by cutting the Gordian knot; in 1629 Charles decided to go it alone and to rule without the benefit of his faithless Commons. The decision was neither without precedent nor without expectation of success and rested on a theory of hierarchic and paternalistic government dear to the king's heart and sense of divine order. The previous five years had revealed the cancer that had possessed the body politic. Parliament had displayed its incompetence and irresponsibility; throughout the previous reign, corruption, greed, and disrespect for authority had flourished; and no one, it seemed, was willing to make personal sacrifices for the sake of long-term public gain. It was clear to Charles that the "time to put brave and noble resolutions into action" had arrived.

The dissolution of Parliament left the king's political enemies without organization or leadership. Of the major parliamentary leaders, the vocal Sir John Eliot was again clapped in the Tower, where he died unrepentant in 1632; Thomas Wentworth recanted his political heresy and entered the king's service; Edward Coke went to his grave, aged eighty-two, still garrulously expounding that "brooding omnipresence," the English Common Law; and John Pym returned to Somerset

---

[3]For more information about this section and the next, see E. S. Cope, *Politics Without Parliaments, 1629–1640* (1987); L. J. Reeve, *Charles I and the Road to Personal Rule* (1989); and K. Sharpe, *The Personal Rule of Charles I* (1992).

to become the treasurer of the Providence Island Company, a Puritan-cum-merchant commercial venture to colonize the New World and to carry on illegal trade in Spanish Caribbean waters. Local Puritan associations and centers of political dissent could always be scrutinized by the Privy Council and, if necessary, chastised by the prerogative Courts of Star Chamber and High Commission. It was just possible that the king might be able to live on his own if strict and scrupulous economy were observed at court and in the government. The country had grown relatively prosperous, and merchants, no matter what their religious ideology, could be expected to pay nonparliamentary duties on imports and exports in preference to not trading at all. There were also new sources of royal income to be cultivated from the historic confusions that surrounded the crown's ancient feudal rights. Most important of all, the custom of paying taxes and of obeying the king were such ingrained social instincts that, as long as Charles could administer a reasonably efficient and popular policy, the success of government without legislative blessing or subsidy was ensured.

What Charles needed most in 1629 was an effective program, honest men to operate it, and money to finance it. Accordingly, he turned to William Laud and Thomas Wentworth to give leadership and direction to eleven years of what royalists call paternalistic monarchy but which parliamentary critics describe as tyranny. William Laud, who was promoted in 1633 from the see of London to the archbishopric of Canterbury, became the king's chief adviser, using his positions on the Privy Council, the Star Chamber, and the Court of High Commission to enforce a policy of "Thorough" on both church and state. His close friend and colleague Thomas Wentworth, the grand apostate of the parliamentary party, became lord president of the Council in the North, lord deputy of Ireland in 1632, and finally earl of Strafford in 1639. Both men stood for the new and invigorated form of monarchical government that seemed to be thriving in Europe. Their policy of "Thorough" was largely a theoretical creed — existing more on paper than in fact. It was a high-minded, if not always effective, attempt by Laud, Wentworth, and a few other royal officials to introduce honesty and efficiency into government, to develop new sources of income that would free the crown from all future dependence on Parliament, to maintain uniformity of faith and politics throughout the kingdom, and to construct a rational and tidy structure of government based on the Elizabethan concept of a balanced, organic, happy, and directed commonwealth.

No policy, no matter how well meaning or well administered, could endure without funds, and in 1629, a campaign was started to increase the crown's nonparliamentary revenues and decrease its expenses. Achieving this goal required economy in administration; pacifism in diplomacy; and, most important of all, fiscal feudalism in taxation. Retrenchment at court was relatively easy to introduce, for Charles had simple personal tastes, even if his ability to curb his wife's extravagances and his courtiers' pleas for pensions, sinecures, and favors was negligible.

A monarch with economical habits, however, was but a trifling advantage; if the government were to survive, it would have to arrange peace with Spain and extricate itself from the Protestant-Catholic wars of the continent. Peace was concluded in 1630, and Charles embarked on a tortuous and fragile foreign policy that lacked force because all the major powers of Europe well knew that he could not make good his threats or go to war without summoning Parliament.

Cutting down expenses was not popular with anyone, except possibly Charles. The government preferred to devise new systems of taxation and to squeeze dry old sources of income; customs rates were raised, new duties were imposed, and the rent paid by tax farmers who collected much of the customs revenues was increased. The most profitable source of income and the one most susceptible to manipulation was fiscal feudalism — the drastic extension of the old Tudor policy of rummaging through long-disused medieval charters and feudal obligations with an eye to monetary profit. In the remote past, the monarch, as the capstone of the feudal pyramid, had claimed a variety of historic privileges, many of which had long since ceased to operate but all of which were capable of being translated into monetary advantage. Under Charles I, purveyance — the right to commandeer food, lodging, and transportation — served as an instrument of blackmail to extract money from wealthy subjects and corporations. Encroachments on the king's forests, the original boundaries of which had been lost to memory, were now suddenly punished, as legal experts chased down the ancient holdings of the crown. The earl of Salisbury confronted a fine of £20,000 for trespassing when Rockingham Forest grew from six to sixty square miles. Likewise, knighthood was transformed into a tidy source of profit. At one time any gentleman who possessed freehold land worth £40 a year had been expected to assume the military burdens of knighthood. For centuries men of property had avoided such a costly privilege, and past sovereigns had allowed the obligation to lapse. Suddenly, in the early 1630s, the gentry was fined for its failure to come forward to be knighted at the time of Charles's coronation in 1626; the proceeds were handsome, even if the hostility engendered was dangerous. Finally, that seemingly bottomless wellspring, wardship, was sucked dry: James had extracted during the final years of his reign £35,000 annually from his wards; by 1641, Charles had raised the ante to £83,000.

Equally irritating and even more politically explosive was the extension of ship money throughout the realm. Traditionally, certain coastal cities had assumed responsibility for naval defense and the maintenance of English sea power. By 1630 the obligation remained; it was expected, however, that the crown would impose ship money, as the levy was called, only at moments of dire national emergency. In 1634 Charles not only declared such an emergency but two years later also extended the obligation to inland cities and counties. Ship money fell within the letter of the law because neither the law nor the royal prerogative had been defined. Nevertheless, it certainly violated the spirit of the past, and it raised a touchy constitutional issue — whether the king was the sole judge of what constituted a state of emergency. Whatever the constitutional debate ship money may have provoked, they placed in the hands of the monarch a source of income that could permanently release him from dependence on parliamentary taxation. The success with which the crown collected this questionable source of income — between 1635 and 1638, the king demanded £673,109 from the kingdom and collected 95 percent of it —seemed ample evidence that the realm had indeed entered a decade of "calm and felicity." Through fiscal feudalism, the customs, and ship money, Charles enhanced his revenues by almost 50 percent and balanced his budget at close to £900,000 without recourse to Parliament.

Makeshift Absolutism: Stuart Paternalism and the Policy of "Thorough"

Had financial extortion and fiscal expediency been accompanied by honesty in administration, the cry against extraparliamentary taxation might not have been so loud. Unfortunately, however, Stuart absolutism and paternalistic approach to government was a shabby, makeshift affair. It had to operate in an economic and demographic atmosphere over which the government had little or no control; and possibly even more important it lacked the two essentials of European despotism — sufficient money and a large, trained, and salaried bureaucracy. With the exception of Thomas Wentworth and William Laud, the king's servants were neither particularly honest nor particularly competent. Richard Weston, earl of Portland, had charge of the treasury, and although he staved off governmental bankruptcy, he was personally corrupt, filled his office with friends and favorites, and had earned the reputation of being a secret Roman Catholic, all of which exposed Charles to the charge of harboring papal spies and corrupt officials. Moreover, as the years of personal rule lengthened, the influence of the queen advanced. To the public she represented the most detestable aspects of foreign rule: she was a Catholic who presided over a priestly coterie at court and maintained her own emissary at the Vatican. Moreover, she constantly urged Charles to model himself and his government on the French pattern.

Laud and Wentworth did their best to implement a policy of "Thorough," but any consistent economic and social planning was doomed from the start because of four factors over which the government had little or no control. First, any policy based on regulation was bound to favor one aspect of the economy at the expense of another. Controlling wages, prices, consumption, production, and social mobility so as to minimize poverty and achieve the ideal of a perfectly balanced and integrated commonweal inevitably resulted in stepping on somebody's financial toes. If the aggrieved person howled loudly enough and possessed sufficient political clout, governmental regulations could be modified, bought off, or ignored, thereby turning what in theory was a well-intentioned social policy into a vast system of jobbery. Second, the crown found it difficult to control industry and commerce, which were growing at unprecedented rates and were increasingly subject to outside European and colonial pressures. As the century advanced, the kingdom was constantly afflicted with a form of economic St. Vitus's dance: uncontrollable booms and busts followed one another with ill-understood regularity. The government responded to periodic hunger and unemployment by asking the impossible. Even when confronted with a glutted or dislocated market, it demanded that both production and wages be kept at a high level to prevent the ultimate and most dangerous expression of social discontent, rioting. Inflation was the third factor that bedeviled all economic predictions and solutions. Although the overall rate had slowed since the days of Elizabeth, pockets of rapid and erratic inflation remained. Finally, the government was confronted by a population that had far outrun the economy's ability to employ it. With so many warring interests to appease and so many economic and demographic pressures to address, it is little wonder that a policy of "Thorough" generated confusion and frustration and undermined confidence in the government. Under James, government intervention had been sporadic and essentially ad hoc, but Charles was far more "Tudor" in his social concepts and, when confronted with the bad harvests and soaring prices of the early 1630s, he favored, as part of his policy of "Thorough," a return to a consistent policy of governmental paternalism. Charles and his Privy Council issued a stream of commands, known as the Book of Orders, directed at justices of the peace to ensure what the book claimed local agencies had ignored: the proper and systematic relief of the deserving poor, the enforcement of apprenticeship regulation, and the organizing of public works for the benefit of the community.

Without a paid civil service, the king's Book of Orders depended for enforcement on the justices of the peace, sheriffs, and local officials — the very men whom the dissolution of Commons had silenced and who complained about fiscal feudalism and nonparliamentary taxation. The case of John Hampden provided an example of the government's potential helplessness if the natural leaders of society ever decided that Charles's "tyranny" had gone too far. Hampden, who was a prosperous Buckinghamshire gentleman closely allied by family and politics to the parliamentary opposition, decided not to pay ship money. He was promptly arrested and in 1637 brought to trial for tax evasion. His legal counsel did not deny the crown's right to raise ship money during a moment of crisis; it merely pointed out that the emergency had been going on for three years and that the king had had sufficient time to call Parliament to raise the necessary money. Therefore, Hampden had been right in resisting what by 1637 had become an improper exercise of royal authority. Although John Hampden lost his case, the seven-to-five decision revealed that even the king's own judges were far from unanimous in their interpretation of historic law or in their approval of ship money. More and more taxpayers in the future would follow Hampden's lead by refusing to pay ship money; and as England approached the end of eleven years of personal rule, the chief condition for rebellion was beginning to materialize — a growing willingness on the part of the gentry to ignore or disobey the king's law.

Money, or more accurately the lack of it, lay at the root of most of the government's troubles. While the Stuarts, especially Charles, brimmed with good intentions, royal idealism was invariably tarnished by squalid fiscal considerations that corroded the government's credibility. Fiscal feudalism was squeezed dry, monopolies were sold or used as blackmail to extract cash from existing companies, the crown jewels were sold, and the government indulged in financial practices that would have brought any other organization into the criminal's dock. As a final desperate measure of arbitrary financing, the government confiscated £130,000 of gold bullion kept in trust for the merchants of London. At the same time, Charles sanctioned the purchase, on credit, of £65,000 worth of pepper, which was then immediately sold for £50,000 in cash — a form of deficit financing that further eroded what little confidence remained in the king's honesty. Zoning proclamations were enforced not to curb or direct London's growth but to extract money from contractors who offended the law or bought licenses to violate it. Enclosure laws aimed at preventing landlords from evicting their tenants, thereby increasing the number of vagabonds, landless farm laborers, and unemployed who were flocking into London, were enforced but often for the wrong reasons. When Thomas Lord Brudenell attempted to turn his estates into a sheep run and evicted his tenant farmers, he was hauled before the Court of Star Chamber and scolded by Archbishop Laud for being a greedy and irresponsible member of the body politic who had "devoured the people with a shepherd and a dog." As punishment and retribution, he was fined £100 and ordered to return the farmland to his tenants. Such high-minded economic moralizing, however, sounded false to the ears of landowners who suspected that it was the £30,000 and more per year that the crown reaped from such fines and not the plight of the evicted and unemployed that inspired governmental policy. Certainly, it was clear to all that Charles's evasion of the Monopoly Act of 1624 — Parliament's final effort to reform the government's abusive use of monopolies without abolishing them altogether — and the reintroduction of commercial regulations had nothing to do with the ideal of a well-regulated society and everything to do with a government so desperate for money that it was willing to barter the goodwill and respect of the ruling elite for a few extra pennies.

Nor did Charles have any more success in convincing lesser folk of the benevolence of his absolutism and social creed. The king sincerely hoped to improve agricultural output and the number of farm jobs, especially by the drainage of crown lands. Although such public works were supported by large local landowners and developers who sensed increased earnings, the crown won the hatred of many smaller people who saw their communal and historic rights violated. The government not only became involved in local land disputes but was also associated in the public mind with profiteering and greed.

In foreign policy the same frantic search for money prevailed. Not only could England be bought, but also it could be bought by the highest bidder. The moment peace was signed with Spain, England became a Spanish errand boy, conveying Catholic gold to the Netherlands and allowing Spanish troops to land at Plymouth and march overland to Dover in order to escape Dutch naval vessels. Finally in 1640, Charles tried to borrow four million ducats from Spain in return for thirty-five English naval ships to convoy Spanish vessels in the channel.

Even when Charles did enforce policy and Laud and Wentworth had their way in administering a program of "Thorough," the results further antagonized the very men on whom the monarchy ultimately rested for support — the landed country gentlemen. In the north, Wentworth labored diligently to maintain the Elizabethan edicts to protect the poor from the rich and mighty. Tudor poor laws and anti-enclosure statutes were enforced, and justice became somewhat less susceptible to influence and corruption. Stuart paternalism, however, was no longer popular in an area that was growing increasingly prosperous and had long since ceased to serve as a military buffer between Scotland and the civilized south. When Wentworth traveled to Ireland to become the king's lord deputy in that difficult and unruly island, he left behind Yorkshire gentlemen who, somewhat optimistically, were delighted by the expectation that his policy of "Thorough" would depart with him. The new lord deputy was certainly more thorough and considerably more successful in Ireland than in the north of England.

By 1633 Ireland had been tamed by Elizabeth and colonized by James. English-Scottish Protestant overlords ruled an Irish-Catholic and landless peasantry. Some landowners were Jacobean and Presbyterian newcomers; others were old English settlers who dated back to the days of the Tudors or before, and who were half Irish in mentality and half Catholic in faith. A strong hand was required to govern such a kingdom, and Wentworth did his best. He assiduously promoted colonization; purged the crown's administration of laxity and dishonesty; made the government financially self-supporting for the first time in a century; raised and trained a small standing army; tried to end the poverty of the church by reclaiming ecclesiastical lands; and sought to introduce the high-church doctrines and rituals so favored by his friend, Archbishop Laud. The results produced laudable efficiency in government and a secret yearning in the hearts of almost everybody of importance to get rid of the lord deputy as soon as possible. Wentworth in Ireland became the personification of the most ruthless and irritating aspects of royal policy, a kind of living warning of what Charles might do in England if he ever got the chance and the financial means to do it.

Stuart paternalism came under attack from all levels of society, provoking political friction and social bitterness. In 1631 the justices of Hertfordshire denounced Charles's efforts to interfere in local affairs when they wrote that "this strict looking to markets is the reason why the markets are smaller, the corn dearer." A variety of laissez-faire economics was in the air, if only because the end of government interference would assure absolute control over local government to the ruling oligarchy of landlords, employers, factory owners, and merchants. Moreover, it would open up the profits of an unrestrained and expanding economy to the most favored, the most ruthless, and the most intelligent — in other words, to the propertied classes. The earl of Clarendon in the middle years of the seventeenth century sadly acknowledged the existence of the new economic spirit when he admitted that money "was entertained as the truest wisdom," and that society accepted as lawful anything "which would contribute to being rich." It is well to remember that the hatred incurred by Archbishop Laud stemmed not only from Puritans who loathed his high-church authoritarianism but also from enclosing landlords who detested his efforts on the Enclosure Commission of 1636–1638, and from profiteers who abhorred his use of the Star Chamber to enforce old-fashioned economic paternalism. When corruption and inefficiency walked hand in hand with a mercantile policy that ran counter to the interests of the moneyed and ruling elite, a major political eruption was only a matter of time and circumstance.

Archbishop Laud and the "Reform" of the Church

It was not, however, fear of a policy of "Thorough" enforced by an efficient Wentworth or the corroding consequences of government by financial expediency that ultimately proved fatal to Charles's rule; it was Archbishop Laud's religious fervor. An old-fashioned and uncompromising disciple of Tudor paternalism, Laud was a high-church, doctrinaire idealist convinced that due proportion and order within the state must begin with uniformity of thought and ceremony in the church. In this he had the king's fervent support; indeed, James I's characterization of Laud as "a restless spirit" who could not "see when matters are well, but loves to toss and change and bring things to a pitch of reformation floating in his own brain," applied as well to Charles as to his archbishop. Above all else, the archbishop wanted a better paid, better trained, better disciplined, and more obedient clergy, and he sought to achieve his purpose by urging the return of church lands and revenues. He fought a long and losing battle with the city fathers of London to have church tithes increased to represent a genuine tenth of Londoners' incomes, and to regain control over the spending of such sums. He used the ecclesiastical Court of High Commission to impose orthodoxy and discipline on the ecclesia, to enforce episcopal decrees and visitations, and to root out Puritan bodies and propaganda within the established church. Under Laud the Puritans received blow after blow. They found themselves persecuted and rigorously forced to conform to the Elizabethan Prayer Book and Thirty-Nine Articles, and they thought the Church of England, with its new stress on ritual and the sensuous beauty of holiness, to be headed for a reunion with Rome.

Some historians argue that Laud's policies dealt a fatal blow to the Tudor-Stuart crown.[4] The tiny trickle of overly conscientious Puritan purists, who had first left the land in 1617 for a new home in the Netherlands and from thence in 1620 had set sail for Plymouth Rock and the New World, now became a steady stream of God's chosen people. By 1640 twenty thousand of them had fled the devil's hand and Archbishop Laud's disciplinary Court of High Commission for Ecclesiastical Affairs. Emigration was more a symptom of heightened religious sensitivity and governmental persecution, however, than a cause of the mounting emotional crisis. The minority that migrated did so not only to escape the wrath of an authoritarian regime but also to avoid the dilemma of conflicting loyalties to God or king. Their less fortunate but far more numerous brethren who remained in England had to struggle with their consciences, and in the end they hearkened to the call of the spirit in preference to the voice of obedience. A community of saints was forming. If treason, civil war, revolution, and bloodshed were necessary, by 1640 Puritans were willing to pay that price. Mr. William Prynne, an ardent pamphleteer, sounded the Puritan cry to battle in 1639. As his cheek was being branded for seditious libel and his ears clipped for having written against Archbishop Laud, he cried out, "The more I am beat down, the more am I lift up." Whether civil war would have erupted without this small but persistent voice of conscience is not even a matter of opinion; it is simply guesswork. But this can be said: Puritanism possessed latent but disturbing potential for political disruption. A creed that exalted the absolute supremacy of the deity denied by implication the serried ranks of hierarchy originating with God and reaching down through the archangels, angels, kings, and magistrates, and sanctioning the authority of parents as well as priests that was so central to the Tudor concept of the cosmos. A faith that insisted on the individual's direct and personal responsibility to and dependence on God's grace for salvation without benefit of church or state placed in question the power of both kings and bishops, should government policy and individual conscience clash. "What is not of faith is sin. . . . Whereby both he [the magistrate] for commanding and making ungodly decrees, and we [subjects] for obeying them, shall be judged." Such dangerously individualistic notions of responsibility were deeply alien not only to Charles's structured view of authority but also to most of early Stuart society, which still believed that obedience stood as "the principal virtue of all virtues." But when

---

[4]N. Tyacke, *Anti-Calvinists: The Rise of English Arminianism, c. 1580–1640* (1987); but see also H. Trevor-Roper, *Catholics, Anglicans, and Puritans: Seventeenth-Century Essay* (1987). Trevor-Roper's portrait of *Archbishop Laud* (2nd ed., 1963) is still the most balanced biography, but see also C. Carlton, *Archbishop William Laud* (1987).

aggravated by economic, political, and social tensions, the faith that avowed "if the prince's laws be contrary or divers to the laws of God, then is not our conscience or body bound by or unto them" had the potential for exploding first into constitutional revolution and then into civil war. Puritanism certainly supplied political rebels with the uncompromising righteousness that induced them to risk their necks in war, and it allied Jehovah on the side of parliamentary supremacy, making victory divine, moral, and predestined.

Possibly even more dangerous was that Puritans did not stand alone, for Laud's policies succeeded in antagonizing moderate as well as radical Protestant opinion, which viewed the transformation of communion tables into altars as a devilish attempt to reintroduce the Catholic mass. Laud and his Arminian followers were branded as "a plotting, undermining and dangerous sect." More and more, as a growing and important segment of society perceived the episcopal structure of the church as an instrument of religious tyranny, the clamor to do away with bishops and diocesan disciplining mounted, thereby jeopardizing the cornerstone of the king's grand design for a perfect commonwealth. Bishops played an even more essential part in Charles's concept of monarchy than they had for his father. He would, he said, rather "suffer all extremities than ever to abandon my religion." He staked and, in the end, lost his kingdom in defense of the episcopal organization of his church.

Although religious frustration may not have caused the Civil War, Laud's tampering with God's Word certainly ended Charles's eleven years of personal rule. To both Charles and his archbishop, the existence of a Presbyterian kirk in Scotland seemed a hopeless anomaly within a divinely inspired monarchy, and a vicious distortion of the perfect and tidy hierarchy of an episcopal church headed by a royal defender of the faith. James I had carried the battle of uniformity as far as he dared but had wisely decided to content himself with an episcopal organization grafted onto a solid Presbyterian base. In 1630, however, Laud and Charles set about anglicizing the Church of Scotland by buttressing the authority of the episcopate and by soft-pedaling Calvinistic doctrine. They then pushed through the Scottish Assembly the Act of Revocation, which decreed the return of all ecclesiastical property that had fallen illegally into lay hands. The first action angered Presbyterian leaders; the second antagonized Scottish lairds aghast at any suggestion that their deeds to monastic and ecclesiastic estates might not be valid. How far out of touch the creed of religious "Thorough" was with the realities of Scottish life was revealed in 1637 when Laud tried to thrust a new prayer book, modeled on the English Book of Common Prayer, down the Calvinistic throat of Presbyterian Scotland. The result was a riot in the Cathedral of Edinburgh, where chairs were hurled at the dean in defiance of the king. A year later, Charles was bluntly told that he must make a choice: either give up his prayer book or send forty thousand armed soldiers to enforce Arminianism on the dour Scots. The king could never forgive re-

**William Laud, Archbishop
of Canterbury**
Archbishop Laud's
religious fervor
"ultimately proved fatal to
Charles's rule." *(Mary
Evans Picture Library)*

bellion, and he determined to safeguard Scotland for episcopacy and the
prayer book.[5]

War and the Collapse of Personal Rule

War was fatal to Charles's system of government; it revealed the rot that
had set in and the isolation in which the king had been living for the past
decade. The treasury was empty, and the king's call for a patriotic loan
from the city of London went unheeded in a metropolis heavily populated with secret admirers of Scottish resistance and Presbyterianism.
Charles traveled north to inspire his troops, who were largely unpaid, un-
trained, and badly led. It soon became obvious, even to an obtuse
monarch, that he could not defeat in open battle an army of enraged
Scotsmen ready to die for kirk and Scripture. In June 1639, he reluctantly
began negotiations with his rebellious subjects and withdrew the offend-
ing prayer book. The king was patently insincere in his peace overtures,

---

[5]For events in Scotland, see M. Lee, *The Road to Revolution: Scotland Under Charles I,
1625–1637* (1985); and D. Stevenson, *The Scottish Revolution, 1637–1644* (1973).

and, on Wentworth's over-optimistic advice, he sent out writs for a new Parliament in April 1640. Charles expected that the presence of an invading army on the border would arouse English patriotism, and in anticipation he called on Commons for £800,000 to discipline his Scottish subjects. What he got was a two-hour speech from John Pym that listed the sins of the government and demanded reform in church and state before a penny was voted to rescue the crown. In anger, Charles dissolved the Short Parliament. A "short" Parliament was merely a prelude, however, to a "long" one, which lasted twelve years and six months, passed from reform into revolution, usurped the authority of the throne, and in the end sanctioned the execution of the king.

Charles was anything but chastened by the turn of events, and he again set out, without a parliamentary subsidy, to teach Scottish Calvinists a lesson in obedience. By July he had scraped together a second force, but in August his troops fled in panic without a fight, and the "general dissatisfaction" with the king's service was dramatically revealed. By 1639 it was perfectly apparent that Charles had lost the respect of the landed country gentleman — that part of society that raised the king's armies, enforced his edicts, and could give essential strength and backbone to the sovereign's faint-hearted troops. The fiscal antics of a bankrupt and irresponsible government had stirred apprehension among men of property and commerce. The government's foreign policy had prompted ordinary Protestants as well as Puritans to wonder whether they could trust Charles to defend the realm against Catholicism; and Laud's tactlessness and doctrinaire notions about uniformity earned the hatred even of those who approved his aims.

The Long Parliament

When a victorious Scottish Presbyterian army invaded England and routed Charles's troops in August 1640, it demanded that Charles pay the Scottish army £850 a day until the two sides could reach a final settlement. The king had no other way to finance these obligations than to summon the Long Parliament. When the first session met in November, the king discovered that an ominous change had taken place: Parliament no longer regarded itself as a temporary body politely petitioning the monarch to redress grievances. An entirely new atmosphere prevailed because the military emergency of 1640 fundamentally upset the historic balance between King and Parliament. Local and regional grievances, which had been festering for over a decade, were now linked with issues of national constitutional reform. The election slogan

> Choose no ship sheriff [ship money collectors],
>   nor court atheist [worldly and cynical courtiers]
> No fen drainer [violators of private property in the
>   name of paternalism and public good],
>   nor church papist [supporters of the episcopacy]

The Execution of Thomas Wentworth, Earl of Strafford His crime was his "support of a concept of royal government in which Parliament had lost confidence and which simply did not work." *(North Wind Picture Archives)*

gave warning that M.P.'s from every sector of the kingdom were willing to make common cause to change an increasingly unpopular system that, as a consequence of the Scottish humiliation, had totally broken down. Even more fundamental, the king proved his ineffectualness by abandoning his traditional prerogative functions; he turned over the job of negotiating peace (foreign policy) and paying the Scots (the disbursement of money) to Parliament. A "new world" was emerging, and John Pym's claim that "a Parliament is that to the commonwealth which the soul is to the body" was coming true. Within the year, legislation passed translating that proposition into legal reality.

A constitutional revolution took place that changed Parliament into a permanent and regular organ of government, stripped the crown of those prerogative powers that had given it fiscal independence, and dismantled the machinery of prerogative rule. The Triennial Act of May 1641 guaranteed the calling of Parliament every three years even without the consent of the king, while yet another act prevented Parliament from being dissolved without its own permission. Tunnage and poundage were forbidden unless sanctioned by Parliament; fiscal feudalism was abolished by legislation that declared all nonparliamentary taxation illegal. Those pillars of Tudor paternalism, the prerogative Courts of Star Chamber and High Commission, were abolished; monopolies were swept away; and the king's evil councillors, Thomas Wentworth and Archbishop Laud, were attainted and sentenced to death — the layman decapitated amidst great fanfare in May 1641, the ecclesiastic executed almost as an afterthought four years later. Their technical crime was treason; their real faults were their loyalty to a king in whom the majority in Commons had no trust and their support of a concept of royal government in which Parliament had lost confidence and which simply did not work.

Charles bowed to the inevitable: he sacrificed his servants to the wrath of Parliament, and he signed statutes that made a mockery of the divinity that doth hedge a king. By August 1641, Parliament had achieved a legal and overwhelming victory without a shot being fired; yet within the year civil war exploded. Once started, the juggernaut of political and religious change was difficult to halt. Unalterably it pushed on, leaving behind the timid of heart and moderate of politics, and giving the advantage to that small minority who wanted to introduce a Puritan revolution and stood ready to risk war to achieve this purpose.

Mistrust, misunderstanding, and the willingness to resort to arms are matters of habit and mind, and throughout 1641–1642, three deeply felt and overlapping emotions pushed the kingdom to the brink of war: suspicion of the king's sincerity, fear of eventual revenge for what had already been achieved, and hatred of Catholicism. Parliament had been suspicious of the king for so long that it continued to suspect the worst out of habit. Each side persisted in misunderstanding the aims of the other. Pym and his followers doubted Charles's sincerity in acknowledging restraints on his prerogative and his outward devotion to the Protestant cause. They took pains to point out that his queen was Catholic; that he had allowed Spanish troops and gold, destined to wage war against Protestants in Europe, to be shipped in English vessels; that his Archbishop Laud had been so high-church that he might as well have been a papist; and that the king himself had sent soldiers to Scotland to destroy the Presbyterian kirk. To Pym and his followers, the king of England appeared to be in league with the forces of Satan and Rome.

Charles's reputation of being "soft" on Catholicism — had he not said publicly "I wish I had rather lost one of my hands" than that the break with Rome should have ever taken place? — must be set against his subjects' instinctive response to the "devilish faith" that he appeared to find so attractive. For Protestants of every complexion, Catholicism was the creed of antichrist, far more pernicious than either paganism or Islam. It was a faith founded upon idol worship and the belief in the magical powers of a priest to perform the miracle of the mass — a mere "superstitious mass of policy under pretext of religion." English men and women knew that they were members of an elect nation, which had, with divine aid, survived medieval papal pretensions and had become the first kingdom to cast off totally its Roman chains. From the moment Henry VIII defied Rome, the citadel of the elect had come under attack by the forces of evil. English Protestants had learned this truth in John Foxe's *Book of Martyrs*, which, along with the Bible and the Book of Common Prayer, could be found in every parish church. Fear of Catholic revenge inflicted by foreign troops in secret league with English recusants, who had refused the Oath of Allegiance and failed to attend official church services, had been the nightmare that had beset the realm throughout most of the sixteenth century. After 1600, however, this specter began to change. The threat was slowly internalized as good Protestants began to think in terms of popish plots in high and sensitive places of government and of secret Catholic infection that thrived on Laudian willingness to compromise with the devil. Ever since that appalling day on November 5, 1605, when Guy Fawkes and his fiendish band of conspirators had attempted to blow up King, Lords, and Commons, English Catholics had been branded as potential traitors. Although modern estimates maintain that no more than 1.5 percent of the population professed Catholicism in the seventeenth century, contemporaries sensed that, when the antichrist was involved, numbers had little importance. English Catholicism had shifted. As it lost ground among the public at large, it gained influence within the governing elite. The peerage may have been as much as one-fifth Catholic, and the old faith so thrived in the great country houses that it has been called the "religion of the gentry." When Charles invited papal envoys to his court, promoted Catholics to high office, sought the company of a Catholic wife, and supported Arminianism in the English church, Protestants accused him of playing with fire, and urged that he be stopped before the entire kingdom died in a holocaust of religious war. The issue did not simply entail politics and constitutional structure; for many it was a matter of the kingdom's salvation.[6]

Throughout the century, fear of Catholicism lingered just below the surface of daily life, erupting during periods of political and economic tension. During the early months of the Long Parliament, the kingdom was tense, experiencing unprecedented change that some had passionately welcomed but that others feared and bitterly resented. Then in October 1641, latent religious hysteria and constitutional crisis merged; reports arrived of bloodthirsty Irish peasants who had risen in the night against their overlords and murdered thirty thousand Protestants in their beds. The figures were the product of overwrought imaginations. The rebellion was real enough, however, and it confronted Parliament with an impossible choice: Catholics and Irish insurgents could not be allowed to go unpunished, but historically the responsibility for military action belonged to the king, and parliamentary leaders did not trust Charles. They feared that instead of commanding an army against papist treason in Ireland, he might turn the military against God-fearing Protestants in England.

Sir Edward Hyde, chronicler of the Civil War, adviser to King Charles, and lord chancellor to his son, was probably correct in his warning that religion was often "a cloak to cover the most impious designs" of men. There is considerable evidence that John Pym may have consciously inflamed credulous London apprentices with the specter of a Catholic bloodbath and rumors of a popish plot to murder the captains of Parliament.[7] Moreover, he may have deliberately goaded the king into violent and illegal action by suggesting that Parliament impeach his Catholic queen. Certainly, religious consciences were tender on both sides. Since people tended to think in spiritual terms, it was easy enough to confuse religious and political issues. The appeal to arms provided a ready solution in an atmosphere of passionate and mutual distrust; and the

---

[6]C. Hibbard, *Charles I and the Popish Plot* (1983), is the best work on the mounting fear of Catholicism.

[7]J. H. Hexter's *The Reign of King Pym* (1941) is still the classic account.

Papists Persecuting Protestants in Ireland, 1642   English Protestant imaginations became hysterical in October 1641 when "reports arrived of bloodthirsty
Irish peasants who had risen in the night against their overlords and murdered
thirty thousand Protestants in their beds." *(Mary Evans Picture Library)*

controversy over the control of the military went to the core of the constitutional struggle, forcing moderates to take sides, and driving a permanent wedge between the king and his Parliament.

Throughout the fall and early winter of 1641, Lords and Commons were swept along by the revolutionary spirit.[8] In September, the lower house voted favorably on a "Root and Branch Bill" abolishing the episcopacy, and it began a highly critical debate on the nature of the Elizabethan Book of Common Prayer. Two months later came the Grand Remonstrance, cataloguing the king's sins since the first day of his succession, describing the deplorable state of the realm, and listing the many reforms still required. Finally, in February 1642, Parliament delivered the ultimate insult to the king's sovereignty and stripped Charles of the last vestiges of his ancient rights by enacting the Militia Bill, which placed all naval and military appointments under parliamentary inspection. In March both houses declared that the statute had the force of law even if the king withheld his signature.

"King Pym" was not without his critics, both in and out of Parliament. Slowly, an isolated, but nevertheless legitimate, monarch in Whitehall found himself once again at the head of a political party as the unanimity that had marked the early months of the Long Parliament began to dissolve. In November, after a long and bitter debate, the Grand Remonstrance passed Commons by only eleven votes; the Militia Bill, by just twenty-three votes. During the winter of 1641–1642, it grew clear that a royalist party was forming. The demand to abolish the episcopacy, the insistence that Commons control the king's advisers as well as his armies, the threat to impeach the queen, the execution of Wentworth in May 1641, and the growing frenzy of the London mobs — all these made men of substance and caution wonder where the process of revolution would end. Lord Paget voiced the alarm of Englishmen who welcomed limitations imposed on royal government but who could never sanction Parliament's blatant seizure of the crown's sovereignty. Thoroughly aroused, Paget said that when he saw Englishmen taking up arms against their king, he resolved to throw himself down at the king's feet "and die a loyal subject." More and more parliamentarians and royalists accused each other of planning bloodshed and war. During December 1641, for

---

[8]The interpretations of the Civil War and revolution have generated a veritable library of scholarship. R. C. Richardson, *The Debate on the English Revolution Revisited* (1989), is a useful starting point. See also R. Ashton, *The English Civil War: Conservatism and Revolution, 1603–1649* (1978); G. F. Aylmer, *Rebellion or Revolution, England 1640–1660* (1986); A. Fletcher, *The Outbreak of the English Civil War* (1981); R. Howell, *The Origins of the English Revolution* (1975); C. Russell, *The Causes of the English Civil War* (1990), and *The Fall of the British Monarchies 1637–1642* (1991); L. Stone, *The Causes of the English Revolution, 1529–1642* (1972); P. A. Zagorin, *The Court and the Country: The Beginning of the English Revolution* (1969); and the essays found in C. Russell (ed.), *The Origins of the English Civil War* (1973), and H. Tomlinson (ed.), *Before the English Civil War* (1983).

the first time, the offensive epithets "Roundhead" and "Cavalier" rang in the streets of the city — the former a phrase of denigration for the shorn heads of the London apprentices; the latter synonymous with *Cavaliero*, the brutal Spanish and Catholic butchers of godly Protestants in Europe.

It was all too easy to counsel violence in an emotional atmosphere that induced a practiced parliamentarian like John Pym to describe Wentworth as a sink of "foulness and unjustness [that] will never be wiped off, neither from his heart nor from his actions." Where reform ended and revolution began is difficult to say. Possibly, the atmosphere of vengeance that had surrounded Wentworth's death poisoned men's minds. More probably, the massacre of Protestants in the Irish rebellion of October swept away reason and restraint. Or again, the English may have found it easier to act than to argue and compromise. Whatever the cause, the sides began to polarize, to indulge in mutual recriminations, and to sanction the appeal to arms.

Deliberately incited by John Pym and his colleagues, and urged on by his wife, who told him, "go, you coward, and pull these rogues out by the ears," Charles was the first to resort to a show of force. On January 4, 1642, at the head of four hundred armed guardsmen, he strode into the chamber where Commons sat and demanded the arrest of Pym and four others. The five members had stayed just long enough to bait the trap and fled minutes before the king arrived, and Charles, as they had planned, was made to look both ridiculous and despotic. All his birds had flown; they could no longer be caught by a pinch of salt and must henceforth be shot down. In February, the queen left for Holland in search of money and friends, and Charles moved north to gather support. By June the drift toward war had gone so far that Parliament sent Charles its Nineteen Propositions — ostensibly a basis for settlement, actually a declaration of war. The propositions placed the supreme authority of government squarely in Parliament; they required that the actions of all privy councillors and royal advisers be subject to legislative review and that judicial, military, and ecclesiastical appointments be open to parliamentary inspection. Then followed the creation of the Committee of Safety as a rival governing agency to the crown; the formation of a parliamentary army; and finally, the declaration, in the summer of 1642, branding Charles as the aggressor.

The king knew his duty. He was determined that if he could not "live as a king," he would "die as a gentleman." War was the only solution, for Charles had announced that he could forgive "no subject of mine who comes deliberately to shed my blood." Parliament had shown its wicked design and its intention to destroy the king, the episcopacy, and the ancient constitution. In defense of all three, on August 22, 1642, Charles raised his standard at Nottingham to the shouts of "God save King Charles and hang up the Roundheads." Civil war had begun.

CHAPTER 13

"This Bloody and Unnatural War"

Slowly, reluctantly, a divided realm prepared for war.[1] The moment of decision had arrived; debate must give way to action, and throughout the land men were called upon to choose sides.

The Anatomy of Rebellion

The controversy over who fought whom and why, and what to call the events of 1642–1660, commenced the moment men made their choice and picked up weapons. Analysts from Hyde, Harrington, and Hobbes to Marx, Stone, Tawney, and Trevor-Roper have sought to find the explanation "in society, not in individuals."[2] Ponderous social and economic forces were undeniably at work, and the specter of class war is certainly discernible. Geographically, the divisions were suggestive. All the cathedral cities save Oxford and Chester sided with Parliament; so did most of the industrial centers, the ports, and the economically advanced regions of the south and east. Conversely, the strongholds of royalty lay in the countryside, the shires, and the backward areas of the north and west. The words *populous*, *rich*, and *rebellious* seemed to go hand in hand. Social alignments reflected geographic divisions, and contemporaries were

[1] The classic multivolume accounts of the early Stuart period and the civil war years are S. R. Gardiner, *History of England, 1603–1656* (18 vols., 1894–1904), and Sir Charles Firth's continuation, *The Last Years of the Protectorate* (1909). For the modern scholarship, see Chapter 12, page 279, footnote 8. See also J. S. Morrill, *The Revolt of the Provinces: Conservatives and Radicals in the English Civil War, 1630–1650* (1976); I. Roots, *The Great Rebellion, 1640–1660* (1966); D. Underdown, *Pride's Purge: Politics in the Puritan Revolution* (1971); J. P. Kenyon, *The Civil Wars of England* (1988); and N. H. Mayfield, *Puritans and Regicide: Presbyterian-Independent Differences over the Trial and Execution of Charles (I) Stuart* (1988).

[2] Edward Hyde, Earl of Clarendon, *The History of the Great Rebellion*, W. D. Macray (ed.) (1888); Thomas Hobbes, *Behemoth: The History of the Causes of the Civil Wars in England*, W. Molesworth, ed. (1840); R. H. Tawney, *Harrington's Interpretation of His Age* (1941); H. Trevor-Roper, "Social Causes of the Great Rebellion," in *Historical Essays* (1957); C. Hill, *Puritanism and Revolution* (1958); P. Zagorin, "The Social Interpretation of the English Revolution," *Journal of Economic History* 19 (1959); and L. Stone, *The Causes of the English Revolution, 1529–1642* (1972).

not unaware of the economic and social interests that were emerging on either side. "Freeholders and tradesmen are the strength of religion and civility in the land," concluded Richard Baxter, and "gentlemen and beggars and servile tenants are the strength of inequity." Not by accident did eighty peers choose the king; twenty others prefer neutrality; and only thirty remain in London, loyal to the "liberties" of Parliament. Men of new wealth, of economic enterprise and capitalistic sentiment, who were busily building industrial and commercial empires, enclosing land, and buying out their less prosperous landed rivals seemed arrayed against "gentlemen of ancient families and estates." As Tawney succinctly put it, an aggressive creditor and capitalistic class "discovered, not for the first time, that as a method of foreclosure war was cheaper than litigation."[3]

It is possible to argue not only that a feudal past was giving way to a capitalistic future and that patterns of economic determination were discernible, but also that England's Civil War harbored yet another element of revolution: the revolt of the poor and downtrodden against the rich and mighty. In 1642 the "heady multitude," always perverse and prone to rioting, grew restive, and dangerous political notions were being voiced as the ramparts of social control began to weaken. "The gentry have been our masters a long time," it was said, "and now we may chance to master them." Men of property directed worried glances at the "commonality" who sought "not only to abuse but [also to] plunder any gentleman." As war and violence progressed, novelty in politics, radicalism in social theory, and extremism in religion intensified. Levellers and Diggers and other "strange voices" grew bold and spoke out against their ancient masters.

Despite the urge to describe England's ordeal as a revolution — social, economic, religious, or political — possibly the older term *civil war* remains the most accurate description. In the final analysis, the choice of sides was personal; it was made by men of the same class, not between classes; and of all private motives, religion may well have been the most personal and the most pressing. God allowed them no choice but to defend the right as they knew it. Yet even when the deity spoke, men and women had to make their own decisions and choose between conflicting loyalties. Sir Edmund Verney made such a choice when he decided that his duty to Charles outweighed his devotion to parliamentary liberties and spiritual purity. "I have eaten the King's bread and served him near thirty years, and will not do so base a thing as to forsake him." The Civil War was fought between men like Edmund Verney who, for reasons of their own, elected different sides.

Cromwell, Charles I, Fairfax, Essex, and Hyde all had one thing in common: no matter what their politics or religion, they were the "natural leaders" of society. They were men of varying degrees of property,

---

[3]R. H. Tawney, "The Rise of the Gentry," *Economic History Review* 11 (1941): 12.

and although they often disagreed violently over who should exercise discipline and who should be obeyed, they concurred that both discipline and obedience were necessary to a well-ordered society. The ancient law, the historic constitution, was not being called in doubt; few questioned that it should safeguard property and "the liberty of all those that have a permanent interest" within the realm. Men of property and rank fought, as William Bradshaw stated at King Charles's trial, not over the law but over "who shall be the expositors of this law." No man of estate had any wish that anyone except men of property should be "the expositors." The royalist Cavalier agreed with the parliamentary colonel who warned that if the master and the servant were deemed equal in law and in vote, then "there may be a law enacted that there shall be an equality of goods and estates" as well.

The community and solidarity of interests among the ruling elements momentarily dissolved, producing civil, not revolutionary, war. But ties of friendship, breeding, and class remained so strong that parliamentarian Sir William Waller could write royalist Sir Ralph Hopton on the eve of battle that "my affections to you are so unchangeable that hostility itself cannot violate my friendship. We are both upon the stage, and must act the parts that are assigned to us in this tragedy. Let us do it in a way of honour and without personal animosities." Up to a point, the old school tie acted as a check to bitterness and passion, curbed some of the horrors of war, and made possible the restoration of the Stuarts in 1660. In the end, after a generation of godliness and violence, the gentry, regardless of whether they were represented by the 236 members of Commons who sided with the king or by the 270-odd who chose Parliament, reunited to restore order and a modified version of the historic commonwealth. They did so when they had finally learned the true cost of war: bloodshed, taxes, and the collapse of respect for authority.

"War Without an Enemy"

At first, the war went badly for Parliament. In November 1644, the earl of Manchester expressed the crux of the matter when he complained that "if we beat the king ninety-nine times yet he is king still . . . but if the king beats us we shall be hanged and our posterity be made slaves." Roundheads were rebels; and despite their control of the navy and their ability to raise money from the prosperous and heavily populated south, rebels carried the stigma of treason. The habit of loyalty to God and king remained strong, and Parliament had the formidable task of building the machinery of war on unconstitutional foundations and of convincing a doubtful nation that God and justice were on its side. The old organs of government could not be used because most of the lord lieutenants of the counties had remained loyal to the sovereign; moreover, the top personnel of the exchequer, the chancery, and the law courts had fled north when Charles left London. Devoid of executive and administrative machinery, Parliament turned to committees to rule the regions under its

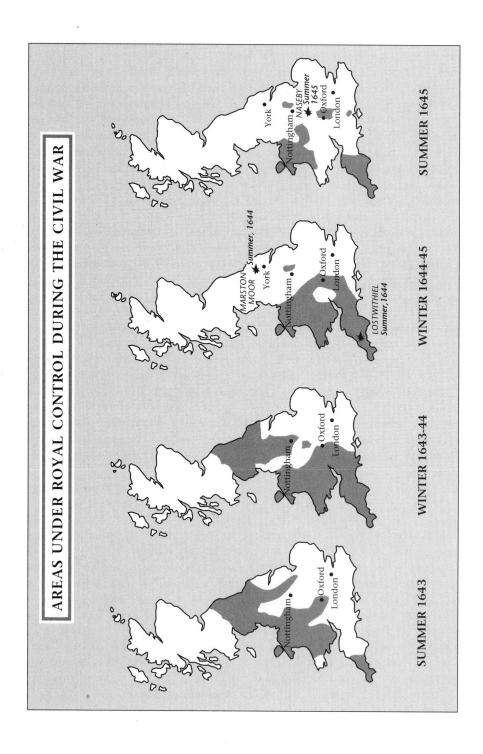

AREAS UNDER ROYAL CONTROL DURING THE CIVIL WAR

SUMMER 1645

WINTER 1644-45

WINTER 1643-44

SUMMER 1643

York

NASEBY *Summer 1645*

Oxford

London

Nottingham

MARSTON MOOR *Summer, 1644*

York

Nottingham

Oxford

London

LOSTWITHIEL *Summer, 1644*

Nottingham

Oxford

London

Nottingham

Oxford

London

control. County committees were organized to administer the shires and muster the local militia, and eventually the Committee of Both Kingdoms became the supreme executive agency responsible to Parliament.

Parliament's difficulties were twofold: Its leaders were determined to be as unrevolutionary as possible, and many of its members were of two minds whether they actually wanted to beat the king. The war, as William Waller said, may have been the work of God, but significantly he added that the "great God" knew with "what a sad sense I go upon this service and with what a perfect hatred I detest this war without an enemy." Conservative parliamentary opinion in both houses had no intention of destroying the monarchy and was aghast at the thought of the dangers of continued violence. Gentlemen schooled in Tudor social mores still retained control. They staffed the county committees and also raised their own tenants and drilled them into military units. In London, Parliament was loath to tax men of wealth too heavily and preferred to finance the war through loans from the city fathers and wealthy merchants. Such a policy, which sought simply to beat the king at his own game, was doomed to failure. The tide of royal victories rolled on until Parliament learned to capitalize on its greater financial potential, and leadership was taken over by men who could recognize the enemy and who steeled themselves to win the war, no matter what the cost in money, men, or time-honored customs.

Parliamentary victory clearly required outside aid, and in September 1643, Commons reluctantly entered into the Solemn League and Covenant with the Scots, promising to reform religion in England "according to the word of God," who presumably spoke the language of Scottish Presbyterianism. Scottish arms helped to win the Battle of Marston Moor in July 1644, with embarrassingly disappointing results. Parliament failed to follow up on the victory, and two weeks later Charles's devoted Cornishmen soundly routed the parliamentary forces at Lostwithiel.

Defeating the king in battle would require more than Scottish arms; a clean sweep from within was needed. The first step was to rid the army of its aristocratic leadership under the earl of Essex and to purge the military of incompetence by enacting the Self-Denying Ordinance, under which members of Parliament resigned their military positions. The ordinance passed through Commons in December 1644 but was blocked by the old guard in the House of Lords until April of the following year. In the meantime, Parliament had created a unique military organization known to posterity as the New Model Army, commanded by Lord Thomas Fairfax, a highly proficient professional soldier, and his lieutenant general, Oliver Cromwell, the most inspired of the new amateur soldiers. Promotion was based on merit, not blood, and the army was staffed with men who "made some conscience of what they did." Parliament had forged a weapon of righteousness and discipline, dedicated to victory. Cromwell had once said that he would rather "have a plain russet-coated captain that knows what he fights for and loves what he knows than that which you call a 'gentleman' and is nothing else." By

March 1645, he had obtained his wish; four months later, at the Battle of Naseby, his raw recruits held firm, and God gave victory to his militant saints.

The New Model Army was not only well disciplined but also, for a time at least, well and regularly financed, because Parliament after 1644 began to use its immense fiscal reserves. It collected the rents on crown lands seized during the war, raised vast sums of money through the customs, imposed first voluntary and then forced loans on wealthy merchants, levied subsidies based on a new and more realistic property assessment, collected what was called the "weekly pay" from all owners of land and chattels, imposed on all basic commodities an excise tax not dissimilar to the old Stuart monopolies on articles of trade, and had at its disposal the vast wealth of confiscated royalist estates. But money alone could not purchase victory; the inspired leadership of such men as generals Harrison, Fairfax, and Ireton was necessary. Above all, victory was achieved by Oliver Cromwell, who started life as a simple country gentleman, justice of the peace, and member of Parliament, and who emerged at the age of forty-three as the one parliamentary leader who could win battles. He proved to be a man of action who could shout back at verbose parliamentarians: "Haste what you can. . . . The enemy in all probability will be in our bowels in ten days." It was his haste and vitality that

> First put arms into religion's hand
> And timorous conscience unto courage manned.

The moment that Parliament mobilized fully for war, Charles's defeat was merely a matter of time. The Battle of Naseby spelled the ruin of the royalist cause, and within the year, on May 5, 1646, a fugitive king elected to surrender his person to his old enemies, the Scots, in the hope that they might remember that he too had been born in Scotland.

The Drift Toward Revolution

There was nothing extraordinary about civil war in England. Rebellion, rioting, and treason were time-honored practices, and in the fifteenth century the crown had become a political football to be kicked and pummeled by the great magnates. Civil disturbances in the past, however, had been of a distinct type; they were waged within the structure of a government and the framework of a society that sanctioned a wide degree of violence. They were fought within a social group to which the king himself, as the greatest baron of the realm, belonged; they were waged not to destroy the crown but to use and control it; and most of the population had little to do with the fighting or the ideological issues at stake. The Civil War started in this tradition. Only a tiny political minority was directly involved; large sections of the gentry — possibly a majority — sought to remain as neutral as they could, and most people, it was said, cared "not what government they lived under so [long] as they may plough and go to market." By the war's end, however, at least a hundred thousand Englishmen had died in battle; cities like Bristol had been sacked, churches and cathedrals desecrated, farms burned, the houses of the poor as well as the rich looted, and family fortunes sacrificed. As the Civil War moved into its second and third years, the tempo of violence and political change increased, drifting steadily from reform to revolution, from limited monarchy to no monarchy. In the end, the customs and restraints of centuries were torn aside, the ancient constitution violated and finally discarded.

The drift toward revolution commenced the moment war broke out, but the Self-Denying Ordinance of 1645 provided the first clear signal that conservatism and caution were giving way to radicalism and extremism. Although self-administered, the ordinance constituted a decisive defeat for the grandees of Parliament, especially for the aristocratic leadership of what remained of the House of Lords. As the military came under the control of men of a lesser social position but with a greater desire to win the war, the composition of the county committees passed to revolutionists of energy, if not of breeding. A basic inherent split — part social, part religious — divided Parliament and the parliamentary party. On one side stood timid constitutional monarchists such as the earls of Essex, Bedford, and Manchester, together with their conservative brethren in the House of Commons, who were inclined to Presbyterianism in religious conviction and who were ready to make almost any compromise with the king in order to preserve some form of the ancient constitution. On the other side were the religious radicals who ranged in politics from the advocates of parliamentary supremacy and limited monarchy to the republicans and devotees of social as well as political revolution.

Although the political radicals tended to be Congregationalists or Independents, the royalist propagandists who tried to equate Presbyterianism with aristocracy and Congregationalism with democracy were considerably off the mark. Some of the most revolutionary leaders in politics were Presbyterians. Conversely, many Independents were politically conservative. Oliver Cromwell may have been no monarchist, but he was certainly no democrat. What distinguished an Independent or Congregationalist from a Presbyterian, and divided a radical from a conservative, was willingness to experiment, desire to act, and readiness to use strong medicine in both state and church. Although few Independents began as republicans by conviction, many, like Cromwell, ended by voting to execute the king out of political desperation.

War had curbed idle tongues and restrained revolutionary ideas, but the moment peace again blessed the land, a host of religious sects and political factions began to voice, and at times to practice, recipes for what they all hoped would be the "godly reformation" just around the corner. Protestantism in the seventeenth century realized the anarchistic potential inherent in its central teaching that salvation was a matter of personal faith and that God's true nature could be understood only by

Christians inspired by divine grace and by reading the Bible for themselves. God revealed his purpose to individuals, not priestly castes, ordained bishops, or sacerdotal institutions. As a result, Protestantism exploded into a myriad of sects or "gathered churches," ranging from Fifth Monarchists, General Baptists, and Muggletonians to Quakers, Ranters, and Seekers. Although they differed widely from one another in creed and militancy, all opposed any form of religious uniformity enforced by the state. They professed liberty of conscience and worship, and they demanded the abolition of compulsory tithes to support an official church. From their point of view, Presbyterianism, decreed in March 1646 by Parliament as the official organization of the church, was just as tyrannical as bishops, archbishops, and a royal Supreme Head. Even the Congregationalists and Independents, both of whom advocated some sort of highly decentralized national religious organization and orthodoxy, were well to the right of what most men of property and social position regarded as a religious lunatic fringe that advocated dangerous social policies. Men and women possessed of God's truth as revealed through the inner spirit did not regard themselves as being bound by human law or morality: "What act soever is done by thee in light and love is light and lovely, though it be that act called adultery."[4]

Closely allied and often overlapping with the religious radicals were secular innovators, generally described as Levellers. Members of this group differed widely in their economic and political ideology but joined together in advocating both freedom from restraint for the individual and the doctrine of inalienable human rights for all. John Lilburne gave this theory its most radical expression when he wrote that "all and every particular and individual man or woman, that ever breathed in the world, are by nature all equal and alike in their power, dignity, authority and majesty." The natural rights of man led logically to a belief in the sovereignty of the people, represented in a Parliament responsible to popular will. Levellers fell out with one another, however, over whom to include among "the people." Some would have limited the vote to middling sorts — artisans, husbandmen, craftsmen, and journeymen — and excluded paupers and servants. Others accepted the logic of their principles and urged universal manhood (not womanhood) suffrage: "The poorest that ever lives hath as true a right to vote as well as the richest and greatest."

The doctrine of human equality led naturally to economic liberalism — the abolition of all restraint on free enterprise and the end of Stuart paternalism. Far more radical were the so-called true Levellers, whom contemporaries branded as Diggers, who sought to construct a

---

[4]There is a current debate over the existence of this religious left wing. J. C. Davis, *Fear, Myth and History: The Rantors and the Historians* (1986), says the wing is a myth; J. Friedman, *Blasphemy, Immorality and Anarchy: The Ranters and the English Revolution* (1987), takes the opposite view.

Christian paradise, devoid of avarice and ambition, in which the land was held in common; law and lawyers were unnecessary; and every man, woman, and child possessed the right to education.

Levellers and religious radicals, even during the height of the revolutionary years of 1646–1649, composed only a tiny minority. Yet their shrill cries for reform, especially their hopes for a godly reformation throughout the kingdom and their pleas for a simpler and cheaper legal system and religious toleration for all, could not be dismissed by the natural leaders of society as the ranting of deranged minds, because their ideas found a sympathetic audience in the army. Soldiers had become profoundly disenchanted with a parliamentary system that, once peace had arrived, not only proved ungrateful to its savior but, worse, showed evidence of planning to rid itself of the military without even paying the arrears owed the rank and file. Cromwell's New Model Army in 1647 was due £600,000, and the army as a whole was owed nearly £3 million. Soldiers and radicals naturally made common cause against a Parliament that seemed bent on restoring the old corrupt constitution and way of life. The army, however, never spoke with a single voice. During the famous Putney Debates in 1648 over the political future of the realm, it became clear that Levellers within the lower ranks and the grandees within the upper echelons fundamentally disagreed over an issue that would remain central to constitutional controversy for the next two centuries: Should all men, as a natural right, have the vote, or should only those who possessed a stake in society, specifically property, represent the kingdom? Despite their political differences, grandees and rank and file agreed that the military would have to protect itself from the actions of a godless Parliament.[5]

The challenge came within a year of the end of fighting. In 1647 the conservatives in Commons struck at the wartime political leadership of such parliamentary radicals as Sir Henry Vane and Oliver St. John, and tried to dissolve the New Model Army. In retaliation, the military occupied London; then in August, the House of Commons was purged at bayonet point of eleven of its most conservative Presbyterian members. Government by coup d'état had commenced, but the final defeat of the conservatives did not come until the summer of 1648. Fearful of mounting political and religious radicalism in the army and growing extremism in Parliament, the conservative Presbyterian members made their last bid to stem the tide of revolution and to turn the clock back to the days of 1641. They made common cause with Charles, who promised to reform the Church of England along Presbyterian lines. They found the military means to defy the New Model Army by alliance with the Scots,

---

[5]The best work on the politics of the army is A. Woolrych, *Soldiers and Statesmen: The General Council of the Army and Its Debates, 1647–1648* (1987). For a general history of the military, see I. Gentles, *The New Model Army in England, Ireland and Scotland, 1645–1653* (1992).

who suddenly remembered that, after all, Charles was a Stuart and a Scotsman. The unholy league of conservative parliamentarians, Scottish Presbyterians, and Anglican Charles Stuart was no match for the soldiers of righteousness, and the Scottish forces were badly defeated in August 1648 at the Battle of Preston Pans.

This "second civil war" changed the rules of the game. Passions had run high ever since Charles had raised his standard at Nottingham in 1642, but when the fighting ended, there had been few criminal charges pressed or punishments inflicted. After the victory at Preston Pans, the army became convinced that it was dealing no longer with men of good yet misguided faith who had fought honorably, but instead with war criminals. Thereafter, the Roundheads did not hesitate to court-martial and execute royalist commanders who held out against God's legions. More and more, the military viewed Parliament as a bastion of antichrist, bent on making a mockery of the sacrifices that God's elect had endured, and determined to strike a deal even at the eleventh hour with that prime war criminal Charles Stuart. Outraged by the actions of what the army regarded as counterrevolutionary forces, a small military clique, headed by Cromwell's son-in-law Henry Ireton, decided on direct action. In November 1648, Ireton persuaded the army council to cleanse Parliament and try the king on criminal charges. In early December, his troops took over London, and on the sixth, Colonel Pride closed the doors of Commons, forcibly evicting 110 of the fearful of heart, the sinful of soul, and the uncertain of politics. Appalled by such violence, 160 other M.P.'s refused to take their seats, leaving only a "rump," scarcely enough for a quorum, to carry on the business of government.

The End of the Old Constitution

The purge had been achieved by a small group within both the army and Commons who were obsessed with a vision akin to millenarianism — the second coming of Christ, who would rectify all that was unjust, ungodly, and irrational in society. In this belief, army leaders like Ireton and Cromwell were one with the Levellers and religious radicals. Supported and protected by the military and urged on by a handful of parliamentary radicals, the Rump launched forth on a revolution that would dismantle the old constitution and, it was profoundly hoped, inaugurate a new millennium. The episcopacy had been abolished as early as 1646 and replaced by a Presbyterian structure of government, but now the tempo of constitutional change attained revolutionary proportions. In January 1649, Commons declared itself to "have the supreme power in this nation," and whatsoever it enacted "hath the force of law . . . although the consent of the king or the House of Peers be not had thereunto." Charles was tried, convicted of war crimes and of being a "traitor to the people of England," and executed on January 30, 1649. A week later on February 6th, the monarchy was declared "unnecessary, burdensome and dangerous"; the Privy Council and prerogative courts of Exchequer and Admi-

The Trial of Charles I in Westminster Hall   The king sits with his back to the viewer, facing the lord president of the court and the high commissioners (135 were appointed by Parliament). Immediately in front of the sovereign are the sword and mace of state, the historic symbols of royal authority, which have now been divorced from the man who inherited the crown. The galleries are packed with spectators and the walls lined with Oliver Cromwell's musket-carrying soldiers. *(North Wind Picture Archives)*

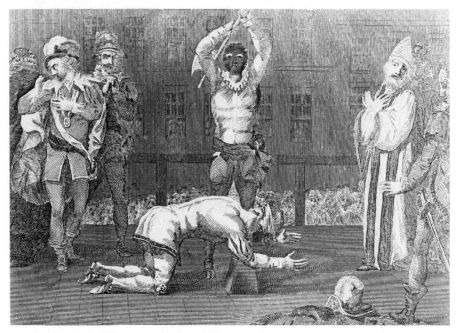

The Execution of Charles I   (An eighteenth-century imaginative depiction.) "In death Charles proved infinitely more dangerous than in life." *(Mary Evans Picture Library)*

ralty were abolished; and on the next day, the House of Lords was legislated out of existence. In their place, England was to be governed directly by the Rump, operating through a Council of State and a series of subcommittees. King, Lords, and most of Commons had vanished. Nevertheless, this was revolution with an important anomaly; in a sense it was only organizational and cosmetic. Shire and parish government remained largely untouched, and the ingrained habits of ruling and obeying continued to operate.

The decision to try and execute the king was momentous. In the past, monarchs had been defeated in war, killed in battle, or quietly murdered in their beds, but never before had a sovereign been executed "as a tyrant, traitor, murderer and public enemy to the good people of this nation." The final decision was Cromwell's, who, for better or worse, was incapable of allowing a decision to go by default. Charles had proved his incompetence in defeat, his untrustworthiness in his alliance with the Scots and Presbyterians, and his sinfulness in the deceit with which he approached any negotiation with the army or Parliament. Cromwell and the leaders of the army faced the dilemma that ultimately confronts all convinced minorities who have acquired the power to impose their will: the question of whether the better part must give way to the more part. God had given his saints victory in war. It was unthinkable to men who believed that they alone could save England from "a bleeding dying condition" that an ungodly majority should snatch the fruits of victory from God's elect. Charles had to be destroyed because he felt in no way bound by sworn promises and would undo God's work just as soon as he could find the means. So determined was Oliver Cromwell that the king must die that he informed the 135 commissioners who tried Charles that, if necessary, he would "cut off the king's head with the crown on it."

In death Charles proved infinitely more dangerous than in life. He died as became a man and a sovereign, and he associated his death with the one principle that could wipe clean a lifetime of political ineptitude: the right of all English men and women to live under laws that had been enshrined in the ancient and historic constitution. He died, as he claimed, "the Martyr of the People," a victim of naked force that denied not only his rights as king but the rights of all subjects, "for if power without law may make laws, may alter the fundamental laws of the kingdom, I do not know what subject he is in England that can be sure of his life or anything that he calls his own."

The Rump Against the Army

After seven years of war, little remained of the ancient constitution except a Rump Parliament that now stood face to face with a military monster of its own creation, which had begun to dabble in politics. England had become a commonwealth ruled by a Council of State of forty-one and a Rump of fewer than seventy-eight members. The council was still relatively conservative in composition, and it continued to reflect the will of Parliament, not of the army, for it was composed of three judges, three army officers, five peers, and thirty M.P.'s. Any serious showdown between the military and the remnants of the Long Parliament was postponed until April 1653, however, because the army was busy crushing mutiny within its ranks and rebellion at home and in Ireland.

Oliver Cromwell had faced a historic decision in ordering the execution of a king; and three months later he made an equally grave choice: the suppression of the left wing of the revolutionary movement. The moment the crust of custom had been broken and the forces of innovation allowed to bubble up, the scent of social revolution from below became stronger and stronger. Although the numbers of Levellers, egalitarians, and religious communists were small, their arguments sounded dangerous to conservative ears. Most of the grandees of the army were gentlemen of considerable substance, and Cromwell informed the Council of State in March 1649 that "you have no other way to deal with these men but to break them in pieces. . . . If you do not break them, they will break you." Both army officers and Rump politicians could make common cause against enlisted men and Levellers who impudently asked, "We were ruled before by King, Lords and Commons, now by a general, court martial and Commons, and we pray you what is the difference?" In May 1649, three regiments mutinied, and General Cromwell followed his own advice: he destroyed the Leveller-inspired uprisings at Burford.

Significantly, five months later the Rump passed legislation to muzzle the press, which had been printing tracts of every imaginable political complexion. Victory over rebellious Levellers was as crucial as Charles's execution in restoring the monarchy, for the Battle of Burford and the return of censorship marked the end of the revolutionary drift toward the left. Both military and political leaders came down hard in favor of social conservatism, which in the end set the stage for conservatism in politics and the restoration of the ancient constitution in 1660.

Once Cromwell had chastened his mutinous troops, the army was called upon to crush rebellion — sometimes referred to as the third civil war — in Ireland and Scotland. Across the Irish Sea, the fire of the uprising of 1641 continued to smolder. Ireland was Catholic, royalist, and seditious — three good reasons to warrant God's vengeance — and in August His instrument, in the shape of Oliver Cromwell, arrived to punish the ungodly and disloyal Celts. At Drogheda the disciplined army of the saints put the hateful heretics to the sword. Within the year, Ireland lay prostrate and bleeding, and by the Act of Settlement of 1652, two-thirds of the land was expropriated, the bulk of the Irish population forcibly transplanted to County Connaught, and the island populated by London land speculators and Cromwellian soldiers. Although the terms of the settlement were never carried out in full, enough was accomplished to embitter English-Irish relations for the next three hundred years and to convince most of the Irish that Oliver Cromwell had come from the land where a man could light his pipe with his finger.

With Ireland safe for the English, Cromwell turned next to Scotland. There, the Stuart dynasty still exercised its ancient magic, and rigid Scottish Presbyterians had risen again in defense of a Stuart king, this time in the person of young Charles II. At the Battle of Worcester in September 1651, God again gave victory to His Roundheads, and Scotland, like Ireland, found itself garrisoned with English troops. The subjugation of Scotland concluded the civil wars. The conflict had taken a prodigious toll. Large areas of England had endured looting, extortion, and wartime assessments; 140 English towns had suffered serious damage; and 190,000 people or 3.7 percent of the population had perished. In the Celtic fringe, the statistics were even worse; 60,000 or 6 percent had died in Scotland, and an appalling 618,000 or 41 percent were butchered in Ireland where the invaders had shown no mercy for the Catholic civilian population. According to one historian, in terms of "gross national product," the cost of the wars "may not have been exceeded until the world wars of the twentieth century."[6]

With all its enemies utterly routed, the army now turned its attention to matters closer to home, for the grandees of the military were anything but pleased with the course of events in London and Whitehall. With each passing year, the Rump seemed more and more unbending,

---

[6]C. Carlton, *Going to the Wars: The Experience of the British Civil Wars, 1638–1651* (1992).

"Be Gone You Rogues. You Have Sate Long Enough."   Oliver Cromwell dissolving Parliament. "The next day, on April 21, 1653, a note was pinned to the door, which read: 'This house to Lett now Unfurnished.' " *(E. T. Archive)*

self-perpetuating, and oligarchical. Its energy for reform had died, and it lacked the respect of the nation. The army officers were disgusted by the spectacle of parliamentary lawyers arguing over legal quibbles and never getting around to such important matters as reforming the church and the legal system or paying the arrears of the military.

Both Rump and army knew that the revolutionary government was becoming less and less representative of opinion in the boroughs and the shires and that it was slipping into incompetence and apathy. Parliament's solution was to enlarge itself with "persons of the same spirit and temper" and allowed existing members to exercise a veto over new recruits. In the army, the spirit of reform and millenarian expectations still lived, and the military's solution was to abolish the Rump entirely and to call into existence an assembly of saints. "We are not a mere mercenary army," they said, "here to serve an arbitrary power of the state." Instead, they had taken up arms "in judgment and in conscience." Technically, the military was the servant of Parliament; but when the master did not "have a heart to do anything for the public good," then it was clear, as Cromwell told the Commons, the Lord was "done with them" and must choose "other instruments for carrying out His work." In almost hysterical tones, Cromwell informed the Rump that "you are no Parliament; I say you are no Parliament; I will put an end to your sitting!" And he did.

The house was cleared at sword's point, and the next day, on April 21, 1653, a note was pinned to the door, which read: "This house to Lett now Unfurnished."

The Search for Legality[7]

When Cromwell justified his coup d'état by arguing that the Rump itself had forced such violence on him, he spoke only part of the truth. The course of novelty had moved from reform to revolution, sweeping away Parliament as well as the crown. When Commons was purged out of existence by a military force of its own creation, the country learned a profound, if bitter, lesson: Parliament could no more exist without the crown than the crown without Parliament. The ancient constitution had never been King *and* Parliament but King *in* Parliament; when one element of that mystical union was destroyed, the other ultimately perished.

The legal authority that had called the New Model Army into existence had vanished, but the army remained. From April 1653 on, the military made a series of sincere, if abortive, efforts to find a legal justification for its authority, and a godly structure of government in which it could participate. Unfortunately, the leaders of the army discovered that the job of clothing naked power with the garments of legality would tax the ingenuity of even the most accomplished political stylist. First, they tried godliness and goodwill, and in July called a Parliament of 144 saints, selected by the army and local church congregations. Ever since, that assembly has been known by the name of one of its members — Praise God Barebones. Never were reformation and reform approached with greater zeal, piety, and confidence of success; never were hopes more bitterly disappointed. Saintliness proved no substitute for political insight or parliamentary experience. Sorrowfully Cromwell had to confess his error in imagining that "men of our judgement, who had fought in the wars and were all of a piece upon that account," would be able to work in accord and achieve God's will. In the end, the general discovered that he was plagued more by pious fools than by devilish knaves. By December the Barebones Parliament had been sent home, bag and Bible.

Faced with the problem of creating some kind of legal government other than martial law, the military unconsciously took the first hesitant steps that eventually led to the restoration of the monarchy. Imperceptibly, men's minds turned back to the idea of monarchy as the single structure of government that offered legality, security, and permanence. The Instrument of Government, drawn up in December 1653, inaugurated

---

[7]Biographies of Cromwell and his efforts to find a legal basis for government are legion, but by far the shortest and most readable are R. Howell, *Cromwell* (1977); B. Coward, *Oliver Cromwell* (1991); and B. Cottret, *Cromwell* (1992). See also M. Ashley, *Charles I and Oliver Cromwell: A Study in Contrasts and Comparisons* (1987). For the search for legality, see G. E. Aylmer (ed.), *The Interregnum: The Quest for Settlement, 1646–1660* (1972).

the drift that ended in restoration. By the terms of the Instrument, Cromwell exchanged the title of lord general of the army for lord protector of the Commonwealth; executive power was placed in a Council of State composed of civilians and army officers who acted as a check on the protector's control; and legislative authority was vested in a single house elected from men of "known integrity, fearing God and of good conversation." God-fearing men were equated with those who had proved themselves careful stewards of the Lord, and the franchise went only to persons worth £200 in real or personal property. The army was too cautious to place its future solely in the hands of the godly; therefore, Cromwell received the right to exclude doubtful individuals from Parliament (a hundred were in fact barred), and a standing army of thirty thousand was written into the constitution.

The Instrument of Government lasted less than two years, for saints proved as unwilling to pay taxes as country squires, especially when the lion's share of the money went to maintain a military force over which they had no control and which was rapidly deteriorating into a self-perpetuating armed caste. By January 1655, relations between the protector and his Parliament had become so strained that Cromwell, like Charles, chose to rule alone.

Charles had succeeded in making his so-called tyranny endure for eleven years; Cromwell's rule of the major generals lasted barely twenty-two months. The difference between eleven years of Stuart absolutism and twenty-two months of Cromwellian dictatorship revealed the underlying weakness of the protector's position: it was easier to rule by legal and historic means than by military force. "If nothing should be done but what is according to law," Cromwell once said, "the throat of the nation might be cut while we sent for someone to make the law." Men who hate, who seek revenge, or who feel close upon them the fire of damnation or the hope of salvation have no time to wait. A decade and a half of indecent haste produced the final irony — there was no law left, and the throat of the nation was cut on the sword forged to protect it. Charles had endured because law, habit, and custom were on the side of monarchy. He collected ship money, wardship, and benevolent loans because subjects were used to paying taxes to a king whom most people continued to accept as divine and who could discover endless precedents for his actions. Sheriffs and justices, constables and lord lieutenants enforced his law and raised money in his name out of a sense of historic duty, even if some of them dragged their feet and opposed royal policy. A king was still a king and had to be obeyed. Only total bankruptcy, produced by the Scottish war, had forced Charles to call his Parliament.

In contrast, Cromwell was neither divine nor legal. His authority did not stem from his title of lord protector, for there was neither precedent nor legality inherent in such a rank. Instead, his power was vested in his command of troops, and in the end he and his military colleagues had to use the army, first, to prop up the crumbling habits of lawfulness and obedience, and then, to take over and operate the administration of government. Under the major generals, the realm was divided into twelve parts, each governed by a military regime determined "to discourage and discountenance all profaneness and ungodliness" and to collect a decimation tax of 10 percent on the estates of former Cavaliers. The results discredited the military and forged a bond among all men of substance, regardless of their politics or religion. Rule by the major generals revealed that only the restoration of the ancient constitution could safeguard property and assure to "the natural rulers" of society their control of local and national government.

To make matters worse, Cromwell discovered that he, like his royal predecessor, could not finance both his government and the cost of war. For the first five years of the Commonwealth's life (1649–1653), the Rump had lived in a fiscal paradise maintained by the sale of confiscated crown, church, and Cavalier lands. Some £7 million had come from these sources, which, when supplemented by occasional subsidies and income from the customs, had carried the government through the first years of its existence and had given it the financial means to suppress rebellion in Ireland and Scotland. In 1653, however, the pinch began on a level unimaginable in the days of the Stuarts. Under the Commonwealth, Englishmen learned for the first time that "an army is a beast that has a great belly and must be fed." Throughout most of the 1650s, the budget stood at £2.7 million, or three times what had been considered feasible under Charles I. The army alone cost anywhere from £1.5 million to £3 million annually, depending on the nature of the government's military involvements. By 1655 the situation was desperate, for the decimation tax was proving unprofitable as well as illegal, and money from the sale of Cavalier estates and fines imposed on royalists was beginning to run out. Moreover, Cromwell faced the added strain of a victorious but extremely costly war against Spain.

A New Foreign Policy

A revolutionary government in 1649 required a new foreign policy; and the moment that Parliament took over first the initiative and then the crown itself, new ideas and interests in foreign affairs began to make themselves heard. With dynastic aspirations dead, the voice of trade rang unchallenged in the halls of Commons. The argument was clearly articulated that the state, by means of war and legislation, should actively seek to expand trade, protect English interests in foreign parts, and formulate a policy of economic aggression. A conscious policy of mercantilism, in which the power of the state was marshaled in defense of chartered trading companies, was accepted by the Commonwealth government, which no longer had to heed the interests of the royal family, courtiers, and favorites. The only debate was the direction of commercial expansion and whether the influence of the Merchant Adventurers or the East India Company should prevail.

Economic aggression and a commercial policy in which English colonies were viewed as "subordinate to and dependent" on the mother

The Horrible Tail-Man   A Dutch satirical depiction of
Cromwell's new foreign policy: "the state, by means of war
and legislation, should actively seek to expand trade, protect English interests in foreign parts, and formulate a policy of economic
aggression." *(North Wind Picture Archives)*

country led to war with Holland in May 1652. Anglo-Dutch relations had
deteriorated ever since England had made peace with Spain in 1604.
Throughout the first forty years of the century, the Dutch tricolors had
dominated the high seas "from China to Peru." The harbors of the world
had been explored and monopolized by Dutch commercial interests, and
the Netherlands East India Company had successfully closed the East Indies to English ships. England continued to resent the so-called massacre
of Amboyna in 1623, when the Dutch seized and tried twelve English
East India Company merchants for treason. Relations between the two
countries soured further with the execution of Charles I, which shocked
public opinion in Holland. Moreover, the Netherlands saw in the enactment of the English Navigation Acts of 1650 and 1651 a direct challenge
to its commercial empire. The Dutch claimed the right to "trade to all
countries and plantations in America and elsewhere, without difference
of people." The Navigation Acts required that English trade be carried in
English ships and that all foreign powers be excluded from the profits of
the empire. Equally serious, England claimed sovereignty over the
channel, and it demanded that foreign vessels strike their flags on
meeting English men-of-war. Although the Dutch had no intention of
accepting the principle of freedom of the seas in the East Indies, which
they controlled, elsewhere they claimed it as the right of all maritime
nations.

The First Dutch War of 1652 proved disastrous to the Netherlands. Its navies were defeated, its commerce disrupted, and its ports blockaded. By February 1654, Oliver Cromwell was in a position to dictate the peace. The Stuart pretender, Charles II, was declared *persona non grata* by the Dutch States-General; Holland recognized English supremacy in the channel and agreed to pay a tribute for fishing in British waters. "The judgment of heaven" had been appealed to, and, although good Dutch Calvinistic merchants had their doubts and would make another appeal eleven years later during the Second Dutch War, the Lord had obviously declared for the English.

War with the Netherlands had never been popular with those economic interests in England that viewed Spain as the national enemy and advocated expansion into the West Indies. Moreover, English Calvinistic republicans were unhappy with the Dutch conflict, which they regarded as a form of religious fratricide. Cromwell and many a country gentleman thought nostalgically of the days of Good Queen Bess, when glory, profit, and righteousness had united to singe the Spanish beard, loot Catholic treasure ships, and strike a blow for God and country. Militant Protestantism, lured on by the ancient myth of cheap and profitable naval war, could not resist the temptation of war against Spain. Cromwell's "design" for English expansion into the West Indies and his grandiose dream of a crusade of all Protestant countries throughout Europe against Catholicism got under way in 1655. In the hope of imitating past glories, English ships again blockaded Cádiz and sought out the treasure fleets carrying the wealth of the New World. Unfortunately, the profits proved meager, and for once England was more victorious on land than on the high seas. England was joined by France in the capture of the Spanish port of Dunkirk in Flanders, a victory that allowed Cromwell to carry "the keys of the continent at his girdle." Had he lived, he might have been tempted to reenact the design of Henry V and carve for England a new European empire. As it was, only the capture of Jamaica from Spain had enduring consequence; it became the center for English domination of the West Indies. Of more immediate concern was the cost of the war, which forced renewed efforts to find a parliamentary government that could ensure a sufficient flow of funds and would cooperate with the military.

Restoring the Monarchy

The army's final solution to the constitutional impasse was called the Humble Petition and Advice, by which the military decided to restore the monarchy in all but name. Cromwell was offered the crown but preferred the less conspicuous title of "his highness"; however, he accepted the right to name his own successor. The ghost of the House of Lords was resurrected in the form of a second chamber nominated by the lord protector and approved by Commons. Even the historic franchise based on forty-shilling freehold land and borough representation was reestab-

Oliver Cromwell, by Joseph Wilton   "The tortured Laocoön, destroyed by serpents called forth by his own actions." *(Victoria and Albert Museum, London)*

lished. The moment, however, that the "natural leaders" of society again sat in the lower house, they proved as difficult as any Stuart Commons. The upper house, which possessed the right of veto, was loaded with generals and Cromwellian friends and therefore could be relied upon. Unfortunately, the lower chamber, with many of its most trustworthy members promoted to the new House of Peers, proved more opinionated than ever. As with his other Parliaments, Cromwell had to resort to force, and in February 1658, he disbanded this final legislative experiment, announcing that he dissolved "this Parliament and let God judge between you and me." The Commons impudently answered back, "Amen." Cromwell had alienated the natural leaders of the realm just as completely as Charles had.

If Oliver Cromwell failed, it was not for lack of courage or endeavor. He has been called a "puzzled Atlas"; he might better be compared to the tortured Laocoön, destroyed by serpents called forth by his own actions. Cromwell's failure was the tragedy of all men of goodwill who recognize evil but find it difficult to describe the good. He and his army colleagues, although masterful men of war who fought with conviction, were innocent in the ways of statecraft. The lord general had had greatness thrust upon him, and he looked to God as his guide. As one of the natural rulers of society, he viewed himself as "a good constable to keep the peace of the parish," and he accepted the post of lord protector "not so much out of the hope of doing any good, as out of a desire to prevent mischief and evil." Cromwell was considerably more than a landed country gentleman, however; he was a Puritan saint, profoundly influenced by the millenarianism of his day. When East Indian merchants, sly lawyers, and ambitious politicians proved that at heart they despised "the cause of the people of God," then the soldier-saint had no choice but to accept the responsibility of forging a New Jerusalem. No matter how often Parliament was resurrected or purged, it always showed itself to be "a worldly constitution, a body fitted for a king . . . and every whit as Babylonish as kingship itself." Cromwell could not escape the conclusion that only the military, the hard core of God's elect, contained the life, the spirit, and the virtue of really good people.

As lord protector, Cromwell represented the best of God's elect, for he achieved a religious settlement unique in its time. He permitted within the state structure of the Church of England an extraordinary degree of toleration, establishing a system that allowed each parish to determine its own style of worship. Even the "gathered churches" of the religious extremists, as long as they did not emulate Ranters and Quakers in violent antisocial behavior, were tolerated. So also were Episcopalians and Catholics, and for the first time since Edward I outlawed Jewry in 1290, Jews were admitted into the Commonwealth. Cromwell's tolerance was dictated in part by practicality; he needed the support of as many religious groups as possible, and he knew that it paid to do business with the Jews. Ironically, it was also influenced by his conviction in his own election and salvation: there was no need for him to encroach upon God's ultimate decision about who was elect and who was damned. Finally, Cromwell also had an abiding, if naive, faith — shared by neither Parliament nor the Council of State — that moderation and tolerance would close the century-old rift between the inner voice of conscience and the obligation to obey in the name of public order.

The more the lord protector labored in the Lord's vineyard, the more evident it became that either men would have to be forced onto the path of righteousness or the old way of life and the ancient habits of thought would have to be restored. In the end, history proved more powerful than the sword, and had Cromwell lived, he probably would have endeavored to restore the monarchy in his own person. As it was, the Stuart court was copied by the protector with one essential exception: Charles I had had only a token military force, but Cromwell dined with every door guarded by armed sentries. Not only was the lord protector styled "his highness" but his children also became princes and princesses, and his country wife had to learn that a queen does not haggle over the price of oranges. Although the new court abounded with the regalia of royalty, Cromwellian monarchy was kingship without conviction or tradition. Only the force of the protector's own personality held the Protectorate together. He never achieved the New Jerusalem, but few doubted his sincerity. His strength rested in his conviction that he was the Lord's instrument and not merely a common manipulator of people and parties. When he died, exhausted but not embittered, the revolution collapsed from within. It had in truth been dead for over a decade. Even in failure, the lord protector remained magnificent. How God ultimately judged between His chosen vessel and the impudent men in Parliament, who forced the protector into greater and greater acts of violence, is not for humanity to record. History has long since given up writing about *Cromwell's Bloody Slauter House* or *The English Devil: Hell's Higher Court of Justice.* Today the verdict is simply that of a "puzzled Atlas" who was eventually destroyed by the means forced on him to attain his ends. The kingdom of God belongs to heaven, the city of man to earth, and not even a Cromwell could unite the two.

The lord protector died on the third of September, 1658, and within eighteen months Charles II reclaimed his throne "without one drop of blood and by that very army which rebelled against him." The bishop of Winchester is not to be laughed at for believing that "never were there so miraculous a change as this, nor so great things done in so short a time. But this is the Lord's doing; no human wisdom can claim a share in it." A peaceful restoration was indeed an extraordinary achievement, for Cromwellian dictatorship had left a legacy of hatred, and the future in 1658 boded nothing but anarchy and further civil war. What the good bishop did not perceive, however, was that both Cavaliers and republicans had had their fill of civil war and military rule, and that no one, not even the major generals, could think of any political solution other than the restoration of the monarchy.

The utter failure of nonroyal monarchy was revealed when Oliver Cromwell's son Richard tried to inherit the protector's authority. What the father could do, his civilian son could not, and in April 1659 the military forced Richard to dissolve the Protectorate and to reinstate the Rump. Incredible as it seems, the Rump proved as unforgiving and as ungodly as ever and promptly defied the grandees of the army by refusing to vote the arrears of pay and to abolish clerical tithes. With the military and the Rump again at sword's point, the realm began the long slide into anarchy. Associations sprang up urging people not to pay their taxes, the law courts ceased to function because the judges had no legal commission by which to act, and the lunatic fringes of the religious sects again distributed their pamphlets and inflamed hungry apprentices and petty tradesmen in the city of London. Confronted with a "giddy, hot-headed, bloody multitude" that was beginning to harken to the voice of religious ranters, the ruling classes came to the conclusion that a state church and a historic king were absolutely essential to the maintenance of social discipline and obedience. As one gentleman complained, "I love old England very well, but as things are carried here, the gentry cannot enjoy much to be in it." With these words, the swan song of revolution was sung.

In an atmosphere of anarchy, and with men of substance putting aside their religious and political disputes to unite in defense of "degree, priority, and place," the army and the Rump continued to harangue each other to death. In May 1659, the Rump cashiered General Lambert and ordered the army to disband. In answer, the military for a second time closed the doors of Parliament. But the army itself was beginning to disintegrate; it was uncertain whether the rank and file would follow their officers against the Rump, and the generals could not unite on a single policy. Some remained loyal to the idea of a protectorate; others sought yet another try at government by God's elect; and still others, such as George Monck, declared for the Rump. In the end it was General Monck who made the crucial decision — he ordered his soldiers out of Scotland and began the long march toward London. Hopelessly split, the military gave in to public pressure and the threat of Monck's approaching troops. "The Lord hath blasted them and spit in their faces, and witnessed against their perfidiousness," and as an act of repentance, the Rump was restored for a third time on December 27, 1659.

What would a thrice-restored remnant of a dead revolution do in the face of the rising clamor for a new and free Parliament? Would it allow new elections or permit the inclusion of excluded old members? In the streets of London, apprentices spitted every steak they could find to signify the "roasting of the Rump." Even so, that body hesitated, for either course of action meant the restoration of the monarchy. In the end, the decision rested with General Monck, whose advance on London became a victory march. He entered the city on February 3, 1660, and immediately commenced the process of unpurging Parliament. On April 21, his soldiers quietly opened the doors to eighty members who had been barred from their seats ten years before by Colonel Pride. The new additions were enough to outvote the diehards, and Commons set up a monarchistic Council of State with authority to invite Charles II back to his native land and to order new elections on the basis of the historic franchise. Having done what General Monck ordered, Parliament then proceeded to dissolve itself. The Long Parliament was finally over and so also was "this bloody and unnatural war."

S INTRA CAMERAM STELLATAM.

Society Restyled

1660 to 1688

On preceding page: THE NEW SCIENTIFIC SPIRIT   The old astronomical observing-room at the Royal Observatory at Greenwich, circa 1675,
where the prime meridian, longitude 0, begins. *(North Wind Picture
Archives)*

CHAPTER 14

Charles II and the Fruits of Revolution

On Friday afternoon, May 25, 1660, Charles II's exile came to an end. Four days later, on his thirtieth birthday, the Merry Monarch made his triumphal entry into the city of London. "The shouting and joy" were "past imagination." Onlookers strewed his way with flowers, bells rang out a noisy welcome, the streets were hung with tapestries, fountains ran with wine, balconies glittered with gaily bedecked ladies, and the procession took seven hours to reach the royal palace of White-hall. There, in the same room where his father had waited eleven years before to walk out onto the scaffold, Charles II was acclaimed by his loyal Commons. King, Lords, and Commons were united in their deter-mination to turn back the clock to the days of 1641. The reality of war, rebellion, and regicide could never be wiped out — indeed, the memory would dominate the political life of the kingdom for the next century — but at law the fiction was maintained that twenty years of treason had never existed. Two decades of civil wars and Cromwellian protectorship became an interregnum, a limbo between periods of legality. The experi-ence of saints and idealists and the advice of Mr. Thomas Hobbes were carefully set aside. The Restoration rested on neither militant godliness nor brutal reason but on safe and comfortable history.[1]

---

[1]The best surveys of the last half of the seventeenth century are G. N. Clark, *The Later Stu-arts* (1934); J. H. Plumb, *The Growth of Political Stability in England, 1675–1725* (1967); and J. R. Jones, *Country and Court: England, 1658–1714* (1979). More specialized are T. Harris, *Politics under the Later Stuarts: Party Conflict in a Divided Society, 1660–1715* (1993); J. R. Jones, *The First Whigs* (1978); D. T. Whitcombe, *Charles II and the Cavalier House of Commons, 1663–1674* (1966); J. Miller, *Popery and Politics in England, 1660–1688* (1973); C. D. Chandaman, *The English Public Revenue, 1660–1688* (1975); R. Hutton, *The Restoration* (1985); and P. Seaward, *The Cavalier Parliament and the Reconstruction of the Old Regime, 1661–1667* (1988). Brief but useful treatments of the reign can be found in J. Miller, *Restoration England: The Reign of Charles II* (Seminar Studies in History, 1985), and K. H. D. Haley, *Politics in the Reign of Charles II* (Historical Association Stud-ies, 1985). The most recent biographies of Charles II are J. R. Jones, *Charles II: Royal Politi-cian* (1987), and R. Hutton, *Charles the Second: King of England, Scotland, and Ireland* (1989). By way of contrast see A. Fraser, *Royal Charles* (1979).

John Milton Versus Thomas Hobbes

The Civil War had produced two great political thinkers: the Puritan poet John Milton (1608–1674) and the rationalist Thomas Hobbes (1588–1679). Each man reflected divergent facets of the Cromwellian revolution, and each was equally unacceptable to the restored monarchy of 1660. Milton had preached tyrannicide and republicanism, claiming that man was born free and that "the power of kings and magistrates is nothing else but what is only derivative" and "committed to them in trust." When monarchs betrayed that trust, the free and godly had a moral duty to revolt. In his last political tract, *The Ready and Easy Way to Establish a Free Commonwealth*, Milton set forth the ultimate justification of the Cromwellian dictatorship. "Nature," he said, "appoints that wise men should govern fools." Wisdom, in Milton's mind, was equated not so much with godliness as with goodwill, and his most enduring treatise was the *Areopagitica* (1644), in which he defended freedom of speech on the grounds that the truth will always prevail over error when both are tested "in a free and open encounter" by men of wisdom and moderation. The truth needed "no policies, nor strategems, nor licensings to make her victorious." Unfortunately, neither the truth, as Milton conceived it, nor men of goodwill had managed to prevent the Cromwellian regime from deteriorating into despotism. Milton's "ready and easy way" proved inadequate, for it presumed the existence of men devoid of prejudice and filled with Christian charity. Charles II could scarcely have been expected to favor a political faith that sanctioned tyrannicide. He and his advisers knew enough about human nature to realize that the Restoration, if it were to endure, could not be built on a Christian dream; it had to be firmly rooted in self-interest and a "vile and sordid love of money."

If Milton was too much the idealist, Thomas Hobbes was too much the realist. Hobbes wrote of the godless Leviathan, the secular state that was the product of social need and naked power. Law and order rested neither on divine precepts nor on the inalienable and historic rights of man, but on the will of the sovereign, which had the strength to secure order and enforce law. Human nature, according to the Hobbesian creed, destined men and women to lust for power and to live in perpetual fear of destruction at the hands of the strong, the intelligent, and the greedy. Self-preservation compelled each individual to convey all rights to a sovereign body, which as a consequence became the source of all coercive authority within society and created and executed its own laws. Rebellion against such a sovereign power constituted the ultimate act of social folly because its destruction meant the end of society and a reversion to a state of nasty brutishness and anarchy.

Hobbes wrote *The Leviathan* between 1641 and 1651 as a defense of the crown and a warning against rebellion, but ironically it cost him his welcome at the exiled court of Charles II. The first Charles had died a martyr to something akin to Hobbes's sovereign — the military might of

The Title Page to Hobbes's *Leviathan* The book depicts the godless "secular state that was the product of social need and naked power." *(The Mansell Collection)*

Oliver Cromwell's New Model Army. Eleven years later, his son claimed the throne of England on the same principles for which his father had died: the law of God and history as enshrined in the ancient constitution. Charles II was no Hobbesian sovereign; instead, he was a legitimate ruler who accepted limitations on his own authority because he recognized the historic rights of his subjects. A godless sovereign, created for reasons of social necessity and claiming absolute authority, was totally unacceptable to the Stuarts and to the seventeenth century as a whole. Charles, as an exiled sovereign returning to his throne at the sufferance of General Monck and public opinion, could hardly have condoned the Hobbesian doctrine that might makes its own right. Indeed, it was England's exposure to the tyrannical consequences of unrestrained political power that so encouraged the restoration of the traditional sovereign. Because men of substance saw in the ancient kingship a safeguard to their property, they applauded a king who could write that "without the safety and dignity of the monarchy neither religion nor property can be preserved."

The Restoration: What Was Restored

In theory, the Restoration was unconditional and limited only by Charles's promises, granted at Breda in April 1660 just before he set sail for England. The Declaration of Breda pledged "liberty to tender consciences," a general pardon for all except those whom Parliament specified, the safeguarding of all land transfers made during the Interregnum until Parliament had decided on a just settlement, and the disbanding of the army. In actuality, of course, the restored monarchy was unconsciously conditioned by the precedent of twenty years of rebellion and regicide. It was clear to all in 1660 that the divinity of kings was fast fading. The Stuart throne had been restored as an act of political necessity, not as the result of divine judgment. If any institution could claim to be the voice of heaven, it was Parliament, not the king. Even as Charles set foot in England, Samuel Pepys recorded the new position of the monarchy. When the king was being rowed to the wharf at Dover, one of his favorite dogs fouled the boat. This mishap, Pepys noted, "made us all laugh and methink that a king and all that belong to him are but just as others are. . . ." If any idea of divine right existed in Charles's mind, it was probably similar to that of the happy pontiff who, on his election to the papal throne, reportedly said, "God has given us the papacy, now let us enjoy it." If nothing else, the new monarch was determined to enjoy what God and General Monck had given him.

England was fortunate in this ugly, big-nosed, "tall man, above two yards high," who stepped ashore at Dover. Like his grandfather, the second Charles was almost a foreigner. Having lived fifteen years in France, he was more French than English in taste and politics. Yet Charles understood England and his English subjects better than any Stuart sovereign before or after him: He instinctively sensed that the rock on which the monarchy stood was popularity. Puritans were revolted by his scandalous self-indulgence, parliamentarians suspected that at heart he was an absolutist, and Protestants were scandalized by his free thinking and shocked by his Catholic inclinations. Yet few Englishmen felt sufficient animosity to act on their hatred, and many thousands saw in Charles the affectionate symbol of "a very merry, dancing, drinking, quaffing and unthinking time." Although the righteous minority had serious doubts, the multitude loved a monarch who could announce that "God will not damn a man for taking a little unregular pleasure by the way."

Charles endeared himself to his subjects because he had a sense of humor and an appreciation for timing, joined with an absolute determination never again to go upon his travels. He had the sensitivity, intelligence, and tact not to drive himself or his enemies to extremes. In victory he was moderate, in defeat he was understanding; and his epitaph, spoken by the marquis of Halifax, has about it the ring of truth: "Let his royal ashes then lie soft upon him, and cover him from harsh and unkind censures; which, though they should not be unjust, can never clear themselves from being indecent." For all his faults, Charles Stuart was never

Nell Gwynn, Charles II's "Protestant" Mistress, Painted by Sir Peter Lely "God will not damn a man for taking a little unregular pleasure by the way." *(Royal Academy of Arts, London)*

indecent in his sex life, his faith, or his politics, and this was all that most men demanded of him. England in 1660 had had its fill of indecent godliness and military rule, and it was satisfied with a sovereign who could learn from the past, yet forget and forgive the bitterness of his experiences.

If fervent royalists thought that the Restoration would bring sweet revenge and that henceforth the sun would shine on their "side of the hedge," they were sadly mistaken. Charles had promised at Breda to pardon all except those named by Parliament, and he kept his royal word. In the end only fifty-seven names were omitted from the Act of Indemnity. Of these, thirty were condemned to die, but only thirteen were finally sacrificed to the demand for vengeance. Although the people greeted the spectacle of hanging and disemboweling with "great shouts of joy," and Mrs. Pepys left her wifely duties to view the hanging of the exhumed corpses of Cromwell and his son-in-law Henry Ireton, the monarchy was not restored in a bloodbath. The men who had committed treason against the sovereign and had cast down the crown were themselves members of the ruling elite, and it had been their disaffection with the revolution that led to Charles's return. They were as useful and necessary to him as his faithful royalists.

The king had scarcely reached London before it became apparent that he would have to reward rebels as well as steadfast friends. Those old Cromwellian military men George Monck and Edward Montagu each earned a peerage. Monck received the coveted Order of the Garter and a dukedom, and Montagu was appointed general of the fleet and created earl of Sandwich. The men who triumphed in 1660 were politic individuals in both camps, able to make the best of all possible worlds. Charles's Council of Thirty in 1661 contained twelve men who had committed treason against his father. In part, forgiveness was deliberate policy; in part it was dictated by necessity, for the king had to have advisers of experience and only the parliamentary party could supply him with what he needed. In all honesty, the new monarch had to agree with Samuel Pepys's conclusion that the Cavalier party could not supply "nine commissioners or one secretary fit for the business." Twenty years of exile had not trained royalists in the art of government. Merchants and Presbyterians, rebellious landlords and Cromwellian generals had ruled the realm for two decades through parliamentary committees; and after the Restoration many of them continued in the service of the crown.

The man who typified the Restoration and its policies was the king's chief minister and lord chancellor, Edward Hyde, the newly created earl of Clarendon. Hyde had opposed ship money and allied himself with Pym when the Long Parliament first met. His purpose in 1660 was to restore to England "its old good manners, its old good humour and its old good nature." This goal did not mean bloodshed, revenge, or the restoration of Tudor-Stuart paternalism. During the years of exile, the earl's greatest accomplishment had been to keep his king free from the religious passions and furious vengeance of the queen mother and hotheaded Cavaliers. He sought a return of King in Parliament that would not be a slavish imitation of the days of Elizabeth but would be instead a constitutional balance reflecting the changes legally introduced during the first years of the Long Parliament. Although royalists might weep for their martyred king, Parliament had dethroned and executed a ruling monarch, and the restored crown had to recognize this unpleasant fact.

The scepter and sword of state returned untarnished, but the crown that rested upon Charles's head was sadly lacking in its ancient luster. The prerogative courts of Star Chamber and High Commission, the two pillars of Tudor-Stuart paternalism, had been legally abolished in 1641 and were not restored. Without the machinery to enforce royal will in church and state or to discipline "the natural leaders" of society in the shires, any pretense of an organic and ordered society began to wither, and the direction of government fell into the hands of men of property. The greatest accomplishment of the earl of Clarendon was his success in associating "the rule of the restored house of Stuart with the sense of universal security for persons and goods." It was exactly here that the royalists' cup of bitterness ran over, for they learned that the Restoration did not mean the redemption of lost estates and rewards for past sacrifices but instead "Indemnity for the king's enemies and Oblivion for his friends."

The Act of Indemnity and Oblivion of 1660, establishing the land settlement, acknowledged the sanctity of private property even when held by rebels, and proved the wisdom of William Prynne's words that "if Charles Stuart is to come in, it were better for those that waged war against his father that he should come in by their votes." Crown lands worth £3.5 million, church property valued at £2.4 million, and the estates of seven hundred royalists, confiscated during the Interregnum, were returned to their original owners. Although many a parvenu Cromwellian officer was stripped of his lands and hard-won social dignity, Cavalier estates, sold to support the king's armies or to pay the fines and crushing taxes levied by the Rump and the military government under Cromwell, were never restored. Between 1644 and 1652, £1.3 million in fines had been extracted from three thousand royalists, and possibly an even larger sum was later raised by the decimation tax. How many Cavalier gentlemen went under, destroyed by debts and loyalty to their king, is beyond reckoning. One study indicates that in Staffordshire half the land changed hands between 1609 and 1669; the highest rate of change probably occurred during the Interregnum years. Certainly, in 1660 the royalists felt that they had been cheated of the fruits of restoration. The wealthy, the influential, the astute, but not necessarily the just, triumphed. Many supporters of the king concluded that they had "endured the heat of the day and become poor," only to be "put off with inconsiderable nothings." Charles himself escaped their hatred, but Cavaliers never forgave Clarendon for what they considered to be outright betrayal.

Although the earl of Clarendon was branded a Judas, he was no traitor to his class, only to an unlucky minority within it. The king's party, he argued, consisted not solely of royalists but of all persons of "considerable fortunes and families in the kingdom." In 1660 England stood on the threshold of 170 years of government of, by, and for the well bred, the well connected, and the well established, in which freedom was equated with property and liberty with privilege. With a single voice, the oligarchy acclaimed Hyde's words that "whatsoever is of civility and good manners, all that is of art and beauty," is the "child of beloved property." Even that excellent Presbyterian Richard Baxter agreed that "want of riches" keeps "men out of freedom."

It was crucial to the defense and security of men of substance that a Parliament dominated by gentlemen be financially and politically supreme, that local government be firmly in the hands of the squirearchy, and that the Church of England be converted into a source of patronage for the oligarchy. All three were in part achieved by the Restoration. The rule of property in government had been gained in large measure when Parliament established its right to act as the sole taxing instrument within the realm. The crown's feudal and historic sources of revenue were never revived. In place of ship money, wardship, and purveyances, Charles II was promised an annual income of £1.2 million for life, only half of what Cromwell had gone bankrupt on, but a third more than his father had survived on during his eleven years of personal rule. The first Restoration Parliament, known as the Cavalier Parliament, loudly voiced its devotion to monarchy, but it was equally determined not to create a financially independent crown, nor to reintroduce the system of direct land and property taxes that had existed in the days of Elizabeth and James I. In the sixteenth century, a parliamentary subsidy had generally been levied at a rate of four shillings to the pound on the assessed value of land, and at the rate of two shillings, eight pence on personal property. By 1628 property assessment had become so outdated that the upper classes had succeeded in escaping the full weight of taxation, and even during the civil war years, Parliament had hesitated to overburden its members. Although subsidies based on a new rate of assessment passed, the Rump and the military preferred to live off the custom duties, excise taxes, and fines imposed on royalists. The Cavalier Parliament of 1661 showed the same reluctance to depend on direct taxation. The last of the ancient subsidies passed in 1663; thereafter, the customs, a hearth tax, and excise levies on beer, ale, tea, coffee, and soap carried the cost of government.

The fiscal supremacy of Parliament produced a tax policy favorable to landlords and merchants. Before judging the class nature of the tax structure, however, one should recall that nearly £1,000,000 was voted in 1660 to pay off the arrears of the army, and that throughout Charles's reign, men of property contributed on the parish level nearly £700,000 a year for poor relief. This was the price that oligarchy was willing to pay for control of local government. The country gentleman had always exercised immense influence in the shires, but after 1660 within his own estate he was "prince." The demise of the Star Chamber and the failure of the Privy Council to discipline and control justices of the peace removed royal influence from the countryside, leaving supreme the sheriff, the high constable, the lord lieutenant, the justice of the peace, and the local squire. At the same time, the abolition of feudal military tenure in 1660 further increased the power of the local gentry by transforming feudal landholding, which in the past had been subject to fiscal and military obligations to the crown, into private property. Copyhold property in contrast remained largely unprotected, and it tended to deteriorate into leaseholds held at the sufferance of the local landowner.

As a further safeguard against a monarchy balanced, and in local affairs heavily outweighed, by oligarchy, Parliament made good its claim to freedom of speech and debate. It demanded that statute take precedence over royal proclamation and that the crown's prerogative be translated into law. The Book of Customs Rates of 1660, for example, was based on statute, not royal decree. Finally, it insisted on the right of habeas corpus, first enacted into law in 1641 and restated in 1679, whereby the critics of the crown were protected and limits were placed on the actions of arbitrary government. England, as the French ambassador noted, had a monarchical appearance because it had a king, "but at bottom it is very far from being a monarchy." Members of Parliament, he said, not only spoke their minds freely but even called "the highest people to the Bar."

The crown was inseparable from religion, and the restoration of the ancient constitution in the state required the resurrection of the episcopacy in the church. Unfortunately, Anglicans and Presbyterians refused to reconcile. Twelve bishops and twelve Presbyterian elders, like Lewis Carroll's maids, could not sweep away the sand of discord. The only thing they could settle on was that "the church's welfare, unity and peace, and His Majesty's satisfaction were ends on which they were all agreed." With the failure of churchmen to find a solution, the Cavalier Parliament of 1661–1662 decided to end the debate; it reestablished Anglican uniformity, episcopacy, and discipline. The Act of Uniformity of 1662 ordered the clergy to give "unfeigned assent and consent" to the Anglican Prayer Book, and possibly 1,800 Puritan pastors were removed from their posts. Those expelled became known as Dissenters or Nonconformists because they refused to revert back to Anglicanism. Having purged the clergy, Parliament struck at the nonconforming ranks of the laity. The Corporation Act of 1661 required all town officials to take an oath of allegiance to the crown and to accept communion according to the rites of the Church of England. The Conventicle Act of 1664 made all meetings of five or more persons for nonconformist worship seditious; and the Five Mile Act passed a year later ordered that no dissenting minister might live within five miles of a town, nor teach unless he had taken the oath of allegiance. Taken together, the religious settlement became known as the Clarendon Code, although in truth it represented the failure, not the triumph, of the earl's policy. Although Clarendon had been responsible for Charles's promise at Breda to grant "liberty to tender consciences," and both he and Charles sought a more moderate and broader religious settlement, the Cavaliers, who had been denied their wish in land and politics, had their say in religion.

In defeat Puritanism found its grandest voice in the blind Milton. Evicted from his position as Latin secretary to the Council of State under Cromwell, silenced as a political pamphleteer, and cut off by law from the comfort of his faith, the poet posed the question hidden in every Puritan heart:

> Now blind, disheartened, shamed, dishonoured, quelled,
> To what can I be useful, wherein serve
> My nation and the work from Heaven imposed?

Satan's triumph in *Paradise Lost* is the cry of blind, disheartened Puritanism; *Paradise Regained* is the hope of inward victory and heaven. Dissent after 1660 turned to pietism, toleration, and finally democracy. Those who could not be persuaded to conform for the sake of political privilege began to close their ranks. Congregationalists, Presbyterians, Quakers, and Unitarians after 1660 stood united in quiet but determined opposition to Anglican episcopacy and the state-enforced uniformity on which it rested.

Militant Puritanism died with the Restoration; so also did Laudian Anglicanism. The restored church became the instrument of oligarchy, not of monarchy, and the alliance of the altar and the throne gave way to the union of the miter and the ermine. Under Archbishop Laud, the church of Henry VIII and Elizabeth had retained one essential feature of its Catholic heritage; ministers were "ambassadors of God" ordained "to supply the room of Christ." The old Tudor-Stuart church had dictated morals and censored opinions. It had constituted a separate caste, and Laud had encouraged the simple parson "to hold up his head in the presence of the country families." Once upon a time, ministers had been "as good as any Jack Gentleman in England," but after 1660 the church became the preserve of the squirearchy.

Although the king continued to be the Supreme Head of the ecclesia and the Defender of the Faith, his powers of discipline had died with the Court of High Commission. Parliament now accepted the burden of ordaining and enforcing religious uniformity, and it removed from the church's hands the right to tax itself. Henceforth the ecclesia lost its position as a divinely sanctioned caste and became a profession, to be taxed and disciplined like any other occupation. The church was worth saving, not for the sake of religion, but because it was one of the pillars of respectability and an essential prop to oligarchical rule. Gentlemen sent their sons to college to "learn the art or trade of preaching." Five hundred years earlier, the church had thundered with the mighty voice of God. By the sixteenth century, it sang an obedient treble to the crown's bass.[2] After 1660 it became the silent and humble partner in that scheme of things so confidently described by the marquis of Newcastle, who "loved monarchy as it was the foundation and support of his own greatness; and the church as it was well constituted for the splendor and security of the crown; and religion as it cherished and maintained that order and obedience that was necessary to both."

Restoration Politics

The Restoration was a brilliant accomplishment, achieved without bloodshed and with a minimum of bitterness, yet the resurrection of the ancient constitution raised almost as many questions as it solved. It remained to be seen whether the treasured Tudor doctrine of uniformity of faith could survive in a society where religious dissent had grown extensive, or whether spiritual orthodoxy was possible in a universe run by the mechanical laws of Sir Isaac Newton's World Machine. Equally problematical was the restoration of the ancient but muddled political formula of King in Parliament at a moment when the English were demanding a more precise definition of the powers of monarchy. The Restoration left the exact relationship between King and Parliament in dangerous obscu-

---

[2]The best pictures of the restored church can be found in J. H. Pruett, *The Parish Clergy Under the Later Stuarts: The Leicestershire Experience* (1978); J. A. I. Champion, *The Pillars of Priestcraft Shaken: The Church of England and Its Enemies 1660–1730* (1992); and J. Spurr, *The Restoration Church of England 1646–1689* (1991).

rity, and by 1666 both crown and Commons were beginning to articulate their own definition of that formula.

The restored crown may have been stripped of much of its divinity, but it still retained many of its ancient prerogatives. The king could prorogue and dissolve Parliament at will, could veto acts of legislation, and was not obliged to account for how much or how well he spent his revenues. He was responsible for the conduct of foreign policy, headed the military forces of the realm, and could choose his own advisers and listen only to those he preferred. Most important of all, the king retained the right to suspend and dispense with any law of Parliament. As James I had put it, "general laws made publicly in Parliament may by [royal] authority be mitigated and suspended upon causes only known to him." The right to pardon is inherent in any executive authority, but the power to suspend the operation of law could, in its most extreme form, have destroyed the fruits of war and revolution for which Parliament had fought.

To counterbalance the weighty authority of the monarch, Parliament possessed the right of impeachment of royal advisers, and it tenaciously maintained its grip on the pursestrings of government. The crux of the constitutional issue was that Parliament had asserted its supremacy but as yet lacked the institutional machinery and the precedents to make good its claim. The right to tax was undisputed, and the crown recognized that its revenues stemmed from Parliament, but the power of appropriation remained in controversy. It was clear that the legislature would never be able to harness the executive unless it possessed the right to allocate money for specific purposes and to require an account of the sums spent.

In the end, the power to tax gave Parliament the power to spend. Charles started his reign with a parliamentary pledge of £1.2 million in revenues; and tradition decreed that, although Parliament supplied the funds, the way the king spent his moneys and the amounts he assigned to the court and the various branches of government were no business of the legislature. Constitutional theory collapsed, however, when Parliament failed to grant the king the full sum promised and refused to vote additional income until it felt confident that the moneys spent reflected its policies, not the whims of royal mistresses and favorites. In the face of bankruptcy, Charles, like his father, slowly surrendered, and in 1665 the principle of appropriation of moneys was reluctantly conceded in theory, if not always in fact. Two years later, Parliament created the crucial piece of machinery necessary to enforce its financial will — the Committee of Public Accounts.

The recurring question of advice underlay the controversy between a restored monarchy and a Cavalier Parliament. The power to impeach royal ministers was a blunt weapon unless Commons knew who was giving "bad" advice to the sovereign. As yet the concept of total cabinet or council responsibility had not evolved, and if the king could do no wrong, it was essential that Parliament know the names and the policies of his most intimate advisers, who might be giving evil advice. Sir Henry Neville urged that the sovereign rely only on councillors approved by Parliament and that "there shall be a register kept of all the votes of these several councils . . . with the names as well of those who consent, as of such who dissented." Charles had no intention of allowing Commons to intrude on the sacred precincts of his council chamber, if only because both he and his cabinet increasingly disagreed with the wishes of Parliament. The crisis came when the architect of the Restoration, the earl of Clarendon, was impeached in November 1667 and fled to France to escape imprisonment and possible decapitation. Clarendon's fall involved three interrelated events: the misappropriation of funds during an ineptly fought Dutch war, Charles's clash with Parliament over the crown's right to suspend the law, and the disasters of fire and plague in the city of London.

War with the Netherlands in 1665 was a continuation of Commonwealth policy. The Cavalier Parliament was as eager as its republican predecessors to enact legislation protecting English maritime and colonial interests. In 1660 the Navigation Act had aimed at establishing a self-sufficient empire and extending the principle of "English ships with English crews" to the colonies. The statute was directed specifically at excluding foreign competition from the colonies and ensuring English commercial dominion throughout the seven seas. Under these circumstances, war with the Dutch was almost inevitable; as Samuel Pepys said, "The trade of the world is too little for us two, threrefore one must down." Moreover, dynastic irritation as well as commercial rivalry entered the picture, for Charles had never forgiven Dutch animosity toward the Stuart cause during the Interregnum. Unfortunately, the war was fought ineptly and highlighted the incompetence of English arms, in contrast to the days of Cromwell and Admiral Blake. Right under English noses, Admiral DeRyter sailed up the Thames in June 1667, set fire to naval installations, and towed away the flagship, *The Royal Charles*. The war was lost from lack of energy and money; Clarendon failed to give the needed leadership, and Commons refused to supply the necessary funds. English military honor also fell victim to the constitutional struggle over appropriations. Charles and his brother James, duke of York, were pictured as leaders "who mind their pleasures and nothing else," and Parliament maintained that it had no intention of granting supplies that might be wasted on favorites, dogs, and mistresses.

Dutch victory at sea did not stem solely from constitutional squabbling between king and Commons and English naval incompetence. The enemy also profited from the bubonic plague that raged through London during the summer of 1666 and from the catastrophic, if purging, fire that destroyed three-fourths of the old city. Indeed, God seemed to be deliberately punishing England. During the 1665–1666 plague, 68,495 Londoners perished. Then followed fire. On the night of Sunday, September 2, 1666, the city went up in flames. St. Paul's Cathedral, the Royal Exchange, the Guild Hall, the Custom House, the halls of 44 trading companies, 87 parish churches, and 13,200 houses were destroyed. The total

The Great Fire of London, Sunday, September 2, 1666 "God seemed to be deliberately punishing England." *(The Granger Collection)*

loss was estimated at over £11 million, ten times the royal income. The fire started in the home of the king's baker in Pudding Lane. Timber houses with plaster walls, pitch-boarding, and thatched roofs went up like torches, spreading their sparks throughout the city. For once the king moved swiftly and decisively. The parishes of the city were divided among members of the Privy Council under the command of the king's brother. Justices of the peace and the local nobility were marshaled; each division received 3 justices of the peace, 30 soldiers, and 100 constables — all intent on demolition, the only possible method of containing the fire. From 5 A.M. to 11 P.M. Charles himself moved from parish to parish, passing buckets, swinging pickaxes, paying workmen, and offering encouragement. The next day a hundred thousand Londoners were homeless, but the flames had died and rebuilding commenced within the hour.

Singed at home and beaten on the high seas, England sued for peace at Breda in July 1667. It regained the city of New York but gave up trying to break the Dutch monopoly over the spice islands of the East Indies, and momentarily withdrew its claim that the channel was an English sea. The earl of Clarendon was held responsible for all the evils of the day. He was held accountable for the king's Portuguese marriage to Catherine of Braganza, which brought with it Tangier in the Mediterranean and

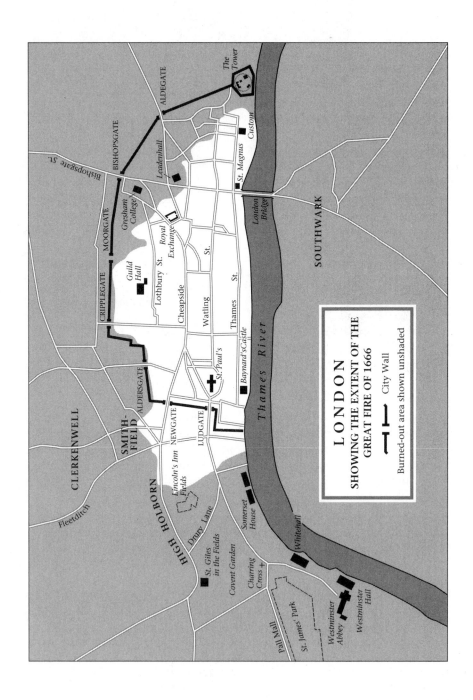

LONDON
SHOWING THE EXTENT OF THE
GREAT FIRE OF 1666

City Wall
Burned-out area shown unshaded

Bombay in India but no children born in wedlock in Whitehall. He was blamed for the sale of Dunkirk to the French in 1662 for £400,000, which was regarded as a deliberate betrayal of the victory won by English arms in the days of Oliver Cromwell. Finally, both Parliament and the king made him the scapegoat for the ignominious defeat of England at the hands of the Dutch.

With Clarendon's fall in 1667, England was ruled by a cabal, or inner council. The age of government by alphabet had begun, for the Cabal took its name from the first letters of the ruling clique — Clifford, Arlington, Buckingham, Ashley, and Lauderdale. Ashley was a free thinker and parliamentarian, Arlington a pseudo-Catholic, Clifford a papist, Buckingham an Independent gone libertine, and Lauderdale a Scottish Presbyterian. Government with five heads floundered almost instantly. The Cabal could agree on nothing except religious toleration, not because it believed in the principle but because each member sought to profit from it. The Cabal, in Charles's view, had but a single advantage; it left him free to develop his own foreign policy and to introduce in 1672 the Declaration of Indulgence suspending the operation of the Clarendon Code.

By 1670 Charles had determined on a pro-French policy. He was himself French by taste and breeding, and his mother was Louis XIV's aunt. He admired the ease, freedom, and brilliance of Louis XIV's absolutism, and he sincerely desired to free English Catholics from the draconian laws of Elizabeth's reign, which still existed, at least in theory. The ultimate purpose of Charles's policy remains in doubt. If he aimed, as some historians have argued, to build a Stuart "tyranny" based on "Catholicism, toleration, a standing army and the French alliance," he never informed those around him. The king was both too lazy and too humorous to be a successful despot or fanatic. Moreover, he was too intelligent to believe seriously that he could get away with it. In all three traits — his laziness, his humor, and his intelligence — he differed from his brother and successor, James II, who was hard-working, humorless, and not overly intelligent, qualities that in 1688–1689 again sent the Stuarts into exile.

In 1670 Charles signed the secret Treaty of Dover with France, by which Louis XIV agreed to relieve his cousin of dependence on Parliament with an annual pension and offered, if necessary, to send troops to make England safe for Catholicism. In return, Charles promised to declare publicly his adherence to the Catholic faith as soon as it was "convenient" to do so. *Convenient* was the saving word, for there is considerable doubt whether Charles seriously imagined that he would ever find such a "convenient" occasion, except possibly on his deathbed. Whatever the ultimate purpose of the treaty, its immediate effect was to put into the hands of an impecunious king a considerable sum of money and a French promise to help England seek revenge against the Dutch. Anglo-French designs on the Netherlands were the only publicized aspects of the treaty, and they led to the Third Dutch War in 1672. The new conflict inaugurated England's entrance into the European system of alliances and realliances to maintain the balance of power.

France dominated the last half of the seventeenth century as Spain had overshadowed the final years of the sixteenth. If any country can be said to have profited from thirty years of European war, during which outrage, atrocity, and aggrandizement on the part of men and states were cloaked in the pious platitudes of religious idealism, that country was France. Almost the moment that the Treaty of Westphalia was signed terminating the Thirty Years' War in 1648, France emerged as the colossus of Europe and sought to extend its dominion to its "natural boundaries" of the Rhine, the Alps, and the Pyrenees. The avowed policy of the French crown was to realize at home and abroad the maxim, "The king first in France, and France first in Europe." Under Louis XIV (1638–1715), that policy seemed on the verge of completion. France was the wealthiest and most stable kingdom in Europe. Paris and the new royal court at Versailles were regarded as the cultural centers of the continent. French became the language of diplomacy and polite society, and every petty dynasty throughout Germany and Italy slavishly modeled itself on the court of the *Grand Monarque.*

French hegemony did not limit itself to the arts and letters. The wealth, security, and economic prosperity of France upset the military balance of power and permitted Louis to train and finance a standing army of a hundred thousand men. Fear of French arms and, at the same time, a willingness to accept French gold became the pivots of European diplomacy. In 1672 French expansion aimed at destroying the Dutch Republic and claiming the Spanish Netherlands in the name of Louis's Spanish wife. It was essential to French plans that the two maritime and commercial powers — England and Holland — not forge an alliance. The offer of gold to finance the Stuart government, the desire for revenge on the Dutch, and Charles's francophilia were sufficient to bring England into the European alliance system on the side of France.

If Louis planned on active and successful English support in the third war against Holland, he was sadly mistaken. Despite the trade rivalry between England and the Netherlands, the war was not popular. English navies were again shamefully defeated, xenophobia against France mounted, and Parliament had strong objections to Charles's pro-Catholic policy. In accordance with his promise to Louis in the secret treaty of Dover, Charles issued his Declaration of Indulgence, in which he suspended the Clarendon Code against Dissenters and the Elizabethan penal laws against Catholics. As a consequence, King in Parliament once again became King versus Parliament because the Cavalier Commons of 1672, although a trifle elderly, was just as fiercely anti-Catholic and anti-Dissenter as ever. In the end, the king faced a choice: either a parliamentary grant of £1.2 million with which to fight the Dutch war and a Test Act (1673) barring all Catholics and Dissenters from civil and military offices, or his Declaration of Indulgence and a bankrupt state. Charles was always one to accept cash in hand in preference to religious scruples in the bush. He withdrew the Declaration and signed the Test Act. The statute was in part aimed at the king's Catholic brother, James, duke of York, who was forced to resign his position as lord high admiral. That resignation became the first skirmish in the long battle to prevent the Catholic duke from succeeding to his brother's throne.

Parliament proved its control over those aspects of foreign policy that involved large sums of money by forcing Charles to conclude peace with Holland in 1674 and to give up the French alliance. Thereafter Charles lived on his secret French pension of over £100,000 a year and the receipts from the customs. In fact, his revenues for the first time reached the £1.2-million level originally authorized by Parliament in 1660. By 1674 the crown finally had achieved a degree of fiscal independence and had successfully weathered the financial crisis of the early years of the reign. Nevertheless, the Stuart monarchy was almost wrecked a second time by the efforts of Parliament to exclude the duke of York from the succession and by the religious and constitutional conflict that culminated in the extraordinary activities of Mr. Titus Oates and the Popish Plot of 1678–1681.

My Lord of Shaftesbury and the Popish Plot

Government by cabal had been replaced in 1674 by the more personal rule of the sovereign and his new chief minister, Thomas Osborne, earl of Danby, who sought to solve the king's monetary embarrassments and to construct in Commons a court party loyal to church and king. The political scene during the Danby years was one of the most convoluted and intrigue-ridden of the entire reign. Behind his ministers' backs, Charles, with the aid of his mistresses, was indulging in petticoat diplomacy, continuing to assure Louis that England was ripe for a Catholic triumph. At the same time, the earl strove to rally support for the monarchy by bribing and influencing members of Parliament. In 1679 it was alleged that 214 M.P.'s were beholden to the earl either for pensions or for offices. It is closer to the truth to say that Danby had £84,000 annually from the Secret Service Fund to spend as he saw fit in organizing the king's friends. Besides the judicious use of money, Danby espoused a pro-Dutch, anti-French, and anti-Catholic policy to weld his party together. As a final measure of confusion, French gold cropped up everywhere, for Louis gave generously to the king's enemies as well as his friends. Out of this quagmire of moral delinquency, political opportunism, and diplomatic chaos, three factors are discernible: (1) the growing resentment against the heir apparent, James, duke of York, and his Catholic faith; (2) the wave of religious hysteria that led even Englishmen of reason and moderation to believe that papists lurked behind every tree, plotting to murder the king and overthrow the Protestant church; and (3) the formation of a country party under the leadership of that spiritual father of ward heeling, lobbying, and bossism, Anthony Cooper, earl of Shaftesbury.

The earl of Shaftesbury was either "the father of liars" and "the favorite of the devil," or the hero of parliamentary supremacy, the father of Whiggery, and the defender of English liberties. The earl was all things to all people and a master at abandoning the ship at the crucial moment. He started life as a victim of the corruption inherent in the ancient constitution, for under Charles I he was robbed of much of his inheritance by the Court of Wards. Nevertheless, he fought for king and church until the royalist defeat at Naseby; he then became a zealous Presbyterian and supporter of the Protectorate until he perceived the drift of events and began working for the return of Charles II. He was rewarded first with the title of Baron Ashley and then in 1672 with the earldom of Shaftesbury. He became a member of the Cabal and lord chancellor of England, but fled the king's government to found the Green Ribbon Club, which became the organizational nucleus for the Whig party and the center of opposition to Charles. What Anthony Cooper believed remains a mystery. What he claimed to stand for was parliamentary supremacy, constitutional and Protestant monarchy, the exclusion of Catholic James from the succession, and an anti-French, anti-Catholic foreign policy. The fact that the earl, like everybody else in Restoration England, was in the pay of the king of France merely muddies the picture further. Whatever his purpose, his achievement was monumental. He forged a political machine whose members were known by their enemies as "Whigs," or Scottish horse thieves. Determined to overthrow Danby, defeat the court or "Tory" party, force a Whig Privy Council on the king, and pass the Exclusion Bill barring the duke of York from the succession, Shaftesbury deliberately used his party machine to spread religious hysteria and fabricate plots purporting to overthrow the "Establishment." Whether he manufactured the Popish Plot remains one of the great mysteries of the century. Certainly Shaftesbury became the ardent supporter of Mr. Titus Oates, whose fertile and unscrupulous mind invented the whole thing.[3]

The earl of Danby fell in December 1678 when, at the height of the hysteria, Charles's negotiations for a French pension were suddenly revealed. The earl had in fact not approved of these secret dealings and had acted only on orders from Charles himself. The king could do no wrong, but his unfortunate minister could, and in December a Whig-dominated Parliament voted to impeach Danby. A month earlier, Titus Oates, a deceiving and defrocked Anglican clergyman who had close but counterfeit contact with the Jesuits, had stood before the bar of the House of Commons and had sworn that the queen and her private physician, Sir George Wakeman, had plans to poison the king and lead a Catholic insurrection. To save Danby and his queen, Charles dissolved Parliament in January

---

[3]Anyone interested in one of the great mysteries of English history and in an exciting account of the Popish Plot by one of the masters of detective fiction should read John Dickson Carr, *The Murder of Sir Edmund Godfrey* (1936), which should be balanced by a more scholarly account by J. P. Kenyon, *The Popish Plot* (1972).

Titus Oates   Many people in 1679–1680 thought this "deceiving and defrocked Anglican clergyman" belonged in the stocks. *(Mary Evans Picture Library)*

1679, but he could not rescue the innocent victims of religious panic, false oaths, and deliberate malice. In all, ten men were tried and executed, largely on evidence supplied by Titus Oates, whose face appeared on ladies' snuff boxes, fans, and handkerchiefs; who received a generous pension of £1,200 a year from a thankful House of Commons; and on whose testimony alone five peers were imprisoned and the queen herself proclaimed a traitor. Imagination knew no bounds. Intolerance and incredulity, unreason and superstition, had been banished from the center of court and social life; but they lurked still in the minds of worthy and upright men educated to fear and abhor Catholicism and in the hearts of tradesmen and apprentices ready to believe the worst, especially when the news came accompanied by free beer supplied by the Green Ribbon Club.

Desperate for money even to feed his immediate family, Charles risked a new Parliament, and elections were called for February 1679. Everywhere Whigs triumphed, and Shaftesbury introduced the Exclusion Bill in the full expectation that it would pass both houses. Although Charles would never fight for his faith, he was willing to risk all to defend his queen and his brother's rightful inheritance. In May, although he

Charles II, 1659, After Sir Peter Lely   "He was more French than English in taste and politics. . . . [But] while the Merry Monarch reigned, England remained safe for Anglicanism." *(National Portrait Gallery, London)*

had received no money, the king prorogued Parliament and in July dissolved it. Then at the height of the crisis, Charles was struck down with fever, and by August it seemed that he was dying. The news shocked the leaders of the nation into sanity and drove home to the Whig party the realization that, should Charles die, the country would again be thrown into civil war between factions supporting Charles's illegitimate Protestant son, the duke of Monmouth, and his legitimate Catholic brother, the duke of York. The memory of civil war and its social consequences prevailed, and the country slowly began to rally to the king.

Time was on Charles's side. Throughout 1680 and 1681, the heat of hysteria receded and men could jokingly remark, "I cannot tell you what today's plot is. 'Tis something to do with yesterday's plot, but I have not heard about yesterday's plot yet." A sure sign of a return to sanity came with the reduction of Titus Oates's pension to £2 a week. By 1681 the king had grown strong enough to order Shaftesbury's arrest on the charge of high treason and to rule without Parliament. The nation's economic prosperity assured him of a handsome income from the customs and excise taxes, and Louis of France decided that French gold would have to restore what it had so nearly destroyed — the Stuart throne. Charles became a French pensioner to the amount of approximately £500,000 a year.

Even in victory Charles was not indecent. He had saved the doctrine of the inviolability of the hereditary monarchy and the right of his brother to the crown, but he introduced no standing army paid with French silver, no Catholic altars built upon swords. Instead, during his final years of personal rule, he outpoliticked the Whigs and beat them at their own game. The king achieved control by giving in to the Tory party and becoming the greatest Tory of them all. French money continued to help sustain his throne, but Charles never tampered with the basic tenet of Tory faith: the union of the honorable and the reverent. While the Merry Monarch reigned, England remained safe for Anglicanism; episcopacy was protected from Catholicism on one side and Dissent on the other. In return, Tories were staunch supporters of the Stuart dynasty.

Charles died in his fifty-sixth year on February 6, 1685, and at the last moment he professed his Catholicism and received the sacraments. He also apologized for taking such an "unconscionable long time" in dying. Although his reign had seen moments of passion and violence, his rule, like his personality, had been restful. On only one subject had Charles been willing to go to extremes — the preservation of the throne for the Stuart line. Nevertheless, he had his doubts about a brother who, he predicted, "would never be able to hold it out for four years to an end." The prophecy proved accurate, almost to the day.

CHAPTER 15

The Triumph of the Oligarchs

The civil wars, which swept Charles I from his throne, had smelled of the social sewer and the fury of religious fanaticism, but the Glorious Revolution, which unseated James II, was safely rational and securely aristocratic.[1] It has been called "glorious" and "bloodless" and "sensible"; it savored somewhat of comic opera, but the events of November 1, 1688, through February 6, 1689, justly deserve the epithet *glorious*, if only because they signify that society can, on occasion, learn from experience. The memory of the revolutionary consequences that followed in the wake of political excess, regicide, and republicanism haunted both Whigs and Tories when they again faced the embarrassing problem of ridding themselves of a monarch whose actions threatened their leadership of society.

James II (1685–1689): A King of "No True Judgment"

If Whig and Tory had ascertained a lesson in the past, the same cannot be said for James II, who learned nothing from his father's martyrdom and his own lean and hungry years in exile. It is difficult to be completely fair to James, either as a king or as a man. If ever a revolution was the result of blundering and misguided good intentions on the part of a single individual, the second and final fall of the house of Stuart is the perfect example. The burden of responsibility rests with James. He was not urged on by hotheaded supporters or goaded into action by radical opponents, for the heat of revolutionary fire was spent. Whigs in Parliament were cautious oligarchs, not militant Puritans or rebels by principle as in the days of King Pym. By 1688 they bore little resemblance to the hot and furious party forged by the earl of Shaftesbury. The Green Ribbon Club boys were dead or exiled. Whigs now listened to the unenthusiastic voices of the earls of Devonshire and Shrewsbury and the reasoned advice

---

[1]Any serious student of the reign of James II will eventually have to turn to T. B. Macaulay's brilliant, if biased, description in his *History of England* (6 vols., 1849–1861). More modern studies include F. C. Turner, *James II* (1948), and D. Ogg, *England in the Reigns of James II and William III* (1955). The best recent biography of James II is J. Miller, *James II: A Study in Kingship* (1978).

of the marquis of Halifax, who preferred the designation "Trimmer" to that of either Whig or Tory. Tories, for their part, were no longer dashing Cavaliers or Laudian ecclesiastics. Instead, they had become well-fed, well-bred defenders of a church that looked to Parliament to enforce its spiritual monopoly and of a restored and legitimate crown that was bound by law to protect property and religion. Tory squires and their cousins, the parish rectors, loudly acclaimed their faith in the divine right of kings and the doctrine of nonresistance to the actions of God's anointed lieutenant on earth. Nevertheless, in the back of their minds, they harbored the reservation that the king and his office were not inseparable. The precedent of 1649 remained, and not even a Tory could escape the riddle, "If the King can do no wrong, somebody did the late King a great deal of wrong." When James II turned on the Church of England and, in the name of a divinely ordained prerogative, violated the sanctity of private property and the rights of the "better part" of society, Tories concluded that a Catholic sovereign could not be protected by the Anglican divinity of kings.

The reservoir of goodwill that lifted James onto his brother's throne appeared bottomless. Not since the days of the first James had the Stuart monarchy seemed more secure and respected. Even though the grandeur of the Tudor throne had vanished, Charles II had succeeded in restoring some of the luster of royalty by mastering the machinery of parliamentary politics. Taking a page from the earl of Shaftesbury's book, Charles had learned a basic lesson of Restoration existence: he could not rely on the faithfulness of his Commons, but he could manufacture it. Neither tradition nor the divinity of kings could guarantee parliamentary obedience unless the monarch controlled the machinery that sent loyal members to the House of Commons. Triumphant over religious frenzy and Whig schemes to limit the king's authority in 1681, Charles had decided to "reform" the source of most of his political difficulties — the boroughs that sent disloyal members to Parliament and placed local government in the hands of those opposed to the Stuart dynasty. Throughout the last years of his reign, borough charters were scrutinized and, if found lacking, were revoked and reissued, giving the crown the authority to nominate town officials and restrict the franchise to holders of municipal office. As a result, local and parliamentary government rested firmly in the hands of the Tories. When Parliament met at the commencement of the new reign, James II had to admit that his brother had done his work so well that "there were not above forty members but such as he himself wished for." Yet within three years, a majority party, predisposed to tolerate the monarch's Catholicism and maintain the prerogative and divine nature of his royal office, joined the Whigs in inviting the king's Protestant daughter and her husband, Prince William of Orange, to replace him on the throne.

It is fashionable for historians to be polite about James, to applaud his aim of toleration but to deplore his means, to bewail his intelligence but to presume his righteousness. Before the accolades are bestowed,

The House of Stuart

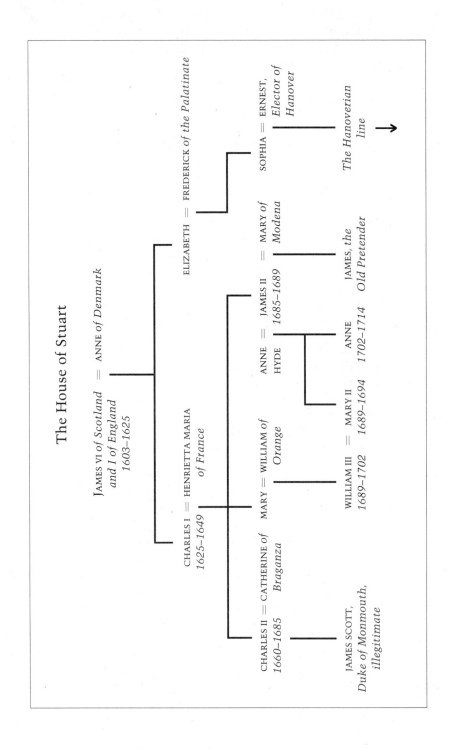

JAMES VI of Scotland = ANNE of Denmark
and I of England
1603–1625

CHARLES I = HENRIETTA MARIA
1625–1649   of France

ELIZABETH = FREDERICK of the Palatinate

SOPHIA = ERNEST,
Elector of
Hanover

The Hanoverian line →

CHARLES II = CATHERINE of
1660–1685   Braganza

MARY = WILLIAM of
Orange

ANNE = JAMES II = MARY of
HYDE   1685–1689   Modena

JAMES SCOTT,
Duke of Monmouth,
illegitimate

WILLIAM III = MARY II
1689–1702   1689–1694

ANNE
1702–1714

JAMES, the
Old Pretender

James II, by Godfrey Kneller "Stodginess, stubbornness, and stupidity were the prevailing characteristics of a man whom Bishop Burnet analyzed as having 'no true judgment.' " *(National Portrait Gallery, London)*

however, scholars might do well to ponder whether James's high regard for toleration was based on principle or was merely a weapon with which to establish an even greater intolerance. Did he speak for the welfare of all subjects or only for a militant and outdated minority who clung to notions unacceptable to the century of enlightenment into which England was moving? Whatever the final judgment, the record of his reign indicates that stodginess, stubbornness, and stupidity were the prevailing characteristics of a man whom Bishop Burnet analyzed as having "no true judgment." In the bishop's view, James lacked his brother's tact and humor; he held to "high notions of kingly authority, and laid it down for a maxim that all who opposed the king were rebels in their hearts." Even his secret dalliances achieved a stuffiness that had once led his brother to remark that one might think his mistresses were "given him by his priests for penance." He took himself, his office, and his duty to God with a seriousness that ultimately destroyed his dynasty. Lord Chesterfield's stiletto-sharp characterization must stand: "Though we have now a prince whose study is his country's glory, whose courage will give him luster without a throne, whose assiduity in business makes him his own chief minister, yet heaven, it seems, has found a way to make this all more terrible than lovely."

In February 1685, no whisper hinted at the thunder to come. Well-wishers of a moral bent noted that "the change upon the face of the English court is very remarkable; in the last King's time mirth, plays, buffoonery, etc., domineered, and were encouraged; now there is little to be seen but seriousness and business." Unfortunately, the new reign did not bring the anticipated "happiness to the nation," because James's Tory supporters made two assumptions that did not materialize: the king would keep his religion private, and the heir to the throne would be Protestant. James II had been born and bred an Anglican. His first wife was the Protestant Anne Hyde, daughter of the earl of Clarendon, and by her he had two daughters, Mary and Anne. Not until 1672 did he publicly declare himself a Catholic. The following year, he married the Italian and Catholic Maria of Modena, but at his succession he was fifty-three and childless by his second wife. The dynasty seemed secure in the Protestant line of Mary and her Stuart husband, the champion of European Protestantism, Prince William of Orange, the stadholder of Holland.

Parliament met in May. The king received for life the same revenues granted his brother, and members of the lower house held it to be in bad taste to embarrass James by asking him to enforce the penal legislation against Catholics. Although Lords and Commons were willing to ignore the Test Act, they adamantly opposed repealing it. In the name of obedience, Parliament was willing to accept a Catholic interlude, close its eyes to the deliberate violation of the law, and wait patiently for James's Protestant daughters to inherit the throne. Unfortunately, the king was not content with religious sufferance. He yearned for a Catholic triumph, the first step of which would be the repeal of the Test Act barring Catholics from civil and military office. Before James could urge Parliament to reconsider its attitude toward Catholics, the realm reeled at the news of a double invasion — the Presbyterian earl of Argyll's descent on Scotland, and the Anglican duke of Monmouth's landing at Lyme Regis on the border between Dorset and Devonshire.

Turning Back the Clock

Argyll's escapade promptly landed him on the executioner's block. Although the Monmouth invasion had no better conclusion, it did involve the last battle ever fought on English soil. The duke — the illegitimate son of Charles II — expected to rouse the countryside in the name of nationalism and Protestantism. Significantly, peasants and artisans flocked to his standard, but yeomen and gentlemen remained coldly aloof. They preferred a sovereign from the right side of the bed and were anxious to do nothing that might restore the hateful days of the Civil War and the Interregnum. Devoid of upper-class support and led by a frivolous fop, the invasion had little hope of success. Parliament granted James £400,000 to finance an army with which to defend his throne, and at Sedgemoor in July 1685, Monmouth's troops were routed. The duke's forces consisted of some 3,000 foot soldiers armed with barbarous but ineffective sickles and scythes, 500 horse troops mounted on plough horses, and 4 Dutch cannons. The royal army, well trained and professional, quickly slaughtered 1,384 of Monmouth's men and two days later ran the duke to ground in a bean field in Hampshire, where he was found cowering, filthy, and hungry. Within the week, he was executed, and James commenced a policy of grim retribution that shocked his Tory supporters out of their unquestioning loyalty to his Stuart person. In September Judge George Jeffreys's Bloody Assizes sat in brutal judgment on peasants, 400 of whom paid with their lives for their folly, and 1,200 of whom were deported to Barbados.

The wages of sin when directed against the Lord's anointed were death, but public opinion was aghast at the sight of common folk dancing their grisly jig three feet off the ground. James's revenge smacked not of deliberate political calculation but of religious hysteria. Many wondered whether the simple sons of Devon were in fact dying for their Protestant faith, not for their treason. Whether Jeffreys's judicial decisions were motivated by religious hatred is beside the point; his actions conjured up the memory of the Smithfield fires and the fate of Protestants under Bloody Mary.

Victorious over his Protestant nephew, James looked to further laurels in Parliament, and he demanded that the Test Act be repealed. Both Lords and Commons balked at such a notion. Even a Parliament packed with royal nominees had expressed shock at the fury of the Bloody Assizes. It grew still more alarmed by the presence of James's standing army, fresh from Sedgemoor and now encamped, thirteen thousand strong, just outside London. A standing army, illegally officered with Catholics loyal to the Stuart dynasty, struck many as the prelude to French-style despotism in England. Throughout Europe, all the signs pointed to a Catholic resurgence. Only a month before, Louis XIV of France had revoked the Edict of Nantes, which protected the political and religious rights of French Protestants. At the same time, James became more and more outspoken in his Catholicism and admiration of his French cousin. In an atmosphere of rising religious tension, Parliament was uncompromising in its determination not to repeal the penal laws against Catholics. For its impudent lack of cooperation, James prorogued Parliament on November 20, 1685, and set forth on a policy that led within two years to the ruin of his house and the loss of his throne.

Unable to catholicize the realm with Tory aid and parliamentary consent, James turned to the suspending powers of the crown to subvert the law and unite Catholics and Dissenters in support of the monarchy. In April 1687, he issued the first of his Declarations of Indulgence, giving freedom of worship to Catholics and Nonconformists, and permitting both denominations to hold public and military office. The king hoped that the two persecuted minorities would stand together against Tory and high-church bigotry and become the prop and stay of the Stuart monarchy. Suspending the law was not enough; the government also had to be catholicized, the Church of England purged and disciplined, and the Tories who controlled the boroughs and shires replaced with Dissenters and Catholics. Military commissions were given to papists, the lord lieutenant of Ireland and the lord admiral of the fleet were Catholics, the papal nuncio was accorded a public welcome in 1687, and the king's Jesuit confessor was admitted to the Privy Council, which became a Roman Catholic cabal. If the realm needed further evidence of his zeal, James appointed as his lord chancellor Judge Jeffreys, who not only possessed a bloody reputation but also had been regarded by Charles II as a man of "no learning, no sense, no manners and more impudence than ten carted streetwalkers."[2]

Having placed the legal system in the hands of a Catholic, James next sought to discipline the church. He resurrected the Court of High Commission for Ecclesiastical Affairs in defiance of parliamentary statute and used it to suspend bishops who allowed anti-Roman preaching in their dioceses. As bishoprics fell vacant, James filled his episcopal bench with high-church Anglicans favorable to Rome, in the hope that the Church of England might be brought back into the papal fold. The ecclesia did not take kindly to such pressure. It renounced its doctrine of nonresistance and showed surprising vigor in defending the Prayer Book, the Anglican communion, and independence from Rome. In retaliation, James struck at the root of the opposition, Oxford University, that seminary of Anglicanism. Christ Church, University, and Magdalen Colleges were placed under Catholic control, and the fellows of Magdalen were evicted for refusing to elect a popish president. When Dr. Hough, the president of Magdalen, was expelled from his office, he complained that the government had illegally deprived him of what was tantamount to private property. Whigs and Tories agreed with him. If Dr. Hough lost his presidency, then no inalienable right was safe, and resistance to royal tyranny was therefore a sacred duty.

Not content with tampering with private property and historic rights, James committed an even worse sin in the eyes of the leaders of society: He tried to wrest local government from the hands of the gentry. His brother had revoked borough charters so that the crown could control the nomination of solid Tory supporters of church and monarchy. Now James used the same means to bully the towns into electing Catholics and Nonconformists and men of no property. Royal commissioners were dispatched into the countryside to inquire whether the local

---

[2]The exposure of prostitutes to public ridicule by carting them about the streets of London.

squirearchy, if elected to Parliament, would favor the repeal of the Test Act and support the Declaration of Indulgence. The evasive and negative nature of the answers persuaded James to purge county administration of its substantial citizens. Whigs and Tories were dropped from the lists of justices of the peace and other shire officials, and Catholics and Dissenters were appointed in their stead. It was bad enough that some of the new appointees could neither read nor write; it was far worse that others had not "one foot of freehold land in England." In London "all the jolly, genteel citizens" were "turned out and all the sneaking fanatics put into their places." James's actions removed the most weighty deterrent to revolution: fear of social upheaval from below. It grew increasingly obvious to the ruling elements that, this time, rebellion might be necessary for the defense of property and order.

The climax came in 1688. In January James ordered home six English and Scottish regiments stationed in the Netherlands, a sure sign to many that the king was preparing to ally England with France against the Dutch. In May he issued a second Declaration of Indulgence and ordered that it be read from every pulpit within the realm. When Archbishop Sancroft and six other bishops refused, on the grounds that the king could not suspend the operation of religious law, he clapped them in the Tower and accused them of seditious libel. Then in June a son was born to James's Catholic wife. The king rejoiced, but Protestant England suddenly lost the single most powerful argument for obedience to the king: the expectation that the succession would pass to Mary and William of Orange. In England and in Holland, men reached the decision to risk revolution, and on June 30, 1688, Whig and Tory magnates sent an urgent appeal to William of Orange to save their land from Catholic domination. If any doubt remained about the overwhelming sentiments of the kingdom, it was dispelled when a London jury acquitted the seven bishops. The king, however, continued to take no notice of the approaching storm, and even Judge Jeffreys admitted that James was guided solely by the Virgin Mary.

The European Scene

In Europe events were synchronizing with those in England, with fatal results. Louis XIV broke the peace of Europe in September and sent his armies against the German empire. Throughout the summer, Prince William had hesitated to accept the invitation to claim the throne of England for fear that Louis might strike first at Holland. When the French finally settled down to a war of siege against Philippsburg, the stadholder decided to risk the invasion of England. He set sail on November 1, 1688, with a carefully organized fleet of 225 vessels and an army of 15,000 men, replete with 4 tons of tobacco, 1,600 hogsheads of beer, 10,000 pairs of boots, his personal coach and horses, a portable bridge, a mobile smithy, a printing press with which to flood England with Protestant propaganda, and a mold for striking new coinage once the invasion succeeded.

Once again an English monarch faced the consequences of having acted as landlord of England, not king; once again an invader arrived under the banner of liberation. What Henry IV had done in 1399, William of Orange, the future William III, did in 1689: He endeavored to transform treason into a crusade against tyranny by championing the liberties of Englishmen and defending property against a despotic government. James II, like Richard II, discovered that legitimacy offered no defense for a monarchy devoid of popular support, and like the last undisputed male Plantagenet, the last male Stuart monarch found himself forsaken and alone. William and his professional troops were not to be compared with the duke of Monmouth and his farm boys, and this time the English gentry came forward to welcome the invader. Even the men in the king's confidence quietly slipped away to join the Dutchman. The standing army, for which James had sacrificed parliamentary subsidies and upper-class popularity, faded away; moreover, the loyalty of the navy was never tested, for a "Protestant wind" kept it harborbound. James himself proved his mettle by attempting impulsive flight, a venture so fraught with ill luck that it took two weeks and the connivance of Prince William to achieve. The queen and her infant son slipped away to France on December 10. Early the next morning, James followed them, dropping the Great Seal of England into the Thames as he headed for the channel. Unfortunately, he was recognized and returned to London, where it had to be carefully arranged for the king once again to escape.

English supporters of William assumed that the stadholder came "only to maintain the Protestant religion; he will do England no harm." Actually, the Prince of Orange had little love for English domestic affairs. His single interest lay in the defense of Holland and the defeat of France. At worst, England had to be kept neutral; at best, it had to be transformed into a weapon with which to destroy Louis XIV. William's concerns centered on England's wealth and her naval and military potential, not Dr. Hough's presidency at Magdalen College. Cold and tight-lipped, William was a fanatic, a soldier who cared nothing for politics and who had little interest in his fellow men except as diplomatic and political instruments or as infantry for his armies. Short, asthmatic, and stooped, with bad teeth and a beaked nose, the prince gave himself and those around him unsparingly to his single obsession — the destruction of France.

The final irony of William's bloodless victory and England's Glorious Revolution is that neither could have occurred without the cooperation of Louis XIV and James II. The Most Christian King of France miscalculated badly; he sent no aid to his Stuart cousin until it was too late, and he failed to redirect his troops against Holland. Instead, he welcomed the Dutch invasion in the mistaken belief that Whigs and Tories would plunge England into civil war, drawing Holland into a hopeless military venture and leaving Europe to French conquest. What Louis failed to discern was that Whigs and Tories, for all their political differences, had one thing in common: They were property owners and therefore the ruling elite of the kingdom. As such, they were united in their opposition to James.

The Glorious Revolution

As for James, he guaranteed the bloodless nature of the revolution[3] by fleeing with his baby son to the security of Louis XIV's court. William of Orange, despite his invitation signed by six solid English peers and an Anglican bishop, was still a foreigner, and plenty of Englishmen remained loyal to the Stuart name. There were many Stuart well-wishers who could not understand "what could make our master desert his kingdom and his friends." Presumably, James lost his nerve, and in doing so he lost his kingdom. The king's flight not only assured a peaceful change of monarch but also solved the constitutional dilemma confronting William and his Whig and Tory supporters: how to legalize the violent overthrow of a legitimate sovereign. The same issue had faced Henry IV, and the same solution was now invoked. James's decision to flee (which received all the help that William could decently give) and his casting of the Great Seal into the Thames were accepted as acts of abdication. Had he remained, the Prince of Orange would have been worse off than Henry IV: he would have confronted the embarrassing presence of a live and legitimate king who possessed a son as heir to his throne.

James's "abdication" solved the crucial problem of how to remove a sovereign; it did not, however, answer the related question of how to replace him with someone else. Without a sovereign, nothing was legal, not even Parliament. Under the circumstances, men did the best they could. William was invited to issue writs for a Convention Parliament that met on January 22, 1689. At one end of the political spectrum stood certain Whig magnates who wanted the throne declared vacant on the grounds that James II had subverted the "constitution of the kingdom by breaking the original contract between king and people"; they demanded the appointment of a successor by act of Parliament. This position proved too much for the Tories, who still clung to the doctrine of hereditary monarchy and opposed any notion of a sovereign who possessed his authority by the grace of parliamentary election. Moreover, William had

---

[3]Scholarship on the Glorious Revolution is particularly rich. See D. W. R. Bahlman, *The Moral Revolution of 1688* (1957); G. M. Straka, *The Revolution of 1688 — Whig Triumph or Palace Revolution?* (1962); S. B. Baxter, *William III* (1966); L. Pinkham, *William III and the Respectable Revolution* (1954); M. Ashley, *The Glorious Revolution of 1688* (1968); G. M. Trevelyan, *The English Revolution, 1688–1689* (1938); S. Prall, *The Bloodless Revolution, England, 1688* (1972); J. R. Jones, *The Revolution of 1688 in England* (1972); and W. A. Speck, *Reluctant Revolutionaries: Englishmen and the Revolution of 1688* (1988). The best biography of William is S. B. Baxter, *William III* (1966); but see also H. Van der Zee and B. Van der Zee, *William and Mary* (1973); and L. Schwoerer, *The Declaration of Rights, 1689* (1981).

William and Mary Accept Their Crowns at Whitehall, 1689, engraving by E. M. Ward   William "dismissed as unacceptable the idea that the crown should pass to his wife as next in line of succession while he became 'his wife's gentleman usher.' He insisted on equal status." *(Mary Evans Picture Library)*

his own views on the subject. He dismissed as unacceptable the idea that the crown should pass to his wife as next in line of succession while he became "his wife's gentleman usher." He insisted on equal status with Mary on the basis of military conquest and his own blood claim as the grandson of Charles I. In the end, the Whig magnates and the Dutch prince both got their way. In February 1689, William and Mary were recognized as joint monarchs but were forced to accept parliamentary limitations on their sovereignty.

Although the fiction of royal inheritance and even the myth of the divine right of kings were preserved in 1689, in reality it was transparently clear that the sovereignty of Parliament had triumphed. Although William III didn't like it, he had to listen to "Honest Tom" Wharton, who tactlessly reminded him, "We have made you king." The crown in theory may have remained unrestrained, but the man and woman who wore it did so on the sufferance of men of property, and statutes were enacted restricting the use of royal authority. The Declaration of Rights, later translated into law as the Bill of Rights of 1689, established no doctrine of limited monarchy or parliamentary supremacy. It merely forbade the use of royal and prerogative rights as they had been exercised in the past by Charles and James. The power to dispense with law was not abolished; it was simply outlawed "as it hath been assumed and exercised of late." The royal claim to maintain a standing army was not denied; only armies raised without parliamentary consent were prohibited. What Parliament enacted was not a statement of rights, but a bill of limitations. To safeguard those limitations, it reverted to the time-honored method of asserting its authority through the purse. William and Mary were offered an annual income of only £600,000, an amount hopelessly insufficient by itself; the rest had to be appropriated yearly by Parliament for specific purposes. In the end, William extracted sums from Commons that no Stuart king had imagined possible; however, such moneys were granted annually, and they were offered only for the purpose of implementing policies agreeable to a majority in Parliament. As a further safeguard, a Mutiny Act was passed, limiting to a single year the crown's right to enforce martial law in the army. The statute thus made it impossible to maintain a military force for more than twelve months at a time without recourse to Parliament.

The final step of the revolution concluded with the Act of Toleration, passed in 1689 for reasons more of political necessity than of principle. William was a Calvinist, his wife an Anglican. He insisted that the Church of England abide by the promise of toleration that had been made to Nonconformists in order to lure them from Catholic James and his Declaration of Indulgence. The tide of religious bigotry had begun to recede, and even Catholics were left in peace, although they and the Unitarians were carefully excluded from the act. On all fronts, men had wearied of emotion. In religion as well as politics, Whigs and Tories were ready to accept the marquis of Halifax's policy of never rocking the political boat. In William and Mary, England found sovereigns uniquely fitted to the temper of the times. Mary was ignorant of history, politics, science, and mathematics. Her spelling was quaint, her grammar faulty. Her mind, her critics maintained, was "as sluggish as an inland river," and she always deferred to her husband's judgment. Still she remained a Stuart, a crucial link with the past. William confessed himself to be "a Trimmer and would continue so," if only because he had come to England in order to trim Louis XIV down to size and redress the European balance of power.

Two bloodless revolutions, almost three hundred years apart, are worth a moment's thought, for one served as the prelude to a hundred years of civil war and anarchy; the other, to the dawn of England's Augustan Age. The kings involved may have had much in common — Richard II and James II were incompetent; Henry IV and William III, unscrupulous — but the men who stood behind royalty, who in fact made the two rebellions, were worlds apart. It is true that both the late fourteenth-century feudal baron and the late seventeenth-century aristocrat attempted to control monarchy, yet while the one found his defense in private law and the absence of government, the other sought protection in the rule of law common to all English men and women. The glory of the Glorious Revolution resided not so much in its bloodlessness as in the security that it offered to all men of property, both Whig and Tory. The real victors of 1689 and the architects of eighteenth-century England were the great estate owners, the lesser gentry, the merchant-princes, and those three vocal apologists of oligarchical respectability — the lawyer, the parson, and the educator. The revolution was their doing. To understand it, it is necessary to turn away from acts of Parliament and the peculiarities of kings to the education of a country gentleman and the commonplaces of country life.

It has been said, with the usual conceit of historical generalizations, that all history is intellectual history, for actions in war, commerce, and government presume at least a modicum of activity on the part of the human brain. Presumably, then, a political upheaval that could sweep away the ordained and organic Tudor state and replace it with a social mechanism contrived by men of good breeding for "the preservation of their property" involved a profound revolution of the mind.[4] Whatever the truth about the causal relationships between thought and deed, this much is beyond dispute — earth and sky, man and God, were judged very differently in 1399 and 1689.

No better symbol of the revolution in mind and spirit exists than the contrast between the old and new St. Paul's Cathedrals. The old, dilapidated structure with its broken spire, vaulted ceilings, and towering Gothic windows — through which the light of God's grace entered — gave visual meaning and comfort to the humble Christians within. The new Classical-Renaissance St. Paul's, designed by Sir Christopher Wren, mathematician, astronomer, city planner, and architect, was intended as a harmonious and lucid momument dedicated to a "philosophic" world view.

Three centuries of history had wrought a revolution in mind and spirit. The ideals and preconceptions most dear to the medieval knight, priest, and craftsman had become as outmoded as feudal kings, guilds, and monasteries. By 1689 Squire Jones and Parson Brown looked out

---

[4]Something of the intellectual ferment of the century can be gleaned from H. Butterfield, *The Origins of Modern Science, 1300–1800* (1949); R. S. Westfall, *Science and Religion in Seventeenth Century England* (1958); C. Hill, *Some Intellectual Consequences of the English Revolution* (1980); M. Hunter, *Science and Society in Restoration England* (1981); C. J. Somerville, *The Secularization of Early Modern England: From Religious Culture to Religious Faith* (1992); D. Cressy, *Bonfires and Bells: National Memory and the Protestant Calendar in Elizabethan and Stuart England* (1990); B. J. T. Dobbs, *The Foundations of Newton's Alchemy, or "The Hunting of the Greene Lyon"* (1975) and *The Janus Faces of Genius: The Role of Alchemy in Newton's Thought* (1991); B. J. Shapiro, *Probability and Certainty in Seventeenth-Century England: A Study of the Relationships between Natural Science, Religion, History, Law and Literature* (1983) and *"Beyond Reasonable Doubt" and "Probable Cause": Historical Perspectives in the Anglo-American Law of Evidence* (1991).

Old and New St. Paul's Cathedral "The old, . . . gave visual meaning and comfort to the humble Christians within. The new Classical-Renaissance St. Paul's . . . was intended as a . . . monument dedicated to a 'philosophic' world view." *(The Mansell Collection)*

upon a new and wonderful kingdom, secure, prosperous, and self-confident. In their thankfulness, they everywhere beheld the hand of God. But the deity whom they worshiped had divested Himself of much of His medieval trappings. Although He continued to reveal His purpose through Scriptures, now three new sources of divine light completely upset the traditional picture of the universe: Nicholas Copernicus's *On the Revolution of the Heavenly Orb* (1543), Robert Boyle's *The Sceptical Chemist* (1661), and Isaac Newton's monumental *Philosophiae Naturalis Principia Mathematica* (1687). Only a generation before, Henry Peacham in *The Compleat Gentleman*[5] was still assuring his young readers that the structure of the heavens consisted of a series of crystal spheres, revolving in majestic serenity around a fixed and stationary earth located at the center of the universe. For Peacham's students, the millennium of faith had not yet ended; although doubt had crept in, man in his own estimation remained God's unique and special creation. The firmaments and all that they contained were presumed to have been established so that humanity could enact the drama of salvation and damnation. Aristotelian physics, which propounded one set of physical principles for man's constantly changing world of earth, water, fire, and air, and another for God's immutable domain of moon, planets, stars, and firmaments, remained supreme. The titans of the new astronomy, Copernicus and Galileo, were suspect, the expounders of a foolish and absurd heresy that, in the words of John Donne, called "all· in doubt." For most of Peacham's gentle readers, the old language of pre-Copernican physics and astronomy accorded with reality. The sun rose and set (the earth certainly did not spin on its axis giving the illusion of moving sun and stars). The pump sucked water up from the well (it was not pushed up by the pressure of the atmosphere). The arrow still fell to the ground of its own accord (it was not pulled down and deflected by the force of gravity). Most men of the early seventeenth century agreed with the royal scholar, James I, who dismissed Francis Bacon's brilliant efforts to invest scientific thought with the cardinal principles of exact observation and reasoned conclusion with the quip, "Like the peace of God, it passeth all understanding."

By 1689, however, Squire Jones and Parson Brown had discarded Aristotelian physics and dismissed the medieval heavens as mere folklore. Bacon's labors were being understood even by untutored dilettantes, and talk of Copernicus and Galileo had become commonplace at the diningroom table. The Royal Society, founded in 1660, had fostered a new generation of gentlemen scientists, who accepted with equanimity the idea of a limitless universe in which earth, sun, and stars hurtled in or-

---

[5]*The Compleat Gentleman* was originally published in 1622, but it remained standard reading down to the time of its last edition in 1661. For a modern reprint, see the Folger Shakespeare Library edition, edited by V. B. Heltzel (1962).

derly but soulless eternity, and who understood the scientific principle of the water pump, which was no longer said to operate on the Aristotelian dictum of nature abhorring a vacuum, but on Boyle's law $pv = C$. The men who made the Glorious Revolution regarded as preposterous the Shakespearean view of the atmosphere as an "excellent canopy" and a "majestical roof fretted with golden fire." Instead, they accepted it as a sea of air that lay heavy upon the earth and exerted an immense pressure on man and beast.

Seventeenth-century minds slowly began to embrace the idea of change in all areas of human endeavor and speculation. The interests of the Royal Society were as varied as its members were brilliant. Originally an "invisible college" meeting in London coffeehouses and taverns, the society included almost every Englishman of intellectual distinction during the second half of the seventeenth century. There were John Evelyn, botanist, coin collector, and political diarist; Samuel Pepys, bureaucrat, commentator, and naval expert; Sir William Petty, "political arithmetician" and father of modern demography; the architect Sir Christopher Wren; the poet John Dryden; Robert Hooke, universal scientist and near equal to Newton; Dr. Edmund Halley, astronomer; John Locke, political theorist; John Aubrey, first of the group biographers; and, of course, Sir Isaac Newton. The existence of such versatility, however, did not mean that conservative country gentlemen or wealthy city merchants had either the intelligence or the economic means to follow in the footsteps of that perfect seventeenth-century aristocratic scientist, the honorable Robert Boyle, promoter of the gospel, government inspector of the mines, director of the East India Company, theologian, inventor, and fourteenth child of one of the greediest English estate owners in Ireland, the earl of Cork. Even the most optimistic reader was discouraged by the titles of Boyle's books. (His famous "law" on the elasticity of gases was first outlined in *New Experiments Physico-Mechanical Touching the Spring of the Air and Its Effects, Made, for the Most Part, in a New Pneumatical Engine* [1660].) Nor did enthusiastic gentlemen have the training to comprehend the mathematical propositions of Sir Isaac Newton and René Descartes. Instead, their imaginations were excited by science fiction and polite popularizations of Newtonian and Cartesian science. They devoured Cyrano de Bergerac's *Voyage to the Moon* (1657) and Bishop Francis Godwin's *The Man in the Moon* (1638), in which they read about a spacecraft powered by forty swans. They learned their Descartes from Fontenelle's *The Plurality of Worlds* (translated in 1688) and came to rely on John Harris for their Newtonian theory. Fontenelle's countess, with her astronomical turn of mind, discoursed on the philosophy of a mechanical universe that was likened to a watch "which is very regular and depends only upon the just disposing of the several parts of the movement." Harris's *Astronomical Dialogues Between a Gentleman and a Lady* presented the Newtonian universe in the elegant language of the day:

O! pray! move on, Sir, said she, this is amazingly fine: I fancy myself travelling along with that little Earth in its course round the gilded Sun.

Although English property owners remained confident in the conviction that they, and to a lesser extent all mankind, were God's special gift to creation, they knew from the books they read that the deity Himself no longer had a secure place in the Newtonian World Machine. He had become little more than a first cause, a divine and marvelous clockmaker who started but thereafter did not tamper with His own universal and eternal laws of motion, inertia, and gravity. Throughout the seventeenth century, the hand of God had been pushed back by the mind of man, and authors branded in their own day as dangerous atheists became respectable philosophers. Sir Walter Raleigh partially removed God from the historical scene, leaving *The History of the World* (1614) as a record of human events and motives. Lord Herbert of Cherbury wrote of *Henry VIII* (1649) as a man, not as God's or the devil's instrument on earth. Francis Bacon offered the new scientific methodology as hope in the struggle to liberate men and women from the consequences of Adam's fall; power over nature, not God's grace, would henceforth lead to a utopia in this world, not the next. In politics, people discussed man-made societies and the inalienable rights of life, liberty, and property, not governments instituted by God or the divinity of kings.

Slowly, the secular, analytical, and categorical mind began to predominate: the habit of thought that conceives of statistical data and accuracy as a positive good, that classifies and breaks down scientific knowledge into its smallest component part, and that delimits and defines every phase of government and society. The seventeenth-century revolution that dissolved the unity of the Tudor state in part grew out of this tendency to view political reality in increasingly exact terms. The age of constitution writing was dawning, and citizens required that the relationship between the executive and the legislature be determined and recorded. Had king and Parliament, royal judges and common lawyers, antiquarians and historians, never sought to define and analyze such formless medieval political equations as "King in Parliament," "the sovereign is over man but under God and law," and "to the king belongs authority over all men, but to subjects belong property," there would have been no controversy over political theory and possibly no appeal to arms. At the same time, the organic Tudor state — a living, breathing, divinely inspired body politic in which each organ knew its social and spiritual purpose and worked together for a common good — receded before a more atomized view of society as a conglomeration of individuals to be counted, calculated, and sorted according to statistical tables and economic function.

By 1689 the statistical and analytical mind had triumphed. Gregory King, in his *Natural and Political Observations and Conclusions upon the State and Conditions of England* (1696), began to count heads and to present population statistics. Consequently, for the first time historians have a fairly reliable notion of demographic growth and breakdown: 5.5 million inhabited England, of whom 2.7 million ate meat daily and 1 million were on poor relief. Two million lived in Ireland, 1 million resided in Scotland, 250,000 dwelled in the colonies, and 500,000 populated London. King estimated that for the year 1688 the average family income of a peer reached £2,800, of a gentleman £450, of a tradesman £45, of a laboring man £15, and of a soldier £14. The average income in England stood at £7 18s per head, in contrast to Holland where it was £8 1s 4d, and to France where the average was only £6. Mr. Thomas Mun displayed the same regard for precision and concern for economic analysis when he concluded in his *England's Treasures by Forraign Trade,* written during the 1630s, that "to sell more to strangers yearly than we consume of theirs in value" held the secret of English prosperity. In country manor and townhouse, table conversation began to take on a modern ring — free trade, human rights, the purpose of government, the rebuilding of London, the control of colonies, and the ebb and flow of finance. No one spoke of usury any longer. Instead, people referred to a decent rate of interest and chatted about trade figures that were duly recorded for posterity: Foreign trade in 1662 was valued at £7.75 million, but by 1688 it had jumped to £11.5 million. In industry and finance, the same attitude of mind prevailed, and the Restoration merchant or country gentleman poured his money into a host of new schemes, each the result of careful analysis of the world — water companies, postal enterprises, paper and glass manufacturing, banking schemes, fire insurance, life insurance, and 236 new patents taken out between 1660 and 1700. Even the gentleman's parkland was subjected to the categorical mind. Tudor gardens, once untamed and almost parvenu in the indecency of their color schemes and designs such as Tudor roses and heraldic beasts, gave way to a more restrained and mathematical approach. Parks, lawns, and garden beds were laid out with geometrical precision — every curve of the flower bed was as perfectly elliptical as any planetary orbit, every shrub in schematic balance with its neighbor, every maze contrived with mathematical exactitude.

The seventeenth-century Englishman was becoming not so much an "economic animal" as a statistical being. Descartes, who declared the reality of human existence to be *cogito ergo sum,* "I think, therefore I am," recorded and distilled into its simplest form the ultimate intellectual conceit. Doubtless, many still hungered for an older and passing way of life that persisted in viewing existence as a spiritual phenomenon and required that governments should strive to achieve a society fit for Christians in need of salvation. But a certain amount of godlessness in the affairs of man and nature seemed a small price to pay for the material, constitutional, and intellectual strides of the century.

For the unwashed multitude, England in 1689 may have remained almost as nasty, brutish, and unhealthy as it had been three centuries earlier. For the oligarchs, the privileged few, however, the kingdom stood on the threshold of an age in which physical discomfort was masked with

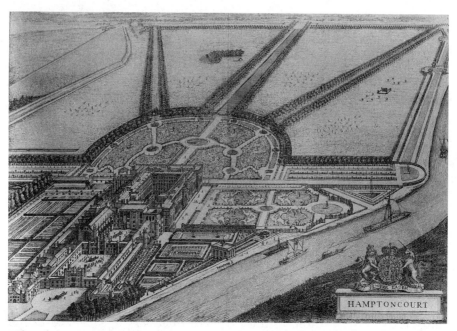

View of the Royal Palace at Hampton Court, Almost Doubled in Size by William and Mary   "Parks, lawns, and garden beds were laid out with geometrical precision — every curve of the flower bed was as perfectly elliptical as any planetary orbit, every shrub in schematic balance with its neighbor, every maze contrived with mathematical exactitude." *(The Mansell Collection)*

massive elegance, religious enthusiasm carefully restrained by the reasoned conclusions of deism, wealth properly dressed in good breeding, and politics predicated on the marquis of Halifax's dictum that "to know when to leave things alone is a high pitch of good sense." England had become a paradise for men of property. Juries, after 1670, could safely hand down verdicts that went against even the interests of the crown. The Habeas Corpus Act of 1679 protected the critics of government from arbitrary arrest. The press, although still answerable to sweeping libel laws, was virtually free to criticize men, policies, and institutions. In religion, it was found necessary to suppress the words of that dangerous iconoclast, Thomas Hobbes, for the oligarchs were not yet willing to accept his argument that salvation was open to all who held to the virtues, "Faith in Christ, and Obedience to Laws." They preferred the more lofty sentiments of Milton — "Give me the liberty to know, to utter, and to argue freely according to conscience, above all liberties." Even after the Toleration Act of 1689, religious nonconformity still suffered political disabilities, but if Catholics, Dissenters, and even Unitarians kept their thoughts to themselves, they were allowed a certain degree of liberty of conscience. Gentlemen of wealth and leisure, however, could and did converse on any subject they chose; they had the time and security, and they were beginning to have the education. The age of Lord Chesterfield, Doctor Samuel Johnson, and Horace Walpole could not lie far in the future, when the Restoration courtier and patron of letters, Charles Sackville, sixth earl of Dorset (1676–1705), could match wits with the dramatist John Dryden. Dorset once proposed at dinner that his guests jot down an "impromptu" and that Dryden should judge each on its literary merit. The playwright, having perused the contributions, proclaimed the earl the victor, and he read the winning entry:

> I promise to pay Mr. John Dryden five hundred pounds on demand.
> Signed, Dorset.

Not only was the world of letters their oyster, to be opened and savored, but so was all of England. Gentlemen could walk safely through the countryside, stick in hand, no longer obliged to go armed with a sword, for their lives were relatively safe and their properties absolutely secure. Two generations of civil war and revolution had transformed England into a kingdom where birth, breeding, and estate had become the pillars of society. The Glorious Revolution guaranteed that government, regardless of party control, would protect the sanctity of private property, reflect its views, and ensure its future.

In achieving such a blessed state of affairs, the leaders of society were fortunate in having a gentleman philosopher who united reason, religion, and good breeding into a philosophical justification for rebellion and who marshaled God and history in the defense of property. Thomas Hobbes had been too secular and shocking; the Levellers and Diggers, too dangerous; Milton, too spiritual; but John Locke, like the porridge in *Goldilocks and the Three Bears*, was found to be exactly right. He presumed the existence of men of birth and self-restraint who joined together to preserve and to defend their inalienable rights of life, liberty, and estate. He advanced the political doctrine that the purpose of government was to achieve a society fit for the dignity of men (preferably gentlemen). States instituted by men and women of good sense and property never deteriorated into tyranny because government was assumed to be a social convenience created to protect every kind of estate — property, wealth, title, and historic position. Society consisted of individuals who possessed rights bestowed by a benevolent deity; and government, be it crown or Parliament, was regarded as nothing more than the trustee of those rights. When the guardian abused the authority conferred on it (as James II had done), rebellion was not only justified, it became a sacred duty. John Locke in his *Two Treatises of Government* (written 1681 and published 1689) had made society respectable to accompany a respectable revolution. The revolution had found a philosophical "Trimmer" as well as a royal one. Together, John Locke and William III guided England into a century of economic prosperity, military triumph, and political self-satisfaction.

Security on such a massive and enduring scale produced confidence in royal government, in the future, in England, and in oligarchy. The

English, said the marquis of Halifax, have "grown saucy, and expecteth reasons, and good ones too, before they give up their own opinions to other men's dictates." And why shouldn't they expect good reasons? Locke assured them that "we are born free and we are born rational." With a Glorious Revolution behind them and 143 years of rule ahead of them, the oligarchs in 1689 stood ready to maintain a government that reflected their wishes, to invest in an economic future that inspired confidence, and to concede the truth of Milton's words about "God's Englishmen":

> Consider what nation it is whereof ye are, and whereof ye are the governors; a nation not slow and dull, but of a quick, ingenious, and piercing spirit; acute to invent, subtile and sinewy to discourse, not beneath the reach of any point the highest that human capacity can soar to.
>
> — *Areopagitica*

Appendix

The English Kings from Richard II to William and Mary

Richard II	1377–1399
Henry IV	1399–1413
Henry V	1413–1422
Henry VI	1422–1461
	(1470–1471)
Edward IV	1461–1483
Edward V	April 9, 1483–July 6, 1483
Richard III	1483–1485
Henry VII	1485–1509
Henry VIII	1509–1547
Edward VI	1547–1553
Mary I	1553–1558
Elizabeth I	1558–1603
James I	1603–1625
Charles I	1625–1649
Interregnum	1649–1660
Charles II	1660–1685
James II	1685–1688
William and Mary	1689–1694

Bibliography

Bibliographies

Keeler, M. F. *Bibliography of British History — Stuart Period.* 1970.
Levine, M. *Tudor England, 1485–1603.* 1968.
Morrill, J. *Seventeenth-Century Britain, 1603–1714.* 1980.
Read, C. *Bibliography of British History — Tudor Period,* 2nd ed. 1959.
Sachse, W. L. *Restoration England, 1660–1689.* 1971.

General Works

Fifteenth Century

Allmand, C. *The Hundred Years War: England and France at War, 1300–1450.* 1988.
Chrimes, S. B. *Lancastrians, Yorkists and Henry VII.* 1964.
Jacob, E. F. *The Fifteenth Century.* 1961.
Kendall, P. M. *The Yorkist Age.* 1962.
Lander, J. R. *Government and Community, England, 1450–1509.* 1981.

Sixteenth Century

Davies, C. S. L. *Peace, Print and Protestantism, 1450–1558.* 1976.
Elton, G. R. *England Under the Tudors.* 1955.
———. *Reform and Reformation: England, 1509–1558.* 1977.
Guy, J. *Tudor England.* 1990.
Hurstfield, J. *Elizabeth I and the Unity of England.* 1960.
Mackie, J. D. *The Earlier Tudors.* 1957.
Palliser, D. M. *The Age of Elizabeth: England Under the Later Tudors, 1547–1603,* 2nd ed. 1992.
Rowse, A. L. *The England of Elizabeth.* 1951.
Smith, L. B. *The Elizabethan World.* 1967, reprinted 1991.
Youngs, J. *Sixteenth-Century England.* 1984.

Seventeenth Century

Clark, G. N. *The Later Stuarts.* 1934.
———. *The Seventeenth Century.* 1961.

Coward, B. *The Stuart Age.* 1980.

Davies, G. *The Early Stuarts, 1603–1660.* 1959.

Firth, C. *The Last Years of the Protectorate.* 1909.

Gardiner, S. R. *History of England, 1603–1656,* 18 vols. 1894–1904.

Hill, C. *The Century of Revolution.* 1961.

Hirst, D. *Authority and Conflict: England, 1603–1658.* 1986.

Jones, J. R. *Country and Court: England, 1658–1714.* 1979.

Kenyon, J. P. *Stuart England.* 1978.

Laslett, P. *The World We Have Lost.* 1965.

Trevelyan, G. M. *England Under the Stuarts.* 1904.

Special Surveys

Alexander, M. V. C. *Growth of English Education, 1348–1648: A Social and Cultural History.* 1990.

Amussen, S. D. *An Ordered Society: Gender and Class in Early Modern England, 1560–1725.* 1988.

Anderson, M. *Approaches to the History of the Western Family 1500–1914.* 1980.

Cahn, S. *Industry of Devotion: The Transformation of Women's Work in England, 1500–1660.* 1987.

Cantor, L. *The Changing English Countryside, 1400–1700.* 1987.

Chambers, J. D. *Population, Economy, and Society in Pre-Industrial England.* 1972.

Chartres, J. A. *Internal Trade in England, 1500–1700.* 1977.

Clark, P., and P. Slack. *English Towns in Transition, 1500–1700.* 1976.

Clarkson, L. A. *The Pre-Industrial Economy of England, 1500–1750.* 1971.

Clay, C. G. A. *Economic Expansion and Social Change: England, 1500–1700,* 2 vols. 1984.

Cockburn, J. S. *A History of English Assizes, 1558–1715.* 1972.

Coleman, D. C. *The Economy of England, 1450–1750.* 1977.

Collins, S. L. *From Divine Cosmos to Sovereign State: An Intellectual History of Consciousness and the Idea of Order in Renaissance England.* 1989.

Cressy, D. *Literacy and the Social Order: Reading and Writing in Tudor and Stuart England.* 1980.

Cross, C. *Church and People, 1450–1660: The Triumph of the Laity in the English Church.* 1976.

Davis, R. *English Overseas Trade, 1500–1700.* 1973.

Fildes, V., ed. *Women as Mothers in Pre-Industrial England: Essays in Memory of Dorothy McLaren.* 1990.

Hatcher, J. *Plague, Population and the English Economy, 1348–1530.* 1977.

Henderson, K. U., and B. F. McManus. *Half Humankind: Contexts and Texts of the Controversy About Women in England, 1540–1640.* 1985.

Holdsworth, W. *The History of English Law,* vol. 4, 3rd ed. 1945.

Houlbrooke, R. A. *The English Family 1450–1700.* 1984.

Jones, N. *God and the Moneylenders: Usury and Law in Early Modern England.* 1989.

Kearney, H. F. *Science and Change, 1500–1700.* 1971.

Kerridge, E. *Trade and Banking in Early Modern England.* 1988.

King, M. L. *Women of the Renaissance.* 1991.

Kussmaul, A. *A General View of the Rural Economy of England, 1538–1840.* 1990.

Levine, D. and K. Wrightson. *The Making of an Industrial Society: Whickham 1560–1765.* 1990.

Loades, D. M. *The Tudor Court.* 1987.

MacFarlane, A. *The Origins of English Individualism.* 1978.

McIntosh, M. K. *A Community Transformed: The Manor and Liberty of Havering 1500–1620.* 1991.

Mercer, E. *English Art, 1553–1625.* 1962.

Mertes, K. *The English Noble Household, 1250–1600.* 1988.

Moran, J. A. H. *The Growth of English Schooling, 1340–1548.* 1985.

O'Day, R. *Education and Society in England, 1500–1700.* 1982.

Orme, N. *Education and Society in Medieval and Renaissance England.* 1989.

Pinchbeck, I., and M. Hewitt. *Children in English Society,* 2 vols. 1969.

Prest, W., ed. *The Professions in Early Modern England.* 1987.

Prothero, R. W. (Lord Ernle). *English Farming, Past and Present.* 1936.

Russell, C. *The Crisis of Parliament: English History 1509–1660.* 1971.

Rowley, T. *The High Middle Ages, 1200–1550.* 1986.

Schubert, H. R. *A History of the British Iron and Steel Industry to 1775.* 1957.

Sharpe, J. A. *Crime in Early Modern England 1550–1750.* 1984.

———. *Early Modern England: A Social History, 1550–1760.* 1987.

Slack, P. *Crisis and Order in English Towns, 1500–1700.* 1972.

———. *The Impact of the Plague in Tudor and Stuart England.* 1985.

———. *Poverty and Policy in Tudor and Stuart England.* 1988.

Slavin, A. J. *The Tudor Age and Beyond: England from the Black Death to the End of the Age of Elizabeth.* 1987.

Starkey, D., ed. *The English Court: From the Wars of the Roses to the Civil War.* 1987.

Stone, L. *Family, Sex and Marriage in England, 1500–1800.* 1977.

———. *Uncertain Unions: Marriage in England 1660–1753.* 1992.

Thirsk, J., ed. *The Agrarian History of England and Wales,* vol. 4. 1967.

Thomas, K. *Man and the Natural World: Changing Attitudes in England, 1500–1800.* 1982.

Waterhouse, E. *Painting in Britain, 1530–1790.* 1953.

Wrightson, K., and D. Levine. *Poverty and Piety in an English Village: Terling, 1525–1700.* 1979.

Wrigley, E. A., and R. Schofield. *The Population History of England 1541–1871: A Reconsideration.* 1981.

Zagorin, P. *Rebels and Rulers, 1500–1660.* 1982.

———. *Ways of Lying: Dissimulation, Persecution, and Conformity in Early Modern Europe.* 1990.

Legal, Constitutional, and Governmental History

Fifteenth Century

Bean, J. M. W. *The Decline of English Feudalism, 1215–1540.* 1968.

———. *From Lord to Patron: Lordship in Late Medieval England.* 1989.

Bellamy, J. G. *Bastard Feudalism and the Law.* 1989.

———. *Crime and Public Order in England to the Later Middle Ages.* 1973.

———. *Criminal Law and Society in Late Medieval and Tudor England.* 1984.

Brown, A. L. *The Governance of Late Medieval England 1272–1461.* 1989.

Carpenter, C. *Locality and Polity: A Study of Warwickshire Landed Society, 1401–1499.* 1992.

Chrimes, S. B. *English Constitutional Ideas in the Fifteenth Century.* 1936.

Cook, D. R. *Lancastrians and Yorkists: The Wars of the Roses.* 1984.

Curry, A. *The Hundred Years War.* 1993.

Dobson, B., ed. *The Church, Politics and Patronage in the Fifteenth Century.* 1984.

Given-Wilson, C., ed. & trans. *Chronicles of the Revolution, 1397–1400: The Reign of Richard II.* n.d.

Goodman, A. *The New Monarchy: England, 1471–1534.* 1988.

———. *The Wars of the Roses: Military Activity and English Society, 1452–1497.* 1981.

Griffiths, R. A., and J. Sherborne, eds. *Kings and Nobles in the Later Middle Ages.* 1986.

Griffiths, R. A., and R. S. Thomas. *The Making of the Tudor Dynasty.* 1985.

Hammond, P. W., and A. F. Sutton. *Richard III: The Road to Bosworth Field.* 1985.

Harriss, G. L., ed. *Henry V: The Practice of Kingship.* 1985.

Horrox, R. *Richard III: A Study of Service.* 1989.

Lander, J. R. *Conflict and Stability in Fifteenth-Century England.* 1969.

———. *Crown and Nobility, 1450–1509.* 1976.

———. *English Justices of the Peace, 1461–1509.* 1990.

———. *The Limitations of English Monarchy in the Later Middle Ages.* 1989.

———. *The Wars of the Roses.* 1965.

Lyle, H. M. *The Rebellion of Jack Cade, 1450.* 1950.

Maddern, P. C. *Violence and Social Order: East Anglia, 1412–1442.* 1992.

McFarlane, K. B. *England in the Fifteenth Century: Collected Essays.* 1981.

———. *Lancastrian Kings and Lollard Knights.* 1972.

———. *The Nobility of Later Medieval England.* 1973.

McNivens, P. *Heresy and Politics in the Reign of Henry IV: The Burning of John Badby.* 1987.

Myers, A. R. *The Household of Edward IV.* 1959.

Pollard, A. J. *The Wars of the Roses.* 1988.

Powell, E. *Kingship, Law and Society: Criminal Justice in the Reign of Henry V.* 1989.

Ross, C. *The Wars of the Roses: A Concise History.* 1976.

St. Aubyn, G. *The Year of Three Kings: 1483.* 1983.

Tuck, A. *Crown and Nobility, 1271–1461: Political Conflict in Late Medieval England.* 1986.

————. *Richard II and the English Nobility.* 1973.

Wilkinson, B. *Constitutional History of England in the Fifteenth Century, 1399–1485.* 1964.

Wolfe, B. P. *Yorkist and Early Tudor Government, 1461–1509.* 1966.

Wood, C. T. *Joan of Arc and Richard III: Sex, Saints, and Government in the Middle Ages.* 1988.

Sixteenth Century

Baumer, F. L. Van. *The Early Tudor Theory of Kingship.* 1940.

Bellamy, J. *The Tudor Law of Treason: An Introduction.* 1979.

Bernard, G. W. *The Power of the Early Tudor Nobility: A Study of the Fourth and Fifth Earls of Shrewsbury.* 1985.

————., ed. *The Tudor Nobility.* 1992.

Brooks, F. W. *The Council of the North.* 1953.

Bush, M. L. *The Governmental Policy of Protector Somerset.* 1975.

Challis, C. F. *The Tudor Coinage.* 1978.

Coleman, C., and D. Starkey, eds. *Revolution Reassessed: Revisions in the History of Tudor Government and Administration.* 1986.

Cross, C., D. Loades, and J. J. Scarisbrick, eds. *Law and Government under the Tudors: Essays Presented to Sir Geoffrey Elton.* 1988.

Davies, C. S. L. "The Pilgrimage of Grace Reconsidered." *Past and Present* 41 (1968).

Dean, D. M., and N. L. Jones, eds. *The Parliaments of Elizabethan England.* 1990.

Elton, G. R. *Henry VIII: An Essay in Revision.* 1962.

————. "King or Minister?: The Man Behind the Reformation." *History* 39 (1954).

————. *The Parliaments of England, 1559–1581.* 1986.

————. *Policy and Police: The Enforcement of the Reformation in the Age of Thomas Cromwell.* 1972.

————. *Reform and Renewal: Thomas Cromwell and the Common Weal.* 1973.

————. *The Tudor Revolution in Government.* 1953. See also Harriss, G. L., and P. Williams, "A Revolution in Tudor History: Dr. Elton's Interpretation of the Age." *Past and Present* 25 (1963).

Fernandez-Armesto, F. *The Spanish Armada: The Experience of War in 1588.* 1988.

Figgis, J. N. *The Divine Right of Kings.* 1914.

Fox, A. *Politics and Literature in the Reigns of Henry VII and Henry VIII.* 1989.

Fox, A., and J. Guy. *Reassessing the Henrician Age: Humanism, Politics and Reform, 1502–1550.* 1986.

Gleason, H. *The Justices of the Peace in England, 1558–1640.* 1969.

Graves, M. A. R. *The Tudor Parliaments: Crown, Lords and Commons, 1485–1603.* 1985.

Gunn, S. J. and P. G. Lindley, eds. *Cardinal Wolsey: Church, State and Art.* 1991.

Harbison, E. H. *Rival Ambassadors at the Court of Queen Mary.* 1940.

Hartley, T. E. *Elizabeth's Parliaments: Queen, Lords and Commons 1559–1601.* 1992.

Hoak, D. E. *The King's Council in the Reign of Edward VI.* 1976.

———., ed. *Tudor Rule and Revolution.* 1983.

Hoyle, R. W., ed. *The Estates of the English Crown 1558–1640.* 1992.

Hurstfield, J. *Freedom, Corruption and Government in Elizabethan England.* 1973.

James, M. E. "Obedience and Dissent in Henrician England: The Lincolnshire Rebellion, 1536." *Past and Present* 48 (1970).

———. *Society, Politics and Culture: Studies in Early Modern England.* 1986.

Janson, S. L. *Political Protest and Prophecy under Henry VIII.* 1991.

Jones, W. R. D. *The Tudor Commonwealth, 1529–1559.* 1970.

Lehmberg, S. E. *The Reformation Parliament.* 1969.

Levine, M. *Tudor Dynastic Problems, 1460–1571.* 1973.

Loach, J. *The Later Parliaments of Henry VIII.* 1977.

———. *Parliament and the Crown in the Reign of Mary Tudor.* 1986.

———. *Parliament Under the Tudors.* 1991.

Loach, J., and R. Tittler, eds. *The Mid-Tudor Polity, c. 1540–1560.* 1980.

Loades, D. M. *The Mid-Tudor Crisis, 1545–1565.* 1992.

———. *Two Tudor Conspiracies.* 1965.

MacCaffrey, W. T. *Elizabeth I: War and Politics 1588–1603.* 1992.

———. *Exeter, 1540–1640. The Growth of an English Country Town.* 1958.

———. *Queen Elizabeth and the Making of Policy, 1572–1588.* 1981.

———. *The Shaping of the Elizabethan Regime.* 1968.

Martin, C., and G. Parker. *The Spanish Armada.* 1988.

Mayer, T. F. *Thomas Starkey and the Commonweal: Humanist Politics and Religion in the Reign of Henry VIII.* 1989.

Morris, C. *Political Thought in England, Tyndale to Hooker.* 1953.

Neale, J. E. *Elizabeth I and Her Parliaments,* 2 vols. 1957.

———. *The Elizabethan House of Commons.* 1949.

Notestein, W. *The Winning of the Initiative by the House of Commons.* 1924.

Parmiter, G. de C. *The King's Great Matter.* 1967.

Plowden, A. *Elizabeth Tudor and Mary Stewart: Two Queens in One Isle.* 1984.

Pulman, M. B. *The Elizabethan Privy Council in the 1570s.* 1971.

Richardson, W. C. *The History of the Court of Augmentations, 1536–1554.* 1961.

———. *Tudor Chamber Government.* 1952.

Samaha, J. B. *Law and Order in Historical Perspective: The Case of Elizabethan Essex.* 1974.

Smith, A. G. R. *The Government of Elizabethan England.* 1967.

Smith, L. B. *Treason in Tudor England: Politics and Paranoia.* 1986.

Starkey, D. *The Reign of Henry VIII: Personalities and Politics.* 1986.

Tittler, R. *The Reign of Mary I.* 1983.

Whitney-Jones, R. D. *The Tudor Commonwealth Men.* 1969.

Seventeenth Century

Ashley, M. *The Glorious Revolution of 1688.* 1968.

Ashton, R. *The City and the Court.* 1979.

——. *The English Civil War, Conservatism and Revolution, 1603–1649.* 1978.

Aylmer, G. E., ed. *The Interregnum: The Quest for Settlement, 1648–1660.* 1972.

——. *The King's Servants.* 1961.

——. *Rebellion or Revolution? England, 1640–1660.* 1986.

——. *The State's Servants.* 1973.

Bahlman, D. W. R. *The Moral Revolution of 1688.* 1957.

Barnes, T. G. *Somerset, 1625–1640.* 1957.

Baskerville, S. *Not Peace but a Sword: Political Ideology of the English Revolution.* 1993.

Beloff, M. *Public Order and Popular Disturbances, 1660–1700.* 1963.

Bosher, R. S. *The Making of the Restoration Settlement, 1649–1662.* 1951.

Brailsford, H. N. *The Levellers and the English Revolution.* 1961.

Brunton, D., and D. H. Pennington. *Members of the Long Parliament.* 1954.

Cogswell, T. *The Blessed Revolution: English Politics and the Coming of War, 1621–1624.* 1989.

Cope, E. S. *Politics Without Parliaments, 1629–1640.* 1987.

Cust, R. *The Forced Loan and English Politics, 1626–1628.* 1987.

Davies, G. *The Restoration of Charles II.* 1955.

Davis, J. C. *Fear, Myth and History: The Rantors and Their History, 1649–1984.* 1986.

Dow, F. D. *Radicalism in the English Revolution, 1640–1660.* 1985.

Everitt, A. M. *The Local Community and the Great Rebellion.* 1969.

Feiling, K. *A History of the Tory Party.* 1924.

Fletcher, A. *A County Community in Peace and War.* 1975.

——. *The Outbreak of the English Civil War.* 1981.

——. *Reform in the Provinces: The Government of Stuart England.* 1986.

Foster, E. R. *The House of Lords.* 1983.

Friedman, J. *Blasphemy, Immorality and Anarchy: The Ranters and the English Revolution.* 1987.

Gough, J. *John Locke's Political Philosophy.* 1950.

Haley, K. H. *Politics in the Reign of Charles II.* 1985.

Harris, T. *Politics under the Later Stuarts: Party Conflict in a Divided Society 1660–1715.* 1993.

Herrup, C. B. *The Common Peace: Participation and the Criminal Law in Seventeenth-Century England.* 1987.

Hexter, J. H. *The Reign of King Pym.* 1941.

Hibbard, C. *Charles I and the Popish Plot.* 1983.

Hirst, D. *The Representative of the People? Voters and Voting in England Under the Early Stuarts.* 1975.

Howell, R. *Newcastle-upon-Tyne and the Puritan Revolution.* 1967.

——. *The Origins of the English Revolution.* 1975.

Hutton, R. *The Restoration.* 1985.

Jones, G. H. *Convergent Forces: Immediate Causes of the Revolution of 1688 in England.* 1990.

Jones, J. R. *The First Whigs: The Politics of the Exclusion Crisis, 1673–1683.* 1961.

——. *The Revolution of 1688.* 1972.

Kearney, H. F. *The Eleven Year Tyranny of Charles I.* 1962.

Keeler, M. F. *The Long Parliament, 1640–1641.* 1962.

Kenyon, J. P. *The Civil Wars of England.* 1988.

———. *The Popish Plot.* 1972.

———. *The Stuart Constitution, 1603–1688.* 1966.

Kishlansky, M. A. *Parliamentary Selection: Social and Political Choice in Early Modern England.* 1986.

Lee, M. *The Cabal.* 1965.

MacCormack, J. *Revolutionary Politics in the Long Parliament.* 1974.

Manning, B. *The English People and the English Revolution, 1640–1649.* 1976.

Mayfield, N. H. *Puritans and Regicide: Presbyterian-Independent Differences over the Trial and Execution of Charles (I) Stuart.* 1988.

Miller, J. *Popery and Politics in England, 1660–1688.* 1973.

Morrill, J. S., ed. *Oliver Cromwell and the English Revolution.* 1990.

———. *Reactions to the English Civil War, 1642–1649.* 1982.

———. *The Revolt of the Provinces: Conservatives and Radicals in the English Civil War 1630–1650.* 1976.

Mosse, G. L. *The Struggle for Sovereignty in England from the Reign of Elizabeth to the Petition of Right.* 1950.

Ohlmeyer, J. *Civil War and Restoration in the Three Stuart Kingdoms: The Career of Randall MacDonnell, Marquis of Antrim, 1609–1683.* 1993.

Peck, L. *Court Patronage and Corruption in Early Stuart England.* 1990.

Pinkham, L. *William III and the Respectable Revolution.* 1954.

Plumb, J. H. *The Growth of Political Stability in England, 1675–1725.* 1967.

Prall, S. *The Bloodless Revolution, England, 1688.* 1972.

Prestwick, M. *Cranfield: Politics and Profits Under the Early Stuarts.* 1976.

Reeve, L. J. *Charles I and the Road to Personal Rule.* 1989.

Richardson, R. C. *The Debate on the English Civil War Revisited.* 1989.

Roberts, C. *The Growth of Responsible Government in England.* 1966.

Roots, I. *The Great Rebellion, 1642–1660.* 1966.

Ruigh, R. E. *The Parliament of 1624.* 1971.

Russell, C. *The Fall of the British Monarchies 1637–1642.* 1991.

———., ed. *The Origins of the English Civil War.* 1973.

———. *Parliaments and English Politics, 1621–1629.* 1979.

Schoerer, L. *The Declaration of Rights, 1689.* 1981.

Seaward, P. *The Cavalier Parliament and the Reconstruction of the Old Regime, 1661–1667.* 1989.

Sharpe, K., ed. *Faction and Parliament: Essays on Early Stuart History.* 1978.

———. *The Personal Rule of Charles I.* 1992.

Solt, L. F. *Saints in Arms.* 1959.

Speck, W. A. *Reluctant Revolutionaries: Englishmen and the Revolution of 1688.* 1988.

Straka, G. M. *The Revolution of 1688 — Whig Triumph or Palace Revolution?* 1962.

Tawney, R. H. *Business and Politics Under James I: Lionel Cranfield as Merchant and Minister.* 1958.

Tomlinson, H., ed. *Before the English Civil War.* 1983.

Trevelyan, G. M. *The English Revolution, 1688–1689.* 1938.

Underdown, D. *Pride's Purge: Politics in the Puritan Revolution.* 1971.

———. *Somerset in the Civil War and Interregnum.* 1973.

Walzer, M. *The Revolution of the Saints.* 1965.

Wedgwood, C. V. *The King's Peace.* 1955.

———. *The King's War.* 1958.

———. *The Trial of Charles I.* 1964.

Western, J. R. *Monarchy and Revolution: The English State in the 1680's.* 1972.

Weston, C. C. *Subjects and Sovereigns: The Grand Controversy over Legal Sovereignty in Stuart England.* 1981.

Witcombe, D. T. *Charles II and the Cavalier House of Commons, 1667–1674.* 1966.

Woolrych, A. *Commonwealth and Protectorate.* 1982.

———. *Soldiers and Statesmen: The General Council of the Army and Its Debates, 1647–1648.* 1987.

Worden, B. *The Rump Parliament, 1648–1653.* 1974.

Zagorin, P. A. *The Court and the Country: The Beginning of the English Revolution.* 1969.

———. *History of Political Thought in the English Revolution.* 1954.

Zaller, R. *The Parliament of 1621.* 1971.

Economic and Social History

Fifteenth Century

Bean, J. M. W. *The Estates of the Percy Family, 1416–1537.* 1958.

Bennett, H. S. *The Pastons and Their England.* 1922.

Beresford, M. W. *The Lost Villages of England.* 1954.

Bridbury, A. R. *Economic Growth: England in the Later Middle Ages.* 1962.

Davis, N., ed. *Paston Letters.* 1971.

Dunham, W. H. *Lord Hasting's Indentured Retainers, 1461–1483.* 1955.

Dyer, C. *Standards of Living in the Later Middle Ages.* 1989.

Goldberg, P. J. P. *Women, Work, and Life Cycle in a Medieval Economy: Women in York and Yorkshire c. 1300–1520.* 1992.

Gottfried, R. S. *Epidemic Disease in Fifteenth-Century England: The Medical Response and the Demographic Consequences.* 1978.

Holmes, G. A. *The Estates of the Higher Nobility in Fourteenth-Century England.* 1957.

Hybel, N. *Crisis and Change: The Concept in the Light of Agrarian Structural Reorganization in Late Medieval England.* 1989.

Kingsford, C. L., ed. *Stoner Letters,* 2 vols. 1919.

Mertes, K. *The English Noble Household, 1250–1600.* 1988.

Poos, L. R. *A Rural Society after the Black Death: Essex 1350–1525.* 1991.

Power, E., and M. Postan. *Studies in English Trade in the Fifteenth Century.* 1933.

Russell, J. C. *British Medieval Population.* 1948.

Thrupp, S. *The Merchant Class of Medieval London, 1300–1500.* 1948.

Sixteenth Century

Ames, R. *Citizen Thomas More and His Utopia.* 1949.

Appleby, A. *Famine in Tudor and Stuart England.* 1978.

Archer, I. W. *The Pursuit of Stability: Social Relations in Elizabethan London.* 1991.

Aydelotte, F. *Elizabethan Rogues and Vagabonds.* 1967.

Beer, B. L. *Rebellion and Riot: Popular Disorder in England During the Reign of Edward VI.* 1982.

Beier, A. L. *Masterless Men: The Vagrancy Problem in England, 1560–1640.* 1985.

———. *The Problem of the Poor in Tudor and Stuart England.* 1983.

Bowden, P. J. *The Wool Trade in Tudor and Stuart England.* 1962.

Campbell, M. *The English Yeomen Under Elizabeth and the Early Stuarts.* 1942.

Caspari, F. *Humanism and the Social Order in Tudor England.* 1954.

Charlton, K. *Education in Renaissance England.* 1965.

Coleman, D. C. *Industry in Tudor and Stuart England.* 1975.

Copeman, W. S. C. *Doctors and Disease in Tudor Times.* 1960.

Davies, R. *English Overseas Trade, 1500–1700.* 1973.

Dietz, F. C. *English Government Finance,* rev. ed. 1964.

Esler, A. *The Aspiring Mind of the Elizabethan Younger Generation.* 1966.

Ferguson, A. B. *The Articulate Citizen and the English Renaissance.* 1965.

———. *The Indian Summer of English Chivalry.* 1960.

Fraser, A. *The Weaker Vessel: Women in 17th-century England.* 1984.

Gough, R. *The History of Myddle.* First published 1834. Ed. D. G. Hey. 1981.

Greaves, R. L. *Society and Religion in Elizabethan England.* 1981.

Hexter, J. H. *Reappraisals in History.* 1961.

Hurstfield, J. *The Queen's Wards.* 1958.

Jordan, W. K. *Philanthropy in England, 1480–1660.* 1959.

Kerridge, K. *Agrarian Problems in the Sixteenth Century.* 1969.

Miller, H. *Henry VIII and the English Nobility.* 1986.

Outhwaite, R. B. *Inflation in Tudor and Early Stuart England.* 1969.

Ramsay, G. D. *English Overseas Trade During the Centuries of Emergence.* 1957.

Rappaport, S. *Worlds Within Worlds: Structures of Life in Sixteenth-Century London.* 1989.

Rowse, A. L. *Sex and Society in Shakespeare's Age: Simon Forman.* 1974.

———. *Tudor Cornwall.* 1941.

Simpson, A. *The Wealth of the Gentry, 1540–1660.* 1961.

Smith, R. B. *Land and Politics in the England of Henry VIII.* 1970.

Stone, L. *The Crisis of the Aristocracy, 1558–1640.* 1965.

———. *Social Change and Revolution in England, 1540–1640.* 1965.

Tawney, R. H. *The Agrarian Problem in the Sixteenth Century.* 1912.

———. *Religion and the Rise of Capitalism.* 1926.

Thirsk, J. *Economic Policy and Projects: The Development of a Consumer Society in Early Modern England.* 1978.

———. *Tudor Enclosures.* Historical Association Pamphlet No. G. 41. 1958.

Wilson, F. P. *The Plague in Shakespeare's London.* 1927.

Wright, L. B. *Middle Class Culture in Elizabethan England.* 1935.

Youings, J. A. *The Dissolution of the Monasteries.* 1971.

Zeeveld, W. G. *Foundations of Tudor Policy.* 1948.

Seventeenth Century

Ashley, M. *The Stuarts in Love.* 1963.

Aylmer, G. E., ed. *The Levellers and the English Revolution.* 1975.

Baxter, S. B. *The Development of the Treasury, 1660–1702.* 1975.

Chandaman, C. D. *The English Public Revenue, 1660–1688.* 1975.

Cliffe, J. T. *The Puritan Gentry: The Great Puritan Families of Early Stuart England.* 1984.

Durston, C. *The Family in the English Revolution.* 1989.

Everitt, A. *Change in the Provinces: The Seventeenth Century.* 1969.

Greaves, R. L. *Deliver Us from Evil: The Radical Underground in Britain 1660–1663.* 1986.

Hughes, A. *The Causes of the English Civil War.* 1991.

MacFarlane, A. *The Family Life of Ralph Josselin.* 1970.

Manning, R. *Village Revolts: Social Protest and Popular Disturbances in England, 1509–1640.* 1988.

Morgan, J. *Godly Learning: Puritan Attitudes Towards Reason, Learning and Education, 1560–1640.* 1986.

Pepys, S. *The Diary,* 7 vols. R. Latham and W. Mathews, eds. 1970–1972.

Rabb, T. K. *Enterprise and Empire: Merchant and Gentry Investment in the Expansion of England, 1575–1630.* 1967.

Rowse, A. L. *Court and Country: Studies in Tudor Social History.* 1987.

Russell, C. *The Causes of the English Civil War.* 1990.

Stone, L. *The Causes of the English Revolution, 1529–1642.* 1972.

Supple, B. E. *Commercial Crisis and Change in England, 1600–1642.* 1959.

Trevor-Roper, H. R. "The Gentry, 1540–1640." *Economic History Review.* Supplement I (1953).

———. "Religion, the Reformation and Social Change" and "The General Crisis." In *Religion, the Reformation and Social Change.* 1967.

———. "Social Causes of the Great Rebellion." In *Historical Essays.* 1957.

Underdown, D. *Fire from Heaven: Life in an English Town in the Seventeenth Century.* 1992.

———. *Revel, Riot and Rebellion: Popular Politics and Culture in England, 1603–1660.* 1985.

Weber, M. *The Protestant Ethic and the Spirit of Capitalism.* 1930.

Wilson, C. *Mercantilism.* 1958.

Wrightson, K. *English Society, 1580–1680.* 1982.

Religious History

Alexander, H. G. *Religion in England, 1558–1662.* 1968.

Ashton, R. *Reformation and Revolution, 1558–1660.* 1984.

Bakerville, G. *English Monks and the Suppression of the Monasteries.* 1937.

Blench, J. W. *Preaching in England in the Late Fifteenth and Sixteenth Centuries: A Study of English Sermons, 1450–1600.* 1964.

Block, J. S. *Factional Politics and the English Reformation 1520–1540.* 1993.

Bossey, J. *English Catholic Community, 1570–1850.* 1975.

Brigden, S. *London and the Reformation.* 1989.

Champion, J. A. I. *The Pillars of Priestcraft Shaken: The Church of England and Its Enemies 1660–1730.* 1992.

Christianson, P. *Reformers and Babylon.* 1978.

Clebsch, W. A. *England's Earliest Protestants, 1520–1535.* 1964.

Collinson, P. *The Birth Pangs of Protestant England: Religious and Cultural Change in the Sixteenth and Seventeenth Centuries.* 1988.

———. *The Elizabethan Puritan Movement.* 1967.

———. *Godly People: Essays on English Protestantism and Puritanism.* 1983.

———. *The Religion of Protestants: The Church in English Society, 1559–1625.* 1982.

Cragg, G. R. *Puritanism in the Period of the Great Persecution, 1660–1688.* 1957.

Cross, C. *The Royal Supremacy in the Elizabethan Church.* 1969.

Davis, J. F. *Heresy and Reformation in the South-East of England, 1520–1559.* 1983.

Delbanco, A. *The Puritan Ordeal.* 1989.

Dickens, A. G. *The English Reformation,* 2nd ed. 1991.

———. *Lollards and Protestants in the Diocese of York, 1509–1558.* 1959.

Doran, S., and C. Durstan. *Princes, Pastors and People: The Church and Religion in England 1529–1689.* 1991.

Duffy, E. *The Stripping of the Altars: Traditional Religion in England, c. 1400–1580.* 1992.

Fincham, K. *Prelate as Pastor: The Episcopate of James I.* 1990.

Finlayson, M. G. *Historians, Puritanism and the English Revolution: The Religious Factor in English Politics Before and After the Interregnum.* 1983.

Foxe, J. *Acts and Monuments of the English Martyrs,* 8 vols. S. R. Cattley and G. Townsend, eds. 1837–1841.

George, C. H., and K. George. *The Protestant Mind of the English Reformation, 1570–1640.* 1961.

Haigh, C. *English Reformations: Religion, Politics, and Society under the Tudors.* 1993.

———., ed. *The English Reformation Revised.* 1987.

Haines, R. M. *Ecclesia Anglicana: Studies in the English Church of the Later Middle Ages.* 1989.

Haller, W. *Foxe's Book of Martyrs and the Elect Nation.* 1963.

———. *Liberty and Reformation in the Puritan Revolution.* 1955.

———. *The Rise of Puritanism, 1570–1643.* 1938.

Havran, M. J. *Catholics in Caroline England.* 1962.

Heal, H., and R. O'Day, eds. *Church and Society in England: Henry VIII to James I.* 1977.

Heath, P. *The English Parish Clergy on the Eve of the Reformation.* 1969.

Hill, C. *Antichrist in Seventeenth-Century England.* 1971.

———. *The Economic Problems of the Church, from Whitgift to the Long Parliament*. 1956.

———. *Intellectual Origins of the English Revolution*. 1965.

———. *Puritanism and Revolution*. 1958.

———. *Society and Puritanism in Pre-Revolutionary England*. 1964.

———. *The World Turned Upside Down*. 1972.

Houlbrooke, R. A. *Church Courts and the People during the English Reformation 1520–1570*. 1979.

Hudson, A. *The Premature Reformation: Wycliffite Texts and Lollard History*. 1988.

Hughes, J. *Pastors and Visionaries: Religion and Secular Life in Late Medieval Yorkshire*. 1988.

Hughes, P. *The Reformation in England*, 3 vols. 1954.

Hunt, W. *The Puritan Moment*. 1983.

Jones, N. L. *Faith by Statute: Parliament and the Settlement of Religion, 1559*. 1982.

Jordan, W. K. *The Development of Religious Toleration in England*, 4 vols. 1932–1940.

Kaufman, P. I. *The "Polytyque Churche": Religion and Early Tudor Political Culture, 1485–1516*. 1986.

Kenny, A., ed. *Wyclif in His Times*. 1986.

Knowles, D. *The Religious Orders in England*, vols. 2–3. 1955–1959.

Lake, P. *Anglicans and Puritans? Presbyterianism and English Conformist Thought from Whitgift to Hooker*. 1988.

———. *Moderate Puritans and the Elizabethan Church*. 1982.

Lake, P. G., and M. Dowling. *Protestantism and the National Church in Sixteenth Century England*. 1987.

Lamont, W. *Godly Rule, 1603–1660*. 1967.

Larner, C. *Witchcraft and Religion: The Politics of Popular Belief*. 1984.

Lehmberg, S. *The Reformation of Cathedrals: Cathedrals in English Society 1485–1603*. 1989.

Loades, D. M. *The Oxford Martyrs*. 1970.

MacFarlane, A. *Witchcraft in Tudor and Stuart England: A Regional and Comparative Study*. 1970.

McFarlane, K. B. *John Wycliffe and the Beginnings of English Nonconformity*. 1952.

McGee, J. S. *The Godly Man in Stuart England*. 1976.

McGrath, P. *Papists and Puritans Under Elizabeth I*. 1967.

Manning, R. *Religion and Society in Elizabethan Sussex*. 1969.

Martin, J. W. *Religious Radicals in Tudor England*. 1989.

Meyer, A. O. *England and the Catholic Church Under Elizabeth*. J. R. McKee, trans. 1967.

O'Day, R. *The Debate on the English Reformation*. 1986.

———. *The English Clergy: Emergence and Consolidation of a Profession*. 1979.

Ogle, A. *The Tragedy of the Lollards' Tower*. 1949.

Owst, G. R. *Preaching in Medieval England: An Introduction to Sermon Manuscripts of the Period, c. 1350–1450*. 1965.

Pollard, A. F. *Thomas Cranmer and the English Reformation*. 1904.

Porter, H. C. *Reformation and Reaction in Tudor Cambridge*. 1958.

Powicke, F. M. *The Reformation in England*. 1941.

Pruett, J. H. *The Parish Clergy Under the Late Stuarts: The Leicestershire Experience*. 1978.

Rex, R. *Henry VIII and the English Reformation*. 1993.

Robson, J. A. *Wyclif and the Oxford Schools*. 1961.

Scarisbrick, J. J. *The Reformation and the English People*. 1984.

Smith, H. M. *Pre-Reformation England*. 1938.

Smith, L. B. *Tudor Prelates and Politics*. 1953.

Solt, L. *Church and State in Early Modern England, 1509–1640*. 1990.

Spurr, J. *The Restoration Church of England, 1646–1689*, 1991.

Swanson, R. N. *Church and Society in Late Medieval England*. 1989.

Thomas, K. *Religion and the Decline of Magic: Studies in Popular Beliefs in Sixteenth- and Seventeenth-Century England*. 1971.

Thompson, A. H. *The English Clergy and Their Organization in the Later Middle Ages*. 1947.

Thompson, J. A. F. *The Later Lollards, 1413–1520*. 1965.

Trevor-Roper, H. *Catholics, Anglicans and Puritans: Seventeenth-Century Essay*. 1987.

Trimble, W. R. *The Catholic Laity in Elizabethan England, 1558–1603*. 1964.

Tyacke, N. *Anti-Calvinists: The Rise of English Arminianism, c. 1590–1640*. 1987.

Watt, T. *Cheap Print and Popular Piety 1550–1640*. 1991.

Whiting, R. *The Blind Devotion of the People: Popular Religion and the English Reformation*. 1989.

Yule, G. *The Independents in the English Civil War*. 1958.

Intellectual and Cultural History

Anglo, S. *Images of Tudor Kingship*. 1992.

———. *Spectacle, Pageantry, and Early Tudor Policy*. 1969.

Auerbach, E. *Tudor Artists*. 1954.

Barker, A. *Milton and the Puritan Dilemma, 1641–1660*. 1942.

Bates, C. *The Rhetoric of Courtship in Elizabethan Language and Literature*. 1992.

Berry, P. *Of Chastity and Power: Elizabethan Literature and the Unmarried Queen*. 1989.

Boas, M. *Robert Boyle and Seventeenth-Century Chemistry*. 1958.

Burgess, G. *The Politics of the Ancient Constitution: An Introduction to English Political Thought 1603–1642*. 1992.

Burtt, E. A. *The Metaphysical Foundations of Modern Science*. 1924.

Bush, D. *English Literature in the Earlier Seventeenth Century*. 1945.

Butterfield, H. *The Origins of Modern Science, 1300–1800*. 1949.

Butterworth, C. *English Primers, 1529–1545*. 1953.

Chambers, E. K. *English Literature at the Close of the Middle Ages*. 1945.

Clare, J. *"Art Made Tongue-Tied by Authority": Elizabethan and Jacobean Dramatic Censorship.* 1990.

Cressy, D. *Bonfires and Bells: National Memory and the Protestant Calendar in Elizabethan and Stuart England.* 1990.

Cruttwell, P. *The Shakespearean Moment and Its Place in the Seventeenth Century.* 1954.

Curtis, M. H. *Oxford and Cambridge in Transition, 1558–1642.* 1959.

Dobbs, B. J. T. *The Foundations of Newton's Alchemy, or "The Hunting of the Greene Lyon."* 1975.

——. *The Janus Faces of Genius: The Role of Alchemy in Newton's Thought.* 1991.

Dobin, H. *Merlin's Disciples: Prophecy, Poetry, and Power in Renaissance England.* 1990.

Dowling, M. *Humanism in the Age of Henry VIII.* 1986.

Dutton, R. *Mastering the Revels: The Regulation and Censorship of English Renaissance Drama.* 1991.

Earle, P. *The World of Defoe.* 1976.

Evans, J. *English Art, 1307–1461.* 1949.

Fink, Z. *The Classical Republicans.* 1962.

Fox, A. *Utopia: An Elusive Vision.* 1993.

Girovard, M. *Robert Smythson and the Elizabethan Country House.* 1983.

Greenblatt, S. *Renaissance Self-Fashioning from More to Shakespeare.* 1980.

Hall, A. R. *The Revolution in Science.* 1983.

Harman, P. M. *The Scientific Revolution.* 1983.

Harvey, I. *Gothic England.* 1947.

Heal, F. *Hospitality in Early Modern England.* 1990.

Helgerson, R. *Forms of Nationhood: The Elizabethan Writing of England.* 1992.

Hexter, J. H. *More's Utopia: The Biography of an Idea.* 1952.

——., ed. *Parliament and Liberty from the Reign of Elizabeth to the Civil War.* 1992.

Hill, C. *The Intellectual Origins of the English Revolution.* 1965.

——. *A Nation of Change and Novelty: Radical Politics, Religion and Literature in Seventeenth-Century England.* 1990.

——. *Some Intellectual Consequences of the English Revolution.* 1980.

Howard, M. *The Early Tudor Country Houses: Architecture and Politics 1490–1550.* 1987.

Hunter, M. *Science and Society in Restoration England.* 1981.

Ingram, M. *Church Courts, Sex and Marriage in England, 1570–1640.* 1987.

Ingram, W. *The Business of Playing: The Beginnings of the Adult Professional Theater in Elizabethan London.* 1992.

Kearney, H. F. *Origins of the Scientific Revolution.* 1964.

King, J. N. *Tudor Royal Iconography: Literature and Art in an Age of Religious Crisis.* 1989.

Laslett, P. *John Locke's Two Treatises of Government: A Critical Edition with an Introduction and Apparatus Criticus,* rev. ed. 1965.

Lewis, C. S. *English Literature in the Sixteenth Century, Excluding Drama.* 1954.

Lovejoy, A. C. *The Great Chain of Being: A Study of the History of an Idea.* 1936.

McAlindon, T. *Shakespeare and Decorum.* 1973.

McConica, J. K. *English Humanists and Reformation Politics Under Henry VIII and Edward VI.* 1965.

McCoy, R. C. *The Rites of Knighthood: The Literature and Politics of Elizabethan Chivalry.* 1989.

McDonald, M., and T. R. Murphy. *Sleepless Souls: Suicide in Early Modern England.* 1990.

Macpherson, G. B. *The Political Theory of Possessive Individualism.* 1962.

Mebane, J. S. *Renaissance Magic and the Return of the Golden Age: The Occult Tradition and Marlowe, Johnson, and Shakespeare.* 1989.

Merton, R. K. *Science, Technology and Society in Seventeenth-Century England,* 2nd ed. 1970.

Millar, O. *The Age of Charles I.* 1972.

———. *English Art, 1625–1714.* 1957.

Ong, W. J. *Rhetoric, Romance and Technology.* 1971.

Pocock, A. *The Ancient Constitution and the Feudal Law.* 1957.

Pomeroy, E. W. *Reading the Portraits of Queen Elizabeth I.* 1989.

Prior, M. E. *The Drama of Power: Studies in Shakespeare's History Plays.* 1973.

Sanderson, J. *"But the People's Creatures": The Philosophical Basis of the English Civil War.* 1989.

Shapiro, B. J. *"Beyond Reasonable Doubt" and "Probable Cause": Historical Perspectives on the Anglo-American Law of Evidence.* 1991.

———. *Probability and Certainty in Seventeenth-Century England: A Study of the Relationships Between Natural Science, Religion, History, Law, and Literature.* 1983.

Sharpe, K. *Criticism and Compliment: The Politics of Literature in the England of Charles I.* 1991.

Shuger, D. K. *Habits of Thought in the English Renaissance: Religion, Politics, and the Dominant Culture.* 1990.

Simon, J. *Education and Society in Tudor England.* 1966.

Smuts, R. M. *Court Culture and the Origins of a Royalist Tradition in Early Stuart England.* 1987.

Somerville, C. J. *The Secularization of Early Modern England: From Religious Culture to Religious Faith.* 1992.

Sommerville, J. P. *Politics and Ideology in England, 1603–1640.* 1986.

Stone, L. "The Educational Revolution in England." *Past and Present* 28 (1964).

Strong, R. *The Cult of Elizabeth: Elizabethan Portraiture and Pageantry.* 1977.

———. *The English Icon: Elizabethan and Jacobean Portraiture.* 1969.

Summerson, J. *Architecture in Britain, 1530–1830,* 2nd ed. 1955.

Sutherland, J. *English Literature of the Late Seventeenth Century.* 1969.

Thurley, S. *The Royal Palaces of Tudor England.* 1993.

Tillyard, E. M. W. *The Elizabethan World Picture.* 1934.

Tittler, R. *Architecture and Power: The Town Hall and the English Urban Community c. 1500–1640.* 1991.

Todd, M. *Christian Humanism and the Puritan Social Order.* 1987.

Walzer, M. *Regicide and Revolution.* 1974.

Watson, C. B. *Shakespeare and the Renaissance Concept of Honor.* 1960.

Webb, G. *Architecture in England: The Middle Ages.* 1956.

Webster, C. *From Paracelsus to Newton.* 1982.

Westfall, R. S. *The Construction of Modern Science.* 1977.

———. *Science and Religion in Seventeenth-Century England.* 1958.

Wolfe, D. M. *Milton in the Puritan Revolution.* 1941.

Yates, F. A. *Astraea: The Imperial Theme in the Sixteenth Century.* 1975.

Foreign Policy, Military, Colonial History, Scotland, and Ireland

Andrews, K. R. *Trade, Plunder and Settlement: Maritime Enterprise and the Genesis of the British Empire, 1480–1630.* 1984.

Bennett, M. *The Battle of Bosworth.* 1985.

Boynton, L. *The Elizabethan Militia, 1558–1638.* 1967.

Brown, J., ed. *Scottish Society in the Fifteenth Century.* 1977.

Carlton, C. *Going to the Wars: The Experience of the British Civil Wars, 1638–1651.* 1992.

Clark, G. N. *War and Society in the Seventeenth Century.* 1958.

Cowan, I. *The Scottish Reformation: Church and Society in Sixteenth-Century Scotland.* 1982.

Craven, W. F. *The Southern Colonies in the Seventeenth Century, 1607–1689.* 1964.

Cressy, D. *Coming Over, Migration and Communication Between England and New England in the Seventeenth Century.* 1987.

Crowson, P. S. *Tudor Foreign Policy.* 1973.

Cruickshank, C. G. *Elizabeth's Army.* 1966.

Donald, P. *An Uncounselled King: Charles I and the Scottish Troubles, 1637–1641.* 1990.

Donaldson, G. *All the Queen's Men: Power and Politics in Mary Stewart's Scotland.* 1983.

———. *Scotland: James V to James VII.* 1965.

———. *The Scottish Reformation.* 1960.

Dunn, R. S. *Sugar and Slaves: The Rise of the Planter Class in the English West Indies, 1624–1713.* 1972.

Edwards, R. D. *Ireland in the Age of the Tudors.* 1977.

Ellis, S. G. *Reform and Revival: English Government in Ireland, 1470–1534.* 1986.

Falls, C. *Elizabeth's Irish Wars.* 1950.

Fissel, M. C. *The Bishops' Wars: Charles I's Campaigns Against Scotland, 1638–1640.* 1994.

Galloway, B. *The Union of England and Scotland, 1603–1605.* 1986.

Gentles, I. *The New Model Army in England, Ireland and Scotland, 1645–1653.* 1992.

Grant, I. F. *The Social and Economic Development of Scotland Before 1603.* 1930.

Howat, G. M. D. *Stuart and Cromwellian Foreign Policy.* 1974.

Kirk, J. *Patterns of Reform: Continuity and Change in the Reformation Kirk.* 1989.

Kishlansky, M. *The Rise of the New Model Army.* 1979.

Lee, M. *Government by Pen: Scotland Under James VI and I.* 1980.

———. *James I and Henry IV: An Essay in English Foreign Policy, 1603–1610.* 1970.

———. *The Road to Revolution: Scotland Under Charles I, 1625–1637.* 1985.

Levack, B. P. *The Formation of the British State: England, Scotland and the Union, 1603–1707.* 1987.

Loades, D. M. *The Tudor Navy: An Administrative, Political, and Military History.* 1992.

Masinnes, A. I. *Charles I and the Making of the Covenanting Movement 1625–1641.* 1991.

McCusker, J. J., and R. R. Menard. *The Economy of British America, 1607–1789.* 1985.

Mattingly, G. *The Armada.* 1962.

Mitchison, A. *A History of Scotland.* 1982.

Moody, T. W., F. X. Martin, and F. J. Byrne, eds. *A New History of Ireland III: Early Modern Ireland, 1534–1691.* 1976.

Rowse, A. L. *The Expansion of England.* 1955.

Ryan, A. N. *England's Sea Empire, 1550–1642.* 1983.

Sanderson, M. H. B. *Mary Stewart's People.* 1987.

Smout, T. C. *History of the Scottish People, 1560–1830.* 1969.

Stevenson, D. *Revolution and Counter-Revolution in Scotland, 1644–1651.* 1977.

———. *The Scottish Revolution, 1637–1644.* 1973.

Wernham, R. B. *After the Armada: Elizabethan England and the Struggle for Western Europe, 1588–1595.* 1984.

———. *Before the Armada: The Growth of English Foreign Policy, 1485–1588.* 1966.

———. *The Making of Elizabethan Foreign Policy, 1558–1603.* 1981.

Williamson, J. A. *The Age of Drake.* 1938.

Wilson, C. H. *Profit and Power: A Study of England and the Dutch Wars.* 1957.

———. *Queen Elizabeth and the Revolt of the Netherlands.* 1970.

Woodroffe, T. *Vantage at Sea: England's Emergence as an Oceanic Power.* 1958.

Woolrych, A. *Battles of the English Civil War.* 1961.

Wormald, J. *Court, Kirk, and Community: Scotland, 1470–1625.* 1981.

Biography

Adamson, J. H., and H. F. Polland. *Sir Henry Vane, 1613–1662.* 1973.

Alexander, M. V. C. *The First of the Tudors.* 1980.

Allmand, C. T. *Henry V.* 1993.

Anderson, F. H. *Francis Bacon, His Career and His Thought.* 1962.

Ashley, M. *Charles I and Oliver Cromwell: A Study in Contrasts and Comparisons.* 1987.

———. *General Monck.* 1977.

————. *The Greatness of Oliver Cromwell.* 1958.

Bald, R. C. *John Donne: A Life.* 1970.

Bassnett, S. *Elizabeth I: A Feminist Perspective.* 1988.

Baxter, S. B. *William III.* 1966.

Beckingsale, B. W. *Burghley, Tudor Statesman, 1520–1598.* 1967.

————. *Thomas Cromwell, Tudor Minister.* 1978.

Beer, B. L. *Northumberland: The Political Career of John Dudley, Earl of Warwick and Duke of Northumberland.* 1974.

Bergerson, D. M. *Royal Family, Royal Lovers: King James of England and Scotland.* 1991.

Bowen, C. D. *The Lion and the Throne: The Life and Times of Sir Edward Coke.* 1956.

Bowles, C. *Charles the First.* 1975.

Brook, V. J. K. *A Life of Archbishop Parker.* 1962.

Browning, A. *Thomas Osborne, Earl of Danby.* 1944–1951.

Bryant, A. *Samuel Pepys,* 3 vols. 1934–1938.

Carlton, C. *Archbishop William Laud.* 1987.

————. *Charles I: the Personal Monarch.* 1983.

Chamber, E. *A Short Life of William Shakespeare.* 1935.

Chambers, R. W. *Thomas More.* 1935.

Chrimes, S. B. *Henry VII.* 1972.

Coquillette, D. R. *Francis Bacon.* 1992.

Cottret, B. *Cromwell.* 1992.

Cowan, I. *Enigma of Mary Stuart.* 1971.

Coward, B. *Oliver Cromwell.* 1991.

Duncan-Jones, K. *Sir Philip Sidney: Courtier Poet.* 1991.

Ferguson, C. W. *Naked to Mine Enemies.* (Wolsey) 1958.

Firth, C. *Oliver Cromwell.* 1900.

Fox, A. *Thomas More, History and Providence.* 1982.

Fraser, A. *Cromwell: Our Chief of Men.* 1973.

————. *Mary Queen of Scots.* 1969.

————. *Royal Charles.* 1979.

————. *The Six Wives of Henry VIII.* 1992.

Gammon, S. R. *Statesman and Schemer: William, First Lord Paget, Tudor Minister.* 1974.

Gillingham, J. *Cromwell: Portrait of a Soldier.* 1976.

Grant, A. *Henry VII.* 1985.

Greenblatt, S. J. *Sir Walter Raleigh: The Renaissance Man and His Roles.* 1973.

Gregg, P. *Free Born John: A Biography of John Lilburne.* 1961.

————. *King Charles I.* 1981.

Gun, S. J. *Charles Brandon, Duke of Suffolk c. 1484–1545.* 1988.

Guy, J. *The Public Career of Sir Thomas More.* 1980.

Gwyn, P. *The King's Cardinal: The Rise and Fall of Thomas Wolsey.* 1990.

Haigh, C. *Elizabeth I.* 1988.

Haley, K. H. *Charles II.* 1966.

————. *First Earl of Shaftesbury.* 1968.

Handover, P. M. *The Second Cecil.* 1959.

Harris, B. J. *Edward Stafford, Third Duke of Buckingham, 1478–1521.* 1986.

Harriss, G. L. *Cardinal Beaufort: A Study of Lancastrian Ascendancy and Decline.* 1989.

Havran, M. J. *Caroline Courtier: The Life of Lord Cottington.* 1973.

———. "The Character and Principles of an English King: The Case of Charles I." *Catholic Historical Review,* Vol. LXIX, April 1983.

Haynes, A. *Robert Cecil, Earl of Salisbury, 1563–1612: Servant of Two Sovereigns.* 1989.

———. *The White Bear: Robert Dudley, the Elizabethan Earl of Leicester.* 1987.

Hill, C. *God's Englishman, Oliver Cromwell and the English Revolution.* 1970.

———. *John Milton and the English Revolution.* 1977.

Howell, R. *Cromwell.* 1979.

Hulme, H. *The Life of Sir John Eliot.* 1957.

Hutchison, H. F. *Henry V, a Biography.* 1967.

———. *The Hollow Crown: A Life of Richard II.* 1961.

Hutton, R. *Charles the Second: King of England, Scotland, and Ireland.* 1989.

Ives, E. *Anne Boleyn.* 1988.

Jenkins, E. *Elizabeth the Great.* 1958.

Johnson, P. *Duke Richard of York, 1411–1460.* 1988.

———. *Elizabeth I: A Study of Power and Intellect.* 1974.

Jones, J. R. *Charles II, Royal Politician.* 1987.

Jones, M. K., and M. G. Underwood. *The King's Mother: Lady Margaret Beaufort, Countess of Richmond and Derby.* 1992.

Jordan, W. K. *Edward VI: The Threshold of Power.* 1970.

———. *Edward VI: The Young King.* 1968.

Kendall, P. M. *Richard III.* 1955.

———. *Warwick the Kingmaker.* 1957.

Kenyon, J. P. *Robert Spencer, Earl of Sunderland, 1641–1702.* 1958.

Kirby, J. L. *Henry IV of England.* 1970.

Lacey, R. *Robert Devereux: The Earl of Essex.* 1971.

———. *Sir Walter Raleigh.* 1974.

Lamont, W. M. *Marginal Prynne.* 1963.

———. *Richard Baxter and the Millennium.* 1979.

Lee, M. *Great Britain's Solomon: James VI and I in His Three Kingdoms.* 1990.

Lehmberg, S. E. *Sir Walter Mildmay and Tudor Government.* 1964.

Loades, D. M. *Mary Tudor: A Life.* 1989.

———. *The Reign of Mary Tudor,* 2nd ed. 1991.

Lockyer, R. *Buckingham: The Life and Political Career of George Villiers, First Duke of Buckingham, 1592–1628.* 1981.

Lynch, M., ed. *Mary Stewart, Queen in Three Kingdoms.* 1988.

MacDougall, N. *James IV.* 1989.

Manuel, F. E. A. *Portrait of Isaac Newton.* 1968.

Marius, R. *Thomas More, a Biography.* 1984.

Marshall, R. K. *Queen of Scots.* 1987.

Martz, L. L. *Thomas More, the Search for the Inner Man.* 1990.

Mason, A. E. W. *The Life of Francis Drake.* 1941.

Mattingly, G. *Catherine of Aragon.* 1941.

Merriman, R. B. *The Life and Letters of Thomas Cromwell*, 2 vols. 1902.

Miller, J. *James II, A Study in Kingship*. 1978.

Muller, J. A. *Stephen Gardiner and the Tudor Reaction*. 1926.

Neale, J. E. *Queen Elizabeth*. 1934.

Palmer, W. *The Political Career of Oliver St. John, 1637–1649*. 1993.

Paul, J. *Catherine of Aragon and Her Friends*. 1966.

Paul, R. S. *The Lord Protector: Religion and Politics in the Life of Oliver Cromwell*. 1955.

Perry, M. *The Word of a Prince: A Life of Elizabeth I from Contemporary Documents*. 1990.

Pollard, A. F. *Henry VIII*. 1902.

Prescott, H. F. M. *Mary Tudor*. 1953.

Ragow, A. A. *Thomas Hobbes: Radical in the Service of Reaction*. 1986.

Read, C. *Lord Burghley and Queen Elizabeth*. 1960.

———. *Mr. Secretary Cecil and Queen Elizabeth*. 1955.

Ridley, J. *Thomas Cranmer*. 1962.

Ross, C. *Edward IV*. 1974.

———. *Richard III*. 1981.

Rowse, A. L. *Sir Richard Grenville of the Revenge*. 1937.

Scarisbrick, J. J. *Henry VIII*. 1968.

Schenk, W. *Reginald Pole*. 1950.

Scott, J. *Algernon Sidney and the English Republic, 1623–1677*. 1988.

———. *Algernon Sidney and the Restoration Crisis, 1677–1683*. 1991.

Seward, D. *Henry V: The Scourge of God*. 1988.

Shapiro, B. *John Wilkins 1614–1672: An Intellectual Biography*. 1969.

Simons, E. N. *Henry VII*. 1968.

Slavin, A. J. *Politics and Profit: A Study of Sir Ralph Sadler, 1507–1547*. 1966.

Smith, L. B. *Elizabeth Tudor: Portrait of a Queen*. 1975.

———. *Henry VIII: The Mask of Royalty*. 1971.

———. *A Tudor Tragedy: The Life and Times of Catherine Howard*. 1961.

Somerset, A. *Elizabeth I*. 1991.

Steel, A. *Richard II*. 1941.

Stone, L. *An Elizabethan: Sir Horatio Palavicino*. 1956.

Storey, R. L. *The Reign of Henry VII*. 1968.

Strong, R. *Charles I on Horseback*. 1970.

Tittler, R. *Nicholas Bacon, 1510–1579: The Making of a Tudor Statesman*. 1976.

Trevor-Roper, H. R. *Archbishop Laud*, 2nd ed. 1962.

Tucker, M. *The Life of Thomas Howard, Earl of Surrey and Second Duke of Norfolk, 1443–1524*. 1964.

Turner, F. C. *James II*. 1948.

Van der Zee, H., and B. Van der Zee. *William and Mary*. 1973.

Wallace, W. M. *Sir Walter Raleigh*. 1959.

Warnicke, R. M. *The Rise and Fall of Anne Boleyn*. 1989.

Waugh, E. *Edmund Campion*. 1935.

Wedgwood, C. V. *Oliver Cromwell*. 1939.

———. *Thomas Wentworth, First Earl of Strafford: A Revaluation*. 1961.

Weightman, C. *Margaret of York, Duchess of Burgundy 1446–1503*. 1993.

Weir, A. *The Six Wives of Henry VIII.* 1991.

Williams, N. *Thomas Howard, Fourth Duke of Norfolk.* 1964.

Williamson, J. A. *Sir John Hawkins.* 1927.

Willson, D. H. *King James VI and I.* 1956.

Wolffe, B. *Henry VI.* 1981.

Wormald, B. H. G. *Francis Bacon: History, Politics and Science, 1561–1626.* 1993.

Wormald, J. *Mary Queen of Scots: A Study in Failure.* 1988.

Index